LOUIS VUITTON

LOUIS VUITTON

THE BIRTH OF MODERN LUXURY

Paul-Gérard Pasols
Translated from the French by Lenora Ammon

Abrams, New York

Vuitton family tree

| Elisabeth GUILLON | Jean-François GUILLON | | Philippe-Louis VUITTON | Colette VUITTON | Danielle VUITTON | | Hervé OGLIASTRO | Bernard OGLIASTRO | | Caroline RACAMIER |

Pierre GUILLON

Andrée VUITTON b. 1907

Josette RATEAU

Henry-Louis VUITTON 1911–2002

Jean OGLIASTRO 1915–1997

Denyse VUITTON b. 1917

Henry RACAMIER 1912–2003

Odile VUITTON b. 1921

Renée VERSILLE

Gaston-Louis VUITTON 1883–1970

Joséphine PATRELLE

Georges VUITTON 1857–1936

Clémence-Émilie PARRIAUX

Louis VUITTON 1821–1892

Victorine VUITTON 1820–?

François-Xavier VUITTON 1793–1888

Claude VUITTON 1759–1807

Pierre VUITTON 1697–1775

Pierre VUITTON Jura, 15th century

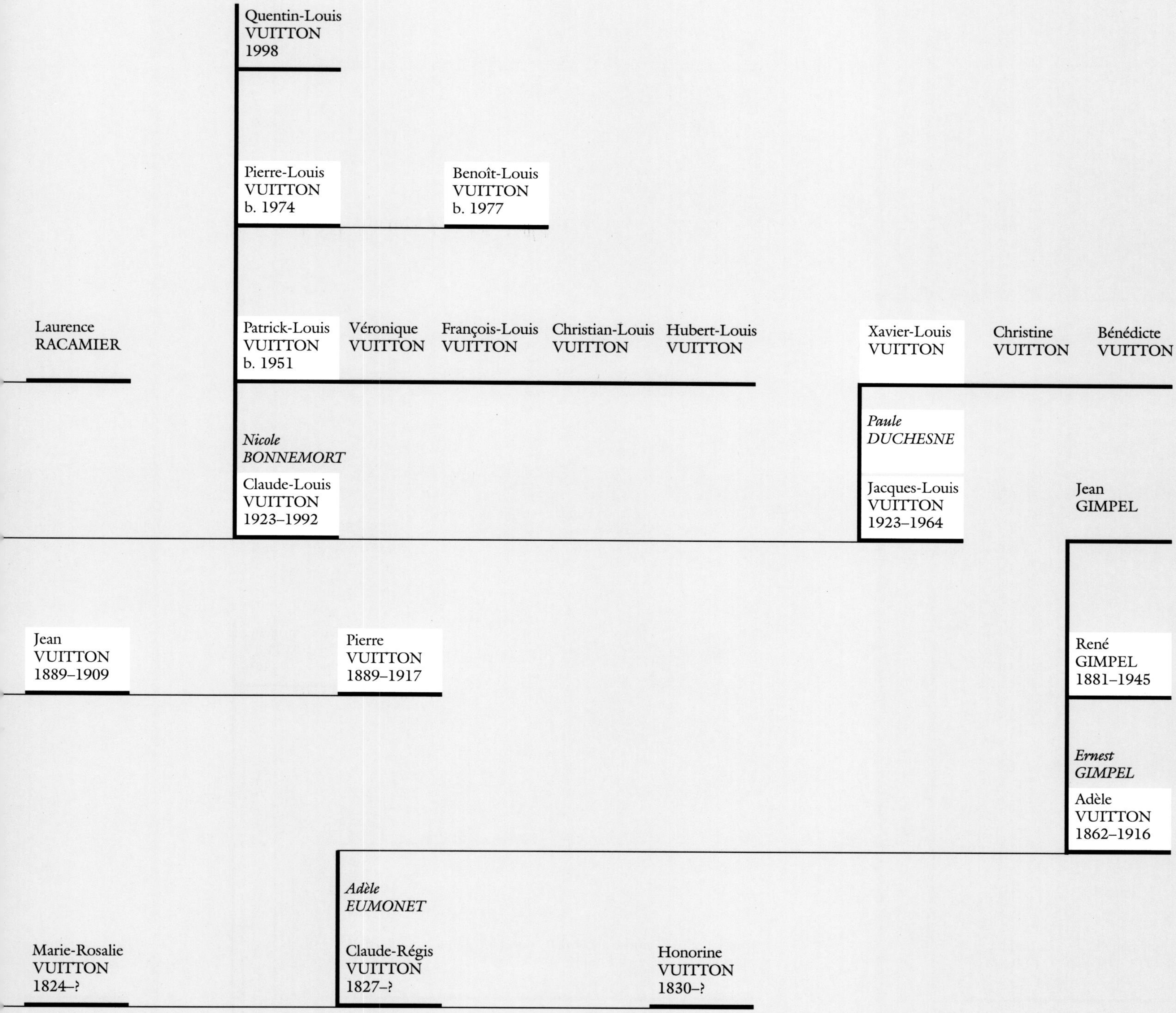

Quentin-Louis
VUITTON
1998

Pierre-Louis
VUITTON
b. 1974

Benoît-Louis
VUITTON
b. 1977

Laurence
RACAMIER

Patrick-Louis
VUITTON
b. 1951

Véronique
VUITTON

François-Louis
VUITTON

Christian-Louis
VUITTON

Hubert-Louis
VUITTON

Xavier-Louis
VUITTON

Christine
VUITTON

Bénédicte
VUITTON

Nicole
BONNEMORT

Claude-Louis
VUITTON
1923–1992

Paule
DUCHESNE

Jacques-Louis
VUITTON
1923–1964

Jean
GIMPEL

Jean
VUITTON
1889–1909

Pierre
VUITTON
1889–1917

René
GIMPEL
1881–1945

Ernest
GIMPEL

Adèle
VUITTON
1862–1916

Adèle
EUMONET

Marie-Rosalie
VUITTON
1824–?

Claude-Régis
VUITTON
1827–?

Honorine
VUITTON
1830–?

The people cited in this work and those active in Louis Vuitton's business are indicated by a white rectangle.

LOUIS

Du quatrième jour du mois d'août à trois heures du matin, l'an mil huit cent vingt-un.

ACTE DE NAISSANCE de Louis

né à Anthay le présent jour
à trois heures du matin, fil de Xavier Antoine
domicilié à Anthay, profession
de cultivateur, âgé de trente ans, et
de Jeanne Gaillard, profession de meunière
âgée de trente ans, mariés.

Le Sexe de l'enfant a été reconnu être de masculin

Premier témoin, Hubert Gentelet
domicilié à Anthay, profession de cultivateur
âgé de trente huit ans.

Second témoin, Xavier Gentelet
domicilié à Anthay, profession de cultivateur
âgé de trente ans, sur la réquisition à nous faite
par ledit Antoine père de l'enfant

Lu aux parties, et constaté suivant la loi par moi, Hubert
Gentelet — Maire d'Anthay faisant
les fonctions d'Officier de l'état civil, soussigné avec lesdits te
et Déclarant Gaillard

Gentelet Gentelet

Gentelet
Maire

Clos et arrêté le premier janvier mil huit cent vingt deux
le Maire d'Anthay soussigné

Gentelet
Maire

A child of the Jura

Louis Vuitton was born in 1821 in Anchay, a hamlet in the Jura, a region of mountains and forests. For five generations his family had been joiners, carpenters, and millers, farming all the while. He was only thirteen years old when he left the family mill in 1835.

It was early spring. The warm air was filled with the scent of forest undergrowth, a mixture of earth and plants. A boy, bag on his shoulder, set forth with a determined gait, his big hobnailed shoes sinking into the softening ground. Behind him, the mechanical squeak of the mill wheel faded away. The murmur of the Ancheronne, a small stream flowing westward, showed him the way. The boy, not yet fourteen years old, did not look back. He had decided to leave the land his family has lived on for generations. And thus began the story, the legend, of Louis Vuitton.

Louis was born at three o'clock on the morning of 4 August 1821, in Anchay, a hamlet in the Jura region of eastern France. The Jura gets its name from a chain of mountains that forms the natural border between France and Switzerland. European monarchs long vied for this backcountry within the province of Franche-Comté. It was ravaged by several wars during the sixteenth and seventeenth centuries before becoming part of the kingdom of France in 1678. The region and its inhabitants were toughened by that history.

They were also toughened by the living conditions there. The Jura has a more extreme climate than elsewhere in France, with scorching summers and winter temperatures that sometimes drop to the polar range. In the nineteenth century the environment was hostile, the mountainous area poorly connected to the rest of the country and difficult to penetrate, with plateaus that were not very fertile. The snow, which lasted many months, immobilized and isolated the local people, making them self-sufficient. Those who were raised in this region had the temperament of mountain people: a sturdy character, independent and courageous, well acquainted with effort and perseverance. Louis would soon be putting those qualities to use.

Wood, stone, water. The hamlet of Anchay is surrounded by two chains of abundantly wooded, medium-high mountains, with the tallest peak rising to 2,625 feet. Wood, stone, and water made up a natural setting that was celebrated by the painter Gustave Courbet. Courbet, a contemporary of Louis, was born in 1819 in Ornans, a village within Franche-Comté north of Anchay. The harshness and power of his native land inspired pictures with dense, vigorous landscapes that have an almost primitive vitality.

People adjusted to this demanding environment and learned to use its natural resources. At the time wood was the main source of energy. It was used as fuel for heating, and also supplied the glassworks and forges that produced iron and cast iron. Wood allowed for the manufacture of all types of objects. Many of the mountain people of the Jura took advantage of the long winter months to devote themselves to making and marketing woodcrafts. Surrounded by snow and frost, they had the free time to make small wooden objects with meticulous attention to detail. Pipes were the exclusive specialty of Saint-Claude, which exported them throughout the world, while toys were the specialty of Moirans-en-Montagne, to the north. Water—the movements of its currents, the force of the falls—provided energy for the processing, textile, and metallurgy industries.

Louis uproots himself. Determined and headstrong, a true child of the Jura, Louis left his native country as a teenager. Extricating himself from the Jura foothills was a revolutionary break with ancestral traditions. Why did he make this radical decision? The family legend recounts that he wanted to run away from his stepmother. He was ten when his

Previous page: Portrait of Louis Vuitton, 1821–1892, founder of the company.

Louis's birth certificate: "On the fourth day of the month of August at ten o'clock in the morning in the year eighteen hundred twenty-one, birth certificate of Louis, born in Anchay on this day, at three o'clock in the morning, son of Xavier Vuitton, domiciled in Anchay, farmer, thirty years old, and to Coronné Gaillard, miller, thirty years old, married.

"The child was recognized as male. First witness, Hubert Gentetet, domiciled in Anchay, farmer, thirty-eight years old. Second witness, Xavier Gentetet, domiciled in Anchay, farmer, thirty years old, upon the request made to us by the aforementioned Vuitton, father of the child."

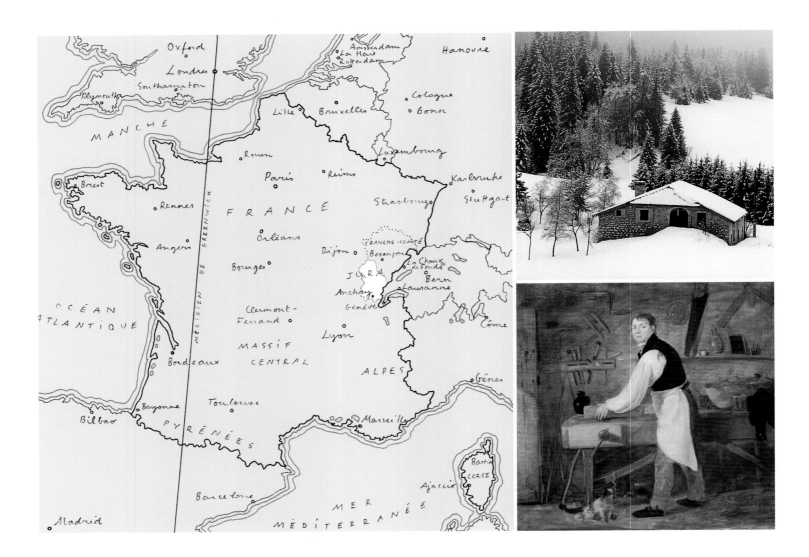

mother died. His father then married a woman who took an immediate dislike to the children from her husband's first marriage—a stepmother out of a fairy tale like *Cinderella*. It seems that Louis did not put up with her severe regime very long, fleeing at the first opportunity. It is easy to imagine the scene. After a long winter, during which he was subjected to the abusive authority of the new head of the household, the first fine days of spring finally arrived, and Louis set off, walking with a bundle on his shoulder.

Escape from a cruel stepmother: fact or fiction? We know, through a letter from Gaston-Louis Vuitton, his grandson, that, once he made it to Paris, Louis was joined by one of his brothers, Claude-Régis Vuitton. Therefore, Louis may have been following the course of many Frenchmen of the nineteenth century, when one son was often sent to try his luck elsewhere, seeking a place with greater opportunities for work and a more promising future. As a kind of scout, he would send for his brothers when he settled down in the big city and found a way to make a living. Louis took an uncommon route, however. Usually those leaving the Jura countryside would go to Lyon, where the silk mills were hiring. So why did young Louis choose Paris? Undoubtedly he already had the driving ambition and the will to forge a unique destiny.

Above left: On the map of France, the Jura is shown in white at the country's borders.

Above right, top: The long, rigorous winters in the Jura region required patience.

Above right, bottom: Woodworking, as illustrated in the painting *Thomas Rogers, Carpenter*, was passed down from father to son. English school, 1830.

Above: The Vuitton family had worked with wood since the sixteenth century and had a water mill whose power enabled them not only to grind grain but also to turn wood. This water mill was painted about 1870 by Gustave Courbet, a contemporary of Louis who also came from the Jura.

Following pages: Like the German painter Caspar David Friedrich—whose 1837 *View from the Crest of Mount Schmiede* is shown here—Louis set his sights beyond the mountains and toward a unique destiny he could already glimpse.

Like a journeyman touring France. When he left Anchay Louis embarked upon an adventure. His yearning for success had not yet taken on a definite form but was flickering like a flame inside him. He began two years of studious wandering. He certainly must have rubbed shoulders with the small, lively, mobile, and very independent society of journeyman workers. Inheritors of a French tradition that went back to the Middle Ages, these young men perfected their apprenticeships by traveling throughout the country. They constituted elite cadres of workers: shoemakers, tawers, tanners, hatters, coopers, cartwrights, ironsmiths, tinsmiths, carpenters, joiners, and stonecutters.

The culmination of their training was to complete a tour of France, staying along the way in guesthouses that provided good food and accommodations. The journeymen were hired by local patrons and along the way they would climb the ladder in the journeyman hierarchy—candidate, accepted journeyman, accomplished journeyman.

Each one was given a nickname that identified him to his colleagues, poetic names that sang of each man's native country and qualities: Avignonnais-la-Vertu (Virtuous Man from Avignon), Poitevin-la-Clef-des-Cœurs (Key of Hearts from Poitou), Languedoc-la-Sagesse (Wise Man from Languedoc). If he hadn't been so young, Louis would surely have earned the name Jura-l'Audacieux (Daring Man from the Jura).

Return to Anchay, 7 April 2004

Patrick-Louis Vuitton, Louis's great-great-grandson, returned to Anchay more than 150 years after Louis's departure, tracking his ancestors beside the Ancheronne River. The forest has reclaimed the vestiges of the family mill.

Louis's great-great-grandson Patrick-Louis Vuitton went to Anchay to encounter the past, the trees that had watched over his ancestor's boyhood, and the ruins of the family mill, which had been one of the largest in the area.

The Vuittons settled for several centuries in Franche-Comté. Their name, of Germanic origin, is found throughout the region. "Vuittons, that's all there is in this country!" joked Denis Picot, an inhabitant of Anchay. "The name appears with different spellings: Vuyton, Vitton, Witton, Vuytton," explained René Vuitton. "It means 'hard head.'" René, one of the many Vuitton cousins from Louis's line, still lives in the Jura. In April 2004 he welcomed some visitors to Anchay, a hamlet of Lavans-sur-Valouse, where Louis Vuitton's descendants gathered to discuss, question, explain, and return to their roots.

Patrick-Louis Vuitton, today the head of special orders for Maison Louis Vuitton, was accompanied on his pilgrimage by author Paul-Gérard Pasols and two longtime employees of the company: Dominique Clemenceau, who is in charge of historical heritage, and the photographer Antoine Jarrier, who

"Vuittons, that's all there is in this region!" The hamlet of Anchay in 2004.

directs the audiovisual department. Denis Millet, mayor of Lavans-sur-Valouse, joined them in the municipal council hall in Faverge.

Three cousins of Patrick-Louis Vuitton were also there: René Vuitton, retired; his wife, Geneviève; and their son, whose name is also Patrick. This Patrick Vuitton, forty-three years old, is a magnetic healer by trade. The Jura is a country of old traditions, and from the dawn of time certain gifts have been handed down from generation to generation.

Henri Vuitton, the town's former mayor, joined the group as well. All the Vuittons are passionate about their genealogy. Patrick Vuitton unwound a genealogical map so large it could not be photocopied or photographed. The visitors leaned over the historic civil registries, which the mayor handled carefully.

The history of the Vuitton family is linked to woodcrafts since at least the time of Pierre Vuitton, the most distant direct ancestor. A joiner, he was born in 1697 in Thorignat, near Lavans-sur-Valouse. He bought the mill near Anchay, on the Ancheronne, a river that flows into the Valouse. A versatile mill—"one of the largest mills in the region," Henri Vuitton

pointed out—it could be used to make flour and, when the winter came and there was no more grain to grind, also to turn wood. The forest was not far away. Hydraulic energy was used to cut down trees and saw boards, thus providing the raw material for cabinetmaking and carpentry. As early as the seventeenth century the wood mill surpassed the manual pit saw, with its hydraulic saw cutting up to four hundred boards a day.

This was the setting, which gives off a rare sort of energy, that the young Louis Vuitton left one spring morning.

On the Dole route, in the Jura, the young Louis set out for Paris on foot. He certainly did not have the means to travel by coach. Lithograph by Victor Adam, about 1840.

Far from home, the teenager did not completely break away from his family's history and traditions. On more than one occasion during his travels, he found the opportunity to work with wood and acquire valuable skills.

Louis's trip was long and slow. If he had walked directly to the capital, averaging 22 miles a day, without taking any days off to rest, it would have taken him about two weeks to cover the 292 miles that separated Anchay from Paris. If he had had the means, he could have taken a horse-drawn coach. He would certainly have cursed the lack of comfort and the lack of privacy—sometimes up to thirty passengers were packed into a single coach— but he would have arrived at his destination in five to seven days. Today, it takes less than five hours to make the same trip by car.

Louis Vuitton's first voyage. The journey young Louis undertook was his first trip anywhere. It was dictated by necessity, not pleasure. Even the notion of a pleasure trip—one not driven by any professional or family obligation—is relatively recent. The idea certainly did not occur to Louis Vuitton as he walked along the paths and roads. Unlike the writer Stendhal, he did not travel by coach or attend the salons then in vogue—in fact, he had probably never even heard of them—nor did he have any idea of the "fashionable" that so fascinated Stendhal at the time. Some months later he would catch up, becoming informed about the capital's latest styles. For now, he was still far from the city and had to make his way to Paris. He walked in the open air and enjoyed his freedom. The future was full of promise.

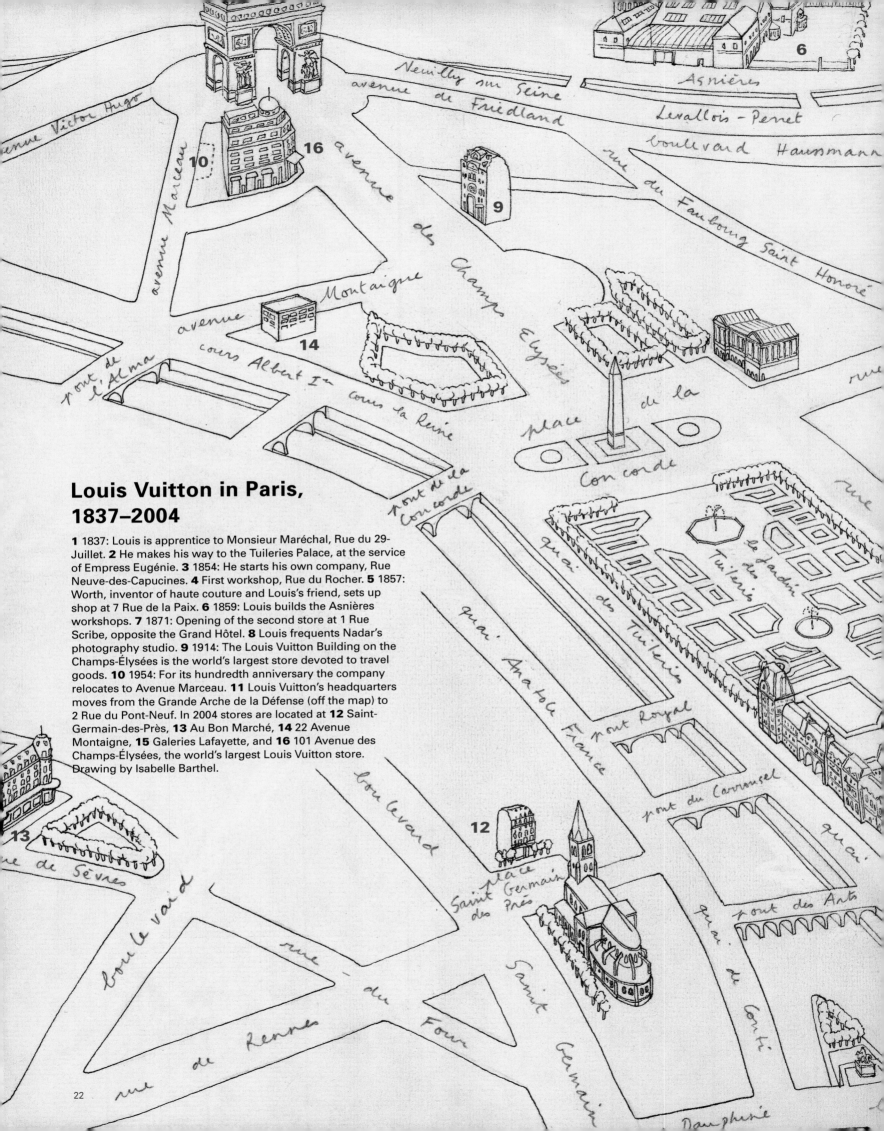

Louis Vuitton in Paris, 1837–2004

1 1837: Louis is apprentice to Monsieur Maréchal, Rue du 29-Juillet. **2** He makes his way to the Tuileries Palace, at the service of Empress Eugénie. **3** 1854: He starts his own company, Rue Neuve-des-Capucines. **4** First workshop, Rue du Rocher. **5** 1857: Worth, inventor of haute couture and Louis's friend, sets up shop at 7 Rue de la Paix. **6** 1859: Louis builds the Asnières workshops. **7** 1871: Opening of the second store at 1 Rue Scribe, opposite the Grand Hôtel. **8** Louis frequents Nadar's photography studio. **9** 1914: The Louis Vuitton Building on the Champs-Élysées is the world's largest store devoted to travel goods. **10** 1954: For its hundredth anniversary the company relocates to Avenue Marceau. **11** Louis Vuitton's headquarters moves from the Grande Arche de la Défense (off the map) to 2 Rue du Pont-Neuf. In 2004 stores are located at **12** Saint-Germain-des-Près, **13** Au Bon Marché, **14** 22 Avenue Montaigne, **15** Galeries Lafayette, and **16** 101 Avenue des Champs-Élysées, the world's largest Louis Vuitton store. Drawing by Isabelle Barthel.

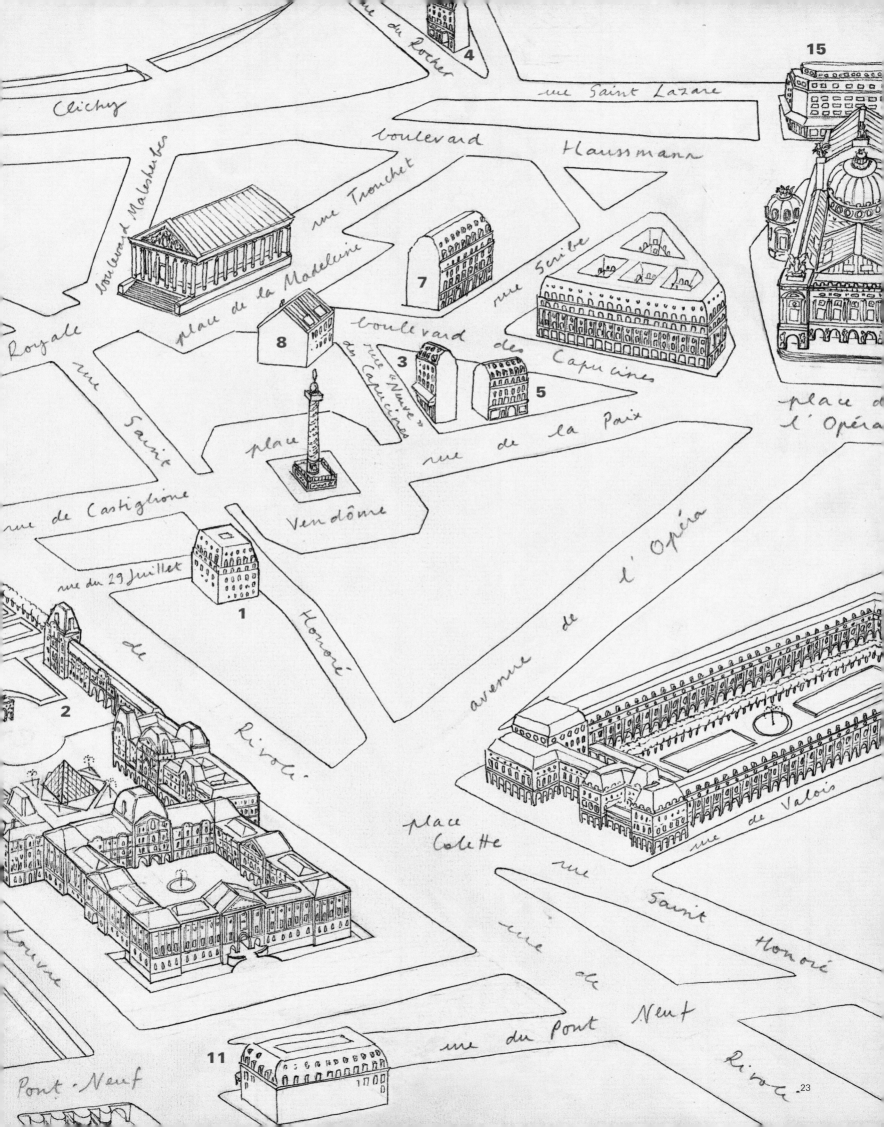

Clichy

rue du Rocher

rue Saint Lazare

4

15

boulevard Malesherbes

rue Tronchet

boulevard Haussmann

place de la Madeleine

7

rue Scribe

Royalle

8

boulevard des Capucines

rue "Neuve" des Capucines

3

5

place de l'Opéra

rue Saint

place Vendôme

rue de la Paix

rue de Castiglione

rue du 29 Juillet

1

Honoré

avenue de l'Opéra

2

Rivoli

de

rue de Valois

place Colette

rue

Saint

Louvre

Honoré

de

Pont-Neuf

rue du Pont Neuf

11

Rivoli

.23

1837, arrival in Paris

Two years of travel, encounters, and experience had given Louis self-confidence. The teenager had matured. He entered Paris astounded by its excesses, stupefied by its contrasts, and convinced that this was where everything would be possible. But first he had to find work.

Louis was sixteen years old. He was far from his native Jura, and what a road he had traveled since his departure two years earlier! Entering France's capital on foot, he hungrily and eagerly took in everything. He didn't want to miss any of the spectacle before his eyes. Astonishing objects and sources of enchantment were everywhere. Louis had heard so much about Paris that he knew even before seeing the capital that it was the most beautiful city in the world. But the reality exceeded his expectations.

Louis probably arrived from the south. He crossed over the remains of the fortified Farmiers-Généraux, a wall that once encircled the city and had fifty-two entrances or tollgates. The layout of the wall, more than fifteen miles long, corresponded roughly to the two subway lines that today connect the Place de l'Étoile to the Place de la Nation. Crossing the Fontainebleau Gate (the present-day Place d'Italie, near the historical center of Paris), Louis discovered an almost rural setting: scattered mills and houses, fields, vegetable gardens and vineyards, paths rather than streets. To the southeast, the Gobelins district is crossed by a stream, the Bièvre, which supplied the mills of tanners and dyers before discharging its polluted water into the Seine. In the vicinity is the Saint-Marceau district, a poor quarter that Victor Hugo grippingly portrayed in his novel *Les Misérables*.

The population increased as he drew nearer to the city center, approaching the Latin Quarter, the student district, which is set between the Sainte-Geneviève hill and the Seine. Across Saint-Michel Bridge was the medieval setting of the Île de la Cité near the cathedral of Notre-Dame, the heart of the city.

"The greatest virtue and the greatest vice." At that time Paris was undergoing remarkable demographic growth. Many young people, most of modest origins, were leaving their native provinces of Nord, Champagne, Burgundy, Normandy, Lorraine, and Auvergne to work in the capital. Paris, which had fewer than 550,000 inhabitants in 1801, now had nearly a million.

The Paris of 1837, Louis Vuitton's Paris, was full of contrasts: the grandeur of palaces and monuments and the beauty of posh neighborhoods up against the grime of the medieval city center, which was overpopulated, stifling, and unhygienic. Five years earlier a cholera epidemic had devastated the district. The pianist Chopin, in a letter to a Polish friend, noted: "Here you find at the same time the greatest luxury and the greatest filth, the greatest virtue and the greatest vice." Around the majestic Notre-Dame crouched a dark, sickly Paris—a Paris of dilapidated hovels, labyrinthine lanes, and disreputable cabarets, a place where it was unwise to venture at night. *Les Mystères de Paris,* a well-known story serialized at the time, described the disturbing setting: "The mud-colored houses, pierced with a few rare windows with worm-eaten frames, almost touched at the rooftops since the streets were so narrow. The dark, filthy alleys lead to even darker, filthier stairways that are so perpendicular they are very hard to climb using a rope attached to the humid walls by iron spikes."

West of the Île de la Cité, Louis crossed the Pont-Neuf, a bridge crowded with sellers of secondhand goods and fried foods, to the right bank. Between the two royal palaces, the Louvre and the Tuileries, he passed through the Carrousel district, a maze of old houses, vacant lots, and groups of shacks where the tooth pullers and the dog shearers worked. To his left, Rue de Rivoli, a street built under Napoléon I, ran toward the west. To his right

In 1832 Giuseppe Canella painted the Île de la Cité and the Flower Market, in the heart of Paris, as they were when Louis discovered them upon his arrival in the capital. In the middle distance is the Pont-Neuf, in front of which today stands the headquarters of Louis Vuitton.

was the Palais-Royal, an entertainment center whose prestige was declining though it housed well-known cafes and restaurants—and more than one gambling dive where one could mix with the riffraff and lose a fortune. Going north Louis came upon Paris's shopping district, whose stylish covered walkways sheltered the stroller from the rain, carriages, and mud of the streets.

Not far from here was the neighborhood of the Madeleine, which at that time had been under construction for several decades. Toward the west, beautiful neighborhoods were developing. Their location was deliberate, as the prevailing winds blew the city center's putrid fumes east. Here it was easy to forget the sordid areas nearby, the Paris of the common people, the dirty streets, and the polluted air filled with the foul odors of the slaughterhouses. These fine neighborhoods would become home to some of Louis Vuitton's future clientele, once he became famous as a box maker and packer and, later, a trunk maker. While the old aristocracy favored the Saint-Germain district on the left bank, the more recently moneyed elite, financiers and businessmen, occupied the new residential areas of the right bank. At the top of the list was the Saint-Honoré quarter, which had been expanding since the eighteenth century. It boasted a succession of magnificent mansions with beautiful gardens and the nearby Avenue de Neuilly—today called the Champs-Élysées—where chic horsemen and fashionable carriages traveled to and fro.

This was Louis's Paris. The teenager was taken on as an apprentice in the workshop of Monsieur Maréchal, a box maker/packer in Rue Saint-Honoré. Close by, at 9 Rue du Faubourg-Saint-Honoré, was the famous fancy goods shop Aux Montagnes Russes, which was owned by Pierre-Alfred Chardon and Marie Lagache. The shop had carefully maintained display windows, shelves of articles from Paris on six floors, and some twenty salespeople. For young Louis it provided an early glimpse of the Parisian life, a sparkling image of success, the fruit of hard work and commercial genius. Chardon and Lagache were perfect role models, with elegant taste, a sense of innovation, and enterprising spirits. Armed with such qualities, they had made a fortune in just a few years, and they donated a great deal of money to charitable works.

On the Boulevards. To the east of the Madeleine were the Boulevards, the golden crown north of the city, the brilliantly animated showcase of Paris during the first half of the nineteenth century. Louis, who lived in the vicinity, could not have missed its seductive powers. It was the place in Paris with the most dazzling reputation. All the elite of Europe dreamed of coming here. According to the German poet Heinrich Heine, a Parisian by adoption, the charm of the Boulevards reached to the heavens: "When the dear Lord gets bored in paradise, he opens the window and contemplates the Parisian boulevards."

Wide, spacious, filled with fresh air, the Boulevards were the favorite destination for Parisian strollers, sensualists, and revelers. The area spreading eastward from the Bastille and along the Boulevards de Beaumarchais, du Temple, de Saint-Martin, and de Saint-Denis had a working-class ambiance. The main attractions were the theaters. They offered mime, vaudeville, and bloody melodramas that gave the place its nickname, the "Boulevards du Crime." Here the stars were Jean-Gaspard Deburau, the pantomime famed for his Pierrot, and Frédéric Lemaître, celebrated for his melodramatic roles. Orchestras accompanied the shows, and in one of them Jacques Offenbach, later known as a composer, made his debut as a cellist. The Boulevards became more aristocratic beginning at the corner of Boulevard Montmartre and Rue de la Grange-Batelière, site of the Jockey-Club, where the cream of Parisian society met. The west side was the most stylish. Among all the streets of Paris, Boulevard des Italiens was the most frequented by fashionable people, artists, and dandies and had the most splendid array of shop windows, clothing, and carriages: "The dandies drove their tilburies, dogcarts, English carts, and cabriolets themselves, while the valets in livery on foot, wearing topped boots and cockaded oilcloth hats, had their arms crossed beside them," wrote Olivier Merlin. He added that in the 1830s English elegance

The Entrance of Charles X into Paris, 6 June 1825, painted by Louis-François Lejeune, was an event as grandiose as the crowning of the king at Reims a few days earlier. The splendor on display presaged the celebrations to come, of which Louis would be an enthralled spectator.

27

set the tone on the Boulevards and "defied any competition: boot makers, tailors, hatters, perfumers, all were branches of London shops."

Nearby, in Rue Le Peletier, was the opera house. After a performance the spectators headed for the fashionable restaurants and cafés where Paris's smart set gathered to make and unravel reputations: the Grand-Balcon, Café Riche, Café Hardy, Café Anglais, Café de Paris, Maison Dorée, Bains-Chinois, and the Tortoni. Here they consumed the punches, sorbets, and ice creams that made the Boulevards famous throughout the world. When night fell, the recently installed gaslights enhanced the brilliant splendor of the surroundings.

The buzzing rumors of the city. Louis, who came from a harsh region where people tended to be taciturn, began to rub up against the thousand and one things that made the capital such a buzzing hive of gossip, a powder keg that exploded at the smallest rumor. The gossip circulating the city was more than just talk—it had real power. It took less than three days, the *Trois Glorieuses* of July 1830, for Parisians to overthrow the reactionary old King Charles X and agree to see a new sovereign ascend the throne. Louis-Philippe I, the Citizen King, was more bourgeois, more affable than his predecessor—no longer the king of France, but king of the French people and, above all, king of the Parisians.

Louis began to taste the spice of the Parisian spirit: lively, easily discontented, feverishly feeding on all the news peddled by the gazettes and by word of mouth, quick to comment on, taunt, or satirize all that was said in the city. In 1837 everyone was still talking about the Obelisk of Luxor, a gift from Egypt that had been erected the previous year on the Place de la Concorde. Could this ancient monument make anyone forget that not so long ago, on the very same square, so many heads had fallen, including those of a king and queen of France? Because France's monument had come from Africa, the newspapers began discussing this little-known continent beyond the Mediterranean Sea. Louis learned that French troops had occupied sites along the North African coast since 1830: Algiers and the surrounding areas, Oran, Bône. He heard about bloody battles that took place in the streets of Constantine in October. He also heard that an ally of France, the Algerian leader Emir Abdelkader, had risen up against the occupation. What was to become the French conquest of Algeria was just beginning.

On the grand boulevards Louis overheard talk on other subjects that animated the conversations of the elite. The English—and those that imitated them through the spirit of dandyism and the taste for the fashionable—were overjoyed by the crowning of eighteen-year-old Victoria as queen of Great Britain and Ireland. Enthusiasts of Italian opera discussed the merits of the tenor Rubini and the bass Tamburini, two great singers who were in the latest work by Donizetti, *Lucia de Lammermoor*, at the opera house on Rue Le Peletier. Tongues were clacking over another wonder: the first passenger arrival platform at the newly opened Saint-Lazare train station, near the Madeleine. Intended to be temporary, it debuted at the same time as the official inauguration of the railroad line between Paris and Saint-Germain-en-Laye, some miles west of the capital. Queen Marie-Amélie took part in the inaugural trip on August 26, but her husband, Louis-Philippe, did not join her, as a precaution: The iron machine was still not very well known and it set off with great speed. An unfortunate derailment would deprive the French of the man who had been their king since 1830.

Opposite, clockwise from top left:

The upper class of Paris mingled with the rabble on the "Boulevard du Crime," as illustrated in Marcel Carné's 1945 film *Children of Paradise*.

On the Boulevards, near the opera house, the latest musical works were discussed. Here is *Boulevard des Italiens*, painted by Thomas Shotter Boys, in 1833.

Rue de Rivoli, painted by Giuseppe Canella in 1850, crosses Rue du 29-Juillet, where Louis worked with Monsieur Maréchal as an apprentice box maker.

Inspired by their queen, Marie-Amélie, who was on board, Parisians were fascinated by the first railroad trip to Saint-Germain-en-Laye. Eighteenth-century engraving.

29

Apprentice box maker/packer

As early as 1690 the trade of box maker was celebrated in an engraving by Nicholas de Larmessin.

Baggage was handled roughly in horse-drawn carriages, boats, and trains. To pack precious items and protect them from the hardships of travel, people called upon a box maker. As an apprentice box maker, Louis made a box for each object.

Monsieur Maréchal took Louis on as an apprentice in the autumn of 1837. He would work there for the next seventeen years. The workshop was at the crossroads of Rue du 29-Juillet and Rue Saint-Honoré, where today a stylish boutique called Colette is located. It is a few hundred yards from the Tuileries Palace, where the king of France and his family lived until 1848. Later the Emperor Napoléon III and his young wife, Eugénie, would also live there.

Young Louis became a highly valued box maker/packer within a few years. These titles and this profession hold little meaning today. However, behind the words lies the long tradition of a rich artisanal industry with specialized skills and techniques that would eventually make Louis's fortune.

An ancient trade

Box maker (*layetier* in French): one who makes boxes and whitewood crates, which are used to package, protect, preserve, and transport. It is an old word for an old trade. It comes from the French word *layette*—diminutive of *laie*, meaning "box" or "case." Before taking on its more limited current meaning, "clothing for a newborn," the layette was a drawer in a wardrobe or a small light trunk where important documents and small personal objects were kept. At the end of the Middle Ages, the poet-musician Guillaume de Machaut thus depicted a lover breaking up with his mistress: "I am sending you back the layette you gave to me when you left, and all that was inside it." The layette contained intimate, fragile, and precious things that could be carried, a portable wealth.

The French words for Louis's trades, *layetier* and *emballeur* (box maker and packer), appeared in the sixteenth century. At this time the court of France led a seminomadic existence, traveling from Paris to Fontainebleau to the Loire valley—not to mention the monarch's regular tours of his kingdom. The box makers and packers, ancestors of today's movers, were often called upon to help those in high places with their travels.

The nineteenth-century box maker custom made each item. He went to the client's home to take measurements of each object: clothing, furniture, jewelry, mirror, table sculpture. Each item had to have its own packaging. It was the only way to transport possessions without damaging them. Traveling also required the skills of a packer.

Packer: one who protects the object, wraps it, and places it in a case specially designed for it.

The packer is also an unpacker: Once the parcels arrived safely, the client would call on the packer, rather than his own servants, to remove each object carefully from its protective case.

An old, urbane, Parisian profession

"The masters of the community of box makers of Paris call themselves master box and case makers of the city and suburbs of Paris." Thus is the profession defined in the *Dictionnaire portatif des Arts et Métiers (Portable Dictionary of Arts and Trades)* of 1767. Evidence shows that box making and packing were clearly delineated trades with their own statutes. They were common to the big cities, especially Paris. Elsewhere, the joiner took on the job of box maker/packer. The box maker's tools were the same as those of the joiner, carpenter, and cooper: saw, plane, trying plane, nails. Wood had to be cut, split, smoothed, fitted, and assembled. The most commonly used wood was poplar, followed by beech and oak. Lagging far behind was a pine called boat wood, which was used to make large crates for packing furniture.

In his workshop, the box maker/packer and his apprentices made boxes and crates that were used to transport precious, carefully packed objects. Detail from a plate of the *Encyclopédie* by Diderot and d'Alembert, 1751–72.

Meticulous attention to detail was equally essential to the fabrication of the box as to the packing of the object, which had to withstand bumpy roads and the jogging pace of a horse-drawn carriage. The artisan's work included lavish precautions. In the 1830s and 1840s, when Louis was an apprentice and later a senior clerk at Monsieur Maréchal's establishment, the Parisian box makers' primary job was to pack elegant clothing. They supplied whitewood crates to dressmakers, who delivered apparel to their clients' residences. Whitewood was a sturdy wood that would not damage delicate fabrics such as satin, silk, taffeta, moiré, muslin, and lace. Each piece of clothing was put in a box or layette specially made for it. In its protective case it would travel without risk, no matter how long the trip.

The origin of the luggage maker's know-how
Louis Vuitton would draw on the box maker/packer tradition years later, when he launched himself as a trunk maker. Many elements of the skills and knowledge he had acquired with Monsieur Maréchal would later inspire him:

• Knowledge of the optimal use of poplar for casks and beech for the slats of rigid baggage

• An understanding of the alliance of solidity and lightness: A case that was too heavy increased transportation costs, but one that was too fragile could suffer from the hardships of travel, and its contents could be damaged. Louis Vuitton, trunk maker, would respond to this challenge by inventing the modern, light, and sturdy trunk.

• The shape of packaging crates, whose covers were rein- forced with pieces of wood, similar to what would become the Louis Vuitton trunk, which was flat and fitted with wooden slats

• The ability to imagine diverse interior arrangements based on the customer's requirements

• The principle of designing the trunk, specially ordered by the customer, around the objects that it would contain, rather than trying to fit objects into an existing trunk design.

The splendors of the Second Empire

In an atmosphere of growth, optimism, and economic development, where energy was dedicated to undertaking innovative industrial, technological, and commercial ventures, Louis Vuitton decided to try his wings.

Charles-Louis-Napoléon Bonaparte, the nephew of Napoléon I who had served as elected president of France's Second Republic since 1848, proclaimed himself emperor in December 1852, ushering in the Second Empire, his reign as Napoléon III, and France's economic revitalization. On 30 January 1853 he married Eugénie de Montijo, a Spanish countess. For Louis it was a pivotal point that gave decisive direction to his life.

Empress Eugénie was young, beautiful, ambitious, and concerned with her appearance. The intense attention she paid to her dress and grooming was not a question of vanity but a matter of state. She conceived her role as France's first lady to be ambassador of beauty and elegance. She customarily called upon Louis's services, entrusting him with "packing the most beautiful clothes" and "in an exclusive way," according to Henry-Louis Vuitton, his great-grandson. In the mid-1850s clothing required elaborate care in handling, transportation, and storage because it had reached an unprecedented level of luxury and opulence. It was the heyday of the crinoline.

The era of the crinoline. The petticoats that increased the volume of women's clothing were made in the 1840s of a fabric of wool and horsehair called "crinoline," a word that came to be synonymous with "petticoat." About 1850 the crinoline was replaced by layers of stiff petticoats made with whalebone. In the mid-1850s this cumbersome, heavy system gave way to a lighter metallic cage, which was still called a "crinoline" or "crinoline-cage," although it no longer used the fabric that had given the undergarment its name. Its enormous, billowing shape obscured the outlines of the wearer's body, which was shrouded in cascades of precious fabrics—silk, tulle, muslin, satin, taffeta, lace, and brocade. Above ample clouds of fabric, pearly white arms, curving shoulders, and swanlike throats were exposed, altogether giving women the appearance of being whirling, unreal, elusive creatures.

Opposite: Golden tones of wood, crimson velvet and silk, a wealth of soft furnishings—the Second Empire was marked by opulence.

Above: Napoléon III's coat of arms, with the imperial eagle that told the world of the empire's power.

Above right: *Reception of ambassadors from Siam by Napoléon III and the Empress Eugénie in the great Henri II ballroom at the Château de Fontainebleau, 27 June 1861* (detail), by Jean-Léon Gérôme.

Above: Extract from the score of *La Vie Parisienne,* a comic opera by Jacques Offenbach, libretto by Henri Meilhac and Ludovic Halévy.

Left: The imperial celebration at its height: *Dîner aux Tuileries,* by Eugène-Emmanuel Viollet-le-Duc.

Following pages: *The Empress Eugénie and Her Ladies-in-Waiting,* by Franz Xaver Winterhalter, 1855, presents a sumptuous image. The empress, in white silk and white tulle, is surrounded by the princess of Essling in pink taffeta, the marchioness of La Tour Maubourg in blue silk and black Chantilly lace, the viscountess of Lezay-Marnésia, the baroness of Pierres, and the marchioness of Las Marismas, all in white muslin and tulle, and the duchess of Bassano in a red dress and black lace.

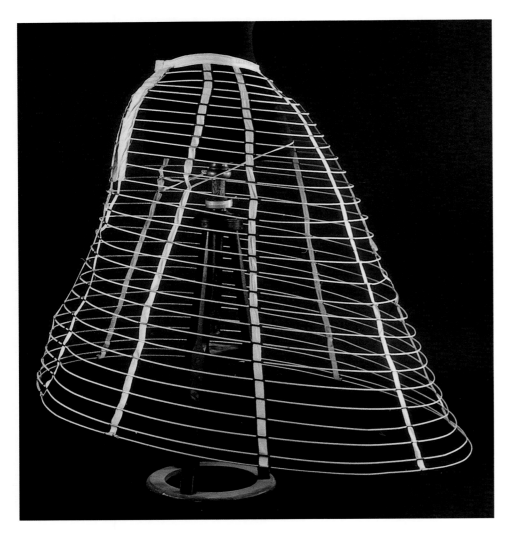

The crinoline was virtually a symbol of the Second Empire, a seductive and fragile banner of the so-called imperial celebration (*fête impériale*). The feverish, exalted atmosphere of the period drew in those swells of Parisian high society whose spirit of adventure—seen in an interest in financial wagering, energetic business affairs, the taste for speculation, quick wealth—was allied to a fierce appetite for opulence, enjoyment, and spending. With ostentation and voracity, people squandered the fortunes they had just audaciously and quickly amassed. As soon as they had the means, these Parisians indulged in a style of living that was princely and extreme, with mansions, lavish horse-drawn carriages, large domestic staffs, and extravagant spending on games, horse races, and receptions. Among society people, wheeler-dealers, courtesans, and adventurers the abundant money circulated rapidly.

The imperial celebration at its height. Emperor Napoléon III and Empress Eugénie were the grand organizers of this nonstop celebration. They were at the heart of court life, its balls, and its travels, which were facilitated by new modes of transportation. It now took only two hours to go from Paris to the Château de Compiègne by train. The new ease of travel and the new desire to vary pleasures contributed to the effervescence of court life. The old aristocracy's routine—spending summers at the provincial castle on family lands and wintering in the mansion in the Saint-Germain quarter on Paris's venerable left bank—

Women's ensembles became increasingly imposing in the mid-nineteenth century. The crinoline, which appeared in 1840, allowed for more ample, voluminous, and heavy dresses. The crinoline-cage, invented in 1850, supported huge volumes of fabric and lace. It became more necessary than ever to call on a box maker to pack such clothes.

gave way to new habits. The court divided its time among the Tuileries Palace, where the atmosphere was somewhat formal, the airier elevations of the Château de Saint-Cloud, where they settled in May, and the chic new seaside resorts—Biarritz, Deauville—where the empress spent the summer, when she didn't go to the spa at Vichy instead. In the fall they all went to Compiègne, Eugénie's favorite place, for hunting parties and walks in the forest followed by a ball or an evening at the Imperial Theater. Of course, clothing and objects had to be transported to and from each of these destinations in packing crates. And that is where Louis's incomparable know-how came into play.

Beneath the splendid appearances was the engine of prosperity. The imperial celebration was driven not only by ostentation, but by determination. The emperor wanted to energize the economy and accelerate the country's modernization. He also wanted to make Paris a dazzling showcase that would rival Great Britain, the leading economic power of the day. The textile industry, for example, expanded along with the emperor's ambition to make Paris the world capital of elegance. The era's constant parties, part of the official promotion of splendid clothing, meant endless demand for women's apparel. The silks of Lyon were revived, as were the wools of Normandy, the laces of Calais, Brittany, and Chantilly, and the ribbons of Saint-Étienne and Roanne. Other businesses, including jewelers, boot makers, glove makers, and feather designers, also benefited from the imperial celebration's highly productive frenzy.

Haussmann redesigns Paris. To make Paris into a metropolis that could rival London, Napoléon III appointed Baron Georges-Eugène Haussmann prefect of the Seine in 1853. He was charged with quickly carrying out a massive urban redevelopment that would transform the capital. Haussmann erased all lingering traces of the Middle Ages and created the look the city still has today. His influential work combined economic aims (such as creating jobs by initiating great construction projects) with public health issues (improving air, water, and living conditions) and political concerns (facilitating the control of urban spaces by the police and army by replacing narrow, twisting streets with wide avenues). On an administrative level, Paris grew to its present boundaries by absorbing eleven adjacent towns. The old, insalubrious town center was opened up and aired out. The architect Victor Baltard was in charge of building the main covered market, Les Halles. Straight new roads, ninety-eight feet wide, were built, paved, and lined with sidewalks. Large arteries were constructed to provide easy access to the new train stations. The city's great east-west-north-south circulation axis was expanded by the eastward extension of Rue de Rivoli, the construction of Boulevard Saint-Michel on the left bank, and the development of Boulevard Sébastopol on the right bank. Areas were cleared around great monuments such as the Louvre, Notre-Dame, and the Hôtel de Ville. Haussmann's assistant, Jean-Charles-Adolphe Alphand, created English-style parks (Bois de Boulogne, Bois de Vincennes, Parc Monceau, Parc Montsouris, Parc des Buttes-Chaumont), added squares throughout the city, and planted one hundred thousand trees. The city of mud, soot, and dirty water that Louis had discovered when he arrived in 1837 was giving way to a much healthier environment. The engineer Eugène Belgrand developed a 373-mile network of sewers that replicated the street plan underground. Plans were organized to supply running water to buildings and to add gas lighting to public roadways. The city breathed. The city sparkled. The city attracted.

To compete with London, which had just organized the first World's Fair at the Crystal Palace in 1851, Napoléon III ordered two similar exhibitions to be organized, one in 1855, the other in 1867. They were showcases of scientific and technical progress as well as national pride, and all the crowned heads of Europe flocked to them.

Paris became the "modern Babylon," where travelers and monarchs converged. Rich Brazilians mingled with Swedish barons. United by their bedazzlement and their enthusiasm, they might very well have disembarked from the train and broken into song as a chorus, much as Offenbach and his librettists imagined at the beginning of his operetta *La Vie Parisienne*.

The textile industry took off with the Second Empire's insatiable demand for silk, wool, lace, ribbons, and feathers, and department stores made their debut.

Empress Eugénie

"One woman seemed to bring good fortune and to be more alive than others in the memories of the people, and this woman was not of royal blood," said Napoléon III of Eugénie. The empress was one of the first people to have confidence in the young Louis Vuitton, with a spontaneous surge of trust that reflected her impulsive character. Though history judges her harshly, she took her role of sovereign very seriously.

Without Eugénie, what would Louis Vuitton's destiny have been? Eugénie quickly came to appreciate the qualities of the box maker/packer of Rue Neuve-des-Capucines. She became a loyal patron and was the first of the Louis Vuitton Company's "prestigious" clients. Perhaps ambition was the common bond between the child of the Jura who was making his way in Paris and the beautiful Spaniard who became empress for love of the emperor.

Born in Grenada on 15 May 1826, Eugénie came from a family of high nobility. Her father was the count of Montijo. In her youth she traveled a great deal throughout Europe and came to love Paris. She crossed Louis-Napoléon's path one autumn day in 1849 as he was reviewing the Satory camp near Versailles. Eugénie, who had gone as a spectator with some friends, immediately caught the eye of the leader of France, who was a connoisseur of feminine beauty. He was enchanted by the purity of her perfectly oval face. Love at first sight was reciprocal, but Eugénie, though impulsive, was not of easy virtue. A stream of official invitations to dinner parties at the Élysée Palace and hunts at Compiègne and Fontainebleau arrived, but the young woman did not surrender to her suitor. When Louis-Napoléon flirtatiously asked her the way to her room, she replied sharply, "By way of the chapel!"

Although his entourage was hesitant, Louis-Napoléon, who declared himself Emperor Napoléon III in December 1852, went ahead. In January 1853 he asked for Eugénie's hand. They married for love at a time when the world favored marriages of convenience.

Eugénie settled into the Tuileries. The morning was her private domain. The empress would receive her suppliers—a couturier like Worth, a milliner, and sometimes her trusted packer Louis Vuitton. Later she would write letters and have her secretary respond to the various requests made of her. If she had time, she visited charitable organizations or read and drew in her office, which the novelist Octave Feuillet described as a "pure dream, a nest for fairies, queens, and bluebirds!" She would then have lunch with the emperor. In the afternoon Eugénie gave official audiences and walked in the Bois de Boulogne.

Dinner followed a strict protocol. In the middle of the evening, while Eugénie abandoned herself to the pleasures of conversation, Napoléon III would slip away to join his mistress of the moment—the stunning countess Castiglione, countess Walewska, or Margot la Rigoleuse.

Posterity has severely judged the Second Empire and has not spared Eugénie. She has been painted as a sanctimonious adventurer, surrounded by a crowd of immoral and mercenary beauties. The reality of the imperial court was more complex. Although the old aristocracy of Saint-Germain may have given her the cold shoulder, she was cosmopolitan as well as versatile.

Eugénie presided over the splendors of a brilliantly social and at times ostentatious life. With the birth of her only son in 1856, she showed an increasing interest in political questions: She worried about the future of the imperial prince, to whom she was passionately attached, and was probably guided by her piety to defend conservative and Catholic interests. She is blamed for her unfortunate influence over Napoléon III's decisions during the last years of the Second Empire, when illness made him hesitant and vulnerable.

After the collapse of the regime in September 1870 Eugénie managed to flee the Tuileries and find refuge in England, where her husband and son joined her. Eugénie would painfully lose both men in her life, surviving them by many decades: Napoléon III died in 1873 and their son, engaged as a lieutenant in the English army, was killed in 1879.

While strolling in London one day in the 1890s Eugénie might have encountered the trade sign of her former box maker/packer, who had opened shop there in 1885. Perhaps seeing the name "Louis Vuitton" revived her memories of imperial glory. Eugénie lived in exile for almost fifty years. She died on 11 July 1920 in Madrid, where King Alfonso XIII had received her as a true sovereign.

In contrast to the conventions of the time, the union of Eugénie de Montijo and Napoléon III was a marriage of love. Their initials are interlaced on the cover of the empress's photo album (above).

Opposite: Empress Eugénie, in a photograph by Eugène Disdéri, was the first crowned head to have an influence on Louis Vuitton's destiny.

Above: A rare image of Empress Eugénie in an exotic outfit in 1860, from the Roger Thérond collection.

Opposite, from left to right and top to bottom: The imperial prince, son of Eugénie and Napoléon III, poses with his mother, on his wooden horse, on his pony, and on the knees of his father in 1858. In his biography of Empress Eugénie (1859) Hippolyte Castille draws a nuanced portrait of Eugénie: "To sketch the imperial and private life of the noble companion of Napoléon III is to retrace a life of beneficence shadowed by the burden of greatness. The empress accepted with piety and devotion, and supported with serenity, the duties of greatness." In the book's frontispiece, the perfect oval of Eugénie illuminates an engraving by Leguay. The imperial court at the Château de Compiègne in 1856, the year the imperial prince was born. Among those close to Eugénie and Napoléon III were Prince Richard de Metternich, ambassador of Austria-Hungary, and his wife, Princess Pauline, photographed by Eugène Disdéri.

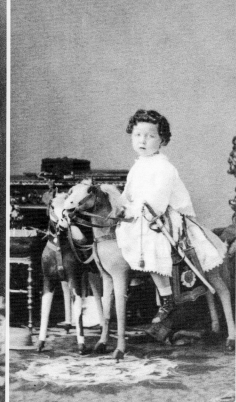

L'IMPÉRATRICE

Opposite: The private life of the imperial family. From left to right and top to bottom: The salon car of the emperor's train in 1863. The young imperial prince at the Château de Compiègne, photographed by Léon Crémière, and in the company of his parents. Empress Eugénie in Biarritz, portrait by Defonds, and (below) with her son on horseback in 1864. Eugénie, here photographed by Gustave Le Gray, was of Spanish origin and deeply pious.

Above: The empress riding on the back of a camel at the inauguration of the Suez Canal on 17 November 1863. Engraving by Alfred Henri Darjou. In his own way, Louis Vuitton participated in the event by providing Egypt's khedive with trunks.

1854 The creation of the company

The creation of the company

It was time to be daring. Louis opened his store and established Maison Louis Vuitton. Always a visionary, he invented the first flat trunk, a model that was ingenious, elegant, and strong—the first modern luggage. Traveling took on a luxurious attribute. A legend was born.

On 22 April 1854 in Créteil, a village a few miles southeast of Paris, Louis married the seventeen-year-old Clémence-Émilie Parriaux. In *La Malle aux souvenirs* (*The Trunk of Memories,* 1984), Henry-Louis Vuitton recounts how his great-grandfather met his future wife. A hard worker, thrifty with his time and his carefully saved money, Louis allowed himself few pleasures. He preferred to devote his leisure to studying the fundamentals of reading and writing. "On rare occasions, and by the express invitation of his employer, he would pass through the tollgate to Vaugirard, to enjoy a pitcher of the white wine that had made the village famous."

During one of those country outings he was introduced to Clémence-Émilie Parriaux. Her father, Nicolas, owner of a mill at Créteil that made wood pulp, had died not long before, in March 1852. This meeting changed something in Louis and led him to take on the role of suitor. Henry-Louis Vuitton imagined his metamorphosis thus: In the winter of 1854, Louis asked his employer for a rare day off: "On that day, in less than two hours, he sacrificed thirty-three francs to purchase a pair of black cassimere pants, a vest, a pair of boots, and a hat at a store named Au Bon Marché, recently opened by Aristide Boucicaut. In the blink of an eye he exchanged the cloth frock and hobnailed shoes of a worker for the courting outfit of the day. The transformation was spectacular, but it required all the know-how of the store's department manager, since Louis's shoulders were much larger than those of Parisian bureaucrats."

Birth of a great company. That same year, Louis made another decision that would have a lasting impact on his future: He opened his own box-making and packing workshop at 4 Rue Neuve-des-Capucines (renamed Rue des Capucines in 1881), near the Place Vendôme. Louis demonstrated skills that surely would have earned him the title "best artisan of France." He described his abilities on a small poster: "Securely packs the most fragile objects. Specializing in packing fashions." Success came quickly, as stylish people sought his know-how. But from the time he opened the store, he knew that the traditional activities of the box maker would not be enough for him. Supported by his knowledge of and love for woodcrafts, he offered trunks to his clientele. He made them himself in the workshop that he set up in Rue du Rocher, in the old, disreputable quarter of Little Poland, which was then in the midst of a renovation that included the enlargement of the Saint-Lazare train station and the construction of Rue de Rome.

Trunk: The French word for "trunk," *malle,* originally meant a supple leather bag. It derived from the Germanic *mal(a)ha* ("pouch," "sack") and the Dutch *male* ("travel bag," "stomach of an animal"). Then came the modern usage: "wooden, leather, or other chest, used to carry belongings."

What did trunks look like when Louis got into the trade? Traditionally, trunk and chest makers at the time made trunks with domed lids. For the exterior casing they favored a leather covering. They usually used the skin of a sow, with the bristle to the outside. The object had a rustic, sturdy, unrefined, almost prehistoric appearance. The sight of one of these old trunks, heavily wrapped in its thick coat, must have given travelers a sense not of the pleasures before them but of cold, uncertainty, pitfalls to overcome, maybe even

In 1854 Louis—shown above in portrait—opened his first store in Paris at 4 Rue Neuve-des-Capucines and founded the company that bears his name.

Opposite: A re-creation of Louis Vuitton's store, as it must have looked in his day. Drawing by Isabelle Barthel.

Following pages: One of the store's first signs promoted special packaging for stylish merchandise.

4, Rue Nve. des

Près la rue

et la Place

Fabrique à l'Héotville, ru

LOUIS V

EMBA

Magasins pour recevoir

Emballe avec sureté
les Objets
les plus fragiles.

Caisses e
et en
Toile C

Spécialité p,r les

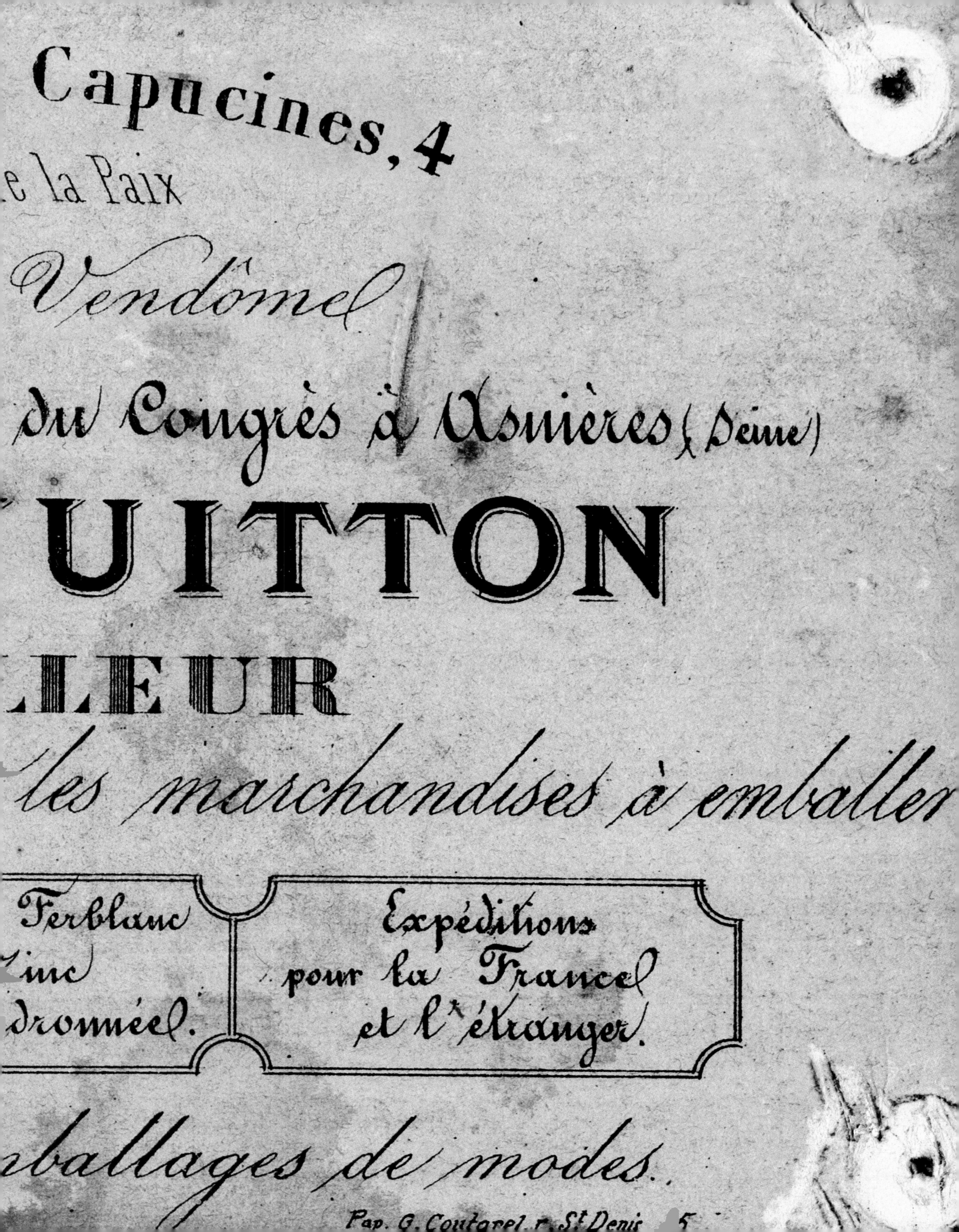

Capucines, 4

e la Paix

Vendôme

du Congrès à Asnières (Seine)

UITTON

LLEUR

les marchandises à emballer

Ferblanc   Expéditions
inc   pour la France
dromée.   et l'étranger.

ballages de modes.

Pap. G. Coutarel r. St Denis 5

packs of wolves to fight off. Louis's first trunk retained the traditional look of the domed lid, but it was already distinguished by lightness (the trunk was made of poplar) and solidity (it was strengthened by metal hooping).

The Trianon gray canvas trunk was born. Louis Vuitton continually came up with practical ideas. He innovated, lightened, simplified. He knew that the leather casing gave off a powerful odor that could impregnate everything inside the trunk. Consequently, he developed a canvas treated with flour-based glue and offered it in a cheerful, discreet, modern color, a light gray called "Trianon gray." The fabric was much lighter than leather and completely waterproof, because the glue penetrating it made it impermeable. Louis offered the trunk in two shapes: the old model with the domed lid and a new model with a flat lid. He firmly believed in his flat-lidded trunk's bright future. In spite of appearances, it was stronger and more solidly built than the trunk with the domed lid. And it was more practical, as its shape was suited to the new means of transportation. Flat and long surfaces assured the luggage's stability, allowing several trunks to be stacked on top of each other. All the trim was of lacquered iron. Henry-Louis Vuitton pointed out that his ancestor had drawn many beneficial lessons from his first trade, noting that the flat trunk was a logical extension of the box maker's crate: "His experience as a box maker and packer taught him that flat and long trunks lent themselves more easily to packing the clothing that was then in fashion, all the more so if they were equipped with compartments for gloves, veils, and fans." This trunk was historic: It was the first Louis Vuitton trunk style.

Success was immediate. In 1858 Louis Vuitton displayed the first series of flat trunks in his store. More appealing, with modern, elegant lines, lighter, more functional, and stronger than traditional trunks, his creations met with immediate success. However, when a dishonest foreman quit to establish his own business marketing trunks that were imitations of the Vuitton model, Louis decided to create a new style that adhered to the same basic principles as the first. His search led him to the slat trunk. Still flat, encircled with iron, and covered with Trianon gray canvas, it was reinforced by nailed beechwood slats. It would revolutionize the travel trunk. Its success was enormous—as witnessed by the fact that it was copied throughout the world, particularly in the United States. Despite the imitations, the original slat trunk was so popular that Louis had to enlarge his business to accommodate the large number of orders for it. The building across the street at 3 Rue Neuve-des-Capucines was available. Louis moved his packing workshop there and devoted the store at 4 Rue Neuve-des-Capucines exclusively to the sale of trunks. Thus creative trunk making supplanted Louis's original activities as box maker/packer. The trunk became

Above left: Before Louis Vuitton, chests usually had domed lids that allowed rainwater to run off. They were often nailed and covered with leather.

Below: In 1854 Louis Vuitton produced his first domed trunks, covering them in Trianon gray canvas.

Opposite: The revolutionary slat trunk in Trianon gray that Louis presented in 1858 was the first luggage of the modern era. Its flat shape enabled it to be stacked in a train's baggage car or in the hold of a ship. Its poplar frame was covered in light gray canvas. More elegant and more functional than any luggage that had preceded it, it brought together the best of Louis Vuitton's know-how—both the art of woodwork and the refinement of the box maker. This photograph shows a trunk made in 1879.

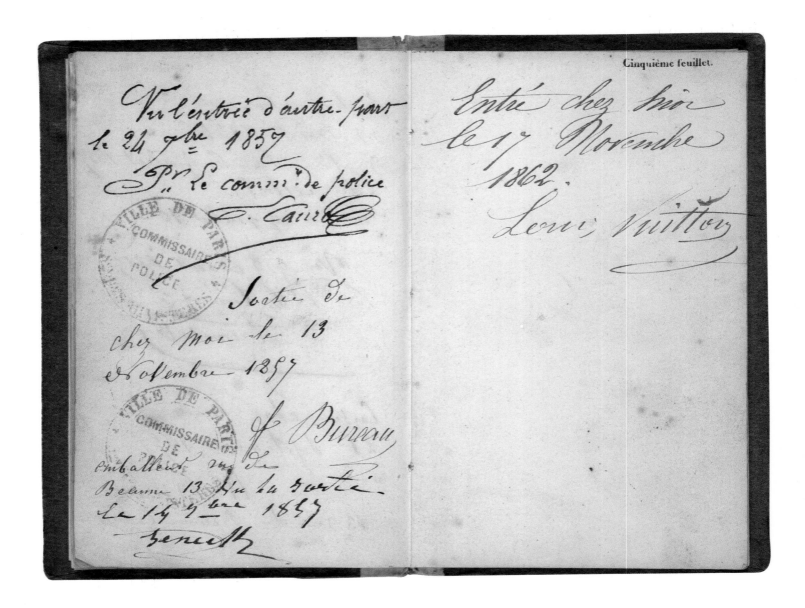

the heart of the company. At the 1867 Exposition Universelle in Paris, Louis—one of 52,000 exhibitors—received a bronze medal for his creations. It was the first official recognition of his work.

Worth, the artist-couturier, as a neighbor. Catering to the tastes and customs of Second Empire high society, Louis brought the concept of luxury to a new level. The idea spread and took hold, paving the way for the likes of Charles Frederick Worth, who would invent haute couture. Worth was an Englishman who had arrived in Paris in 1845 at the age of twenty to work in a fancy-goods shop. He launched his own company in 1857, in association with a young Swede, Otto Gustav Boberg, at 7 Rue de la Paix, a few steps from Louis Vuitton's store. The following year he designed for Princess Metternich an evening dress in white tulle woven with silver and adorned with a pattern of clustered greens and pink-centered daisies. Impressed, Empress Eugénie summoned the couturier to the Tuileries, and Worth's career was established. He became the favorite of fashionable women, and his fame spread from Paris across the international stage. He invented the principle of the designer's collection as well as that of the model (then called a *sosie*, French for "double"), who was selected as a representative of the primary clients' physical type. His taste was for women's clothing with forms more supple than the crinoline-cage, but his designs retained a fantastic fullness. A dress of the 1850s and 1860s, with or without crinoline, required a great deal of fabric. A Worth creation took some fifteen yards of material.

In 1857 Louis's growing success required him to increase his staff to handle the large number of orders. Above: One worker's employee booklet, signed by Louis's own hand. It is the only record of his handwriting.

Opposite: Countess Greffulhe inspired the character of the duchess of Guermantes in Marcel Proust's *Remembrance of Things Past*. In this photograph by Paul Nadar (about 1900) she is dressed by the illustrious Charles Frederick Worth, Louis's friend and neighbor and the inventor of haute couture.

The transportation revolution

In the middle of the nineteenth century the world transformed itself. Within a few decades a technological and industrial society would emerge, revolutionizing living and working conditions. It was the beginning of a modernity to which the birth and rise of Maison Louis Vuitton was intimately linked.

It all started with a revolution in energy and technology. Until this point in history, man had relied upon his own strength to work and to manufacture. He was aided by animals for labor and transportation, by water power for some production (metallurgy, textiles, joinery), and by wind propulsion for travel by boat. The introduction of the steam engine radically transformed those traditions. Developed at the end of the eighteenth century, the steam engine was in widespread use by the nineteenth century. It was powered by coal, which became the primary source of energy. Coal extraction steadily rose, from 90 million tons in 1850 to 1.34 billion tons in 1913. The increase in the power available and the heavy use of machinery changed the fundamental principles of production. Metallurgy, among other industries, experienced a spectacular expansion, with an increase in both the quantity and the quality of metals produced. There was no turning back: The production of steel facilitated the manufacture of steam-powered machine tools, which accelerated the mechanization of human activities.

Full steam ahead. The railway quickly followed the advent of the steam engine. It was based on two inventions, the locomotive and the rail, which was first made of wood and then, at the end of the eighteenth century, of cast iron. In 1825 the English engineer and inventor George Stephenson opened the first railway line. Within a few decades railroads would appear in all developed countries. By 1850 Great Britain had a rail network of nearly 6,835 miles. France's railroad development lagged behind, thanks to King Louis-Philippe's cautious policies. However, by the end of the 1840s the Parisian business world was investing in railways: In 1846 financier James Rothschild created the Société des Chemins de Fer du Nord (Northern Railroad Company) after gathering together two hundred million francs of capital and twenty thousand shareholders in a matter of weeks. But it was up to Napoléon III, in 1851, to stimulate with conviction and determination the enormous investments in railroads that would enable France to catch up to England. The state backed the creation of a national railroad system divided among six large private companies. Within two decades a network had been constructed, with Paris at the center: 2,175 miles of railroad in 1852 grew to 10,750 miles by 1869, leaving only small local lines to be added later.

There was also a revolution in maritime transportation. Steam came to the assistance of wind as a means of propulsion. In 1819 a crossing of the Atlantic by steamship took twenty-seven days. Cunard, the cruise line founded in Great Britain and the first company to offer regularly scheduled transatlantic crossings, significantly reduced travel time: less than fifteen days in 1840 and nine days in 1862. By replacing the paddlewheel with the propeller and perfecting machines that consumed less coal, steamships reigned supreme on the ocean in the second half of the nineteenth century. In France maritime navigation was the province of two large companies: Messageries Maritimes, in Marseilles, provided connections to the Orient and South America, and the Compagnie Générale Transatlantique, in Le Havre, was in charge of connections with North America. In 1870, when London's port handled four million tons of merchandise, two million tons of goods trafficked through Marseilles and one million tons through Le Havre. To compete with England, the state supported the enlargement and improvement of its ports.

Louis Vuitton observed society's great transformation in the mid-nineteenth century. Railroads were built in all the developed countries. In 1869 a 10,750-mile network of railroad tracks covered France. Opposite: The inauguration of a section of railroad in the United States.

Following pages: A meeting at sea of a sailboat and a steamship off Le Havre, photographed by Gustave Le Gray in 1857. Steamships took part in the transportation revolution by reducing travel time.

A new kind of traveler appeared, in quest of adventure. Most of these travelers needed new kinds of baggage for new uses. Opposite: Preparation of a hot-air balloon, photographed by Nadar about 1900.

The transformation to an industrial society required ever-increasing investments. The family-style banking structure shattered, making way for commercial banks and stockholders' shares (above).

The revolution in trade. The railroad's development accelerated the modernization of financial structures capable of supporting large investments. A new type of banking firm was modeled after the pioneering Crédit Mobilier, which was established in 1852 with a capital of sixty million francs. Backed by Napoléon III, Crédit Mobilier's founders, the Pereire brothers, broke from the tradition of family-style banking by offering stock to shareholders and soliciting deposits from a great number of customers throughout France. This approach provided the sizable funds required for industrial investment. Although it was much criticized, the Pereire model was quickly imitated, even by those who had opposed it, giving rise within a few years to large banking corporations: Crédit Industriel et Commercial in 1859, Crédit Lyonnais in 1863, Société Générale in 1864. The financial revolution that took place between 1850 and 1873 also included the introduction of new forms of payment. The promissory note came into common use, and the check was introduced in 1865. Trade intensified throughout the world along with the growth in production.

In the major cities the most spectacular change was the appearance of the large department store. It offered a luxurious setting and a wide variety of merchandise, which was classified into departments and sold at attractive prices. Trade names flourished, and most of them still exist today: Au Bon Marché, founded in 1852, had a sales volume of twenty-one million francs in 1869. The Grands Magasins du Louvre was created in 1855, followed by Le Printemps in 1865 and La Samaritaine in 1869. La Belle Jardinière opened in 1867 at 2 Rue du Pont-Neuf, the present-day headquarters of Maison Louis Vuitton. Small boutiques and merchants did not disappear, but expanded and specialized in the face of the new competition.

The modern world that was emerging seemed like a colossus, a constantly changing and elusive Proteus. Louis Vuitton observed it carefully. In Paris he had the advantage of being well and quickly informed, giving him a good sense of the future. He thought about

his own direction. With his courage and experience, what place could he make for himself in a world undergoing a complete transformation?

The extraordinary voyage. " 'Around the world,' murmured Passepartout.

'In eighty days,' replied Mr. Fogg. 'So we haven't a moment to lose.'

'But the trunks?' gasped Passepartout, unconsciously swaying his head from right to left.

'We'll have no trunks. Just a carpet bag. Inside, two woolen shirts, three pairs of stockings. The same for you. We'll buy along the way. Bring down my mackintosh and my travel rug, and take sturdy shoes, though we will do little walking. Go.' "

Published in 1873, Jules Verne's *Around the World in Eighty Days* captured the tone of the period. Verne's hero, the Englishman Phileas Fogg, accompanied by his French servant Passepartout, accomplished the trip in record time. He had against him all the unforeseeable circumstances of traveling, but they were greatly offset by the reliability of the new means of transportation. After leaving London and reaching Calais by boat, he took the train to Brindisi, where he caught the Indian Mail train. It went from Italy to France through the Mont-Cenis tunnel, which had just been inaugurated in September 1871. He traveled on a steamship that took him to Bombay through the Suez Canal, opened three years before. He crossed India to reach Calcutta via the Great Indian Peninsular Railway, completed in 1870—with an interlude on the back of an elephant. Finally, to cross the United States from San Francisco to Chicago to New York, Fogg got aboard the transcontinental railroad, the Grand Trunk, completed in May 1869. Other novels in Verne's series *Extraordinary Voyages* depicted the wonders of travel by land, sea, and air. *Five Weeks in a Balloon* detailed a flight over Africa. *A Floating City* put the reader on board the *Great Eastern,* the world's largest ocean liner, on which the novelist made a round trip between Europe and the United States. *Claudius Bombarnac* followed a great reporter across Asia, traveling by rail between Tbilisi and Peking and crossing the Caspian Sea by boat. That itinerary was largely imaginary. Verne invented the Grand Transasiatic Railway that stretched 3,728 miles through Pamir, Chinese Turkestan, and the southern Gobi Desert, connecting Paris to Peking in thirteen days. In reality, Russia in the 1890s, pursuing an eastward expansion across Asia, would build a trans-Caspian railroad to Samarkand and Tashkent and plan the trans-Siberian line, completed in 1904, via Omsk and Irkutsk to Vladivostok.

The birth of wanderlust. In the last decades of the nineteenth century the transportation revolution accelerated across the globe. Trips were regularly organized over large distances, across oceans, through territory that had been previously impenetrable. The scheduled

itineraries of transatlantic or transpacific steamers stimulated a desire to travel and even inspired emigrants, enabling them to discover a new world or invent a new life.

The new ways of moving about opened the world up like a large fan. The whistle of the locomotive, the foghorn of the steamship, and the clackety-clack of steam engines all promised reliable travel to faraway lands. They were calls to relocate, to search for virgin landscapes, to contemplate unknown skies. Going to the other side of the globe was no longer a pipe dream. You could travel anywhere on the map where railroad lines or steamship routes were drawn, and the time the trip would take could be accurately measured. It was now a matter of mere weeks or days, fixed schedules, and guaranteed connections. Going around the world was no longer the life-risking adventure it had been for James Cook or La Pérouse in the eighteenth century. The expedition still held the thrill of the unknown and the unforeseeable but it could be planned and organized. After all, even Phileas Fogg always carried with him the modern traveler's new bible, *Broadshaw's Continental Railway Steam Transit and General Guide*.

Faces of the explorer. The Earth gave way to the appetites of incredibly diverse travelers. The search for El Dorado, the hunt for gold and spices, and the quest to save souls were motivations then as they are today, but new faces appeared in the company of the gold seekers, traders, and missionaries. They included explorers drawn to the remotest or most extreme regions—equatorial or Saharan Africa, the interior of China, the depths of the tropical forests, the North and South Poles. There were also colonial officers, conquerers and builders of empires on behalf of Old Europe. And, most of all, there were the well-to-do tourists who inspired the term "globetrotter." Their affluence and the new means of transportation made it possible for them to travel the world freely. Leaving behind their bourgeois comforts, they sought the heightened emotions, the rare sensations, even the new scents that travel to exotic locales could provide. They were sensualists, aesthetes, and adventurers at the same time.

Traveling to faraway places meant carrying a great deal of supplies—everything necessary to combine freedom with comfort. Very few people followed Phileas Fogg's example and left home without trunks. Even he had to recognize their utility when he saved Mrs. Aouda, a ravishing young Indian woman, from her aged husband's funeral pyre. "Since Mrs. Aouda accepted his offer to take her to Europe, Phileas Fogg had to think about all the details that such a long voyage entailed. That an Englishman like him could travel around the world with one bag was possible; but a woman couldn't undertake such a trip under these conditions. Thus, it was a necessary to buy clothes and the articles needed for travel." Louis Vuitton understood this need very well and strove to create luggage that was adaptable to all situations.

Above: *The Great Eastern,* 689 feet long, was the world's largest ocean liner when it made its maiden voyage in 1860. Jules Verne, who took a round trip from Europe to the United States aboard the ship, described it as a veritable floating city. Robert Howlett photograph, before 1858.

Below: First illustrated edition of *Around the World in Eighty Days,* by Jules Verne, 1873, from the Hetzel collection.

Isma'il Pasha and the Suez Canal

At the 1869 inauguration of the Suez Canal, Isma'il Pasha, khedive of Egypt, topped the long list of heads of state who made Louis Vuitton their preferred supplier and gave him special orders. His exceptional articles developed an elite following.

Port Said, east of the Nile delta, is where the African continent meets the Sinai peninsula. On 17 November 1869 the khedive of Egypt welcomed there all of European high society, as well as a number of celebrities from beyond Europe, to celebrate the official opening of the Suez Canal. Eight hundred guests—including the sovereign of the Ottoman Empire, the khedive's suzerain—arrived for the inaugural festivities, complete with cannon salutes, flag-bedecked ships, blessings, official speeches, toasts, libations, and balls. Paul Morand, in his *Route des Indes,* brought the scene to life: "The Sultan Abdülaziz himself has deigned to participate in the celebrations; honored by the visit of his suzerain, the khedive receives him on bended knees, then accompanies the imperial carriage on foot, one hand resting on the door as a sign of vassalage. Empress Eugénie steps down from a camel and Emperor Franz Josef, wearing a blue veil, smokes rose-scented tobacco in a hookah with a mouthpiece of diamond-studded amber. The princess of the Netherlands tries on pants gathered at the ankle, and Emir Abdelkader tastes jams offered to him by the grand mufti of Cairo." Also present were Archduke Victor of Habsburg, the royal prince of Prussia, and the crown prince of Hanover, while absent sovereigns made sure they were represented by their ambassadors.

The contrasts were dazzling: luxurious clothing and accessories, laces, pearls, carriages, and thoroughbred horses mixed among the picturesque local people and exotic beasts—fellahs, sheiks, dancing girls, goats, buffalo, and dromedaries. Two worlds collided to celebrate the new maritime route that would bring Europe and Asia closer together.

Ferdinand de Lesseps alters geography. For the Frenchman Ferdinand de Lesseps, the canal's project manager, it was a glorious day. "The Suez Canal was the great passion

Previous pages: The arrival of the prince of Wales at Port Said. The world's sovereigns attended the inauguration of the Suez Canal in 1869, and their great ships were on procession there. Empress Eugénie arrived aboard the imperial ship *L'Aigle.*

For Isma'il Pasha, the khedive of Egypt (pictured right), Louis Vuitton created a trunk with racks to transport fresh fruit (left). It was one of the company's first special orders.

An enlightened sovereign, Isma'il Pasha commissioned Giuseppe Verdi to write an opera. The composer produced *Aida.* The Egyptologist Auguste Mariette designed the sets. The model shown here (far right) is part of the collection of the Bibliothèque-Musée de l'Opéra de Paris, whose renovation was funded in part by Maison Louis Vuitton.

of his life," noted Paul Morand. When he was appointed vice-consul of France in Alexandria, in 1832, Lesseps took up a project first conceived during Napoléon Bonaparte's Egyptian campaign: a plan to cut through the Suez isthmus, connecting the Mediterranean and the Red Sea. By chance he became a close friend of Crown Prince Muhammad Sa'id Pasha. Once Sa'id Pasha ascended Egypt's throne in September 1854—a momentous year—he solicited Lesseps's ideas on the country's development. Within only a few weeks Lesseps had convinced his friend of the canal's importance. Lesseps obtained the exclusive right to create a company that would build the canal and oversee its operation. Despite the opposition of the British, who were concerned about controlling all routes to India, and in spite of the technical difficulties and exorbitant cost, the work, which began in April 1859, advanced rapidly. Lesseps could count on the support of the Egyptian government, which put at his disposal twenty thousand workers, who had been requisitioned as forced labor. However, in 1863 Sa'id Pasha died. His nephew and successor Isma'il Pasha was not hostile to Lesseps but he was a more modern "canalist" than his uncle and did not want to offend the British. The work was suspended to renegotiate the conditions of the contract between Egypt and the Compagnie de Suez. It took Napoléon III's intervention for the two parties to reach an agreement, in July 1864, and work finally resumed. At last, in August 1869 the two seas were joined: the Mediterranean at Port Said and the Red Sea at Suez.

Louis Vuitton, the khedive's supplier. The khedive of Egypt had gone to Paris a few months earlier, in June 1869, to discuss the canal's inaugural ceremonies. Empress Eugénie would be given the seat of honor, as she had continuously supported the ambitions of Lesseps (who was her cousin) against the British. She had pleaded his cause to her husband, Napoléon III. Lesseps had privileged access to the Tuileries Palace. As a preferred supplier, no doubt Louis Vuitton did too. His reputation for excellence had already been established in imperial Paris. Although it is not known whether the empress personally recommended her favorite box maker/packer to the khedive, one thing is sure: Isma'il Pasha called upon Louis's ingenuity to fill several special orders for trunks, which were to be delivered at the time of the Suez Canal's inauguration. Louis Vuitton customized his creations for the khedive with special racks for storing, preserving, and transporting fresh fruit. History does not tell whether the fruit that Isma'il Pasha served his eight hundred guests in November was transported in the newly made Louis Vuitton trunks.

Empress Eugénie at her zenith. In September 1869 Eugénie left her residence at Saint-Cloud and went to Venice. There she boarded the *Aigle* to Istanbul, where she was received with pomp by the sultan, ruler of the Ottoman Empire. She sailed on to Egypt, where Isma'il Pasha had completely furnished a palace for her with goods from France. The Egyptologist Auguste Mariette took her to visit ancient monuments, including the Temple of Luxor and the pyramids at Giza. Her arrival at the inauguration was a triumph for the empress: Aboard the *Aigle* she entered Port Said escorted by a glittering armada of sixty-eight ships carrying other crowned heads. Eugénie was acclaimed. After participating in a double benediction, officiated by both a Christian and a Muslim, she boarded the emperor of Austria's ship. They passed beside the Spanish frigate *Berneguela*, where the officers broke into Andalusian songs in her honor. The next day the festivities culminated with a ball. Against the rhythm of Viennese waltzes, Eugénie was the most sparkling jewel. She wore a gown of nasturtium-colored satin dotted with flowers and trimmed with point lace from Alençon and silver lamé netting. She was participating in one of the last great international events to parallel the splendors of the imperial celebration. When she returned to Paris a few weeks later the capital was frozen by the winter cold. Everything seemed sad. Perhaps Eugénie had a presentiment that the year that had just arrived, 1870, would be terrible.

La Tribune des souverains à Port-Saïd, painted by Riou, echoes Paul Morand's description in *La Route des Indes.* "Despite all opposition, the canal is built. 17 November 1869 is the inauguration day. All Europe, now convinced, is represented here. Cannon salutes, musket fire, fluttering flags, blessings, the speech of Napoléon III at the opening of the chambers, telegraphed congratulations, *Te Deum* in Paris, verses from the Koran in Port Said. . . . Isma'il Pasha lavished millions; he had to feed eight hundred guests in the middle of the desert; his yacht made of precious wood had ebony, mother-of-pearl, and ivory doors with silver hinges; he invited all his subjects and arranged them into ethnic groups around the canal."

Asnières, cradle of the Vuittons

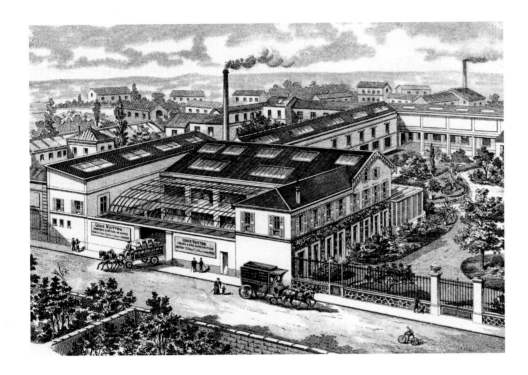

Louis had to expand his operations to keep up with his success. In 1859 he moved his workshops to Asnières, a village in the countryside that was just over a mile from the gates of Paris and near the train station and the barges of the Seine. His family eventually would move there too.

The success of Louis Vuitton's trunks made his Rue du Rocher location too cramped. Just as a growing Paris could no longer be held within the boundaries of the Fermiers-Généraux wall, Louis was stifled within the confines of his workshop. At about the same time that Paris expanded to its present-day borders, Louis looked for a spacious lot where he could set up a new workshop with room for future expansion. Anticipating the success and growth to come, he needed a site that would keep pace with his ambitions. In a strategic business move, Louis chose a plot of more than 48,500 square feet in Asnières, a village northeast of the center of Paris and less than three miles as the crow flies from the Opéra district. Asnières was easily accessible by train from Paris's Saint-Lazare station. In addition, Asnières's site along the Seine provided convenient access to the barges that would carry the raw materials. Louis needed large quantities of poplar wood to manufacture his trunks' framework, and river transport was less expensive than transportation by road. He obtained his stock in the Oise valley, north of the Île-de-France, where the fertile, humid conditions were especially favorable for growing poplars.

Asnières, workshop for social progress. On the site he acquired on Rue du Congrès, in the district of Héotville—named for a former owner—Louis Vuitton began constructing his manufacturing shop. He adopted the most modern architectural principles of the

In 1859, to keep pace with his trunks' growing success, Louis opened new workshops in Asnières, northwest of Paris. Located along the Seine, the village of Asnières (pictured opposite) was also accessible by train from Paris's Saint-Lazare station. The engraving (above left) appeared on the back cover of the company's 1897 catalogue.

Following pages: The heart of the Asnières workshops, pictured about 1888, when the company had about thirty employees. On and around the delivery truck are the trunks whose quality made Louis, his son Georges, and their workers proud. Louis's grandson Gaston-Louis lies upon a trunk-bed.

time, using a metal framework and combining iron and glass in the style used by Baltard at Les Halles and by Gustave Eiffel for his famous tower in 1889 and other works. The Asnières workshop would expand regularly to accommodate Maison Louis Vuitton's manufacturing and commercial development. In the 1880s a metal hall was erected, and about 1900 two rows of workshops were constructed alongside the existing building. These expansions of the work site followed steady increases in the work force. In 1859 twenty people worked at Louis's Asnières workshop; in 1880 there were nearly thirty employees; in 1900 almost one hundred people worked in six workshops. From that point until the outbreak of the First World War, in the summer of 1914, the company's domestic and international expansion (it had four shops in France, one in London, and fifteen agencies in other countries) was reflected by a rapid increase in personnel at Asnières: 125 workers in 1908, 200 in 1911, and 225 in June 1914. All employees benefited from an internal system of social security. The company had established in November 1891 a philanthropic Mutual Aid and Retirement Fund for the Asnières staff. The fund was supported by workers' contributions (one percent of their salaries) and payments by the employers, which "Messieurs Vuitton reserve the right to increase at their convenience." The fund's benefits included a reimbursement of fifty percent of the cost of a doctor's visit, full reimbursement for pharmaceutical costs, and daily compensation at half pay after the third day of a work stoppage. Moreover, the retirement fund provided a pension to employees who had been with the company at least fifteen years when they "stopped work due to an incapacity linked to age or infirmity duly recorded."

A family residence. Asnières was not only a manufacturing site, it was the Vuitton family's home for several generations. At the suggestion of his wife, Émilie, Louis had a

Above: The factory's metal and glass construction bathed the work space in light. This innovative structure, built like the Eiffel Tower, held to the same standards of quality and comfort as did all Louis Vuitton products.

Louis's first consecration: At the Exposition Universelle of 1867 his designs were awarded a bronze medal. Always on the cutting edge, even in his advertising, Louis produced a small poster (opposite) to announce both that award and a silver medal won in the International Maritime Exhibition of Le Havre in 1868.

pied-à-terre constructed above the workshop, although the Vuittons remained in their Paris home on Rue Neuve-des-Capucines. Their son Georges was born in 1857. He was put in the care of a wet nurse in Asnières, close to his parents' property. In 1862, at the age of five, "he was led some five hundred yards from there and put into a boarding school," which he would leave only on Sundays and during school vacations. Georges remained at that school until the end of the Franco-Prussian War of 1870–71, when he was sent to continue his studies at a high school in Jersey. At that time Louis and Émilie left their Parisian residence to live in Asnières. In 1880, when Georges married Joséphine Patrelle and assumed important duties at the company, the family residence changed its appearance. Louis freed up the upstairs living quarters so the workshops could expand. He had two villas built in the garden adjoining the factory. One, which he kept for himself, was spacious and equipped with numerous guest rooms; the other provided lovely quarters for Georges and his wife.

In Louis's eyes, Asnières had a double advantage: It was part of the city, where one climbed to success, and also part of the countryside, where his roots were (though it was far from the Jura, to which he would never return). Here the Vuittons lived, worked, and gathered together, achieving personal and commercial success. A letter from Louis's grandson Gaston-Louis to his cousin Jean Gimpel (son of the renowned art dealer René Gimpel and grandson of Louis's niece Adèle Vuitton) described the residence in Asnières as a real family home where a circle of close family members visited religiously. "Asnières was in the countryside, and at my grandfather's every Sunday he had an open house, a pot-au-feu, and all four [Adèle, her two sisters, and Miss Marqua, a sales clerk for Worth] regularly attended these gatherings."

After Louis's death in 1892, Georges, his wife, Joséphine, and their three sons moved into the grand paternal home. He invested in modernizing the interior decor, following a botanical style made fashionable by Louis Majorelle. Georges had made Majorelle's acquaintance and through him discovered the decorative splendors and technical feats achieved by the glassworks school of Nancy, especially the works of artists like the Daum brothers and Émile Gallé. Joséphine Vuitton lived at the house in Asnières until her death in 1964.

Lights from the Île-de-France. In 1859, when the Vuittons settled there, Asnières still had its rural character. Not far from the Saint-Lazare station and along the banks of the Seine, it lay amid the gentle and colorful countryside of the Île-de-France, which the new school of Impressionist painters was glorifying. Beginning in the 1860s the Impressionists left their studios to capture the special out-of-doors atmosphere, the variations in light throughout the day and the seasons, the play of water and its reflections, the perpetually changing passage of clouds, the shapes of the landscapes, the color and movement of boats and sails—a thousand sources of stimulating impressions for the artist's eye.

In Asnières the river set the pace for daily life. It was not just a circulation route but also a place for amusements and relaxation. Impressionist painters fixed upon their canvases festive scenes of sailboat races, of open-air music cafés, of dancers swirling by the water's edge. A nautical company based at the Asnières bridge organized regattas on the river. Like true locals, Louis Vuitton and his son Georges took part. Those two tireless workers, whose output was entirely devoted to travel objects, found a pleasant escape just a few steps from home. Rowing on the river on a sunny Sunday afternoon was an idle time stolen from their daily labors.

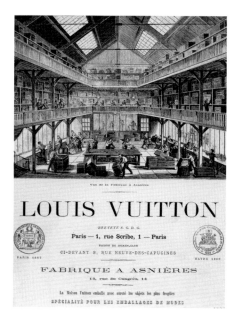

The poplar boards used to manufacture trunks were transported aboard the Louis Vuitton barge on the Seine (above). They were put out to dry after arriving in Asnières, shown (opposite) in 1902.

1871, Rue Scribe

The 1870s began in ruins and tears. The Franco-Prussian War led to the fall of Napoléon III and the long, brutal siege of Paris. The Empire gave way to the Paris Commune, a socialist government, and a bloody, destructive civil war. Louis Vuitton had to rebuild on new foundations.

It took only a few weeks in the summer of 1870 for the Second Empire to collapse. After being drawn into war against Prussia and confronting Chancellor Otto von Bismarck's unwavering determination to unify Germany, Napoléon III capitulated on 2 September in Sedan. He went into exile in England. With the fall of the Empire came the proclamation of the Third Republic. The Republicans took power in Paris but they could not stop a German invasion. Although surrounded by Prussian forces, the capital resisted. The Siege of Paris lasted four months—a long, severe winter during which the people suffered bombardments and food shortages. Henry-Louis Vuitton described, in his *Malle aux souvenirs,* the dedication and energy with which his great-grandfather Louis took charge of organizing supplies in the Capucines district. Food was rationed quickly, with about ten ounces of poor-quality bread distributed to each person each day. Horsemeat, limited to an ounce a day, sold at eleven francs a pound. When the meat started running out, people took to eating anything: Rat sold for two francs a piece, and more exotic animals—including two elephants from the Jardin des Plantes, Castor and Pollux—were slaughtered on 30 December. The next day Louis, who had witnessed their sacrifice, noticed near his residence on Boulevard Haussmann that the English butcher Roos was selling the elephant trunk at the exorbitant price of seventy-three francs a pound. The besieged city struggled not only to find nourishment but also to communicate with the rest of the country. Parisians resorted to sending messages by balloon. Manufacturing these aerostats required a lot of canvas, and Louis's stock was requisitioned for that purpose.

The headstrong Louis starts over. When Paris surrendered on 28 January 1871, Louis was able to return to Asnières. What he discovered there was devastating. The buildings, workshops, and apartment had been used as military quarters and were damaged. The soldiers had used the entire inventory of poplar as firewood. Even worse, all the tools had disappeared, and the staff had been dispersed by the war. Fifteen years of work were reduced to nothing.

It would take more than that to discourage a strong-willed son of the Jura. He used the personal and national disaster as the springboard for a fresh start. He could have thrown in the towel and returned to his native region, as his brother Claude-Régis did. Claude-Régis's grandson, the art dealer René Gimpel, reported the circumstances of his grandfather's return home in his *Journal d'un collectionneur.* According to the story handed down to René by his mother, Adèle Vuitton, Claude-Régis had gone to Paris to join Louis, who was six years older. Together they embarked upon their venture manufacturing and selling trunks. "The Franco-Prussian War ruined my grandfather, because a lot of people didn't pay him, but he paid his own debts," René explained. "He didn't have the strength or courage to start over." He returned to Anchay, where his daughter Adèle regularly visited him, and led a quiet life, spending most of his time hunting with his dog. The reality may have had a less heroic tint than the family legend. With Asnières devastated and everything needing to be redone, Claude-Régis—indolent by contrast to the hard-working Louis—chose to return to the gentle pace of provincial life. That's the version of the story Gaston-Louis Vuitton offered his cousin Jean Gimpel in a letter dated October 1965.

Louis and his wife, Émilie, had a greater vision and made bigger plans. They not only rebuilt the workshops of Asnières but expanded them. They decided to sell the two shops

Paris endured a four-month siege by the Prussian Army and a popular uprising during the Commune. The Capucines quarter was devastated, the Vendôme column was knocked down, the Tuileries Palace was set ablaze.

Previous pages: A barricade on Rue Royale, photographed by Collard. The village of Asnières was not spared, and Louis Vuitton's workshops were ruined.

Louis did not lose courage. He had the workshops at Asnières rebuilt and opened a new shop at 1 Rue Scribe, across from the Grand Hôtel. Below: A handbill advertises the shop's change of address. Its specific mention that English is spoken shows an early outreach to a foreign clientele.

Opposite: Horse-drawn carriages deliver the trunks that were made in Asnières.

on Rue Neuve-des-Capucines. Once Paris settled down, after three months of bloody civil war, they moved to a new building. Though not far from their former address, they had symbolically crossed the border of the Boulevards. The new premises they bought at 1 Rue Scribe would be Maison Louis Vuitton's Paris address until 1914.

In the heart of the new Paris. Even before Louis Vuitton's arrival, 1 Rue Scribe had an aura of prestige: It was home to the aristocratic Jockey-Club—a sophisticated social club attached to the Society for the Encouragement, Improvement, and Perfection of Horseracing in France, founded by Lord Seymour in November 1833. This members-only men's club, reserved for the elite of the Saint-Germain district, occupied part of the Hôtel Scribe, which opened in 1860 at the corner of Boulevard des Capucines and Rue Scribe. The ground-floor corner housed the Grand Café. Louis's shop, in the Jockey-Club's former saddle room, had thirty-six feet fronting the street and a depth of twenty-six feet. Three bays faced the street, two devoted to trunks and travel items and the third to packing. Louis Vuitton presented himself as both trunk maker and box maker/packer.

In terms of marketing strategy, the choice of Rue Scribe was a good one. To get a foothold there was to be part of the heart of the new Paris. The shop was across from the Grand Hôtel and the new Place de l'Opéra, where the architect Charles Garnier was completing an enormous theater that would replace the old Académie de Musique on Rue Le Peletier. The quarter was being completely renovated, and the events of the Franco-Prussian War and the Paris Commune were being quickly forgotten. It was a modern district.

The travelers at the Grand Hôtel. From the very beginning the Pereire brothers, who were active in real estate as well as finance, conceived their Grand Hôtel as a destination

for elite international travelers. The investment in its construction was colossal: twenty-one million gold francs. The building, designed by architect Alfred Armand, took shape on a triangular site of 86,000 square feet bordered by Boulevard des Capucines, Rue Scribe, and Rue Auber. The work, which lasted from April 1861 to June 1862, created the largest hotel in Europe, with eight hundred rooms and apartments that provided the "peak of comfort." It was also the most luxurious and most modern hotel, filled with the latest innovations, including a hydraulic elevator serving all floors from six in the morning to midnight, and bathrooms, showers, and a hydrotherapy spa on the mezzanine. Lighting was provided by 4,000 gaslights (replaced in 1890 by electric lights); heat, produced by 18 furnaces, was distributed by 354 heating registers (central steam heating would be introduced in 1901). In 1911 a telephone would be installed in every room. It was a Parisian hot spot where travelers enjoyed the latest advancements in technology, science, and the arts. A guide published at the time praised the hotel's excellence as worthy of the most distinguished guests: "The Grand Hôtel provides the best accommodations Paris can offer to foreigners. Sovereigns traveling unofficially found princely accommodations at the Grand Hôtel, for themselves and their attendants, as numerous as they may be. Its location in the center of the new Paris, or to put it more aptly, the true Paris, is near to all the amenities of Parisian life." It was a microcosm of high society, a cosmopolitan hive. Here one could rub shoulders with the entire world and hear every language spoken: "From six in the morning to one in the morning, the courtyard is an ever-changing kaleidoscope: Cars bring travelers from every country, wagons loaded with luggage, omnibuses from the railroad, caleches with high-spirited horses, horsemen, horsewomen, strollers, interpreters, couriers, sommeliers."

A new quarter focused on travel. The train stations were not far away from the Grand Hôtel. Saint-Lazare, just at the end of Rue Auber, provided a connection to the ports, where travelers embarked for England and America. The entire quarter was devoted to the most

The much-admired Opéra de Paris (at right above) remains the Second Empire's architectural jewel and a model for opera houses throughout the world. It was the masterpiece of architect Charles Garnier (below, photographed by Nadar).

On the same square, the famous Grand Hôtel, built at Napoléon III's request, received a clientele of rich cosmopolitan travelers, who also visited the Louis Vuitton shop.

refined tourism, its elegance, and its pleasures. And at its heart, a few steps from the Louis Vuitton shop and across from the Grand Hôtel, stood the new Paris opera house, named the Palais Garnier for its architect, Charles Garnier. The Opéra was the nerve center of the Parisian art world, where the forces of artistic life and high society met and mingled. There was as much to see in the boxes, salons, and lobbies as in the orchestra pit and on the stage.

Paris builds itself an opera house. The official decision to construct a new opera house was made in September 1860 and, for the first time in the history of public architecture, a competition for its design was held. Each submission had to respect detailed specifications. To everyone's surprise the commission went to young Charles Garnier, who had won the Grand Prix de Rome in 1848, over architects as influential as Viollet-le-Duc. Work on the project was soon underway but would take fifteen years to finish. It was an expensive and formidable undertaking. The government estimated the total price at thirty-three million francs, knowing that it would actually cost twice as much. The marshy land required drainage on a vast scale and still demanded technical innovations that would enable it to support a great structure: The opera house was built on a three-story foundation, with the bottom level, filled with water like a reservoir, working to ballast the structure. Politics also presented challenges to the construction project. Work was partially stopped in 1867 when the imperial regime, shifting its social policy, favored financing the Hôtel-Dieu, the "refuge of the suffering," at the expense of the Opéra, a "temple of pleasure." Three years later work was completely stopped by the Franco-Prussian War and the collapse of the Second Empire.

A "blessed" accident led to the fiery destruction of the opera house on Rue Le Peletier in October 1873, and work recommenced at the Opéra Garnier three years after it had been stopped. The new theater was brilliantly inaugurated on 5 January 1875. A select international audience gathered for the occasion. Attending with Patrice de Mac-Mahon,

The photographer Nadar, another of Louis's friends and neighbors, received celebrated members of Parisian high society in his studio at 35 Boulevard des Capucines (opposite). That is where an anecdote cited by Henry-Louis Vuitton in *La Malle aux souvenirs* took place: "In April 1874, Nadar put his photography studio at the disposal of a group of practically unknown Impressionist painters. They included Monet, Renoir, Pissarro, Sisley, Cézanne, Degas, and Berthe Morisot. Louis and Georges were also among the first to have laid eyes on a canvas by Claude Monet entitled *Impression, soleil levant,* painted in 1872 [pictured above]. A few days later, it inspired Louis Leroy, a journalist at the *Charivari,* to coin the term 'Impressionist.'"

president of the young Third Republic, were the lord-mayor of London, the king of Spain, and the burgomaster of Amsterdam. As Martine Kahane, the illustrious chief curator at the Bibliothèque-Musée de l'Opéra de Paris, noted: "This formal opening constituted one of the first demonstrations of the Revenge. The government of the Third Republic wanted to make a public act of national pride to affirm the renaissance of France, which a few years before had been defeated and humiliated in the grip of foreign occupation and civil war."

Garnier's masterpiece stupefied and shocked some with its wealth of ornament. The architect had used all the resources of his art to mask the building's metal framework under exuberant decoration. The Opéra soon took on the stature of a Parisian monument. It aroused "an immense public curiosity, and for ten years the entire world paraded past to wonder at its sumptuousness and beauty," wrote Martine Kahane. "This same sumptuousness was an object of criticism, and caricaturists had a field day using it to make fun of the bourgeois dazzled by the gold covering the walls of the Palais Garnier, sparkling to its ceiling."

Stripes, the signature of luxury. In tune with his setting in a district devoted to the modern and welcoming the world, Louis Vuitton distinguished himself with his creativity. The 1870s, years of radical reform in France, saw the company blossom anew. The 1850s and 1860s had been characterized by the invention of modern luggage and the widespread acceptance of the flat trunk. The 1870s would be marked by the introduction of luxury luggage. Henry-Louis Vuitton explained with an expert precision, "For the protection of edges and corners, Louis Vuitton replaced metal fittings with leather. The removable frames, which permitted a functional distribution of belongings inside the trunk, kept the stretched canvas bottoms, but the lids were lined with diamond-shaped padding, and a small nail with a golden head attached each intersection of binding. The luxury trunk was born." The success of the Trianon gray canvas had spurred many imitations, so beginning in 1872 Louis Vuitton offered his clients a canvas of red stripes printed on a beige background: a simple, cheerful, and singular pattern that once again charmed his customers and launched a fashion for striped canvas. Again asserting the company's originality in the face of imitation, Louis Vuitton changed the color range four years later, introducing in 1876 a monochrome canvas with alternating stripes of light and dark beige. From that point on a monochrome palette of beige and brownish beige was Maison Vuitton's graphic signature. It would be used again for the Damier canvas and the Monogram canvas years later.

Reflecting on the significance of stripes and striped fabrics in the West, the historian Michel Pastoureau wrote in his book *L'Étoffe du diable* that the stripe had been perceived as evil, even diabolic, in the Middle Ages. It changed its status during the Renaissance, becoming prestigious and aristocratic, especially the vertical stripe; horizontal stripes were a sign of lowly position. At the end of the eighteenth century the stripe, whose uses expanded from clothing to decorative fabrics and furniture, experienced an unprecedented vogue. The neoclassical taste saw in it sobriety, rigor, and elegance. Appreciation of those virtues persisted, signifying man's desire to inscribe order on the objects around him, and the vertical stripe remained popular. By its rhythm and its alternating play a stripe could evoke a sense of organization amid domestic chaos. Perhaps something of this notion was at work in the striped canvas of Louis Vuitton trunks: a dynamic sensation of movement, a rigor of shape and design, all suggesting that the profuse belongings inside were well contained, even mastered.

This striped canvas was officially produced until the end of the 1880s, but in reality it was manufactured longer than that for Madame D. A., a loyal client smitten with it. This woman's family had been among the company's first clients. Georges Vuitton had known her as a young girl, and his son, Gaston-Louis, remembered meeting her in 1889, at the time of the Paris Exposition Universelle. She inherited the striped trunks her forebears had purchased in the 1870s and had an inflexible taste exclusively for the striped canvas, even when it disappeared from the Vuitton catalogue. "It was especially woven for Madame D. A. until 1929. The striped canvas had become her canvas," Gaston-Louis wrote.

The wardrobe, luggage for seagoing voyages. For an extraordinary voyage, exceptional luggage! To meet the needs of people going on long journeys, Louis's products combined functionality and elegance. In 1875 Louis Vuitton created his first wardrobe, which would prove itself a classic in the coming years. It was a vertical wardrobe-trunk that opened into two sections. The wardrobe had several variations. In its "compartment" version, one side of the trunk was a wardrobe for hanging clothes, and the other was divided into several compartments. The women's model was fitted on the wardrobe side with special hangers, including some in the shape of an anchor for long dresses; in the opposite section, two drawer compartments could be inverted, one atop the other, providing enough space to store hats. The "all wardrobe" version had both sections arranged for hanging clothes. The owner could, in the limited space of a trunk, bring everything that would be necessary to confront all seasons and withstand all climates in all parts of the world, and be assured that those items would not be damaged in transport.

The wardrobe trunks, logically equipped with wardrobes and drawers, meant that travelers no longer needed to unpack everything at each leg of their journey. The system for opening the trunks, the quality of materials, and the finish of Louis Vuitton products were much better than anything that previously had been offered on the luggage market. As for strength, testimonials abound from Louis Vuitton clients who took the time to write to their favorite supplier, expressing satisfaction and admiration. One of these globetrotters was cited in *La Malle aux souvenirs:* "From Karachi, W.-C. Sandeman thanked Georges for the strength of the two trunks that accompanied him for over six thousand miles, from the United States to India, across Japan, Korea, Tonkin, Cochin China, Siam, Burma, on

The much-imitated Trianon gray trunk gave way to one covered in canvas with red stripes on a beige background. In 1876 the canvas with light and dark beige stripes entered the scene. The model shown here was made for Sultan Abdülhamid II.

Louis Vuitton created wardrobe trunks for elegant travelers like the woman depicted in *Camille, la dame à la robe verte* (opposite), painted by Claude Monet in 1866. Shown above is the compartment version, with wardrobe and drawers.

the backs of elephants, camels, ox, horses, and mules. Six months later, he even announced triumphantly from Colombo that, during the unloading of a steamship on which he was traveling, a considerable amount of luggage fell to the bottom of the hold from the upper deck, and that his trunk was the only one to come out of this catastrophe intact while all the others were completely smashed." Another example is the traveler of the "grand highway" who lavished praise on his Vuitton trunk "because it had not only successfully resisted the brutal and terrible treatment inflicted on it from Paris to Algiers through Italy, Switzerland, Germany, France, England, and across the ocean, but also the heedless, even malicious, handling that our luggage busters practice here when transferring baggage compartments." The Vuitton trunk resisted everything. It was capable of confronting untimely derailments, attacks by savages, strong gales at sea, and the somewhat too "athletic" unloading of cargo onto the quay. Its strength would be the foundation on which the shop on Rue Scribe built its success.

DATE	LOCK	N°	DETAIL OF GOODS BOUG
1877			
1ᵉʳ Août		602	90 haut cuir homme
1878			
4 Mai	M	1381	100 homme cuirée
10 Août		1750	70 Cab. cuirée
21 "		1721	75 homme cuirée

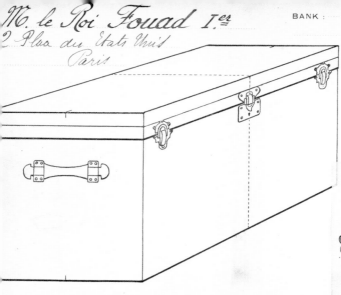

M. le Roi Fouad I.er
2 Plce du Etats Unis
Paris

BANK:

couronne Royale 3/6.td

F
lettre Noire

Louis could be proud of his success as the nineteenth century came to a close. Maison Louis Vuitton was well established, and its know-how and innovation had transformed the art of traveling. Louis had earned the trust of men in high places throughout the world, from crowned heads to renowned artists. His son Georges would assure the company's continued prestige through his own creative talents.

Louis Vuitton customers, from left to right and top to bottom: Czar Nicholas II and the czarina, 1896. Naonobu Sameshima, Japanese ambassador to France, 1873. Béhanzin, last king of Dahomey, 1892. Client record of Fuad I, son of Isma'il Pasha and king of Egypt, 1923. The sculptor Auguste Bartholdi, creator of the Statue of Liberty, painted by Jean Benner, 1886. The Italian singer Adelina Patti. A few client records. Robert de Montesquiou, painted by Giovanni Boldini, 1897. Goto Shojiro, statesman during Japan's Meiji government. Sarah Bernhardt, photographed by Nadar, about 1870. King Alfonso XIII of Spain and two of his children. Samuel Morse, inventor of the telegraph, about 1860. Yvette Guilbert, French singer, painted by Henri de Toulouse-Lautrec, 1894. Emma Calvé, French singer, in *Salome*.

GEORGES

The heir learns the hard way

Louis, the founder, was succeeded as head of the company by Georges, who was just as determined and ambitious as his father. He had joined the firm in 1873, trying his hand at all the trades involved in good trunk making. Five years later Louis put him in charge of the store on Rue Scribe.

Georges, Louis and Émilie Vuitton's son, was born in 1857. He spent his childhood in Asnières and in 1871 was sent to Jersey to continue his studies and learn English. One of the Channel Islands, Jersey was a slice of the British Empire only a few miles from Saint-Malo and Granville, off the northwest coast of France. Victor Hugo, the great poet and novelist, had just spent some years in exile at Hauteville House on the nearby island of Guernsey, where he had castigated the regime of Napoléon III (who had banished him in 1851) in scathing verse and asserted himself a champion of the common people in *Les Misérables*. Georges was a boarder at Eden House School in Saint Clements for two years, until December 1872. He distinguished himself by making good grades and returned to France crowned as valedictorian of his class. Georges would follow those first steps in the British Isles with many others, which would be critical to the future and the expansion of Maison Louis Vuitton.

Time for apprenticeship. Louis had handed down to his son a passion for woodwork, an activity that combined manual skills and inventiveness. When Georges was a child Asnières must have seemed like an enormous playground to him, rather than a work place—there was no need for toys or carpentry sets. Upon his return from Jersey, in January 1873, Georges became an apprentice at Asnières. He wanted to learn everything about trunk

Previous page: Portrait of Georges Vuitton by Eugène Pirou.

Georges studied at an English school in Jersey. Left: *Keats Lane, Eton College,* by Georges Moore, 1895.

Opposite: Georges Vuitton and Joséphine Patrelle, who married in 1880, with their children, Gaston-Louis and the twins Pierre and Jean.

making. Henry-Louis Vuitton noted, "He wanted to acquire the accomplished craftsman's sureness of movement and manual dexterity. He longed to introduce innovative ideas and present his own creations. With his youthful enthusiasm he went from workshop to workshop. He found some of the older craftsmen who, before the war, would give him a piece of wood or lend him a chisel or plane. They all enjoyed having 'little' Georges at their sides again and showing him how to adjust a cask with a rasp file or hammer in a rivet." This idyllic description left out the harsher aspects of apprenticeship. Gaston-Louis Vuitton's journal, reviewing George's writings, indicated that he felt considerable pressure: "Under incessant supervision, he learned the secrets of manufacturing and packing." The heir was well guided, but with an attentiveness and benevolence that were undoubtedly burdensome at times.

Georges soon divided his workday between Asnières and Rue Scribe, where his father taught him salesmanship and introduced him to suppliers and the most important customers. He worked as a packer, salesperson, deliveryman, and cashier, learning all the skills he needed to become an expert trunk maker. His great-grandson Patrick-Louis Vuitton observed that Georges inaugurated the family tradition requiring the Vuittons to learn their trade at the Asnières workshops before going to the store. A dogged worker, Georges had little time for leisure, only managing a rowing trip on the Seine on Sunday afternoons. Perhaps this was one of the marks of his British education.

A young, determined new boss. In 1878 Louis put his son in charge of the store on Rue Scribe. The following year, in the summer of 1879, Georges became engaged to Joséphine Patrelle, the daughter of a businessman who had amassed a fortune and built his reputation on L'Arôme Patrelle, an aromatic coloring for stocks and sauces made from glucose, meat extract, and onions. Georges's athletic rowing sessions undoubtedly gave way to hours of romantic boating and intimate conversations on the riverbanks. The wedding took place in 1880. Louis took advantage of the event to reorganize his company. He sold the store on Rue Scribe to Georges and Joséphine and decided to devote himself to manufacturing at Asnières. Georges was twenty-three years old when he took over the store from his father.

The young couple had five children, only one of whom survived them—Gaston-Louis, their eldest son, born in 1883. Two of his siblings died as very young children, and both of the twins born in 1889 met early ends—Jean after an illness in 1909, and Pierre in the First World War, on the front in Champagne. Gaston-Louis vividly described his father's moral and physical dimensions a short time before Georges passed away, in a piece dated 24 November 1934: "He has a full healthy face, rosy cheeks, a walrus mustache, and short hair. He has blue eyes and a lively, kind expression. Large in stature, broad shouldered, with a high stomach, he walks slowly, leaning on a walking stick. When in the company of others he charms them with the vivacity of his conversation and his shrewd common sense. He speaks loudly and expresses his opinions with great frankness, which sometimes makes him appear gruff. This is because his opinions are sincere and he does not attempt to hide them. He explains his opinions, describes his reasons, and tries to convince people. He never talks about himself or what he has done. His confident and aggressive bearing makes many fear him. Yet his friends and family know the infinite kindness beneath his harsh exterior."

When Georges returned from England, he apprenticed in his father's workshops in Asnières. The whole family's life was based on the rhythm of work, interrupted by short outings on Sundays to the Seine. The river was set in a landscape that inspired Impressionists and pointillists like Georges Seurat, who painted *Une baignade, Asnières* about 1883.

Conquering London

English-made travel goods enjoyed worldwide renown and commercial
dominance. Georges opened a store in London in 1885, introducing
the French trunk with the intention of supplanting the English one.

Georges decided to launch his attack from inside the opposing camp. It was actually a counter-attack. The English were already concerned by the success of Vuitton trunks and looked askance at the continued development of French products. In 1884 they decided to deal a fatal blow to Louis Vuitton creations, which were already famous for their canvas coverings, by introducing all-leather trunks with cardboard frames. Georges reacted with panache. On 1 March 1885 he opened a store in the heart of London, at 289 Oxford Street, one of the city's most prestigious thoroughfares.

The English campaign. Georges wanted his skills and know-how to help spread France's influence abroad. In that proud, slightly chauvinistic spirit, he incorporated the tricolor French flag in his signage. He put such a sign on display in the brand-new window of his London store, along with one of the Vuitton trunk-beds that French officers took on their missions overseas. On the mattress of the open trunk-bed he placed a model wearing the uniform of the French Zouaves. Londoners reacted strongly, as Henry-Louis Vuitton described: "A crowd gathered immediately, making comments and discussing the matter. The press reported 'the incident,' describing it as scandalous and provocative. It almost caused a diplomatic incident but Georges held firm, and for several weeks the Vuitton window attracted London crowds."

He had landed in England, but he still had to conquer it from a commercial standpoint. The same year the store opened on Oxford Street, a world's fair of inventions and patents was held in London. Louis Vuitton won a silver medal outside competition, the only prize awarded to travel articles, even though competing products from English manufacturers were represented, including some from Harrods department store. This first encouraging victory needed to be seconded. Georges put everything he had into the long struggle. Between 1885 and the beginning of the 1900s he divided his time among Paris (Rue Scribe), Asnières, and London. He traveled every week to England to spend a day at the Oxford Street store. Gaston-Louis recounted the speed at which his father ran his life during this

Louis Vuitton opened its first London store in 1885 on Oxford Street. The second was established on the Strand in 1889, opposite Charing Cross Station (above left). The third was at 149 New Bond Street (shown opposite in 1924). Maison Louis Vuitton, established since 1982 at 17–18 New Bond Street, has maintained a high profile on that avenue of luxury.

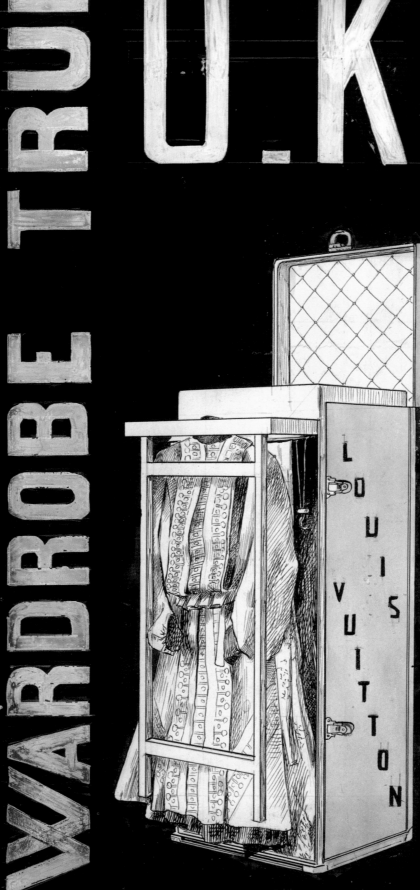

LOUIS' VUITTON'S WARDROBE TRUNK O.K SCRIBE PARIS - 1 RUE SCRIBE LONDON - 149 NEW BOND S[t]

LOUIS VUITTON

period: "To save time he used to leave Paris by train in the evening, crossing the Channel on boats like the *Petrel* and the *Fowl*—these were terrible boats whose names are still engraved on the memories of a few old sailors from the north coast of France. He arrived in London in the morning, left in the evening, and was only away for one day. He spent two sleepless nights, but that didn't matter."

One can imagine the rough crossings between Calais and Dover on the *Petrel*, a boat named after the bird that heralds storms and loves violent winds. One can also imagine Georges's steely determination as he pursued his "London idea," with never a thought of the raging elements.

Establishing a beachhead. Among the eventful moments in Georges Vuitton's conquest of England are two particularly important dates—1889 and 1900. The sales at the Oxford Street store had proven disappointing, and Georges realized that its location was not ideal.

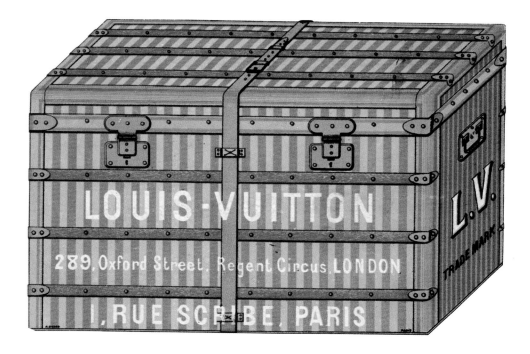

Oxford Street was more of a thoroughfare than a shopping district. He decided therefore to go directly to his customer, the traveler, and lie in wait for him as he got off the train. He chose a new site for the store opposite one of London's main railway stations, Charing Cross, and near Trafalgar Square, one of the city's chicest areas. The new, more luxurious store opened at its prestigious address, 454 Strand, on 1 December 1889, proudly exhibiting the sign "Louis Vuitton Trunks and Bags." It was a few hundred yards from Nelson's Column, a monument honoring the English admiral who had defeated the French navy in 1805—which might have been a foreshadowing. Within a few years sales at the Strand store were stagnant, although American Vuitton agents were increasingly successful. In 1900 Georges had to admit that he had made a mistake locating his store near a station. As Henry-Louis Vuitton said, with British-style humor and pragmatism, "You don't buy luggage a few minutes before getting on the train!"

Reflecting the sophistication of his trunks, wardrobes, and bags, Georges decided to relocate to the heart of London's luxury goods district. In 1900 he opened a store at 149 New Bond Street. All his neighbors were suppliers to Her Majesty Queen Victoria, and he hoped to become one himself.

The new branch occupied the entire building, as did the store that opened on Paris's Champs-Élysées a few years later. This third attempt in London was a success. It had taken years of hard work, time, capital, and disappointing results to establish the company there. Georges had remained resolute and fought hard. Gaston-Louis wrote, "He was overjoyed when, at the beginning of the twentieth century, the Americans copied his products and in their ads called their Louis Vuitton counterfeits French trunks. This really made him feel he had won, not only for his own company but for all French trunk manufacturers." London had served as the beachhead that allowed the company to conquer America. Without the London branch, Maison Vuitton would not have been able to build such a strong international reputation.

The quality and functionality of Louis Vuitton wardrobes and trunks won over the British clientele. Making a name for itself in the country with the world's largest population of demanding customers was quite an accomplishment for the company.

Opposite: The cover of the 1901 Louis Vuitton catalogue in English.

Above: A label used between 1885 and 1890.

1890, the tumbler lock

Wardrobes and flat trunks attracted burglars. To thwart them, Louis transformed his creations into safes. He devised an impregnable lock and a unique numbered key that opened all the luggage belonging to a given customer—an invention to confound Houdini himself.

A trunk has been stolen! What's hidden inside? A pile of gold, a cascade of jewelry, or maybe a treasure map with clues leading to a trove? Perhaps the unpublished manuscripts of an unknown genius? But there is blood on the trunk—oh, how horrible! Maybe it contains a dried-out corpse, grinning like a mummy! But before gasping at the contents in delight or fear, you have to force the trunk open. And with Louis Vuitton trunks, that's no small task. In fact, it's next to impossible.

Reassuring travelers. In the 1900s travelers carried in their trunks all their essentials— important papers, bank notes, jewelry, everything they needed to deal with the uncertainties of life far from home. Rich tourists faced a dreadful mob—outrageous, unpredictable people like the characters who appeared in the serialized stories of the time: Rocambole, Arsène Lupin, Fantômas, and other burglars and tricksters. Nothing would stop them from getting their hands on a fortune or a precious stone. Nothing could resist their inventive resourcefulness, their taste for technological innovation, their ability to disguise themselves and blend into the decor, or their incredible mobility. They might appear in a luxury express train, then disappear on an ocean liner, seeming to transform themselves and to be everywhere at the same time. Frightened by fictional references, travelers were anxious and in need of reassurance. They had to be persuaded that their luggage was impregnable and convinced that they could entrust it to strangers, provided they kept full control of the key that gave access to their secrets and treasures. The trunk had to be a sanctuary.

First inspirations for unpickable locks. Two locks reinforced by a strong leather strap protected the 1872 trunk model, which was covered in striped canvas. In the late 1880s Louis and Georges tried to perfect the trunk closing system. In 1886 they made important modifications to all the company's products by adopting a single lock with two spring buckles. The following year a lock fitted with mobile disk tumblers replaced it. Finally, in 1890, with the help of two Parisian locksmith artists, Foucher and Delachanal, Georges developed a lock patented by Louis Vuitton. Each brass tumbler was registered and assembled to form an inviolable locking mechanism. Louis was undoubtedly this tool's real inventor. He was a skilled locksmith and until 1892 reigned over the workshops at Asnières with his ingenuity. The new closing device revolutionized luggage locks. A bit later the trunk maker invented a pushbutton lock that provided a quick and easy opening for handbags. It satisfied the needs of elegant travelers who, with a simple push of two buttons, could open their bags without spoiling their nails.

For the 1890 lock, the tumblers were put together in a metal case, allowing a multiplicity of combinations. The principal behind this mechanism is still used today in Louis Vuitton baggage. The lock's first advantage was the sturdiness and complexity of its arrangement, which made it unpickable. The upper and lower parts of the trunk were attached and impossible to separate. The lock's second advantage was the serial number written on it. It enabled all the locks of one particular customer to be harmonized. The customer was the exclusive owner of one unique key capable of opening all his present and future Louis Vuitton luggage. The personalized serial numbers, jealously guarded in Louis Vuitton's registry of orders, made it possible to duplicate a lock for new luggage or make a new key to replace a lost one. The traveler no longer would be weighed down with a bunch of heavy,

In 1890 Georges created a revolutionary system: the tumbler lock, fitted with a set of unique, numbered keys (opposite). This model has survived the passage of time. The multidisk tumblers now used for rigid luggage are based on the five-tumbler lock.

Below: A poster advertising Vuitton's historic challenge to the famous illusionist Houdini.

clinking keys. A single key and an exclusive serial number were real privileges for the cosmopolitan traveler.

A challenge for Houdini, king of escape artists. The new Vuitton lock was soon put to the test. In September 1890, the year the lock was developed, a Louis Vuitton trunk belonging to a traveler staying in one of Dieppe's best hotels fell prey to a burglar. The crook struggled with the lock and vainly tried to force it open. He tried to pull the top off the trunk, but this also failed. Somebody finally saw him and he ran away empty-handed. In New York a few months later another thief resolutely tried to break open one of Vuitton's French trunks. His pliers, pincers, and scissors came up against too much resistance. The story goes that the town's locksmith was called upon to open the trunk but was unable to force the lock "despite its apparent simplicity."

A few years later Georges—confident in his trunks' solidity and their security system's efficiency—dared to challenge Harry Houdini, the great American illusionist and escape artist. Houdini was mad about films, spiritualism, and aviation and he had a keen sense for publicity. Georges Vuitton—with his own keen sense for image promotion—publicly challenged the great Houdini by publishing the following message in a newspaper: "Sir, I believe the box you use in your act has been prepared for this purpose and I take the liberty of setting you a challenge. It involves escaping from a box of my own making, which will be closed, after you have gotten into it, by one of my staff." We do not know Houdini's answer, but like to imagine that he inquired into the solidity of the trunks and the reliability of their locks and then gave up.

Above: A securely locked case.

Following pages: In 1894 Georges published *Le Voyage, depuis les temps les plus reculés jusqu'à nos jours,* a history of travel—and luggage—since ancient times. Georges identified himself as "Louis Vuitton Son" in tribute to his father, who had died two years earlier.

Opposite: The cover of the book, by Charles-Henri Pille (1844–1879). The illustration conveys the late-nineteenth-century passion for the Middle Ages. The sign reads, "Loys Vuitton, huchier," a twelfth-century Latin term meaning "chest maker."

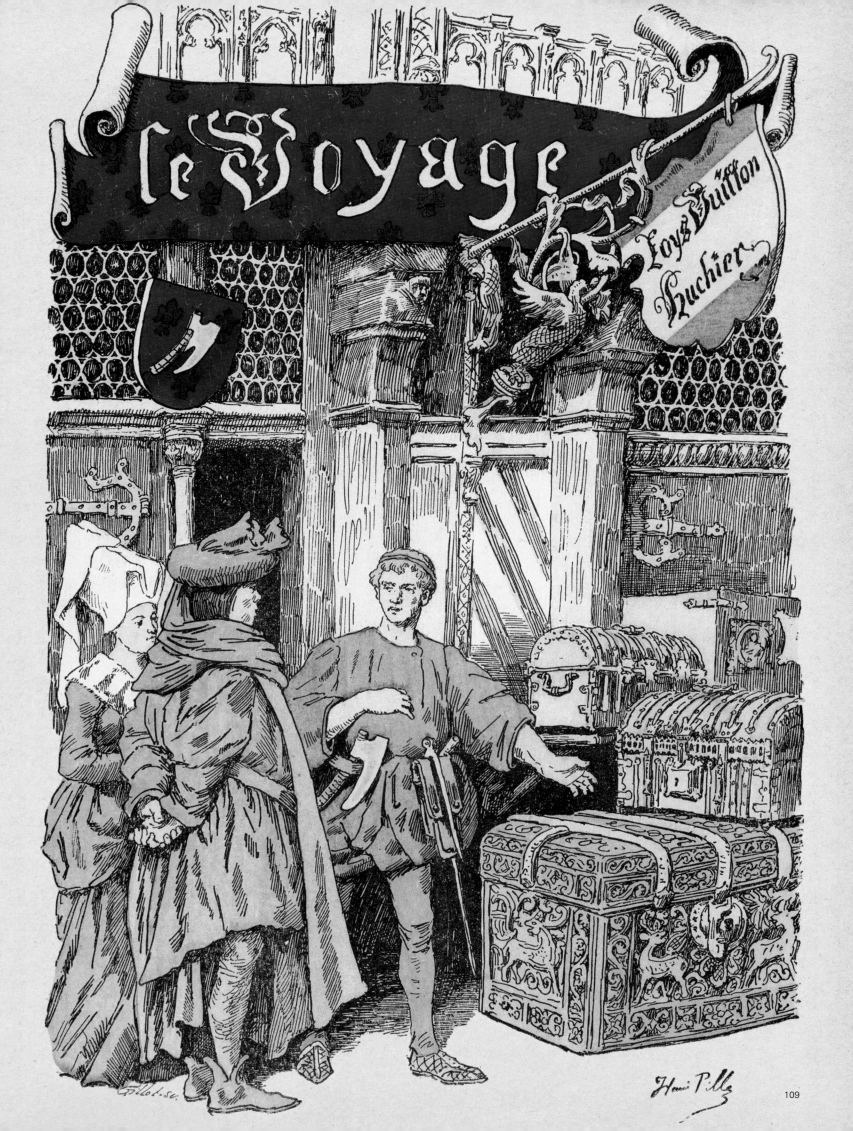

le Voyage

Loys Vuitton
Huchier

Louis VUITTON Fils

LE VOYAGE

Depuis les Temps les plus Reculés jusqu'à nos Jours

ILLUSTRÉ DE QUARANTE GRAVURES SUR BOIS
ET DE DEUX PORTRAITS A L'EAU-FORTE

PRÉFACE PAR ÉMILE GAUTIER

PARIS

E. DENTU, ÉDITEUR

LIBRAIRIE DE LA SOCIÉTÉ DES GENS DE LETTRES
3 & 5, PLACE DE VALOIS PALAIS-ROYAL

1894

In 1892 Georges set about to write a history of travel and luggage. Leaping into the past, he ventured far from his own family's history back to humankind's origins.

George's book, *Le Voyage, depuis les temps les plus reculés jusqu'à nos jours (Travel from Olden Times to Our Time),* with a preface by Émile Gautier, a journalist for *Le Figaro,* was published in September 1894. Two years later, on 26 August 1896, it earned him the honor of being named an officer of the Academy. His work was inspired by Viollet-le-Duc's illustrated dictionary of French furniture through the ages. Georges treated his subject chronologically, presenting a panorama of travel—and, naturally, luggage—through history. The first chapters evoked the remotest eras, such as those of Celtic Europe, the Hebraic Middle East, and the early Mediterranean civilizations—the Phoenicians, Carthaginians, Greeks, and Romans. He then discussed the long medieval era and its master chest makers, the ancestors of modern-day trunk makers. The Renaissance and the age of discovery brought distant voyages. In time an official policy of organized transportation developed, with frequent stops, post coaches, and royal roads. During the age of Louis XVI luggage took on the form it essentially retained through the late nineteenth century, when Georges wrote his book. The stagecoach era lasted until the 1850s, eventually giving way to steamships and railways—and the period that saw the creation of Maison Louis Vuitton and the invention of modern luggage.

The work is richly illustrated with detailed engravings, and picturesque objects from the past stream before our eyes. They range from the simple bundle fixed to long poles and pulled by a horse or ox, to early-nineteenth-century trunks and travel bags marketed by famous Parisian manufacturers—for example, Lavolaille, which specialized in traveler's chests fitted to berlins and post chaises, and Franc-Comtois Pierre Godillot, who founded the Travel Emporium. Among the images is one of a trunk whose decorative details herald the stylized motifs of Louis Vuitton's Monogram canvas, which would appear in 1896. The book thus linked the distant past with the near future, explaining where we came from to provide a better understanding of where we are going.

Opposite: The litter, a simply designed mode of transport, consisted of a wooden frame covered with a dome of fabric. It could be richly decorated and was used in the thirteenth and fourteenth centuries to carry noblewomen and clergymen.

Following pages: Some travel chests from the fourteenth century contained four cases in which dishes, linen, clothes, and weapons were stored (top left). Each of these cases was divided into three drawers. For example, the case for dishes held separate compartments for silverware, jewelry, and spices. Bottom left: A thirteenth-century ivory casket edged with thin strips of engraved copper. According to Viollet-le-Duc, it was one of the oldest caskets to survive into the late nineteenth century. Right: Chest locks like this one were made in one piece, and then decorated with welded metal ornaments.

UNE LITIÈRE AU XIVe SIÈCLE

(Extrait du *Dictionnaire du Mobilier*, Viollet-le-Duc, t. II).

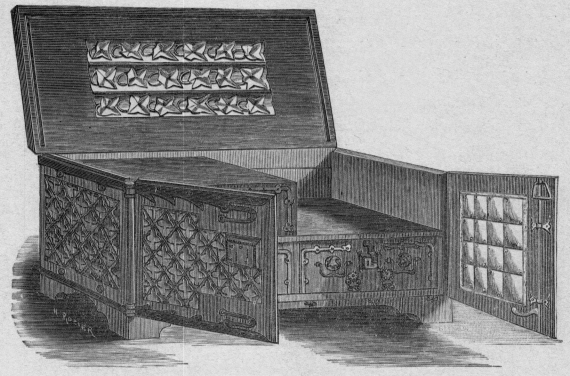

GRANDE HUCHE de voyage en bois de châtaignier, XIVe siècle (d'après nature)

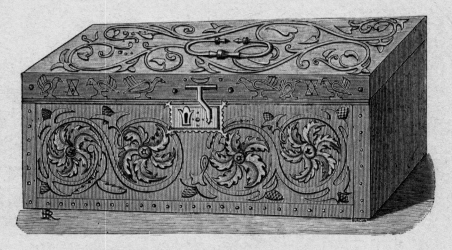

COFFRET DU XIIIe SIÈCLE

Provenant de la Collection du prince Soltykoff (d'après nature)

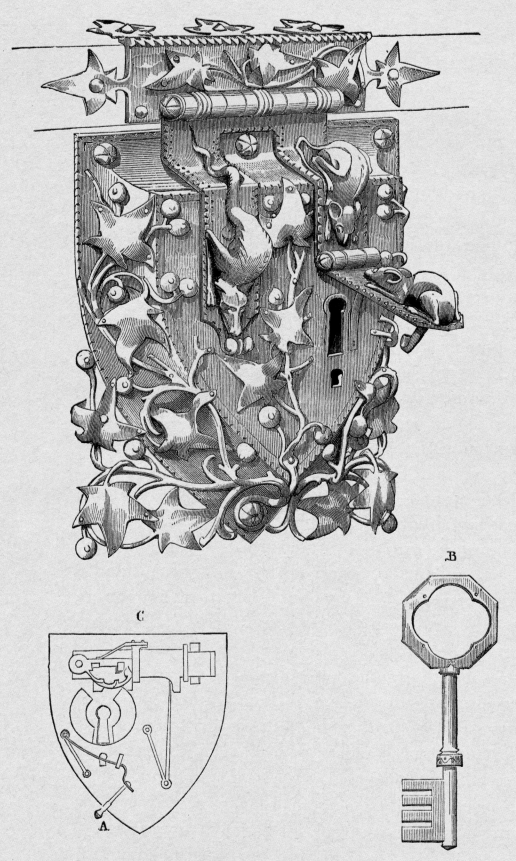

SERRURE A BOSSE, de coffre de voyage, au XIVᵉ siècle
(*Dict. du Mobilier,* Viollet-le-Duc, t. I).

FRAGMENT DU BAHUT DU MUSÉE DE CLUNY

(Extrait du *Dict. du Mobilier*, Viollet-le-Duc).

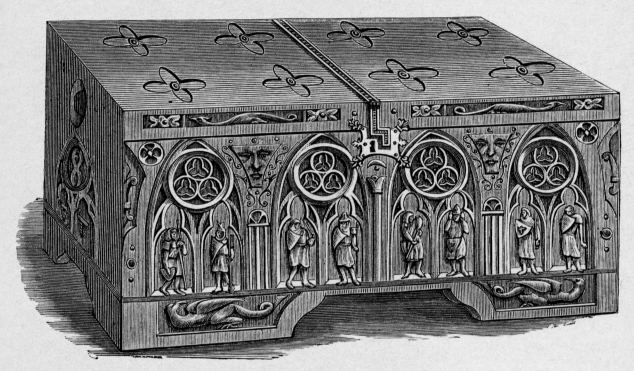

BAHUT DU XIVe siècle,

Musée de Cluny (d'après nature).

This chest (above) is one of numerous nineteenth-century reproductions. Its lock is shown
opposite. The chest's decoration attracted the attention of both Viollet-le-Duc and Georges Vuitton.
On its top are four-petal flowers like those on Vuitton's Monogram canvas, created two years after
this book's publication.

The Damier canvas

In 1888 Louis Vuitton created a canvas that Georges presented one year later at the Exposition Universelle in Paris. They intended the design to seal the company's image and also to deter counterfeits. "L. Vuitton registered trademark" appeared on the company's canvas for the first time.

The Damier canvas occupies a special place in the company's history as founder Louis Vuitton's last creation. He revolutionized the history of luggage in 1854, when he came up with the idea of covering his trunks in his Trianon gray canvas. Trying to stay ahead of imitators, he launched a different canvas in 1872—the first striped one, with four thin red stripes repeated on a beige background. It was just as successful as the Trianon gray canvas, which again led to many counterfeits. Something had to be done. In 1876 Louis modified the striped canvas, designing a beige monochrome with alternating stripes of light and dark beige. The imitators were not deterred. With Georges's assistance Louis set out to create several new patterns, finally choosing one with alternating brown and beige squares—the Damier canvas. Created in 1888, it was presented at the Paris Exposition Universelle in 1889 in the shadow of the Eiffel Tower, which had been inaugurated for the occasion. For the first time in the company's history the words "L. Vuitton registered trademark" appeared on the canvas, written diagonally across one of the checkered squares. Until that point, Louis Vuitton had never patented his designs. This new precaution did not prevent counterfeiting, but Louis Vuitton nevertheless used the Damier canvas for nearly a decade to cover rigid luggage, tall trunks, cabin trunks, wardrobes, and hatboxes. It was reintroduced in 1996 and was an immediate success. Damier today remains one of Louis Vuitton's principal lines.

The Damier canvas bears the company's signature. Created in 1888 and brought out again in 1996, its checkerboard pattern is a hallmark of Louis Vuitton design.

The birth of the Monogram canvas

The continuous cycle of innovation, success, and imitation drove Georges to decisive measures. It led to the incredible graphic daring of the Monogram canvas, which incorporated his father's initials into its design. The Monogram became the company's emblem and one of the earliest symbols of modern luxury.

The precautions taken in the creation of the Damier canvas failed to thwart plagiarists. It too was widely copied. To protect its goods, the company had to react, either defensively or creatively. Georges, who had been controlling Maison Vuitton's destiny since his father's death in 1892, chose to take the offensive. He put an end to the exploitation of the Damier pattern in 1896 with the creation of the legendary Monogram canvas. The company would no longer use traditional motifs with simple geometric stripes or checkered squares, as they were too easy to reproduce. It needed instead to create an entirely new pattern specific to Vuitton. Georges worked on his ideas for several weeks, making endless sketches and revisions before creating the pattern we now call the Monogram. It did not mark a complete break from previous designs. There was continuity, for example, in the choice of the two colors, brown and beige, that had been used in both the striped and checkered canvases. The name "L. Vuitton" had already appeared on the checkered Damier design, almost as a decorative element punctuating the canvas—the first time a manufactured object had a brand name visible on its exterior. The Monogram expanded upon these elements, enriched them, and gave them a completely innovative singularity.

Flowers, letters, geometry. The Monogram canvas's global fame has grown so great since its introduction that it is now as familiar to us as an old acquaintance. We hardly take the time to examine it, but the Monogram pattern is worth studying in detail. It is made up of four ornaments—three stylized floral motifs, combining the geometric with the botanical, plus the monogram of the company's founder—the interlaced initials of Louis Vuitton. Their strong graphic style is based on a rhythmic interplay of horizontal and oblique lines that draw two incomplete triangles—almost identical, but inverted, so the base of the L supports the point of the V. The first floral motif is the brown star with four curved points—or could it be a flower with four pointed petals? The second floral motif is the reverse image of the four-pointed star—light beige points or petals with a dark beige dot in the center. The last motif is a brown four-petal flower inside a light beige circle. At the center of the flower is another small light beige circle or dot. The stylized motifs and the formal interplay of their echoes, whether obvious or simply suggested, create a strongly graphic

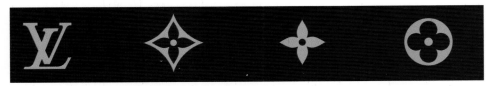

In 1965 Gaston-Louis recounted how his father, Georges, had created the motifs on the Monogram canvas:

"First of all the initials of the company—L V— interlaced in such a way as to remain perfectly legible.

"Then a diamond. To give a specific character to the shape, he made the sides concave with a four-petal flower in the center.

"Then the extension of this flower in a positive image.

"Finally, a circle containing a flower with four rounded petals."

RÉPUBLIQUE FRANÇAISE.

MINISTÈRE DU COMMERCE ET DE L'INDUSTRIE.

CONSERVATOIRE NATIONAL DES ARTS ET MÉTIERS.

MARQUES DE FABRIQUE ET DE COMMERCE.

OFFICE NATIONAL DE LA PROPRIÉTÉ INDUSTRIELLE.

DURÉE DU DÉPÔT : 15 ANS.

Duplicata

La marque ci-dessous sert à désigner des articles de voyage, malles, valises etc, fabriqués par le déposant. Elle s'imprime à volonté à plat en relief et en creux sur les toiles, cuirs, cuirs factices, papiers etc dont sont recouverts les articles de voyage dont s'agit, aussi bien que sur ces articles eux-mêmes, et sur tous emballages au besoin.

Greffe du Tribunal de Commerce de Paris
N° 89139

Dépôt du 21 mars 1905 à 1h ½ de M. Louis Vuitton, fabricant d'articles de voyage à Paris, rue Scribe N° 1. représenté par M. Ernest Parmentier, ingénieur-conseil, boulevard Magenta, 29. à Paris. Mandataire suivant pouvoir s.s.p. enregistré et annexé.

Destiné à des articles de voyage, malles, valises etc.

Signature du Déposant,
Signé : E. Parmentier Mandre
Signature du Greffier en Chef,
Signé : Bourgoin

Signature du Déposant,
Signé : E. Parmentier Mandataire
Signature du Greffier en Chef,
Signé : Bourgoin

Exemplaire certifié conforme :

Paris, le Quatre Décembre Mil neuf cent onze.

Le Directeur de l'Office national de la Propriété industrielle,

772-39-1910. [3080]

perfection that is reinforced by the motifs' layout. It is simple, clever, and strict. The separate shapes are unified by a precise scansion, a rigorous order. Scanning the canvas from left to right and from top to bottom, we discover a structuring motif—the light beige four-pointed star. It forms a regular grid, appearing on every other vertical and horizontal line of the canvas. The other ornaments alternate inside of that grid.

Georges's stubborn conviction. The canvas pattern was registered and the trademark registration regularly renewed. The entry in the *Official Gazette of Trademark Rights* did not specify the colors, so Louis Vuitton is entitled to use any color. In fact, the text accompanying a copy of the design stated, "This brand can be placed or printed in any way and in any color." Before achieving success and global renown, the Monogram canvas met with some resistance. Gaston-Louis Vuitton noted that "the public was initially reticent and demanded the checkered and even the striped canvas, but my father stood firm." He was as stubborn as his father, Louis, who had followed his intuition and imposed the flat trunk. Georges imposed the Monogram canvas with the same tenacious conviction. The combination of Georges's powers of persuasion and the strength of the design finally won out, overriding conservative attitudes. The Louis Vuitton signature was born.

Previous page: A 1911 duplicate of the 1905 certificate showing the registration of the Monogram canvas as a trademark at the National Office for Industrial Property: "The trademark is used to indicate the travel articles, trunks, suitcases, etc., manufactured by the registrant. It can be printed as required, flat, embossed, or stamped on canvas, leather, imitation leather, paper, etc., covering the travel articles in question and on the actual articles themselves, as well as on any packaging as required."

The Monogram canvas created by Georges Vuitton in 1896 lived on through the twentieth century and to the present day. Even in its sometimes bold colors and variations, it continues to serve as Maison Vuitton's lasting symbol. Opposite: A trunk used for the first time in 1897.

GEORGES

The secrets of the Monogram

Distinctive and instantly recognizable, the Monogram asserts Maison Louis Vuitton's identity through the power of an image. Its amazing longevity gives rise to questions and interpretations.

The clearly identifiable Monogram is not only a means of protecting the company from imitators, it is also an invitation to travel. To explore its sources of inspiration, let the mind wander. The Monogram is first of all a representation of filial piety. Georges was working on the design of the new canvas soon after succeeding his father, who died in 1892. The initials "LV" are his tribute to his father, the company's founder, and the ornaments are flowers he scatters to crown Louis's work. Still within the context of the family, it is possible to associate the floral ornaments with decorative elements in the Vuittons' home. There had been Gien earthenware tiles in the house at Asnières since Georges was born, and they may have influenced, even unconsciously, his quest for the perfect design. Maybe his insistence on drawing four-petal flowers and four-point stars that resembled four-leaf clovers was a superstitious gesture, meant to ward off ill fortune.

An artist's signature. The canvas was called Monogram because of the intertwined initials, which also revealed a great ambition. A monogram is the symbolic signature an artist uses to mark his work, to authenticate it, to make it unique. It is a centuries-old tradition. The finest example was probably that of Albrecht Dürer in the sixteenth century. He marked his drawings and paintings with his initials: his famous "A," which resembled a torii (a Japanese gateway), protectively rising above his "D." The monogram is an artist's privilege. By adopting it, Georges Vuitton asserted that luxury goods, as extraordinary objects, had an artistic dimension.

To be a trunk maker is not simply a matter of mastering a technique. It means deploying a creativity that goes beyond know-how to engage in a form of art.

An aristocratic sign. More profoundly, elements of the Monogram pattern that became the company emblem in 1896 derive from the rules and traditions of heraldry. It can perhaps be seen as a coat of arms. It has the simple structure of the first coats of arms, from feudal times, which were meant to be visible from a distance, in the heart of a melee, in the middle of the battlefield.

Above left: Stars and four-petal flowers like those featured on the Monogram canvas appeared fifteen centuries earlier on this fragment of a fourth-century polychrome Coptic tapestry from Cairo, Egypt, kept at the Cluny Museum in Paris.

Opposite: Architectural detail of the Doges Palace in Venice, with the quatrefoil in stone. The motif appears in numerous civil and religious medieval, Gothic, and neo-Gothic monuments throughout Europe.

As the documents on these pages show, the Monogram's motifs are found in works by various civilizations, from the fourth to the nineteenth century. It is this universal character that accounts for its amazingly timeless appeal.

Opposite, left: Detail of Saint-Germain-l'Auxerrois Church in Paris, first built in the seventh century and rebuilt from the twelfth to the sixteenth century.

Opposite, top right and bottom right: These stained-glass windows, dating from the beginning of the thirteenth century, are from the chapel of Notre-Dame de Semur-en-Auxois. Viollet-le-Duc admired them in 1843 and reproduced their motifs, similar to those of the future Monogram canvas, in his *Medieval Encyclopedia*. We know how much Georges Vuitton enjoyed Viollet-le-Duc's work.

Above: A small repeating pattern of four-leaf figures made of gold-plated copper and cloisonné enamel adorns a reliquary at the Saint-Pierre abbey church, Corrèze. Limoges silversmith, about 1210–30.

Below: Thistle tiles, manufactured in Gien in 1882, adorned some of the walls in the Vuitton family's house in Asnières.

Warriors' coats of arms are designed to be noticed. According to historian Michel Pastoureau, "The figure is simplified, and everything that helps identify it is underlined or exaggerated: the geometric shape of figures, heads, legs, animal tails, leaves, and fruit on trees." In the Western imagination, coats of arms have since medieval times been a privilege of nobility—though theoretically anyone can use them. The brand promotes itself by displaying its coat of arms.

The Monogram functions as an aristocratic sign to identify luxury goods, a sign of distinction, excellence, and rarity.

A timeless, universal code. Some have suggested that the Monogram reflects the aesthetic trends that were in vogue at the time of its creation—that Georges might have more or less consciously appropriated the contemporary atmosphere for his canvas. It was a time when the Nabis painters insisted on the decorative dimension of painting, simplifying shapes and giving them the power of symbols, a time when distant influences traversed time and space. A fascination with the Middle Ages had been influencing art and design since the Romantics brought back into fashion Gothic "barbarity," with its carved filigree and gargoyles.

Viollet-le-Duc led a Gothic revival in architecture and restored many medieval buildings in France. Georges Vuitton was interested in his work. His book on travel through the ages constantly referred to Viollet-le-Duc's illustrated dictionary of French furniture and included several engravings of ancient objects that had appeared in Viollet-le-Duc's book, such as a sideboard from the Cluny Museum's collection in Paris. The connection between the design on this sideboard and the Monogram canvas's four-petal flower is strikingly obvious. The quatrefoil pattern was omnipresent in Paris's artistic environment and throughout Europe. It is also visible on a fragment of polychrome wool tapestry in the Cluny Museum that was made by fourth-century Egyptian Copts. It was carved into the stone of the cathedral in Barcelona (late thirteenth–late fifteenth century), Saint-Germain-l'Auxerrois Church in Paris (twelfth–sixteenth century), and the Doges Palace in Venice (fifteenth century).

The vogue for *japonisme*. Since the opening of Japan to the West in 1854 and the Paris Exposition Universelle in 1867, Japanese art had permeated Europe. In the 1870s and 1880s it sparked such a passion among the public and among artists that everything shaped by Far Eastern influences was referred to as *japonisme*. Japan has a tradition of family crests called "mon," which are similar to European coats of arms and play the same social role, identifying individuals and lines of descent.

"The escutcheon or mon is usually round, but can also be square, rectangular, diamond-shaped, or hexagonal like a tortoise shell, with its edges and corners rounded," wrote René Le Juge de Segrais. "Sometimes, especially when the arms are intended to decorate fabric, the mon's ring is eliminated." Le Juge de Segrais's twentieth-century analysis of mon made clear their connections to the Monogram's motifs. There is the disconcerting coincidence between the Japanese word "mon" and the first syllable of "Monogram." Moreover, the stylized floral motifs that abound in the coats of arms of feudal Japanese nobility are very similar to the figures Georges drew. Is this one of the reasons Vuitton has been so well received in Japan over the past few decades? Rather than seeking a direct affiliation between *japonisme* and the Monogram, the Japanese connection can be understood thus: The Monogram canvas presents a group of signs with universal power. The secret of its lasting success lies in this universality. The design touches everyone, without necessarily evoking the same response. It catches people's attention, but is interpreted differently by all who see it. There are as many ways to understand and sense the origins of the Louis Vuitton canvas and its decorative motifs as there are cultures and individuals. Is this an assurance that it will remain timeless, that it will outstrip and transcend fashion? Could it be a guarantee of eternal youth?

The historical puzzle of the Monogram. A recent study by Atsushi Miura, a professor at the University of Tokyo, confirmed our hypotheses on the invention of the Monogram. "These findings show that the Monogram canvas should be placed in the artistic and cultural context of late-nineteenth-century France. Georges Vuitton would definitely not have copied a particular Japanese motif. Medieval art is another source of inspiration that should be considered. Georges may have been inspired by French art of the Middle Ages, as seen through the neo-Gothic eyes of the nineteenth century, modifying and adjusting it to suit his own artistic intentions. Although we cannot deny the influence of *japonisme,* it would be better to consider the Monogram canvas in a wider historical context.

"It was above all the modern movement of decorative arts and industrial design that dominated the scene at the end of the nineteenth century in France: furniture, faiences, fabrics, wallpaper. . . . It was also the period of Art Nouveau. The general structure of the Monogram canvas is inspired by the grammar of decorative arts. Moreover, we should remember that Georges was exposed to new influences at the Expositions Universelles of 1878 and 1889. Therefore, we should integrate the creation of the Monogram canvas into the artistic and aesthetic context of the period. In the history of art, it is poised between a national tradition and a universality."

Above left: The Honchodori main road in Yokohama. Detail from a Japanese print made by Ichiyusai Kuniyoshi in 1860.

Below: A series of Japanese mon. Family crests similar to European coats of arms, mon were used to identify individuals and lineage.

Opposite: Georges Vuitton examines a flower box in Monogram canvas. This little trunk, equipped with a zinc tub filled with flowering plants, was a gift to very good customers, who could return it to the store to be transformed into a box for cigarettes or jewelry.

Following pages: The four historic canvases. Clockwise from top left: The Monogram canvas (1896), the Damier canvas (1888), the Trianon gray canvas (1854), and the striped canvas (1872).

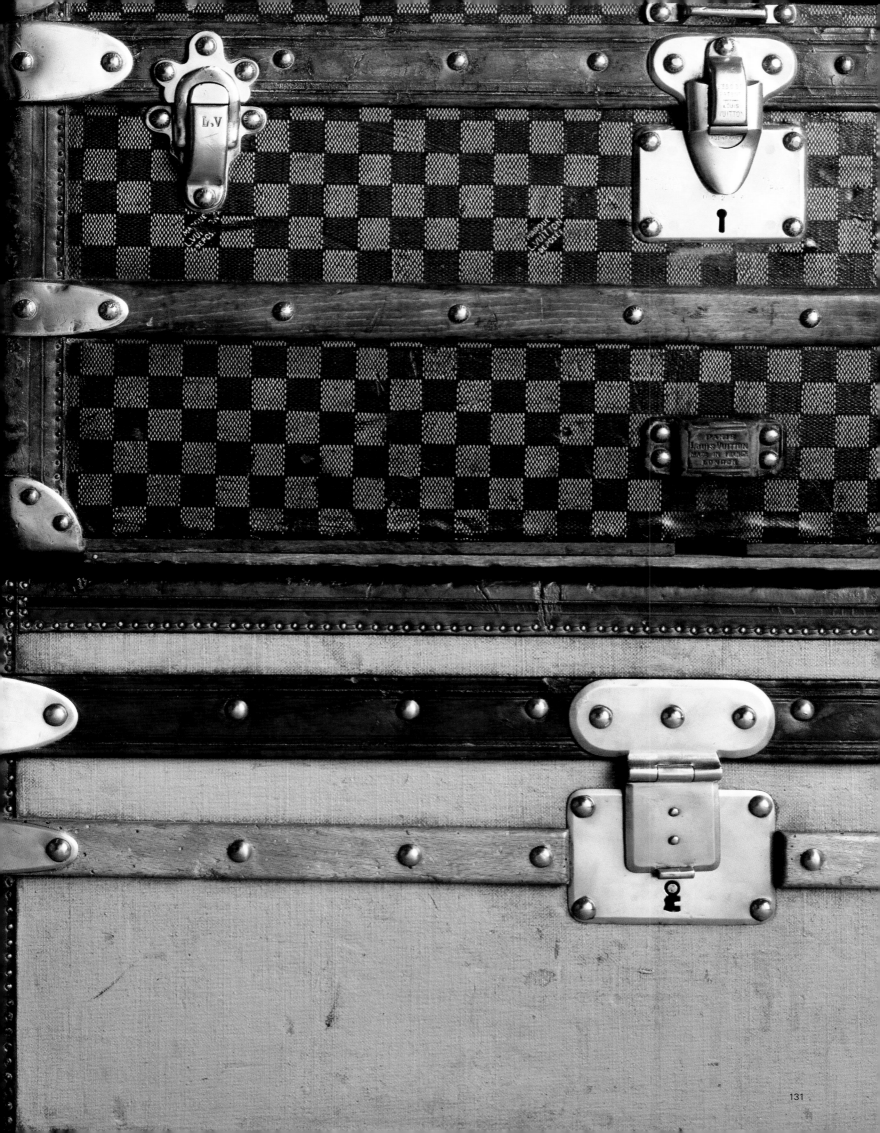

The art of train travel

With the introduction of Pullman sleeping cars on the Orient-Express in 1883 and on the Trans-Siberian railway some years later, railways were pushing back frontiers and inciting people to travel. Luggage piled up on platforms around the world, waiting to be stowed discreetly in compartments. Along with toiletry sets and hatboxes, luxury was on the move.

"In the first years of this century, a travel agency in Avenue Nevsky exhibited an oak-colored model of an international sleeping car approximately thirty-five inches long. Its meticulous resemblance to the original was so much better than the painted model train I had at the time. Unfortunately, it was not for sale. Inside the train we could see the blue padding, the embossed leather covering the compartment sides, their shiny panels, fitted mirrors, tulip-shaped reading lights, and other overwhelming details. Large windows alternated with narrower ones—they were single or double—and some were made of frosted glass. In some of the compartments the beds were made. The magnificent and enchanting Nord-Express of the time, composed exclusively of railway cars like this and with only two departures per week, linked Saint Petersburg and Paris." In his memoir *Other Shores,* the writer Vladimir Nabokov creates an image of his aristocratic, cosmopolitan childhood in Saint Petersburg. The train took him on long pleasure trips across Europe to fashionable French and Italian resorts like Biarritz, Nice, and Venice.

Pullman opens the way. "International sleeping cars"—the very expression sets one thinking about traveling and sleeping, traveling and dreaming. The mind wanders while the body, drifting off to sleep, rushes through the night, sheltered by the cozy cocoon of a berth on the luxury express. With the development of railways travelers became more demanding. In the second half of the nineteenth century railway companies tried to outdo each other in the care they lavished upon their passengers. In 1859 the American inventor George Mortimer Pullman sought to ensure that riders in his railway cars were comfortable. Now that they were making journeys that lasted days rather than hours, he offered them real sheets to sleep on, with soft pillows like the ones they had at home. His railway car could be converted into a sleeping car, requiring only a few minutes to change the decor. At the beginning of the 1860s the pioneering Americans introduced restaurant service as well. Pullman inspired an enterprising Belgian, Georges Nagelmackers, to improve upon the principle. He kept the idea of a sleeping car with berth but added other amenities, such as a toilet and a dining car. The train became a mobile palace in 1883, when Nagelmackers

Opposite: Traveling artists were Louis Vuitton's favorite customers. Among them was the grande dame of the theater, Sarah Bernhardt (1844–1923). She achieved early success with her spectacular interpretation of *Ruy Blas* in 1866 and went on to worldwide renown. Her lilting voice enchanted Victor Hugo, who baptized it the "Voice of Gold." She is shown here in the lounge of her private train.

Left: Drawing by P. F. Grignon, 1921.

Following pages: The reception lounge of the Mexican presidential train.

International Sleeping-Cars inaugurated the legendary Orient-Express (initially called the Train-Express-Orient).

The Orient-Express. The track was not yet complete that first year, going only as far as Vienna, capital of the Austro-Hungarian Empire. Soon, and for nearly a century, it would lead as far as Istanbul, the Ottoman Empire's Sublime Porte. The very term held the promise of enchanting places, a Thousand and One Nights, the richness of the Orient. Syllable by syllable, stop by stop, station names became less and less familiar as the journey progressed, propelling travelers toward strange music and exotic colors—Épernay, Châlons, Bar-le-Duc, Nancy, Strassburg (with the German pronunciation, since the Reich annexed Alsace between 1871 and 1918), Karlsruhe, Pforzheim, Stuttgart, Ulm, Augsburg, München, Wels, Linz, Amstetten, Sankt Pölten, Wien, Györ, Komarom-Ujszöny, Budapest, Kiskorös, Ujvidek, Zimony, Beograd. The full journey lasted several days and at first included a voyage by sea. In Giurgiu, on the Danube in Romania, passengers transferred to another train that took them to the Black Sea, where they caught a boat to Istanbul. In 1906, when the Simplon tunnel opened, the Orient-Express could travel through northern Italy, then straight on to Belgrade, Sofia, and Istanbul. After experiencing the exhilaration of traveling on these express trains, the writer Valéry Larbaud celebrated them in *Le Vagabond Sédentaire* (published by La Quinzaine Littéraire–Louis Vuitton):

> *You slide through the night, through illuminated Europe,*
> *Oh luxury train! And the agonizing music*
> *That rumbles through your golden leather corridors.*

Trains become luxurious. The model sleeping car that young Nabokov contemplated in the window on Avenue Nevsky reproduced the real ones in minute detail, with excellent materials and skillful layout worthy of princely accommodations. It was similar to the sleeping car on Napoléon III's imperial train and the presidential cars the Compagnie des wagon-lits provided for Czar Nicholas II's official visit to France in 1896. Travel in those days was accompanied by a sense of romance that brought luxury even to the wait before the train departed. Grand restaurants opened within the terminals, such as the Station Buffet (later called the "Train Bleu"), which was inaugurated on 7 April 1901 at the Gare de Lyon. The huge restaurant embodied the Belle Époque style with a sumptuous, dramatic decor, plentiful gilding, and allegorical representations. Huge paintings depicted lemon picking in Nice and grape picking in Burgundy. Smaller lounges decorated in Algerian and Tunisian styles prepared southbound passengers for the change of scenery that awaited.

As for train travel itself, luxury was the order of the day. Nagelmackers was designing palaces on rails. Maison Louis Vuitton, planning a line of luggage and new interiors for its famous trunks, was keeping up with the times and adapting to new ways of traveling. The luggage's size and weight were reduced without compromising its strength. The flat trunk became firmly established in the company's catalogue. It could easily be slipped under train seats and into the inevitably limited storage spaces on board. Above all, the trunks' interior layout was designed to be refined and functional: Removable racks and holders cunningly provided optimal storage for clothes and accessories (hats, gloves, ribbons, canes, fans, parasols, veils), while inner padding kept all the contents perfectly in place—legacies of Louis Vuitton's early work as a packer. The design allowed travelers to pack a great deal in a small space.

As Henry-Louis Vuitton admiringly wrote, "The list of things some models can carry is quite impressive. A lady's hat trunk measuring about 35 x 22 x 28 inches allowed Mrs. D to take between eighteen and twenty-five hats with her, while her husband contented himself with a model carrying four hats. The edges of the hats were placed upside down on two thin, velvet-covered cords and strapped into place. The shoe trunks contained up

Above: The Folies Bergère's famed *Revue Nègre* (1925) starred the exuberant, talented, and somewhat provocative Josephine Baker (1906–1975). She caused a sensation singing and dancing half-naked in the show. She inspired painters like Van Dongen, Foujita, and Picasso. Above, Baker during a 1928 trip on the Orient-Express.

Opposite, right: Attractive and seductive, the diva Marthe Chenal (1881–1947) was the talk of the town. Passionate and patriotic, she sang the "Marseillaise," draped in the French flag, on the steps of the Opéra on 11 November 1918, the day the armistice was signed. For this loyal customer Maison Louis Vuitton designed a toiletry case (opposite, left) in the 1920s. It was a dazzling artistic creation of crocodile skin, tortoiseshell, crystal, and gold.

to six pairs of ankle boots and one pair of boots on a shoe tree. If more room was needed, the two boxes containing the shoe kit could be removed, allowing a few more pairs to be carried. As for the wardrobe-trunk belonging to Mrs. S, it could easily carry fifteen to eighteen dresses and coats!" There was special luggage for shorter trips, such as dinner and a night spent with friends, when only a few things were needed. Instead of the high trunks used for great seafaring expeditions, the company offered low trunks and travel bags with rigid built-in compartments that could be removed and used as toiletry kits.

The excitement of departure. During the last few decades of the nineteenth century and the beginning of the twentieth century, travel was a way of life for members of high society. Although nowadays we consider travel rather ordinary, it was seen then as a major event that required detailed planning. Preparing for a train journey was like preparing for a grand party. As Countess Jean de Pange recounted in *Comment j'ai vu 1900,* "Some of the luggage was transported eight days in advance in a special slow freight car, reserved several weeks beforehand. One freight car was not always sufficient when you consider that each servant (there were at least fifteen) had a trunk and my mother alone had thirteen, as well as her hat boxes, needlepoint frames, and an arsenal of paint boxes and more or less folding easels. She had some things sent ahead—her cushions, stools, foot warmers, screens, flower vases, and travel clock—as if we were going camping in the desert, when in fact the house in Dieppe was full of furniture. My nurse used to cram miscellaneous objects into two enormous trunks with domed lids that must have dated back to the stagecoach days. Although the journey from Paris to Dieppe took only four hours, we settled ourselves in as though we were going to China. We would take several baskets of supplies and an array of 'travel' utensils. Folding knives and forks, tumblers that could be flattened like opera hats, small bottles of salt, eau de cologne, mentholated alcohol, fans, shawls, small rubber cushions, and an awful rubber chamber pot that made me feel sick just to look at it."

A trunk maker like Maison Louis Vuitton no longer had to worry about providing

CHEMINS DE FER PARIS-LYON-MÉDITERRANÉE

FLORENCE
PAR LE TRAIN DE LUXE ROME·EXPRESS

Above: A poster from the 1910s for the Paris-Lyon-Mediterranean line.

Going on vacation was a great occasion requiring days of preparation. The new travelers packed superfluous things as well as essentials. Maison Louis Vuitton offered travelers all sorts of wardrobes, trunks, and garment bags. Opposite: Gaston-Louis Vuitton's luggage on a station platform in 1933, photographed for the magazine *Chemins de fers français.*

crinoline cases. The Second Empire had come to an end. Women's clothes were simpler, narrower, and lighter, which made storage and transportation easier. During the second half of the nineteenth century, suits became more practical and adapted to people's increased mobility. Clothes also became more specialized. Suits for train journeys were made of material that tended to be "crease-resistant, fresh, and pleasant to wear, strong enough to withstand inevitable little accidents, dust, and smoke," as the magazine *Art et la Mode* noted in 1891. There were raincoats, costumes for walking in the forest or the mountains, costumes for spa patrons, and clothes for riding bicycles. Certain colors were recommended for traveling, particularly "shades of dust"—gray, tobacco-brown, and beige—which were thought to be more resilient. Tourists were advised to wear tartans and plaids because they "brought a dash of cheerfulness to more severe outfits."

The exhilaration of rail travel. In 1891 Nicholas II, the future czar, initiated the construction of a new transcontinental line—the Trans-Siberian railway. The western section opened five years later. It stretched from the Urals to the banks of the Ob. The following year the eastern section, between Vladivostok and Khabarovsk, opened. By 1904 the line was almost complete, allowing people to travel from Moscow to Russia's Pacific coast. Only the bypass around Lake Baikal was missing—so railway cars were loaded onto boats to cross the lake. The Trans-Siberian opened new regions for globetrotters to explore. They were in search of novel and powerful sensations. Along with their luggage they brought with them their memories, hopes, dreams, and fantasies. Many books written in the 1900s convey the poetic influence that railways exercised on creative spirits. Railways symbolized youth and a life of adventure.

They also symbolized erotic energy. Guillaume Apollinaire wrote an unbridled Sadian account in *Les Onze Milles Verges* (1907), in which a railway orgy ends in a double murder in a compartment on the Orient-Express. In 1925 Maurice Dekobra immortalized what had become a literary stereotype, almost a cliché of popular serials, in his novel *The Madonna of the Sleeping Cars.* Rail travel also conjured up danger, spies, plots, and murders. Novelists and film directors from Agatha Christie (*Murder on the Orient-Express*) to Alfred Hitchcock (*The Lady Vanishes* and *Strangers on a Train*) took advantage of the train's simultaneously closed-in and mobile nature to suggest an imprisonment of the body and freeing of the spirit that led to savagery and perversity. The distant horizons of rail travel unleashed imaginations. Blaise Cendrars, a Swiss poet with a roaming spirit, celebrated those aspects of travel in *The Prose of the Trans-Siberian and of Little Jehanne of France* (1913), a work that made him famous. In 1904, at age seventeen, he was one of the first to try his luck by crossing the wild Orient east of the Urals. The spirit and heart leapt, jolted by the metallic symphony of singing axles and rattling steel:

> I was very happy, carefree
> I pretended I was playing robbers
> We had stolen the Golconda treasure
> And we were going on the Trans-Siberian to hide it on the other side of the world
> I had to defend it against the Ural thieves who had attacked Jules Verne's traveling acrobats
> Against the khoungouzes, the Chinese boxers
> And the High Lama's furious little mongols
> Ali Baba and the forty thieves
> And those loyal to the terrible Old Man of the Mountain
> And, of course, against the most modern things
> The hotel rats
> And the specialists from international express trains.
> Blaise Cendrars, *Panama, or the Adventures of My Seven Uncles and Other Poems.*

The great sea crossings

The open sea! Passengers on the high seas lived to the rhythm of the ocean swell. The chiming of the ship's bell punctuated the hours of the crossing. It once took weeks if not months to cross an ocean, but steam power had cut the travel time.

A few centuries ago sea travelers' greatest concerns were pirate attacks, an absence of wind that could dangerously stall the journey, or violent winds that could dash the vessel—and the hopes of all aboard it. Though rough weather could still provoke fear of shipwreck, steam-powered ocean liners had now narrowed the range of anxieties. One could only hope that no wandering icebergs or other sea giants awaited liners as they advanced quickly through the fog, for a collision would be inevitable.

Passenger travel by sea had steadily increased since the seventeenth century, when ships transported mail across the English Channel between Dover and Calais. The English called them "packet-boats"—"packet" meaning "parcel." This early enterprise was the forerunner of large maritime shipping companies. The ships carried passengers as well as mail. The numbers of passengers gradually grew until they were occupying most of the boats' available space.

The Blue Ribbon races. With the development first of steam propulsion and then engines, and with innovations like metal hulls and propellers, liners became much faster and more reliable than sailing ships. Shipping lines were established in the major Western countries, including Compagnie Générale Transatlantique, Cunard Line, White Star, Black Ball Line, Guion Line, Imman Line, Hamburg Amerika Line, and Norddeutscher Lloyd. They provided regular liner service on transoceanic trips to America, the West Indies, Africa, the East, and Asia (service between Marseilles and Yokohama was launched in 1883). The North Atlantic route between Europe and the east coast of the United States was especially busy and competitive, reflecting massive population movements. Large numbers of emigrants were leaving Old Europe for the New World, just as "American Uncles" were returning from the States to their homelands, proud of the success they had achieved in America, basking in the glow of their newly earned fortunes, and eager to be back in Europe to enjoy the rich cultural life that was now within their reach.

The shipping lines began trying to outdo each other in speed in 1850. Once a year, when the weather was favorable, shipowners would set off, full steam ahead, on a mad chase across the North Atlantic in vessels nicknamed "publicity liners." The goal was to better the previous year's fastest crossing time and use the new speed record to promote the company. The challenge was very costly in terms of fuel, and it was dangerous. Liberties were taken with safety measures. But the public loved knowing who held the Blue Ribbon, the large pennant the winning ship displayed for one year. The time of the "lightning" crossing was calculated between Bishop Rocks—a rock with a lighthouse in the Scilly Isles, off England's southwest coast—and the Ambrose Lightship in New York Harbor. The distance was 2,938 miles and competition was fierce, especially between English and French ships.

In addition to the speed races, a race was on for ships' size. Companies vied to develop ever larger vessels. In the middle of the nineteenth century the *Leviathan,* the first transatlantic giant, inspired French poet Victor Hugo with a prophetic vision of its future ruin, which was the theme of his poem "Pleine Mer" in *La Légende des Siècles.* A few years later it was transformed into the *Great Eastern,* which encountered many difficulties but was celebrated by novelist Jules Verne. The title of his book, *A Floating City,* aptly described the *Great Eastern*'s colossal size. Liners' passenger capacity continued to swell. At first they

From the beginning of the nineteenth century transatlantic liners took exceptional care of their wealthy clients, with great luxury and abundant comfort everywhere. Over time liners came to resemble great floating palaces. Above: The staircase of honor on the *Champlain.* Federico Fellini lyrically evoked these grand maritime settings in his famous 1983 film *And the Ship Sails On.*

carried several hundred people, then a thousand, and soon almost two thousand. In April 1912 the *Titanic*, touted as the world's largest ocean liner, sank during its maiden crossing. Nearly fifteen hundred passengers and crew drowned, and seven hundred others survived the shipwreck. But even that catastrophe did not dampen the public interest in ships or stop the race to break speed records. The Blue Ribbon remained a coveted pennant for some time.

Floating palaces. Shipping companies also sought to outdo each other in the luxuriousness of their onboard facilities, the excellence of their cuisine, and the variety of entertainment they offered their wealthy clientele. Liners took on the appearance of floating palaces. One such was *La Provence*, owned by the Compagnie Générale Transatlantique and launched in 1906. The liner was designed to carry 450 passengers in first class, 200 in second class, and 900 in third class. The crew comprised 14 officers; 300 seamen, mechanics, and stokers; plus a 150-person service staff of chambermaids, cooks, headwaiters, and so forth. The magazine *L'Illustration* avidly promoted the liner and tried to entice readers: "The most affluent American multimillionaires could not dream of anything better for a sea crossing than the six luxury apartments put at their disposal, each of them equipped with a bathroom and very decorative electric hearths, bringing together the most refined of modern comforts."

Although all passengers traveling on a given ship were subjected to the same rough seas and squalls, they were not all on equal footing. They came from a range of social classes,

Opposite: The Steamer bag, a historic Louis Vuitton creation. Designed in 1901 as an accessory, it could be easily folded and stored in a wardrobe compartment. It is considered the forerunner of the soft-sided bag. This one bears the initial of its owner, Gaston-Louis Vuitton.

Above: On deck, the moment the ship approached land was always exciting.

by which they were strictly segregated. The emigrants confined to the tween decks never bumped into the high-society passengers traveling in first class. For some the voyage was a transition to a land promising a better future, while for others it was a business cruise or an adventure—the difference between a future full of hope and a present filled with pleasure.

For each category of traveler life on board followed a precise ritual. Travelers had to abide by a daily agenda and follow established rules of etiquette. Nothing was improvised on board; everything was controlled—except the weather, the condition of the sea, and the wind's strength.

Women were not welcome on deck before 10 a.m., although men were allowed. At lunchtime passengers who were not feeling well were served lunch in their cabins. Others went to the dining room, where appropriate attire was required. At midday the captain gave an up-to-the-minute report and informed passengers of the ship's position. After lunch, between 2 p.m. and 5 p.m., was a time for socializing—conversation, board games, musical entertainment, reading, or lounging in chairs on the promenade deck. Dinner was announced at 6 p.m. First-class passengers had to follow a prescribed dress code for every moment of the day. For men, three outfits were recommended, one each for morning, daytime, and eveningwear. Detailed instructions on eveningwear were provided: "A navy blue dinner-jacket with black silk lapels, a white waistcoat with one row of gold buttons, a matching pair of trousers with an embroidered black silk stripe, and a black tie."

The cabin trunk and steamer bag. Under such a regime, travelers had to plan their packing carefully and not skimp on clothing. In a poem called "Baggage," Blaise Cendrars listed everything in his trunk when he boarded the *Formose:*

Above: Maison Vuitton designed the nested trunk, called the Idéale, for elegant men. It could hold exactly five suits, one overcoat, eighteen shirts, underwear, four pairs of shoes, a hat, three canes, and an umbrella.

Opposite, from left to right and top to bottom: Some of the company's famous traveling customers. French writer and diplomat Paul Morand, in the 1920s. American screen stars Douglas Fairbanks and Mary Pickford on board the *Europa* in 1910. Stage actors Sacha Guitry and Yvonne Printemps (sitting on one of her Louis Vuitton trunks, marked with her initials) and composer André Messager prepare for their trip to the United States in 1927. French boxer Georges Carpentier in 1920. Writer Paul Claudel, French ambassador to Japan in 1921, with his daughter on board the *Duquesne.*

Above: Souvenir of a crossing on a liner bound for the Americas. Georges, pictured in the center, found that his travels inspired future creations.

Opposite: The stairway for first-class passengers on the *Laos,* owned by the Compagnie des Messageries Maritimes, about 1900.

They say that people travel with heaps of luggage
Me, I only bring my cabin trunk and already I find
that it's too much, that I have too many things
Here is what my trunk contains. . . .
My late-model Remington typewriter
A packet containing some small things I have to give back to a woman in Rio
My babouches from Timbuktu that bear the marks of the great caravan
Two pairs of splendid shoes
One pair of patent-leather shoes
Two suits
Two overcoats
My heavy sweater from Mont-Blanc
Small toiletries
A tie
Six dozen handkerchiefs
Three shirts
Six pajamas
Kilos of blank paper
Kilos of blank paper
And a charm
My trunk weighs fifty-seven kilos without my gray hat.

At 57 kilos (125.6 pounds), Cendrars's trunk was quite a piece of luggage. Even if a liner's cabin was luxurious, space was always limited and luggage couldn't be too large. Maison Louis Vuitton therefore developed a cabin trunk that was specially designed to slide under passenger bunks, making the cabin feel more spacious. Since the cabin trunk was not very high, it had only a single beech board for reinforcement. Several different models were available, all with the same standard height. The Excelsior, which Georges designed during his first Atlantic crossing, offered complete accessibility. It had a side flap and sliding drawers that enabled travelers to open the trunk without having to pull it out from under the bunk. The Saint-Louis had a frame for clothes and racks for hats, shoes, underwear, and an umbrella. Its name referred to the Saint Louis World's Fair, which Georges attended in 1904 as president of the jury for travel articles.

Vuitton created the soft-sided Steamer bag in 1901. It was originally designed as a laundry bag into which travelers could stuff their dirty linens during the crossing. Made of canvas and completely foldable, it conveniently and easily slipped into trunks and other hard-sided luggage. It became one of the company's classic catalogue bags, then evolved into a carryall. The Steamer bag has become a piece of luggage in its own right that can be loaded into the trunk of a car or taken onto a plane as carry-on luggage.

Offshore letters. The days slipped by on the great ship. People chatted, played, changed their clothes, ate, and slept. They became somewhat bored. They thought of the people

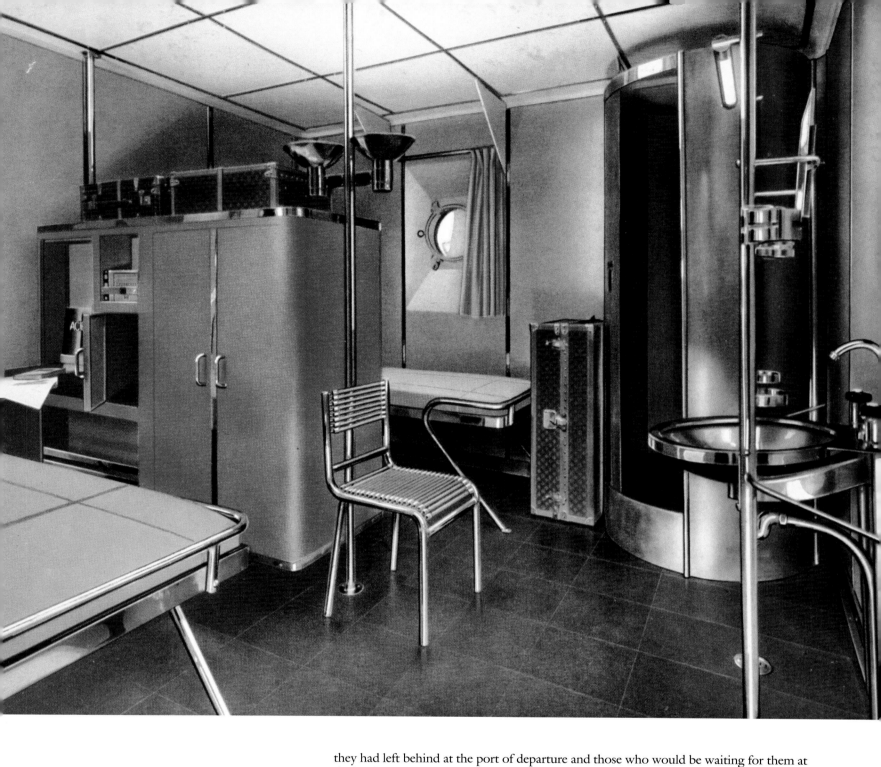

During the long crossings daily activities followed a well-organized schedule. Opposite: In 1900 Vuitton created a writing desk on which passengers could write "ocean letters."

At the 1934 Autumn Salon in Paris the Technical Office for the Use of Steel presented this liner cabin (above), which was designed by René Herbst. The modernity of its lines and materials are perfectly integrated with the timeless Monogram motifs on the trunks.

they had left behind at the port of departure and those who would be waiting for them at the landing. They contemplated letters to those on land, perhaps reminding them of their arrival. The days of packet boats were over, but liners were able to communicate with land and continued to provide messenger services. Passengers in the middle of the Atlantic had plenty of time to compose poetic "ocean letters." Does it seem a strange term? Cendrars, whose writing flourished amid the spray of the open sea, clarified it in his 1924 poem "Feuilles de Route":

> *The ocean letter was not invented for making poetry*
> *But when you travel when you start out*
> *when you are on board when you send ocean letters*
> *You make poetry.*

The ocean letter was not only poetic; it was also modern: Ships broadcast passengers' messages via radio and Morse code. Those on land would reply in the same way, with just a few words. They would be at the dock the day the liner arrived. They would be delighted to welcome the French trunk maker. In 1893 the *Touraine* entered New York Harbor after a seven-day crossing. A Vuitton would soon take his first steps on American soil.

Those magnificent men in their flying machines

Throughout history, the dream of Icarus—whose wax wings melted when he flew too close to the sun—inspired poets and artists alike. Then it stimulated the imagination of inventors, first during the era of hot-air balloons, then during the age of aircraft.

Between the Renaissance and the Enlightenment, from Leonardo da Vinci to the Montgolfier brothers, creative technological dreams became realities. The flying machines the Italian master designed on paper in the late fifteenth and early sixteenth centuries were succeeded by real hot-air balloons, which made their first ascent in 1783. In Europe and the United States at the end of the nineteenth century all sorts of crazy Icaruses got carried away. The dream of flying inspired inventors who were as reckless as they were creative, and the airplane was born. It took only a few years, between 1900 and 1914, to lay the foundations for a new means of transport.

The hot-air balloon was invented more than a century before the airplane. On 4 June 1783 Joseph and Étienne de Montgolfier presented one of the earliest of these contraptions in Annonay, south of Lyon. In November of the same year Pilâtre de Rozier and the marquis d'Arlandes were airborne for just under thirty minutes. Hot-air balloons made wonderful observation posts and were useful for terrain reconnaissance, so geographers and the military enthusiastically adopted them. It is well known that the Republican politician Léon-Michel Gambetta used one to flee the Prussian troops during the siege of Paris in 1870. It is less well known that the French were already using the device to spy on the Austrian enemy at the Battle of Fleurus in 1794. At the end of the nineteenth century technical improvements led to the creation of dirigibles, which could not only rise up into the air but could also be steered, using wind currents. Alberto Santos-Dumont proved its merits in 1901, when he elegantly circled the Eiffel Tower in a hot-air balloon he had designed himself.

The engineer Clément Ader coined the French word *avion* (airplane), using the term in a patent application in 1890. On 9 October of that same year he also managed to lift his *Eole* off the ground in Armainvilliers and fly 164 feet. The *Eole* was an engine-propelled wood and canvas structure with a batlike appearance; it looked like a stage prop from the studio of film director Georges Méliès (*Le Voyage dans la lune,* 1902). Meanwhile, in the suburbs of Berlin, Otto Lilienthal was making numerous flights with gliders. The first truly controlled flight was performed on 17 December 1903 in Kitty Hawk, North Carolina, where the Wright brothers made four very short but successful flights, one after the other, in their *Flyer.* The last of these flights lasted nearly one minute and covered more than 852 feet. Two years later the Wrights flew for thirty-eight minutes and more than twenty-four miles.

From pioneering feats to regular air flights. From that time on, progress was rapid, encouraged by the enthusiasm of the public, entrepreneurs, and newspaper owners. Air shows were organized and prizes offered. Aviators were designers, manufacturers, and pilots at the same time and they were treated like modern-day heroes. They performed one feat after another, trying to outdo each other, and breaking records for speed, altitude, and distance. The first night flights were conducted in 1908. Louis Blériot was the first to cross the English Channel, on 25 July 1909. Three years later an American army captain named Albert Berry was the first to successfully jump from a plane using a parachute. In 1913 Roland Garros made the first nonstop flight across the Mediterranean Sea.

Industrialists mobilized capital to promote this new method of travel through the air. In 1909 Paris organized an international air show at the Grand Palais that brought together nearly four hundred exhibitors. The Vuittons were enthusiastic spectators and participants

For the pioneering passengers of the skies, the Aéro trunk could carry two suits of clothes, one overcoat, ten shirts, three nightshirts, three pairs of underwear, three undershirts, six pairs of socks, twelve handkerchiefs, one pair of shoes, eighteen detachable collars, gloves, ties, and one hat. It measured 31½ x 18 x 13 inches and weighed only 57 pounds (26 kilos) when filled— quite a feat! Below: A 1923 ad for the Aéro.

Opposite: Otto Lilienthal, a pioneer of gliding, floating in a biplane about 1891. The French aviator and aircraft manufacturer Henri Farman made the first one-kilometer airplane flight at Issy-les-Moulineaux in January 1908.

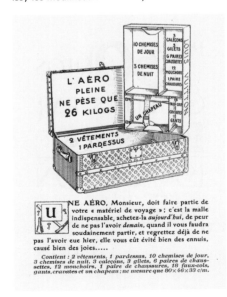

in this conquest of the skies. Georges's twin sons, Pierre and Jean, represented the company at the Grand Palais with a helicopter they had designed. The onset of World War I—the first war in history to be fought in the air—contributed to an acceleration in planes' mass production and performance improvements. By the end of the war planes could fly at a speed of 124 miles per hour.

The end of the war led to a propitious period for civil applications of aerial navigation. In 1918–19 aircraft manufacturer Pierre Latécoère organized commercial mail transport flights between Toulouse and Morocco. At the end of the 1920s Latécoère, in association with the Bouilloux-Laffont brothers—Maison Vuitton customers—set up the Compagnie Générale Aéropostale to serve South America. These routes had their heroes—Mermoz, Saint-Exupéry, Guillaumet—who were just as famous as the prewar pioneers of the air. The planes transported passengers as well as mail. Regular airline service linked European capitals and also linked Europe to some of its colonies. Stewardesses came on the scene in 1930. In 1933 the French commercial companies merged to become Air France. Two classes of travel were instituted, and plane interiors' safety and comfort were improved by soundproofing, air pressurization, better seating, and more.

Airline luggage. Even before regular airline service was available to passengers, the Vuittons had imagined luggage that would be suited to planes and dirigibles. About 1910 Maison Vuitton created the Aéro trunk. Two of them could be fixed to the basket of a hot-air balloon—one on each side, to balance the vessel. The Aéro was above all designed to be light, compact, and versatile. It weighed only fifty-seven pounds when filled.

The odyssey of Charles Lindbergh. From 1919 on, aerial routes were explored and conquered: between Europe and Australia in 1919, across the southern Atlantic in 1922, and between Japan and the United States via Alaska in 1931. The most dazzling of these feats was American aviator Charles Lindbergh's flight on May 20–21, 1927, when he flew nearly 3,700 miles from New York to Paris, with no radio to guide him, no parachute, and in dreadful weather conditions. His monoplane, the *Spirit of Saint Louis,* flew directly from one city to the other in thirty-three and a half hours. Parisians gave Lindbergh an exuberant welcome. According to an account by his son, Henry-Louis Vuitton, Gaston-Louis acted as an amateur "bodyguard" for the occasion: "On the afternoon of May 21, the telephone rang in Gaston-Louis Vuitton's office. It was his friend, the minister Maurice Bokanowsky, asking him to go to Le Bourget immediately. He jumped into his car and raced to the airport, where a crowd of people was already invading the runways and building roofs. Monsieur Bokanowsky explained that because of his height and stature, he was just the person they needed for the cordon of bodyguards they were organizing to protect the American pilot from an over-enthusiastic welcome that could become rough." Lindbergh's arrival at 10:24 p.m. and the delirious welcome of the crowd at Le Bourget airport are described in *Diary of an Art Dealer,* by René Gimpel, Gaston-Louis's cousin: "Two hundred thousand people were waiting for him. The indescribable enthusiasm was so great that eight people were injured and taken to the hospital. He is twenty-five years old and it is his first visit to France. He had only a few sandwiches and no radio. He was bored stiff, shut up in the plane with only a periscope to see through. He knows next to nothing about navigation and had only an insignificant, minuscule compass. It is difficult to understand how he was able to navigate. He also had a poor map of the French coast. However, he dived straight for Paris. That's how he always navigates—using what we could call his intuition. There are men who are like birds, like Icarus—who have a feeling for the skies. The crowd at the Opéra was just as dense as it was on the evening of the Armistice."

Gaston-Louis Vuitton, welcoming Lindbergh with the other "strong-arms," was able to get close to the hero. Before returning to the United States by ship, Lindbergh visited the Vuitton store on the Champs-Élysées, where he bought two wardrobe trunks. He became one of those illustrious customers who helped establish Maison Vuitton's lasting reputation across the Atlantic. Three years after Lindbergh's feat the French pilots Dieudonné Coste and Maurice Bellonte flew from Paris to Dallas in a plane named *Point d'interrogation (Question Mark)*. A new era in aviation was opening as planes began outpacing travel by sea. On 30 July 1939 a plane called the *Ville de Saint-Pierre* overtook the *Normandie,* a ship that three days earlier had left Le Havre bound for New York. The era of floating palaces was coming to an end.

The Aéro trunk was a great success, as it was suitable for all situations and all types of aircraft. Above left: Drawing by Pierre Legrain, 1910.

Maison Vuitton showed a passionate interest in air adventures, and many of its heroes were also its customers. Opposite: Those magnificent men in their flying machines. From left to right and top to bottom: Louis Blériot after his first flight over the English Channel, Dover to Calais, 25 July 1909; Charles Lindbergh, in front of the *Spirit of Saint Louis* at Le Bourget airport after his Atlantic crossing on 21 May 1927; customer record of Count Zeppelin, the inventor of the dirigible balloon of the same name; aviator Roland Garros (pictured in 1910), who was the first to fly over the Mediterranean in 1913; Edmond Audemars, seen at the controls of his *Demoiselle* in 1910; Alberto Santos-Dumont, the Brazilian air pioneer and airplane builder, made the first officially recognized flight in Europe in October 1906.

Vuitton aircraft

In the effervescence of the dawning century's aeronautic development, the Vuitton twins were not left behind. In Asnières they designed and built prototypes of a helicopter and an airplane from start to finish. But their talent and promise would be destroyed by war and death.

The early years of the twentieth century were exciting and turbulent. Rapidly developing technologies seemed to offer a bright, promising, serene future. Progress, peace, and happiness were the inspiring words of the day. It was still a time of optimism; the new technologies had not yet revealed all their potentially destructive forces. Before Europe turned into a vast and bloody battlefield, it was a brilliant playground, full of creativity and hope. People were enthusiastic about electricity, internal combustion engines, automobiles, and flying in all its forms. Much ingenuity was devoted to developing and improving rudimentary machines that were capable of moving on wheels or in the air. The inventors would summon all their courage, throw caution to the wind, and attempt to put theory into practice. They would head for a road, an open field, a hilltop—and off they went. If they failed, it was humiliating for the spirit and injurious for the body.

The twins lay down the law. The Vuitton twins, Pierre and Jean, though still in their teens, had strong characters. Like many young Europeans and Americans of the Belle Époque they had a great passion for innovation and discovery. They shared a love for mechanical inventions. First they designed a small car, and then they began working on another means of transportation—the helicopter. A French engineer, Paul Cornu, had just succeeded in launching this type of machine in Lisieux on 13 November 1907. His device was like one of "those magnificent men's" strange "flying machines" and nothing like a modern-day helicopter. It had huge propellers over a very light structure of cables and tubes that supported an engine and, next to it, a pilot's seat. The whole contraption rested on four wheels that might have been taken from a baby's carriage . . . but it worked! It was Cornu's success that encouraged Pierre and Jean to bury themselves in calculations, sketches, and sophisticated experiments.

Asnières was their den, and the atmosphere was highly charged. "The twins laid down the law! As the workshop was not up to their ambitions, they lopped or felled a few trees and put some concrete down in a corner of the yard. They strictly controlled access to this area. It was soon filled with a strange tangle of wing spars and cogwheels housing an engine topped by twin horizontal rotors—a helicopter they had designed from scratch and built with their own hands." The machine probably never flew but it was exhibited. Indeed, in September 1909 the first model of the helicopter, the *Vuitton-Huber,* was presented to the public at the first aeronautical show at the Grand Palais, officially called the Exposition Internationale de Locomotion Aérienne et de Navigation Automobile. A note in the *Encyclopédie de l'aviation,* published in October of the same year, briefly described it as "A frame supporting the engine and the aviator, surmounted by two counter-rotating propellers measuring 16½ feet in diameter. There is a vertical propeller at the rear measuring 6½ feet in diameter." This recognition seemed like only the beginning for them. As it turned out, the *Vuitton-Huber* was Jean Vuitton's legacy.

Shattered dreams. On 22 September, three days before the show's opening, the young man died, worn out by illness. His brother's sudden death at age twenty did not keep Pierre from continuing the project they had undertaken together and improving the machine. He built two more models—the *Vuitton II* and the *Vuitton III.* In 1910 Maison Vuitton had another exhibit at the Exposition de Locomotion Aérienne, held at the Grand Palais once again. Two of the creations the twins had worked on together were presented—the heli-

In the workshops at Asnières the twins Pierre and Jean (above) demonstrated extraordinary inventiveness. Ideas burst forth and sketches were made on the corner of a workbench. Their work produced a helicopter and an airplane that were presented at the Exposition Internationale de Locomotion Aérienne et de Navigation Automobile in Paris, at the Grand Palais, in November 1910, shown on the following pages. Georges gave the model of the Louis Vuitton helicopter to the Musée des Arts et Métiers, in Paris, at the end of the same year.

Opposite: The *Vuitton III* helicopter, listed in the 1910 Louis Vuitton catalogue.

copter and the airplane. But the 1914–18 war put an end to Pierre's experiments. Like other young Europeans rushed off to the front and trapped there, Pierre fought in the war for more than three years. He was a lieutenant in the 101st Infantry Regiment. This unit was frequently exposed to enemy fire, and Pierre's action in combat won him the Military Cross with Palm and the cross of the Legion of Honor. On 28 September 1917, during a sortie in Billy-le-Grand, he was fatally injured.

All that remains of the Vuitton twins' dreams of flight are sketches, models, and photos. Their designs seem like fragile structures, scarcely more complex than large kites, but they are accurate and elegant. They remind us of the excellent drawings that sprang from the hand and the visionary imagination of Leonardo da Vinci. They preserve the youthful passions of two young men lost to illness and war.

Automobiles off to a good start

Anticipating the development of automobiles, Georges Vuitton prepared for customers' new needs. In 1897 he presented the first prototype of the auto trunk. A line of accessories and luggage would follow, including the roof trunk and the driver's bag. There were even Louis Vuitton vehicles, including the auto-camper, an ancestor of the mobile home.

In the mid-1880s two German inventors, Gottlieb Daimler and Carl Benz, each developed a combustion engine fueled by petroleum gasoline. Daimler sold his patent to two Frenchmen, René Panhard and Émile Levassor, who in 1891 built the first automobile with the engine mounted at the front of the chassis instead of under the driver's seat. This invention, which established the automobile's basic structure for the next eighty years, was an immediate success. Another Frenchman, Armand Peugeot, soon imitated Panhard-Levassor, and the automobile industry was born. Maison Louis Vuitton quickly developed a passion for this new machine.

It was not long before rivalry between the first major French manufacturers broke out at sporting events. The 1894 Paris-Rouen competition, organized by the *Petit Journal,* was the first big motor race. Twenty-one vehicles were arranged at the starting line at Porte Maillot, ready to set out on the seventy-eight-mile race. It was 8 a.m. on Sunday 22 July. They were expected to reach Rouen at 8 p.m., after a stopover for lunch at Mantes-la-Jolie from 12:00 to 1:30 p.m. The marquis of Dion, maintaining an average speed of eleven miles per hour, won the race in one of his steam-powered Dion-Bouton vehicles. The event attracted huge crowds.

Gasoline overtakes steam. The competitions helped build the reputation of the winning car models and also helped establish the superiority of one source of power over another. Which would come out on top for this new means of locomotion—steam, electricity, or gasoline? In 1895 a more selective race of 744 miles from Paris to Bordeaux and back brought together twenty-two competitors: five steam-powered cars (including models by Dion, Serpollet, and Léon Bollée), one electric-powered vehicle by Jeanteaud, fourteen gas-powered cars (by Panhard-Levassor, Peugeot, and others), and two gas-powered bicycles. Panhard-Levassor won the race in forty-eight hours and forty-seven minutes, with an average speed of just under 15.5 miles per hour. The car's performance proved that the fuel it used was the most efficient. Within just a few years, automobile performance—top speeds and average speed per hour—improved significantly.

It was in France that the automobile world first took shape. A prestigious club—the Automobile-Club de France (ACF), founded in 1895 by Paul Meyan, the marquis of Dion,

Above: This 30 HP Mercedes is decked out in all its finery, with Louis Vuitton luggage taking the place of honor—a Steamer bag on the step, a driver's bag on the roof, and trunks in Vuittonite canvas on the luggage rack and in the trunk.

The French automobile industry satisfied the public's passion for the new machines. Below: Robert Peugeot, French manufacturer and Vuitton customer, in one of his cars in 1897.

Opposite: Drawing by P. F. Grignon, 1921.

and Baron Zuylen de Nyevelt—promoted its interests. ACF opened its headquarters in the elegant heart of Paris, in the Hotel de Plessis-Bellise on Place de la Concorde, next to the present-day Hotel Crillon and near the Louis Vuitton store. *France Automobile,* a weekly magazine launched in February 1896, supported its activities. The club began organizing events that would make history. In 1897 it mounted a show exhibiting the newfangled machines as well as bicycles, and the following year the automobile reigned supreme at the Tuileries Salon de l'Auto. On 27 June 1906 the ACF organized its first Grand Prix, near Le Mans. Drivers raced six laps around a triangular circuit and covered about 64.5 miles. The winner was a Hungarian man driving a Renault at an average speed of 63 miles per hour. At the same time, brands of automobiles were beginning to emerge, including Panhard, Peugeot, De Dion-Bouton, Mors, Delahaye, Bollée, Berliet, De Dietrich, and Renault. Thanks to coachbuilding firms like Kellner and Labourdette (which were often customers of Maison Louis Vuitton), the awkward "monsters" of the early days gave way to comfortable, enclosed cars and limousines, as well as convertibles. In 1900 France produced about four thousand vehicles.

Georges Vuitton creates luggage for automobiles. The automobile was born in France, so Georges Vuitton was well positioned—in the front row—as a witness to its birth. His intuition rarely failed him. He foresaw the importance of the transportation revolution under way. There was still only a small number of manufacturers and users of automobiles but they formed an elite of well-informed pioneers. Georges Vuitton created new models of accessories and luggage expressly for them.

In 1897 he presented the first prototype of the auto trunk. The Paris-Rouen race three years earlier had been very instructive for the design process. Clouds of dust, specks of soot, and lubricating oil had soiled the clothing of the distinguished competitors, who had been sporting derby hats or boaters. How could motorists be assured that their belongings would not be damaged under such conditions? Motorists initially had a strong, even exclusive, preference for wicker trunks, but Georges Vuitton resisted the fashion. He obsti-

LE "SAC CHAUFFEUR" DE LOUIS VUITTON

nately rejected wicker and succeeded in imposing his preference for dust-resistant auto trunks. Their design, from which sprang all future automobile baggage, was inspired by the zinc trunk Louis created for exotic countries. What a success it was! Guaranteed waterproof, the rain could beat down and the dust could fly—the trunk was completely sealed off from the harmful elements.

At the 1898 Salon organized by the Automobile-Club de France—officially called the Exposition Internationale de l'Auto, du Cycle, et de Sports—some of the models exhibited by hundreds of participants were equipped with optional Louis Vuitton auto trunks. The Parisian trunk maker improved, diversified, and adapted its range of products to the new means of transportation. There were trunks for the flat roofs of the cars and trunks for the luggage rack, usually at the rear of the vehicle, as well as luggage that fit on the side step. The trunks were covered in black canvas or leather. Henry-Louis Vuitton provided a detailed description of his grandfather's creations: "He offered a set of stackable trunks for the rear that neatly fit into the curves of the bodywork. He also offered a large trunk with a front flap, which contained several cases so that each passenger could have his or her own suitcase. For the roof he designed trunks with flat tops and arched bases, to evenly distribute the load and protect the roof."

The further development of the automobile gave rise to another specialized creation by Maison Vuitton. John Boyd Dunlop, a Scotsman, had invented pneumatic tires and patented them in 1888. They were used only for bicycles until the Paris-Bordeaux race in 1895, when the Michelin brothers tested their pneumatic tires on a car called the Éclair. The test was conclusive but demanding. The tires were thin and fragile. The roads were rough and strewn with sharp flint, so punctures and flats were constant risks. In response to that need, and to ensure the car's efficiency, Maison Louis Vuitton launched the driver's bag—a round case containing a spare tire and inner tube as well as a smaller round case to hold the driver's gear. The driver's bag was perfectly waterproof and could be used as a tub if the driver wanted to have a quick wash. This elegant and functional product was just as attractive as the auto trunk. The king of Spain, Alfonso XIII, who was the company's customer from 1905 to 1907, ordered three auto trunks and one driver's bag.

The automobile conquers the world. Just like the creations of Louis Vuitton, which were shipped to distant customers and appreciated by royalty around the world, French cars were exported. Other countries responded to the innovation quickly. In the early years of the twentieth century the automobile industry was established in most developed countries. Some of the prestigious brands that were introduced then still exist. The German makes included Benz, Lutsman, and Daimler, which in 1900 launched the first Mercedes (named for the daughter of a customer, Emil Jellinek). Great Britain's auto industry began with Lanchester, Wolseley, Arrol-Johnson, Austin, and Rolls-Royce. In Italy, Giovanni Agnelli founded Fiat in 1899. Detroit, Michigan, became the automobile capital of the United States, home to many manufacturers: Ransom Eli Olds, creator of the Oldsmobile, the Dodge brothers, David Buick, and Henry Leland, who created the Cadillac, which was named after A. de La Mothe Cadillac, the Frenchman who founded Detroit in 1701. Henry Ford, a customer of Louis Vuitton (as were many in his industrial empire's dynasty), launched the legendary Ford Model T in 1908 and, most important, implemented assembly-line mass production in 1913.

Sporting events also took on an international dimension, whether they were rallies combining tourism and speed tests or distant treks, modern-day epics that caught the fancy of newspaper readers and set them dreaming. In 1898 the first major international race was organized, from Paris to Amsterdam. The Paris-Berlin race was introduced in 1901, and the Paris-Madrid in 1903. These races were eventful and sometimes tragic. They revealed the talent of legendary figures like Gaston de Chasseloup-Laubat, Camille Jenatzy, Henri Farman, and the Renault brothers. An American sponsor, the fabulously wealthy James Gordon Bennett, financed an event every year. His father had founded the *New York Herald*, and he was a loyal customer at the Vuitton store on Rue Scribe and then at 70 Avenue des Champs-Élysées. The Gordon Bennett Cup, a motor race between competing national automobile clubs, was first held in June 1900 and went from Paris to Lyon. Frenchman François Charron won the race in a Panhard. On 15 July 1902 the Renault company triumphed at the Paris-Vienna event; seven of its cars completed the race. Marcel Renault won first place overall, driving in the "light car" category. It took him twenty-nine hours and thirty minutes to cover about 893 miles. That was four hours faster than a high-speed train. Rail transport had everything to fear. Roads had a great future ahead.

Above: Keen inventors, Jean and Pierre Vuitton had a passion for all the newest machines, whether flying in the skies or rolling along the road. Here they are testing the roadster they designed themselves.

An advertisement (opposite) for the driver's bag, which is shown open below. "It protects the tires from bad weather, it contains hats. When empty, it can be used as a shower tray."

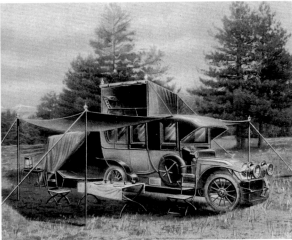

The twins are ace mechanics. There were two kinds of automobiles being developed, one for performance (high-speed cars) and one for tourism (vehicles designed as mobile palaces). Maison Louis Vuitton not only outfitted other manufacturers' cars, it offered its own automobiles. Georges Vuitton's twin sons, Pierre and Jean, who had proven brilliant at aeronautical invention, were just as interested in automobiles. Maison Louis Vuitton financed their research at Asnières. The young men fitted a Stabilia chassis with a roadster body and they built a small, light vehicle called a "voiturette," which they equipped with accessories from the Vuitton automobile catalogue for the 1909 exhibition. "On the left-hand step is a very small trunk containing spare parts and on the right-hand step, the tool box. At the rear we find Louis Vuitton's new patented washbowl and one of its automobile lunch sets. Between the top of the car's trunk and the petrol tank is the long, wide, and spacious clothes trunk." This description demonstrates Vuitton's special art of making the most of all available space.

An exceptional limousine. The auto-camper of 1908, known as the "H.K.V." (for Hogan Kellner Vuitton), was even more surprising in terms of innovation. Fully equipped with Louis Vuitton trunks and bags, it was exhibited at the 1908 Salon de l'Auto, along with thirty-five cars by major manufacturers and coachbuilders. It was a kind of luxuriously designed camper. The automobile magazine *Omnia* described the auto-camper experience as vastly superior to touring by car: "Imagine: You set out very early in the morning and you're getting close to the inn. You stop once or twice on the way for Madame to pick some flowers. When you set off again, there's a sweet-scented breeze, so you leave a window open. A few locks of hair are blown about by the wind—you can't sit down for lunch in that state, darling! There's no decent bathroom at the hotel—we'll have to rent a room. What a bore! It will smell musty, there'll be traces of the previous occupant and maybe bugs and more. Everyone will be in a bad mood at lunch and the day will be ruined. Don't let this happen, say Kellner and Vuitton. Park the vehicle near a woods a mile or so from the inn. Open the rear door and, presto, you're in a bathroom that has not been defiled by any dubious predecessor. Apart from the fact that you just reach out and open any of your trunks without disturbing the others, you have everything you could imagine within reach. Absolutely everything is at hand. If you want even more independence from the inn, you can put lunch or tea into one of the suitcases, which will keep you going until dinnertime. A table and campstools can be fitted into another case, if you don't want to sit on the grass. Maybe you don't fancy dining or sleeping at the inn. Here is a complete camping kit with tent and bedding that you can fasten to the roof of the limousine. What a limousine!" Long live the freedom of the road with Louis Vuitton auto equipment!

Inventors—including Georges Vuitton—were mad about the automobile. In collaboration with the Kellner coachbuilding company he created the auto-camper (above), which he exhibited at the 1908 Salon de l'Auto. Upon opening the rear door, the visitor discovered a washbasin, a three-sided mirror, a wardrobe containing four suitcases, a toiletry case, a trunk for six ladies' hats, a trunk for men's hats, a first-aid kit, two clothes trunks, and the mechanic's trunk. The tool kit was located under the driver's step, and the driver's bag was at the front of the roof. But that was not all. The car opened up to become a room and dining area, with a bar inside and additional sleeping space on the roof. It provided everything needed to cope with the unexpected.

Right: As this advertisement shows, the first auto trunks could be attached and removed from the rear of the vehicle, in the days before cars were designed with the storage compartments we know as trunks.

EN COMMANDANT VOTRE
UNE MALLE-AUTO VUITTON.
ACTUELLE DEPEND MOINS DE
QUE DE LA CONCEPTION DE SON
QU'ELLE EMPORTE. C'EST EN
LOUIS VUITTON REALISE DES
COMPLEMENTS INDISPENSABLES

VOITURE, COMMANDEZ
LE RAYON D'ACTION DE L'AUTO
LA PUISSANCE DE SON MOTEUR
CONFORT ET DES BAGAGES
VERTU DE CE PRINCIPE QUE
MALLES-AUTO IMPECCABLES
DE LA VOITURE DE TOURISME.

LOUIS VUITTON
PARIS 70 CHAMPS ELYSEES
NICE 12 AV. DE VERDUN_CANNES 10 R. DES BELGES
VICHY RUE DU PARC_LONDON 149 NEV BOND STREET

A.S. PUBLICITE

Vacation time

In the nineteenth century the affluent discovered the beneficial effects of open air and iodized sea breezes. They began devoting leisure time to swimming in the ocean, excursions to the mountains, and the virtues of hot springs. Louis Vuitton stores opened in the provinces to support the upper class's fancy.

The Second Empire played an important role in the development of seaside resorts and thermal tourism in France. Napoléon III and Empress Eugénie acquired and expanded on a taste for sea and spa vacations that the English were the first to cultivate. Although British travelers had already discovered Biarritz, the imperial couple put it on the map, establishing it as a place for high society and boosting its economy. The Pereire brothers were responsible for developing Arcachon, the resort on the southwest coast, while the English became infatuated with Dinard, in Brittany. Within only a few decades, from 1850 to 1900, this small fishing port on the Rance River was transformed into an upper-crust, cosmopolitan, and "artsy" destination with beautiful and extravagant villas. Casino gambling, horse racing, and regattas alternated with parties and receptions frequented by such notables as Claude Debussy, Paul Valéry, Auguste Renoir, and Winston Churchill.

Deauville, Trouville, and Cabourg. The coast of Normandy, meanwhile, had an almost irresistible attraction: It was not far from Paris. The duke of Morny, a close relation of Napoléon III, "invented" Deauville, as Jean-Marie Rouart recounted: "It was Doctor Olliffe, the quack who supplied him with aphrodisiac pills, who first drew his attention to this small village in Normandy. The idea of creating a pleasure town based on the new fashion for sea bathing appealed to this builder, who had always been keen on hydrotherapy. He drew the plans, designed the hippodrome, and even started planning a commercial port that would compete with the English ports. He only had time to complete the first part of this ambitious program. Work began in 1860. Morny built a sumptuous villa, named 'La Sergewna' after his second son. On 14 August 1864 the hippodrome, which had been built on reclaimed marshlands, was inaugurated." Within a few years Deauville was well established as a place for entertainment and high society. Two neighboring towns competed with Morny's town. One was Trouville, which was very close by. The other, about 12.5 miles to the west, was Cabourg, Marcel Proust's favorite spot. Gaston-Louis Vuitton spent many summers in Cabourg, where he owned a villa. Gaston-Louis's cousin René Gimpel, who also loved Cabourg, had the opportunity to meet Marcel Proust when they both stayed at the Grand Hôtel in 1907 and 1908. However, it is unlikely that Gaston-Louis ever met Proust. The writer and the entrepreneur did not keep the same hours. In any case, medical hygienists considered bathing in cold water advantageous to adults and children alike: "In the summer, bathing in rivers or even in the sea is a good alternative to hot baths. In the right season, this type of bathing is very beneficial because cold water removes harmful excess heat from the skin, has a tonic effect on all bodily functions, and restores muscular strength."

The Côte d'Azur. Farther from Paris than the Normandy coast, the Côte d'Azur attracted the elite of England and Russia. Cannes and Nice were health resorts reputed for their mild winters, just like the Italian Riviera. They promised a mild climate, a pleasant life, and plenty of lounging in general. Maison Vuitton decided to open a third store, after its Paris and London locations, on the Côte d'Azur in 1908. "In early December Georges went to Nice, where his son had negotiated the purchase of business property, ideally located near the Promenade des Anglais. Opening a second store on French territory was a real stroke of genius when you con-

In 1925 Maison Louis Vuitton created this travel kit (opposite, below) for Polish pianist and statesman Jan Paderewski (shown below in 1923). Made from precious and innovative material—snakeskin and sealskin made to look like walrus leather, silver, and macassar ebony—it was a masterpiece.

Opposite: *Plage de Cabourg (Cabourg Beach)*, painted by René-Xavier Prinet, 1910.

The Côte d'Azur was very fashionable. In 1908 Georges Vuitton opened a third store in Nice, painted by Paul Huguenin in 1911 (opposite). Louis Vuitton trunks were an absolute must for people going on trips. Right: An illustration by Paguoy, published in *La Gazette du Bon Ton* in 1914.

At the beginning of the twentieth century the Normandy coast was a hive of artistic activity. Visitors painted and wrote, and sometimes even went swimming. Marcel Proust (below) stayed in Cabourg, where the Vuitton family spent vacations. René Gimpel, Gaston-Louis Vuitton's cousin, met the illustrious writer, but it is unlikely that Gaston-Louis did. Louis Vuitton developed a keen literary interest during this period. In the 1990s it published, in collaboration with La Quinzaine Littéraire, the "Voyager avec . . ." ("Travel with . . .") book series, including one called *Voyager avec Marcel Proust*.

sider how much the Russians, English, Americans, and Germans loved our Côte d'Azur, where they came to spend three months every winter." The store was entrusted to Gaston-Louis, which enabled him to become acquainted with the Russian imperial family and the aristocrats of Saint Petersburg. They were all loyal customers until the First World War and the 1917 Revolution changed their destinies and habits. Other well-known figures, some of whom were Maison Vuitton regulars, stayed at the Hôtel Ruhl or the Negresco: billionaires like John Pierpont Morgan and the Aga Khan, adventurers like the singer and dancer La Belle Otero, and famous musicians like the pianist Paderewski and the composer Camille Saint-Saëns.

The benefits of the mountains. As with seaside resorts, Empress Eugénie did much to promote spas and resorts near the mountains, one of which—Eugénie-les-Bains—was named after her. Well-off city dwellers were attracted by the health benefits of mountain air and mountain water, and mountain resorts made the most of their interest. Many villages became both chic and modern, including Eaux-Bonnes, Bagnères-de-Luchon, Bagnères-de-Bigorre, and Cauterets in the Pyrénées; Le Mont-Dore in Auvergne; and the famous Vichy in Bourbonnnais, where Louis Vuitton opened a store about 1921. Vichy waters' therapeutic virtues had enjoyed a widespread reputation since ancient times. Thanks to the convenience of modern transportation, the town now attracted a large clientele, especially travelers from other parts of the vast French colonial empire. Gaston-Louis rented a site on Rue du Parc and had it decorated in Art Deco style. Several years later he put his eldest son, Henry-Louis, in charge of the store. In 1930 the writer and traveler Valéry Larbaud, who was born in Vichy, proudly described his birthplace: "It seems to me that this name looks and sounds cheerful and somewhat exotic—Hungarian or maybe Czech—and this suits the large, cosmopolitan spa town it refers to. Yet in fact it is a very old French name meaning a fortified town in the Bourbon duchy, and you know the geographic center of France is located on Bourbon territory. Vichy is such a famous name that it is used, more or less illegally, in faraway countries. In these distant lands, as soon as spring water is found with properties vaguely similar to Vichy spring water, a few hotels are built next to brand-new basins and people proudly proclaim, 'Here is our Vichy.'"

Brazza, the colonial hero

The legendary explorer Pierre Savorgnan de Brazza was a prominent figure in the foundation of the French colonial empire. He gave his name to the capital of Congo, Brazzaville. A loyal Louis Vuitton customer, he also gave his name to an illustrious trunk.

"Suddenly, a tall, emaciated European was standing there on his long legs, looking like a devil. He had disheveled hair, a long, thin, swarthy face with a beard and two bright eyes. His thin, long-nailed fingers constantly tormented the cigarette in his mouth. He looked nonchalant and remarkably vigorous." He was leaning on a long stick and wearing espadrilles on his feet and a dirty hat on his head—so dirty, one would scarcely imagine that it had originally been white. As he emerged from the African bush, this is how Pierre Savorgnan de Brazza appeared to the surprised and admiring eyes of Alfred Fourneau, a French traveler just arrived in Congo.

Destined to be an explorer. Brazza was born into an aristocratic Italian family in Rome in 1852. At the age of sixteen he enrolled in the French naval academy as a foreign student. Two years later, in the French navy, he was involved in the Franco-German war. He obtained French citizenship in 1874. After completing a reconnaissance mission along the Gabon coastline and with the support of the minister of the navy, he was put in charge of exploring the Ogooué River. The Ogooué flows into the Atlantic Ocean about 124 miles south of Libreville and 310 miles north of the mouth of the Congo River.

During the first expedition, between 1875 and 1878, Brazza ascertained that the Ogooué could not be used as a waterway inland from the coast. As he headed for the Alima, a tributary of the Congo, Brazza met with opposition from the local people. Since he believed in negotiation and nonviolence, he decided to turn back. Aware that Europeans were beginning to covet the immense Congo basin, Brazza persuaded the French government to send him back to Africa. During this second mission, from 1880 to 1882, he explored the northern banks of the great river, ahead of the English explorer Henry Morton Stanley. Brazza signed a friendship treaty with King Makoko of the Batekes, which placed the territories under French protection. After that he set up an outpost that would become Congo's future capital city—Brazzaville. This was the start of what would become French Equatorial Africa. When Brazza returned to Europe he received much public acclaim, and the name "Makoko" became very popular.

The Brazza trunk-bed. Before setting out on his first expedition Brazza placed several special orders for trunks and travel articles with Maison Louis Vuitton. Louis created a trunk-bed for the yet-unknown man who would later become a chivalrous hero of the French colonial adventure. Maison Vuitton had developed the first model of its trunk-bed about 1868. A cot—with a customized canvas stretched around a hinged frame and a comfortable flat mattress—folded to fit inside a compact trunk. It was a practical invention that was later widely copied, as Louis had failed to apply for a patent. The trunk-bed's success was so widespread that after Henry Stanley conquered Congo for the Belgian king it became known as the "Belgian bed." It was displayed at the Congo Museum in Brussels under this misleading name. Brazza ordered different trunk-beds on various occasions, and Louis adapted them to his customer's dimensions, which were as imposing as his moral stature.

From exploration to colonization. Brazza's campaigns in Congo were part of a series of explorations undertaken by Europeans in the second half of the nineteenth century that led to the establishment of vast colonial empires. The explorers of the time had a purely

It was the time of expeditions to faraway places. Men, whether adventurous or just curious, would set out on long and sometimes dangerous voyages. Pierre Savorgnan de Brazza (above) was one of these men. After being sent on two missions to explore the Ogooué River, between 1875 and 1882, he had Congo placed under French protection. His generous and idealistic personality and his greatness of soul won him the population's respect. The future capital of Congo would be named after him—Brazzaville.

Opposite: In 1888 the expeditionary photographers George Huebner and Charles Kroehle set off on foot for a photographic report on the Amazonian forest.

J. C. Kroehle

Feeling cramped within its borders, Old Europe set out to conquer new lands. The trunk-bed (opposite), one of Louis Vuitton's cult objects, was first designed about 1868, years before Pierre Savorgnan de Brazza went on his expedition to Congo. However, his popularity and fame were such that the piece came to be known as the "Brazza trunk." The explorer ordered several original travel articles from Louis Vuitton, including a portable desk with a secret compartment.

The Europeans struggled bitterly over the distant lands they hoped to colonize, competing to win the allegiance of a tribe, discover a strategic river, or occupy a region. Above right: About 1900 General Jean-Baptiste Marchand went on a mission to Africa to occupy the upper Nile, but was preempted by the English. His march through Africa enabled him to develop special relationships with chiefs of the tribes he encountered.

geographical curiosity—a desire to reduce the number of unknown regions on maps. Europeans ventured into unexplored areas of Africa in particular. Between 1849 and 1873 the English explorer David Livingstone traveled up and down the equatorial and southern regions of the continent, went on an expedition on the Zambezi River, and discovered Victoria Falls. Between 1850 and 1855 the German explorer Heinrich Barth traveled the Sahara and the Lake Chad region, getting as far west as Timbuktu. In 1858 the English explorers Sir Richard Burton and John Hanning Speke discovered Lake Tanganyika, and in the 1870s Henry Stanley surveyed the same region. Some of the explorations carried out by missionaries were clearly aimed at evangelizing the population, but all of them led to political and economic ambitions in European countries. The discovered lands contained rich supplies of raw materials and unexploited resources. They offered the opportunity to invest in territories beyond Europe. Moreover, on a worldwide scale they became the terrain where national rivalries were played out. Every major European power wanted to control vital trading routes and establish strategic naval bases. Having a powerful colonial empire was a way to assert national strength. In 1914 most of the African continent was under European domination. France was present in western and central Africa—Algeria, Morocco, Tunisia, French West Africa, and French Equatorial Africa—and on the island of Madagascar. French influence in Asia spread in the 1880s from Cochin China, in southern Vietnam, to the colonies and protectorates that made up the vast territories of Indochina—Annam, Tonkin, Laos, and Cambodia.

Louis Vuitton creates articles for faraway lands. Empire building mobilized soldiers, civil administrators, entrepreneurs, and adventurers. Maison Louis Vuitton offered a wide range of articles designed to facilitate their travels in distant lands where the climate could be inhospitable and the insects voracious. The famous trunk-bed attracted more than a few enthusiasts, of course. Louis Vuitton archives contain the names of many notables, military as well as civil, who went to distant lands for pleasure or official duty and always took the precaution of traveling with the Louis Vuitton trunk-bed: General Torrico in South America, General De Couvay in Tonkin, the duke of Blacas, and Baron Benoist-

Méchin. An officer stationed in Tamatave, on the east coast of Madagascar, wrote the company a thank-you letter. After a ten-month campaign, he was the only person in his regiment who still had a bed to sleep in, and he was very pleased he had made the purchase in the store on Rue Scribe. Louis Vuitton also offered the zinc trunk, which was airtight and waterproof. It was designed for travels in exotic countries, especially India and Africa. Patrick-Louis Vuitton compared it to the company's other products: "It was the same as the classic Louis Vuitton trunk, but the canvas was replaced by zinc or copper to prevent rodents and insects from attacking clothes. The inside was often lined with camphor wood instead of fabric," as camphor was a powerful mite and moth repellant. The zinc trunk won a silver medal at the 1868 Exposition in Le Havre. In January 1885 Georges registered a patent of invention based on its principles, which his father had developed. He described it in his memoirs as "a kind of hermetically sealed trunk built to protect its contents from the effects of humidity and even accidental submersion, from insects and the introduction of any foreign bodies into the trunk, however insidious they may be. The entire outer surface of the trunk is reinforced with sheet metal that leaves no part of the structure uncovered." Maison Vuitton also offered a trunk for photographic equipment, "designed especially for expeditions into the bush." To make it easier to carry while walking, the handles on each end were replaced by pieces of rope. Two porters could slip a bamboo pole through the ropes, rest the pole on the shoulders, and carry the trunk.

The last mission. Pierre Savorgnan de Brazza embodied a noble, peaceful, and idealistic approach to colonization, but not all colonizers shared those qualities. Brazza's rival Stanley, for example, was noted for his aggressive and harsh behavior. He was essentially as acquisitive as the big colonial companies, which had a greedy appetite for raw materials like rubber and ivory and sought to divide up the recently conquered territories and monopolize operations there. Brazza clashed with these companies when he was appointed commissioner general to the Congolese government in 1887. Opposed to dividing up French Congo, he ended up being dismissed in January 1898.

However, in February 1905, the minister of the colonies had to confront the concessionary companies' cruelty toward the Congolese population, including abusive work conditions, slave labor, and acts of violence. He decided to have the matter investigated, and Brazza was appointed to the task. Before leaving Brazza placed an order with Louis Vuitton for two large tin trunk-beds fitted with horsehair mattresses. The finest piece of luggage he had made was a portable desk. It was described in detail in the magazine *Illustration*: "From the outside this piece of furniture looked just like an ordinary but solidly built trunk. It was made from well-seasoned wood, covered with dark green painted copper, and reinforced with strong strips of the same metal. It had heavy-duty rope handles, which allowed the trunk to be hung from a few poles or bamboo sticks and carried on the shoulders. Yet, when placed on a table with four foldable iron legs, this trunk became a real desk. Once set up it had racks for folders, some drawers, a compartment for stationery, and a drop leaf that provided a writing surface. This piece of furniture had a secret compartment, a complicated mechanism, concealed in the lower part of the desk, that allowed only those who knew the secret to open it." That was where Brazza would put his confidential documents—notes for the report he was commissioned to prepare and the accounts he had collected from administrators, concession agents, and Congolese workers.

Brazza was on his way back to France when he fell ill. He died in Dakar in September 1905. His portable desk was repatriated. Officials knew that it had a secret compartment, but nobody was able to open it. The minister of overseas territories summoned Georges Vuitton. He instructed him to open the impregnable drawers in his presence and release the papers Brazza had collected. What did they discover? What did the explorer-investigator's notes reveal? We do not know. The report was shelved.

The public was fascinated by the explorers' expeditions, and Louis Vuitton closely followed their discoveries. In 1868 the company created a copper-clad trunk that was "hermetically sealed for the Indies and the colonies. These trunks are essential for protecting clothes from insects and humidity."

The great world's fairs

Glittering international expositions presented the latest products to a cosmopolitan crowd. Inventors and manufacturers who exhibited at the world's fairs competed for prestigious prizes, and an impressive procession of notable people streamed past their displays. The world's fairs were Maison Louis Vuitton's surest way to become known throughout the world.

"Today we went to the Crystal Palace," wrote Valéry Larbaud in *Le Vagabond sédentaire* (Édition La Quinzaine Littéraire–Louis Vuitton). "It is a large building of iron and glass just outside of London, as big as a whole city, with many shops and all kinds of objects (automobiles, bazaars, dressmakers, steamboats, paintings, perfumes, etc.). In addition there are three theaters, cabarets, cafés, restaurants, all in the same building. All around are large gardens with waterfalls, artificial rivers, panoramas, open-air fairs, and all kinds of games. The "Russian Mountain" is an extraordinary ride: By the force of the descent, the wagons go up in the air, with the people inside, in such a way that at one instant they are upside down. It seems very dangerous, but it appears there haven't been any accidents yet. There is also the "Shooting Boat," which descends on rails very fast from the top of a steep slope with a force that makes the passengers go very far into the water."

Larbaud's description conveyed a sense of novelty and wonder upon first experiencing the Crystal Palace and its festival atmosphere in September 1902. At that point, however, the Crystal Palace was more than fifty years old. It had been built to house the Great Exhibition of 1851 and moved from London's center to its outskirts in 1854.

Two sovereigns' creative rivalry. The first world's fairs resulted from a friendly rivalry between two nations and their rulers: Victoria, queen of England, and Napoléon III, emperor of France. The original plan to exhibit works of art and industry "for the world" from "(almost) all over the world" was French and dated to the summer of 1849. Political problems put an end to its development, so the very first world's fair was held in London in 1851. For the occasion architect Joseph Paxton designed the Crystal Palace, a vast glass and iron edifice originally built in Hyde Park, which attracted some six million visitors.

In 1855, a year after Louis Vuitton founded his company, Napoléon III's France responded to the British challenge. The Paris Exposition Universelle took over the Champs-Élysées district, where it built impressive temporary palaces: a Palace of Industry, a Palace of Beaux-Arts, a machine gallery. The emperor announced a lofty ambition of "bringing people together to extinguish hate." Five million people arrived to view 24,000 exhibits from thirty-four nations, a vast display of inventions, art objects, and diverse manufactured goods: American Colt revolvers, a washing machine, Peugeot's household appliances and tools, huge mirrors manufactured by the Saint-Gobain glassworks, floral displays by horticulturalist Louis de Vilmorin, and paintings by Ingres, Delacroix, Courbet, and Horace Vernet.

Louis Vuitton arrives on the scene. The next world's fairs were the 1862 exhibition in London and the 1867 Exposition Universelle in Paris. The latter was a great occasion for the Second Empire. It took place on the Champ-de-Mars, where Frédéric Le Play built a huge circular palace, and drew some ten million visitors. Leading figures from around the world responded to Napoléon III's invitation: Czar Alexander II, Sultan Abdülaziz, Oscar of Sweden, Sophie of the Netherlands, Franz Josef of Austria, and the brother of Japan's emperor. The Élysée Palace was completely remodeled to accommodate them.

Crowds turned out for world's fairs in Paris, London, Brussels, Vienna. Opposite: Napoléon III, the imperial family, and all the crowned heads present at the 1867 event in Paris helped distribute the awards. Some ten million people visited the exposition. It was an extraordinary showcase for Louis Vuitton, which was honored by a bronze medal. The company has been similarly recognized at many world's fairs.

Above: Vuitton's first known English-language catalogue, from 1892.

It was also an important event for Louis Vuitton, as it was the first time he displayed his trunks in such a formal environment. He made a fine impression among the 52,000 exhibitors, and his functional and elegant goods were awarded a bronze medal. The trunk maker seized on the opportunity to build a cosmopolitan and selective clientele.

Celebrating progress. The world's fairs that followed in Paris (1878, 1889, and 1900), Vienna (1873), Philadelphia (1876), Amsterdam (1883), Chicago (1893), London (1894), and Saint Louis (1904)—all magnificent in their own ways—paid homage to scientific and industrial progress, to strength, power, and speed, and to the technological mastery of the forces of nature. An intoxicating passion for engineering was embodied in spectacular objects such as steam machines, locomotives, submarine cables, elevators, combine harvesters, giant forge hammers, microphones, and retractable bridges. Colossal sanctuaries were built of glass, metal, and stone to house these new idols of mechanization. The 1900 Paris exhibition, which undoubtedly marked a peak for this type of event, had a magical palace blazing with the brilliance of twelve thousand lamps to celebrate electricity, the "invention of the day," which was seen as a kind of supernatural being. "Much like morphine in the boudoirs of 1900, [the Electricity Fairy] triumphed in the exhibition; it seemed to come from the heavens, like a true ruler," wrote Paul Morand in *1900,* his book of essays (Flammarion). "At night beacons swept the Champ-de-Mars, the Château d'Eau flowed with the colors of cyclamen and looked like a green cascade, orchid jets, water lilies of flames, orchestrations of liquid fire, debauchery of volts and amperes. The Seine was violet, dove-colored, and beef-blood red. Electricity was accumulated, condensed, transformed; it was put in bottles, held in wires, rolled in spools, then it was discharged in water, on the fountains; it was released on the roofs; it was unleashed in the trees: It was the scourge, the religion of 1900."

Discovering civilizations. The principle of the world's fair was to bring together in one city scientific inventions, artistic creations, and traditions from all around the world. For a few months at a time it gave the public the opportunity to enjoy a far-reaching overview of the diversity of human civilizations and cultures. Nations began building their own representative pavilions for the expositions, creating all kinds of picturesque constructions, architecture both typical and temporary. Only a few steps from a Chinese pagoda would be a Japanese temple or an African hut. The visitor might walk through an exotic Indian or South American setting to the more familiar but also folkloric spectacle of an Alpine chalet or an Italian loggia. The colonial pavilions manifested the European empires' geographic extent. The Exposition Universelle offered a vision of the world in a scale model.

These exhibitions, which had begun as a celebration of progress, sometimes took on an aspect of pure entertainment, becoming much like today's amusement parks. The Exposition Universelle of 1900 transported the public to a reconstruction of a medieval street in Paris, with stalls, taverns, and troubadours. It also presented an animated panorama of the Earth by the painter Louis Dumoulin, who had just finished ten years of travel and study, "containing both decor taken from nature and indigenous peoples from all the countries represented." At the exposition's "Maréorama"—an early virtual reality ride—spectators seated on an ocean liner's rocking chairs took a simulated trip on the Mediterranean between Villefranche and Constantinople, complete with the sway of the ship, light effects, and "a brisk sea breeze, iodized and salty, that whips the traveler's face," according to a press report. Those who preferred the pleasures of rail travel replicated a ride on board a Trans-Siberian train: "The spectators were seated in luxurious train cars that vibrated, simulating motion. On both sides and at the doors, a complete panorama of all the countries between Moscow and Peking unfurled, with stops at the main stations."

Sometimes the exhibitions introduced, like a kind of revelation, the values and aesthetics that would come to wield wide influence. The world's fairs not only celebrated technology but also guided and focused the period's fashions and artistic sensitivities. For example,

One of the most prestigious world's fairs ever was held in Paris in 1900. The city was transformed by new construction, much of which still exists: the Gare d'Orsay, the Petit Palais, the Grand Palais, the subway system, and the Gare de Lyon. Georges Vuitton was responsible for organizing the travel and leather goods section. Opposite: Vuitton's stand, draped in velvet, stood at the center of the section.

PARIS. - 1, Rue Scribe **LOUIS VUITTON** 454, Strand. - LONDON

Opposite: An unusual encounter in Paris, 1878: The head of Auguste Bartholdi's Statue of Liberty alongside Isidore-Jules Bonheur's *Bull*.

Louis Vuitton's stand (above right) at the 1910 Brussels world's fair, where it presented the innovative designs that were judged "hors concours," or without equal. The prize certificate is shown below.

Japan, opened to the West since the mid-1850s, gradually permeated Western tastes and awareness. After a preliminary display in London in 1862, the first official presentation of Japanese objects was a major event at the 1867 Paris exhibition. Members of the Parisian elite were enthusiastic about the Japanese tradition, which was all the more attractive since it was new to them. Many came to share their infatuation, a vogue that led to the coining in 1876 of the term *"japonisme."* The 1878 Paris Exposition Universelle prominently featured Japan's pavilion of art objects. Large crowds went to see the bronzes, ceramics, ancient lacquer ware, and prints so appreciated by painters like Manet and the Impressionists and by writers like Goncourt and Zola. Similarly, the exposition of 1900 marked the consecration of Art Nouveau, whose excesses did not escape the piercing eyes of writer Paul Morand: "The gourd, pumpkin, marshmallow root, and the wreath of smoke inspire illogical furniture on which pose a hydrangea, bat, tuberose, and peacock feather, the invention of artists in the grip of a mistaken passion for the symbol. This furniture resembles the illnesses studied by the clinical psychologists of the time. They thought to be inspired by nature—the sunshade, shellfish, bones, or seeds—but had never been so far from it."

The city gets a makeover. Organizing an event of international scope is a heavy investment that mobilized the city in the years and months leading up to the exhibition. Accommodating visitors and building the gigantic exhibition spaces required works to modernize and improve amenities. The host cities' appearances were transformed. Not everything built for the events was temporary. Paris retained several superb monuments from its exhibitions. The Palais du Trocadéro of 1878, with its two tall minarets, graced the landscape of west Paris for fifty years

before being replaced by the Palais de Chaillot, which was built for the 1937 exhibition and stands to this day. Also in 1878 the sculptor Frédéric-Auguste Bartholdi unveiled his Statue of Liberty, which France had planned to give the United States for the hundredth anniversary of its independence. In 1885 it arrived in New York Harbor, where it remains today; a small-scale version stands in the Seine near Paris's Grenelle Bridge.

The 1889 Exposition Universelle was completely dominated by the Eiffel Tower, begun on 1 January 1887 and inaugurated on 6 May 1889. At a height of 984 feet, it was built of 18,000 pieces of iron and 2.5 million rivets installed while hot. It took twenty-six months to erect, and the workers found themselves at heights never before reached. This was engineer Gustave Eiffel's masterpiece, scarcely tarnished by the lamentations of old aesthetes who found the iron in poor taste. While the Eiffel Tower became one of the world's best-known monuments and a lasting symbol of Paris, the 1900 exhibition changed the city's face and pace forever. The first line (Vincennes-Maillot) of the subway system designed by engineer Fulgence Bienvenüe began to travel through the city, both underground and above. Hector Guimard designed the stations in a defining Art Nouveau style, which was ridiculed by Paul Morand. Other elements of the exhibition contributed to the transformation of the entire area between the Champs-Élysées and the Invalides. The Grand Palais and the Petit Palais, built for the exhibition, are now public galleries housing temporary exhibitions. Nearby, the lovely Alexandre III Bridge still spans the Seine. The architect Victor Laloux created the Gare d'Orsay, a train station and hotel, which is a museum today. Architect Marius Toudoire completely rebuilt another Paris train station, the Gare de Lyon, then the property of the Compagnie PLM. Its buffet was replaced by the still famous restaurant Le Train Bleu, with its luxurious decor, stucco, and garlands—a theatrical setting and romantic prelude for departures.

The Vuittons' diligence rewarded. Beginning in 1867 Louis Vuitton participated in every Paris world's fair but the one of 1878. It was an opportunity to compete for and regularly win awards. It was also an excellent way to build an international clientele of discerning patrons who could compare Louis Vuitton products to those of its competitors. After visiting one exhibition the Spanish court became a customer; King Alfonso XII confirmed his order for a series of trunks a few weeks later. At the 1889 event the Damier canvas, developed the previous year, decorated all the models displayed, and Maison Louis Vuitton won a gold medal and a grand prize for its wardrobes and garment bags. At the sumptuous

Above: An invoice on Louis Vuitton letterhead, dated 31 December 1894.

Opposite: The Eiffel Tower (shown at the early stage of construction) was the real star of the Paris Exposition Universelle of 1889. Louis Vuitton displayed the Damier canvas at that fair and won a gold medal as well as the grand prize for its wardrobe trunks and garment bags.

Exposition Universelle of 1900, which attracted forty-eight million visitors, Georges Vuitton was charged with organizing all the "travel articles and leatherwork." His stand had an ideal location, in a huge carousel, in the center of the section. Once again success rewarded Louis Vuitton's spirit of excellence, and it was classified "hors concours," or without equal.

Elsewhere in Europe and on the other side of the Atlantic, Louis Vuitton received an equally positive welcome and similar awards. Its trunks and suitcases won first prize at the exhibition in Anvers in 1894, at the Exposition Universelle of Liège in 1905, and in Milan the following year. The Franco-British Exposition of London in 1908 was an opportunity to show the latest products available at the store at 149 New Bond Street: the office trunk, the men's Idéale trunk, and the women's hat trunk. The last great fair before the war was held in 1913 in Ghent, where the French trunk maker's own individual pavilion displayed its newest items: the Aéro trunk, the Escapade suitcase, the Inviolable bag, and new models of wardrobe trunks.

From the end of the nineteenth century Louis Vuitton articles developed a high profile across the Atlantic as well. They were displayed at the Chicago 1893 world's fair, which was called the World's Columbian Exposition to commemorate the four hundredth anniversary of America's discovery. Georges Vuitton went to America in 1904 for the Saint Louis World's Fair. He was named president of the jury for travel articles, a testament to the company's world-renowned reputation. Louis Vuitton received awards at successive fairs in the New World, including first prizes in Portland, Oregon, in 1906; at the Alaska-Yukon-Pacific Exposition in Seattle in 1908; and in Buenos Aires in 1910. The United States government invited France to participate in the Seattle event, which Georges Vuitton attended as president of the French section's advocacy committee.

The end of an era. The outbreak of the First World War put a stop to the procession of peaceful and festive international fairs. The West's confidence in progress and faith in the machine were suddenly confronted with the reality of war. Technological innovations showed their murderous potential on the battlefield. Nevertheless, all hope was not lost. A world's fair took place in San Francisco in 1915. In the face of the barbarism soaking Europe in blood, it demonstrated the optimism of resistance. The press took up the message of indomitability, noting that the fair exhibited "a microcosm so complete that, if the whole world were destroyed, it could be reproduced using the samples exhibited here."

Adventure opens new roads

The latest mechanical developments launched a new age of adventure, and Louis Vuitton became involved in exciting exploits. The company was associated with the first automobile rallies, which roared through hundreds of miles of inhospitable terrain. These races were a kind of test, a proof of reliability in extreme conditions.

The Peking-Paris race was the first rally in automobile history. It took place in the summer of 1907, and Louis Vuitton was well represented. Charles Godard, without a doubt the most extravagant of the five competitors, had his Spyker vehicle outfitted with trunks specially ordered from Georges and the Asnières workshops. The race crossed the vast, distant deserts of Central Asia, where the drivers made their way by improvisation and resourcefulness. Godard did not win but he demonstrated a temperament that earned him the nickname in the press of Tartarin of the Gobi. (The moniker referred to the likeable but boastful protagonist of Alphonse Daudet's book *Tartarin de Tarascon*.) The next year Louis Vuitton equipped the New York–Paris rally, which like the previous event was organized by the newspaper *Le Matin*. It was a journey of nearly 25,000 miles across America and Asia. It subjected six teams—three French, one American, one German, and one Italian—to trying climatic conditions. The teams departed on 12 February, in the middle of a harsh New York winter, and headed to Chicago, then San Francisco, where they traveled by boat to Japan. They went on to Vladivostok and Lake Baikal through snow, ice, and mud. The only ones who finished the entire race were the four Americans in a car built by the Edwin Ross Thomas factory in Buffalo, New York. They arrived in Paris on 30 July 1908.

Alliances between Louis Vuitton and Citroën. In the period between the two world wars Louis Vuitton got involved in the legendary automobile odysseys organized by the car maker André Citroën. Citroën, whose company was based in the Javel district of southwest Paris, decided to use his automobiles to establish the fastest connections among France's African colonies. His ambitious aims were political as well as technological. Public authorities were interested in his first project, which took place between December 1922 and March 1923 and resulted in the first crossing of the Sahara. Citroën vehicles equipped with caterpillar belts traveled round trip between Touggourt and Timbuktu. This type of expedition required special outfitting, and Maison Vuitton's know-how proved invaluable. Following the example of Louis, who had developed a hermetically sealed zinc trunk for explorers and colonial travelers, the company in the 1920s designed luggage that protected even the motorists' most fragile objects from the extreme conditions, dust, sand, shock, and humidity.

The Croisière Noire. In 1923 Asnières began developing a whole series of travel articles for the great auto rallies. Citroën's next rallies, the Croisière Noire (Black Journey) and Croisière Jaune (Yellow Journey), were even more ambitious than the first. The Croisière Noire would cross not only the Sahara but the whole African continent, from the northwest, south of Algeria, to the southeast and Madagascar. Despite the "journey" in its name, the adventure had little in common with the increasing nonchalance of modern travel, wherein tourists ambled from one stopover to the next. It pursued serious objectives that were both economic—to establish links among the French colonies in Africa, especially between French West Africa and Madagascar—and scientific—to take topographical readings, draw accurate maps, and conduct ethnological research. The French government backed the undertaking, which was sponsored by the Ministry of the Colonies, the Museum of Natural History, and the Geographical Society of France. Two men led the Croisière Noire:

Great rallies kicked off the new automotive age: Experienced men faced unknown routes and extreme conditions. Georges-Marie Haardt and Louis Audoin-Dubreuil (top) during the Croisière Jaune, 1931–32. G.-M. Haardt's customer record (above).

Opposite: The Croisière Noire used half-track Citroën vehicles to cross the Algerian Sahara in 1924.

Georges-Marie Haardt, André Citroën's right-hand man, and Louis Audoin-Dubreuil, who had experience driving in the desert. The fourteen other members of the team were photographers, ethnologists, scientists, and mechanics. The sixteen of them rode in eight half-track vehicles made by Citroën, each with a poetic name and an identifying logo: Scarabée d'or (Golden Beetle), Pégase (Pegasus), Colombe (Dove), Croissant d'argent (Silver Crescent), Escargot ailé (Winged Snail), Soleil en marche (Moving Sunshine), Eléphant à la tour (Elephant at the Tower), and Centaure (Centaur). They carried an impressive cargo of objects and materials, all packed in a set of Louis Vuitton luggage that was just as astonishing: countless suitcases, tool bags, lunch boxes, first-aid kits, camera cases, Thermos boxes, and driver's bags. The eight-vehicle team departed from Béchar in southern Algeria at the end of October 1924. It continued on a southern course across the desert, then east, through places

Above: Pierre Teilhard de Chardin, theologian and paleontologist, during the Croisière Jaune. Always in search of remote cultures, he participated in many scientific expeditions in the Far East.

Opposite: Pegasus, Golden Beetle, and Winged Snail . . . the poetically named vehicles confronted increasingly hostile terrain on the Croisière Noire. They carried some 150 suitcases and other luggage designed by Louis Vuitton, mostly by special order. Left: A poster for the event.

Following pages: Louis Vuitton accompanied the participants of the 1907 Peking-Paris rally to the steppes of Central Asia.

where no roads had ever been traced. The vehicles had to make their own roads through a changing natural landscape of dunes, brush, high savanna grasses, rivers to be crossed in canoes, virgin equatorial forest, and marsh, where the cars got stuck. Many months and more than 12,400 miles later, the motorized caravan made its way to Tananarive, the capital of Madagascar, in June 1925. The Croisière Noire was a resounding success.

The Croisière Jaune. The rally also must have proven its equipment a success because five years later, when Citroën organized a new rally, it called once again upon Louis Vuitton. In April 1931 the Croisière Jaune set off in the tracks of Marco Polo, from the Mediterranean to the China Sea through the Middle East. Its purpose was to connect Beirut to Peking. Soviet Russia prohibited the vehicles from entering its territory, so they were forced to cross

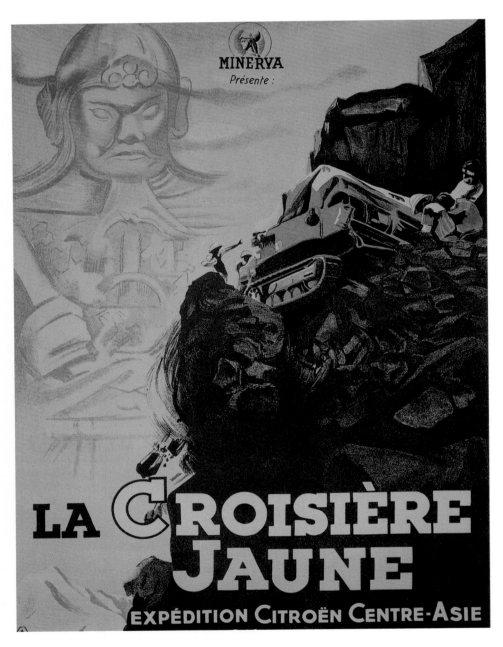

the Himalayas. Like the African adventure, this one was sponsored by Haardt and Audoin-Dubreuil, but it was put together on a grander scale. There were forty travelers, heavy vehicles especially designed for the transcontinental expedition, and seven lighter vehicles that were easier to handle and could be disassembled. Hundreds of pounds of materials, including technical, scientific, and cinematic equipment, were packed into Louis Vuitton trunks, accompanied by tool bags, toiletry kits, folding tables, and trunk-beds manufactured in Asnières. Two groups made the trip, departing from different cities. The Pamir group, led by Haardt and Audoin-Dubreuil, left Beirut and headed east. The China group, led by Victor Point and including the scientist, philosopher, and Jesuit priest Pierre Teilhard de Chardin, left from Peking and headed west. It planned to meet up with the Pamir group after crossing the Himalayas, but quickly confronted great technical difficulties and polit-

Louis Vuitton used new materials—zinc, wood, and copper—for items that would have to stand up to extreme conditions, such as those encountered on the Croisière Jaune. Opposite: A poster for the event.

Above: The 1908 New York–Paris rally. Photo from the 1909 Louis Vuitton catalogue.

ical unrest. The group was taken hostage in the Asiatic regions that were in a state of rebellion. Meanwhile the Pamir group, which followed the ancient silk route across Persia, advanced without much difficulty to Srinagar, in Kashmir. But the Pamir group had to lighten its equipment to cross the Himalayas. Only the two light cars could handle the steep slopes and high-altitude peaks, especially the Burzil Pass—at 13,800 feet, the trip's highest point—so the rest of the Pamir group returned to Europe. However, even the two cars had to be abandoned in Gilgit (in Kashmir), and the journey continued the old-fashioned way, on horseback, until the remaining members of the Pamir group met up with the China group. The rough odyssey was very trying for the men as well as their luggage. Georges-Marie Haardt, who had been in all the great Citroën rallies, died at the end of the trip, in Hong Kong, of pneumonia.

The Vuitton Building

In 1914 Georges opened the largest store for travel articles in the world, the Vuitton Building, at 70 Champs-Élysées. It would be the company's Paris address until 1954. Forty-four years after its departure, Maison Louis Vuitton would return to this world-renowned avenue.

From its eighteenth-century beginnings the Champs-Élysées (which means "Elysian Fields") was reserved for walking and entertainment. Along its length were elegant restaurants in pastoral settings, such as the famous Ledoyen (near the Jeu de Paume in the Tuileries Gardens), where Parisians went to dance, listen to music, ice skate, and enjoy theater or circus performances. The north end, at the bottom of the avenue, near the Saint-Honoré district, was the first area to be adorned with lovely private mansions. The real embellishments were undertaken after 1828, when the state transferred the avenue to the city of Paris. Sidewalks and an asphalt street were added to the Champs-Élysées, eliminating the "field of mud and dust" that had daunted the sturdiest coaches and most valiant pedestrians. Now some 1,200 gas candelabra lit the avenue through the night. Though the evening pleasures were attractive, it was still more chic to be seen there in the afternoon.

The promenade, prelude to the voyage. People would traverse the entire length of the Champs-Élysées, then continue on to Avenue du Bois (today's Avenue Foch). Members of Paris's smart set recognized each other in their carriages. They waved, they watched. Dandies paraded on expensive mounts, showing off their horsemanship. Elegant women let themselves be rocked by the rhythm of their pleasure carriages—coupés, victorias, and phaetons. Parisian high society rolled and trotted in orderly lines. The stated purpose was to go out for some fresh air on the bridle paths of the Bois de Boulogne before returning to the city at sunset. Of course, they all got their fresh air, but the goal, first and foremost, was to display a new conquest, a new outfit, or a new horse-and-carriage. In his book *202 Champs-Élysées* José Maria Eça de Queirós (1845–1900), a great Portuguese writer and a Parisian by adoption, presented a lively portrait of this slice of society. "To the Bois, the city goes every afternoon for a healthy test of energies, finding there, thanks to the presence of duchesses, courtesans, political and financial figures, generals, academics, artists, and clubmen, the comforting certainty that everyone is present in number, with vitality and responsibility, and that no element of its grandeur had disappeared or faded." The businesses along the avenue were in part linked to high society's daily routines. In the 1820s a horse dealer opened there, and all kinds of stores devoted to horseback riding soon followed, including saddleries, harness makers, and coachbuilders. This marked the first commercial activity on the Champs-Élysées. In 1863 Mühlbacher, the luxury coachbuilder founded in 1780, moved from the venerable Saint-Germain district to the Champs-Élysées. The coachbuilders along the avenue had such a fine reputation that in the 1880s they could compete with the top English manufacturers.

The opening of 70 Champs-Élysées. The horse-drawn carriage declined with the arrival of the automobile age. Stores specializing in horses and harnesses gradually disappeared from the landscape, making way for the first big automobile dealerships. Display windows were filled with brand names like De Dion, Panhard-Levassor, Hotchkiss, Berliet, Rolls-Royce, Mercedes, Peugeot, and Renault.

In the early years of the twentieth century Maison Vuitton was growing so fast internationally that it needed a larger store. Georges Vuitton decided to leave the Rue Scribe building in the Opéra district and in June 1912 purchased land at 70 Champs-Élysées from a Mercedes dealer. The address was located in the middle of this dynamic thoroughfare of

Georges showed double daring with the Vuitton Building (opposite), in terms of both architecture and location. The building, whose facade is now classified as a landmark, represents its era's latest trend, halfway between Art Nouveau and Art Deco. Georges's bet on the Champs-Élysées, then undergoing a complete transformation, would be rewarded by the store's great success.

Georges and his son Gaston-Louis certainly knew how to draw attention to their store. They seized every opportunity to create lively windows on travel themes, such as the automobile (above). Other eye-catching displays included acrobatic performances, giant tortoises, and Father Christmas's sleigh.

Following pages: Part of the company's heritage is the iconic representation of its original Champs-Élysées store (left). The building bears an amusing resemblance to Louis Vuitton's shoe trunk (right).

VUITTON BUILDING

modern travel, newly studded with showcases for all types of cars, including the most innovative. The Champs-Élysées was also where the large luxury hotels were locating. The Élysée-Palace opened in 1898 at No. 101; the Wanamaker, in 1905 at No. 127; the Carlton, in 1907 at No. 119; the Astoria, in 1907 at No. 131, near Place de l'Étoile; and the Claridge, in 1914 at No. 74, near the new Vuitton store. The land Georges bought covered an area of 5,380 square feet, on which Georges had a seven-story building constructed. He entrusted the plans to the architects Bigaux and Koller, who had just worked on the Ritz. Within a few months an Art Deco building rose, with the two basements, ground floor, and mezzanine reserved for Louis Vuitton. The upper floors were rented to a well-known dress designer, Jenny, who set up her workshops and fashion showrooms, designed by Mallet-Stevens, there. Jenny's choice of the Vuitton Building was representative of couture houses' westward movement. They were leaving the district around Rue de la Paix for Avenue Matignon, Avenue Montaigne, and the Champs-Élysées, where very chic boutiques had opened, including two famous English boot makers, Phillips and Thomas and Son, and James, the dressmaker. The great perfumers were arriving on the same wave. Guerlain left Rue de la Paix and had a building erected at 68 Champs-Élysées at the same time as Vuitton.

The Vuitton store opened on 15 May 1914. At the time it was the largest store in the world dedicated entirely to travel articles. Henry-Louis Vuitton underscored his grandfather Georges's flair and daring: "The naysayers predicted and swore that customers would never go that far, that they would refuse to go farther than Place de la Concorde, the gardens of the Champs-Élysées, and the Rond-Point to come all the way to the middle of the avenue. First of all, their curiosity was very strong. It must be said that Georges and Gaston had been stirring it up for months. In fact, success came more quickly than anticipated. To be precise, it was immediate."

The confidence the Vuittons had in the area, which would be their location for forty years, inspired them to make a commitment to its future. With other tradesmen and inhabitants they created an association in 1916, Les Amis des Champs-Élysées. Its purpose was to ensure the Parisian artery's rank of most beautiful avenue in the world by protecting it from deterioration and ugliness. The Vuittons were especially active, helping to stop the Champs-Élysées from being renamed Avenue Clemenceau, improve the lighting, destroy the unsightly public urinals, and strictly regulate advertising and illuminated signs—limited to white—along the entire avenue, from Place de la Concorde to Place de l'Étoile.

Giant tortoises, a yo-yo, and a torii. Vuitton's store windows sparkled with beauty and astonished with their inventiveness. Gaston-Louis Vuitton's fertile and artistic imagination produced extraordinary windows to enliven and promote the store while surprising customers and passers-by. In the early 1930s the store window was transformed into an enormous terrarium, where two giant tortoises frolicked. A sign indicated their meal times. Twice a day crowds gathered around the store to watch the distribution of lettuce leaves and small fish be gobbled up by the two antediluvian beasts. The display was a sensation. But there were complications behind the scenes, noted Henry-Louis Vuitton. "The dimensions of the glassed cage were such that serious problems with watertightness became apparent right away, and the rug was soon transformed into a sponge."

It would take more than that to discourage Gaston-Louis. For another window he replaced the tortoises with crocodiles. Another time, during the summer of 1932, he highlighted the yo-yo at 70 Champs-Élysées. This toy, which dates back to ancient China and Egypt, was all the rage in the 1930s. Every afternoon the company employed a juggler to stand behind the large bay window of the Vuitton Building and play with his wooden yo-yo, which rose and descended on a long string held in one hand. The crowd of onlookers seemed as tenacious and patient as the artist, a veritable marathoner, who spent several hours a day yo-yoing among the trunks on display. The following winter the store windows celebrated the holidays with Father Christmas's three-horse sleigh and a few animated

Statesmen and other notables have long traveled with Louis Vuitton luggage. Clockwise from top left: Queen Astrid of Belgium in 1934. Farouk, the young king of Egypt, about 1936. Calouste Gulbenkian, the British financier and art collector of Armenian origin. Raymond Poincaré, president of France, with Prime Minister Georges Clemenceau in 1918. Lady Mendl, the American interior decorator born Elsie de Wolfe, who had her trunks marked with a white wolf. Hirohito, the future emperor of Japan, during his 1921 visit to Paris. Walking along the Champs-Élysées, he admired the Vuitton store window that was decorated with a torii—an ornamental gateway for Shinto temples—in honor of his visit.

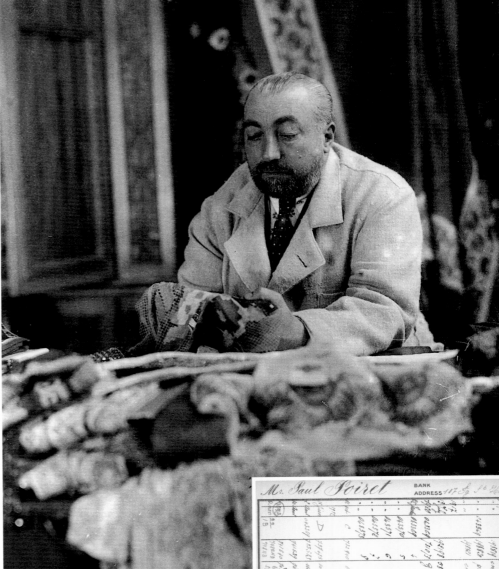

figures in a snowy, frosty setting. In April the ice gave way to something equally glittering. The store window became a huge jewel box in which bloomed dozens of bouquets of lilies of the valley, crafted of crystal. The most remarkable window was the Japanese garden of June 1921, designed in honor of Imperial Prince Hirohito's visit to France. Gaston-Louis Vuitton recounted the circumstances of the design: "A visit from the son of the emperor of Japan had been announced some time before. How to connect this visit with our products? I had studied the art of Japanese gardens and I had the ambition to create a Japanese garden in our store window. I went to see Lemonnier (Maison Ferard), then located at Rue de la Pépinière, who was my personal plant and seed supplier. He had an open and cultivated mind and agreed to help me. We consulted with Weiss from Saint-Cloud, who was a specialist in cultivating Japanese trees. I had a splendid torii made at the factory. We rented a lantern. The Japanese ambassador was pleased to draw the characters for 'welcome' on a pine board. A painted canvas represented Fujiyama in our window display. A stairway of a few steps led to the temple. Thus was put in place a Japanese garden, which met with incredible success." The 2 June 1921 report of the imperial prince's visit in the *Excelsior* newspaper confirmed his account. "About five o'clock the prince received the president of the Republic at the embassy on Avenue Hoche, and then took a walk through Paris. Going down the Champs-Élysées, his attention was especially attracted by a Japanese torii in Louis Vuitton's store window."

The atmosphere along the Champs-Élysées changed in the 1950s. Movie theaters and brasseries replaced the luxury goods stores. Consequently the Vuittons chose to relocate, moving away from the commotion on the avenue to an area that reflected the elegance and discretion of their traditional clientele. The new store was in a town house at 78 bis Avenue Marceau, where Louis Vuitton celebrated its hundredth anniversary in 1954. It remained there for decades. But the Champs-Élysées regained its luster after a renovation in 1994 and is again worthy of the title "world's most beautiful avenue." It became the "in" place to be. The prestigious brands that had deserted it returned, enhancing the brilliance of this vast showcase of contemporary urban life. Louis Vuitton moved back in 1998 with a new store at 101 Avenue des Champs-Élysées.

Artists, perfumers, and couturiers called upon Louis Vuitton. Opposite, from left to right and top to bottom: Jean Patou with a group of models in 1924. Jean-Jacques Guerlain's customer record. Madeleine Vionnet. The entertainer Mistinguett. Paul Poiret (and his customer record). Jeanne Lanvin. Customer record of Gabrielle (Coco) Chanel, 1918–20.

Above right: A 1923 advertisement.

Below: The Japanese garden Gaston-Louis Vuitton designed for the Champs-Élysées store window to honor Imperial Prince Hirohito's 1921 visit to Paris.

GASTON-LOUIS

Creative passion

A sickly childhood gave Gaston-Louis an early love of books. He also enjoyed writing, recording his impressions of his travels and maintaining a diary. He kept sketchbooks and made drawings and collages. His curiosity naturally led to an interest in design.

Gaston-Louis represents the third generation of Vuittons. He was the only one of Georges's three sons to survive the cataclysm of the First World War. Jean died of an illness before the war and his twin, Pierre, perished on the front in 1917. Though he was very involved in the management of family affairs, Gaston-Louis had many diverse interests, which his father considered secondary. He was an esthete, a businessman, and a financier. His particularly keen business sense was obvious in the way he managed the Champs-Élysées store, giving it a brilliant visibility. His taste for beautiful things inspired his passion for collecting.

A studious youth. Gaston-Louis was born on 30 January 1883 in Asnières at 15 Rue de la Comète, where he would spend his entire life. Coincidentally, on the day of his birth the store on Rue Scribe recorded an order from a Japanese official, Goto Shojiro. The child's health was delicate. "According to my mother, the imprudence of a wet nurse made me contract bronchitis," he later wrote. "It left my bronchial tubes extremely sensitive, and this affected my whole life." As a result, his attendance at the local school in Asnières, then at a private school, and finally at the Lycée Condorcet was sporadic. However, Gaston-Louis had a great appetite for all types of knowledge, and his curiosity extended in every direction. "The leisure time that resulted from treatments in different spa towns allowed me to develop an interest in geology, botany, and zoology. I had a thirst to know history and the arts, and I was a regular at all the Parisian painting salons and museums." During that time he also became interested in photography.

In January 1897 he began two years of training at the Asnières workshops. "With the doctor's advice, my father took me on as an apprentice at the plant, on the sole condition that I always work in front of an open window, which at the time was very easy to do." Following the family tradition, he then went to work in the store. "On 15 May 1899 I started out in sales at our store on Rue Scribe and, for me, selling immediately seemed like a sport. It's an opinion that I still hold and will defend always." He remained there for eight years. Military service did not interrupt his career as he was declared unfit, "due to thoracic insufficiency."

Vuitton et Fils. In 1906 Gaston-Louis married Renée Versillé, the daughter of a public works entrepreneur. She was a childhood friend whose family had been close to the Vuittons since Louis's generation. The following year Georges brought his eldest son into the company's management and on 1 March created a partnership of which he was principal stockholder. That company's trade name was "Vuitton et Fils."

Gaston-Louis was twenty-four years old at the time. Tall, thin, and elegant, he had, according to his son Henry-Louis, "a determined face, barred with a magnificent moustache. Tall like his father, he was, however, infinitely less robust." At fifty Georges still had an impressive build. He was a "six-foot-tall, strapping fellow who could lift the biggest wardrobe trunks with a mere turn of a wrist." In addition to height, Gaston-Louis may have inherited from his father a love of traveling. He already knew English when he went to England for the first time, in 1901. In 1905 and 1906 he traveled through Switzerland and the Savoy region of the Alps. In 1908 he visited the Jura, Dauphiné (in southeastern France), and Egypt. Curiosity and the desire to tackle subjects that directly or indirectly related to the future of the family business were his guides. He would study tree species, or take an interest in the commercial structure of retail sales or expor-

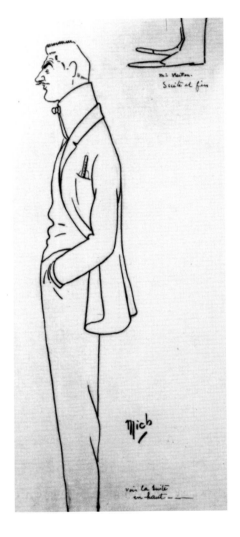

Previous page: Portrait of Gaston-Louis Vuitton.

Opposite: Gaston-Louis and his wife, Renée, in 1950. A collector and aesthete with great intellectual curiosity, Gaston-Louis was interested in all art forms. His inventiveness would push the company in directions it had not previously explored.

Above: A caricature of Gaston-Louis by Mich in 1908.

tation, or experiment—winter or summer—with a new type of vacationing called camping.

In 1908 Gaston-Louis negotiated the purchase of a business in Nice, near the Promenade des Anglais—a fashionable seafront avenue lined with hotels and cafés and much frequented by the English and wealthy Russian aristocrats. His first child had been born the year before, in 1907. In honor of his first grandchild Georges had his most skilled worker make a baby's trunk, an exact replica of one an American multimillionaire had ordered four years earlier for a newborn's layette. Gaston-Louis ultimately had seven children, but one daughter died at an early age. His other daughters were Andrée, Odile, and Denyse, and his three sons were Henry-Louis and the twins Claude-Louis and Jacques-Louis.

Gaston-Louis managed the company at his father's side until Georges's death in 1936. It was up to him to ensure the company's survival during the difficult years of the Second World War and the German occupation of 1940–44. In his biographical notes of 1963 he recounts those years in a succinct, telegraphic style: "War of 39–45. Son mobilized. Order of military canteens—the exodus, the regrouping in Sologne, the dispersion, Cognac, Vichy, Isle-Jourdain, Nice." After the war he directed the company to leave its Champs-Élysées location and move to a new store on Avenue Marceau. It opened in 1954 for Maison Louis Vuitton's hundredth anniversary and closed in 1970.

A taste for beauty. Gaston-Louis was an erudite man full of curiosity, as well as a collector. His sense of beauty led him just as often to objects from the past as to contemporary artistic pursuits. He began developing an interest in collecting as a child, when his health was delicate and his school attendance sporadic. "If my intermittent instruction was rather neglected due to my sickly state, it allowed me, thanks to my mother's intelligence, to direct my childhood activities toward reading and collecting. I learned geography through stamp collections and I avidly followed our colonial era through the exploits of Faidherbe, Morès, Flatters, Livingstone, Stanley, and Barth in the *Journal des Voyages*."

At an early age he began collecting trunks and old travel articles, which he searched for in antiques and secondhand shops and auction rooms. He collected the tools used to make trunks and cases, craftsmen's shop signs, and the labels that large hotels usually stuck on their customers' trunks.

Gaston-Louis had other interests and enterprises as well, many related to the printed word. "A keen taste for reading led me to bibliophilia and in particular to typography. After founding Les Exemplaires [a publishing company for limited editions] with a few friends, I wanted to pursue fine printing further. We founded the Compagnie Typographique, whose presidency I assumed for several years." Gaston-Louis was also a member of the National Committee of Illustrated French Books and the Société Archéologique, Historique et Artistique Le Vieux Papier. Writing was like breathing for him. He left behind a large quantity of notes, diaries, and book projects. Under the pseudonym Gaston Hellevé he published essays for a magazine called *l'Intermédiaire des chercheurs et des curieux* (*The Intermediary of Seekers and the Curious*—two words that aptly described him).

A precocious love of art pushed him toward the cutting edge. In the early 1900s, when the Exposition Universelle of Paris established a taste for Art Nouveau, Gaston Louis did not merely appreciate it as a connoisseur. "Won over by modern art from its beginnings, in 1901 I designed, under the influence of the School of Nancy, the furniture for my bedroom, which I had made in teak wood. Of course, the floral motifs, irises, and very ornate style of the period found a place there." The same "very ornate style" and other intertwined plants can be seen today in the decoration of the family residence at Asnières (now a museum). Art was not just a pastime for Gaston-Louis. It nourished his activities and innovations as a trunk maker. He conveyed his sense of architecture and design in store windows displays, new models, and artistic collaborations (with designers like Legrain, Lebourgeois, Rulance, Conversat, and Puiforcat) that produced objects both functional and aesthetic, including small cases, flasks, toiletry kits, and cutlery.

Gaston-Louis was always in charge of the Champs-Élysées store. He is shown here about 1965, flanked by his sons Henry-Louis (at left) and Claude-Louis, examining new products. A bust of his father, Georges, is in the background.

Window displays

Every week the store windows were reinvented. The following pages show some of the numerous drawings found in the sketchbooks of Gaston-Louis Vuitton, who wrote in 1927, "You're talking about displays? Why, the action is better than the word, and instead of talking about it, I would rather make the window displays. It's an enjoyable preparation involving the arts of architecture and stage direction. Judge me by what I have done and not by what I can express here. Let me point out that after twenty-eight years of practice, setting up a lovely display is a real pleasure for me and I am just as passionate about it now as I was on that long-ago day when I was sixteen and made my first window display. I only hope it will still be the same in another twenty-eight years."

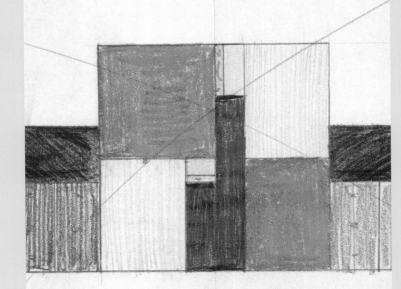

Above: Photograph of the Champs-Élysées store window in 1926.
Right, opposite, and following pages: Sketches from the 1920s.

Executé le 24 mai 1927 Mardi

Photo n°. 1204

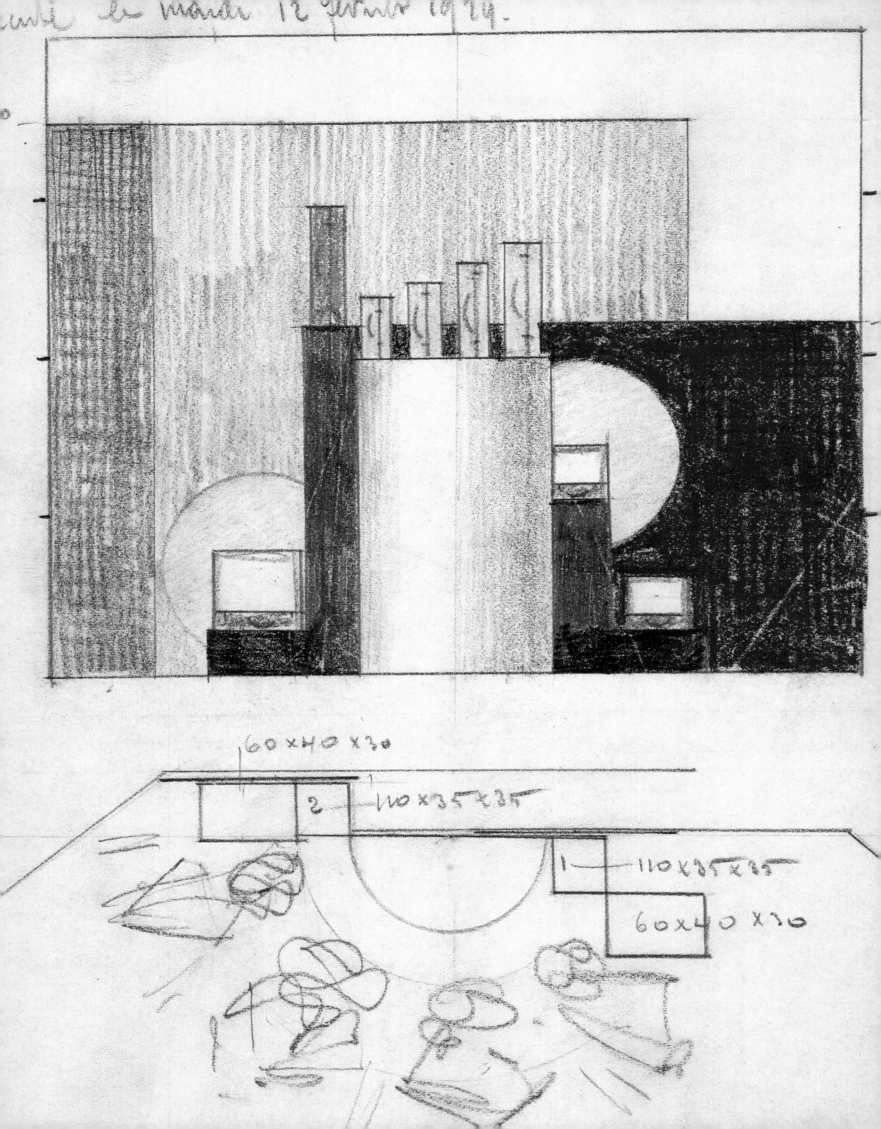

60 x 40 x 30

2 ——— 110 x 35 x 35

1 ——— 110 x 35 x 35

60 x 40 x 30

Four of Gaston-Louis's drawings in pencil and watercolor for the store window at 70 Champs-Éysées, conveying the aesthetic of the twenties.

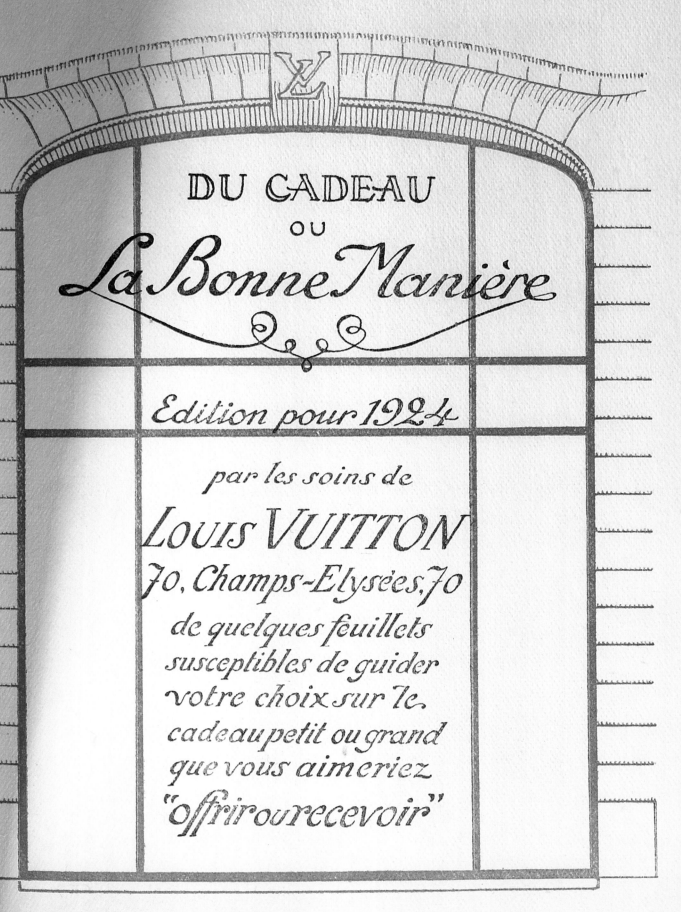

DU CADEAU
ou
La Bonne Manière

Edition pour 1924

par les soins de

Louis VUITTON
70, Champs-Elysées, 70
de quelques feuillets
susceptibles de guider
votre choix sur le
cadeau petit ou grand
que vous aimeriez
"offrir ou recevoir"

The art of display

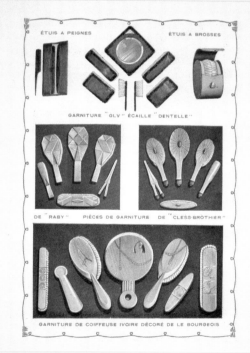

"Du Cadeau ou La Bonne Manière," Louis Vuitton's 1924 catalogue, contained an array of handbags, clutch bags, toiletry bags, perfume bottles, and more. The booklet (7¼ x 5½ inches) was adorned with an elegant green cover illustrated to recount milestones of the company's history.

Gaston-Louis VUITTON

Voyage iconographique autour de ma Malle

Extrait du *Bulletin de la Société archéologique, historique et artistique*
LE VIEUX PAPIER

LILLE
IMPRIMERIE LEFEBVRE-DUCROCQ
1920

Collecting, reading, and writing were three of Gaston-Louis Vuitton's passions. He wrote a speech for a conference of the Société Archéologique, Historique et Artistique Le Vieux Papier, entitled "Voyage iconographique autour de ma malle" (Iconographic Voyage Around My Trunk)—a wink at Xavier de Maistre's *Voyage autour de ma chambre* (Voyage Around My Room), published in 1795. Gaston-Louis's speech, published in 1920, explained the origin, use, and value of the travel decals that were then commonly affixed to luggage:

"Maybe happiness exists only in train stations. I would like to let you circulate there amidst trunks, crates, baskets, suitcase, etc., just to examine the papers stuck on the baggage. What can you find on old luggage? You can find imprints of the means of transportation used, the voyages made, the visits carried out, all this recorded by old papers, by the labels of railroad companies, special trains, grand international expresses. You can also find labels from cruise lines, companies providing transport between train stations and domiciles, from customs and expeditors, from storerooms and furniture storehouses—all the places through which the trunk has passed. Finally, there are hotel labels. This is what you can find on used trunks. Putting aside the first of these categories, I would like to show you some hotel luggage labels and accompany them with a few comments. We are going to follow them and in so doing we will take a trip around the world.

"To designate hotel luggage labels I propose the name 'mini-poster,' with the following definition: a small printed poster that hotels stick on their customers' luggage for advertising purposes.

"And let me add, it's advertising with a triple effect. The mini-poster acts through memory, attraction, and suggestion.

1. Through memory: It reminds the owner of the trunk on which it is affixed which hotel he or she stayed at in which place.

2. Through attraction: It indicates to other tourists where the owner of the trunk usually stays, with the hope that they will follow the example.

3. Through suggestion: Like a real advertising poster, it should inspire the desire for the hotel and if possible even the desire for the country.

"When did mini-posters first appear? They were first made by Maison Boutillier about 1890, and Maison Richter began making them in 1900. Some journalists noticed a few trunks that were extravagantly covered with mini-posters and reproduced them to illustrate an article enumerating the countries visited. Here is a trunk that set out on 8 July 1911 and returned 25 July 1912 after traveling to Austria, Germany, France, England, America, Hawaii, New Zealand, Australia, the Philippines, Hong Kong, China, Korea, Japan, Siberia, and Russia—a complete trip around the world. The article was published in three different newspapers in February 1913. Trunk makers thought that

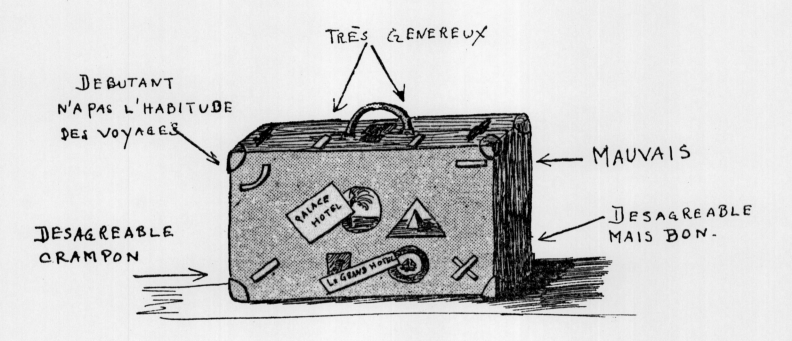

TRÈS GENEREUX

DEBUTANT N'A PAS L'HABITUDE DES VOYAGES

MAUVAIS

DESAGREABLE CRAMPON

DESAGREABLE MAIS BON.

the numerous stickers were a testament to their products' value and did not hesitate to include a trunk so decorated in their catalogues.

"There were many flags, either from the country where the hotel was located or from the foreign or distant land that was the trunk owner's home. We are filled with emotion when we look at the French flag of the Métropole Hotel in Hanoi or the Oriental Palace in Yokohama.

"Some wanted to read into the way the mini-posters were affixed, imagining a code that allowed hotel employees to communicate with each other and to signal the customer's value in terms of tipping. If we can believe the *American Examiner,* there's nothing to it—chalk marks were used for that purpose.

"A quarter circle in the upper corner of a suitcase meant 'a novice, who hasn't traveled much'—he or she must be treated well. A straight line on each side of the lock meant 'very generous.' A horizontal line in the upper right-hand corner meant 'bad.' That line accompanied by a V meant 'very bad.' A diagonal mark on the bottom corner was a 'disagreeable leech'; a cross in the lower right-hand corner meant a 'leech, but generous.'

"With a good deal of wit, the article explained how you would be treated in the hotels according to the sign on your luggage. It frankly demonstrated that hotel employees had a hundred refined ways to make miserable the man who didn't give tips, while those who tipped enjoyed enviable comforts and luxuries.

"As we said, the mini-poster is an advertisement—advertising that the hotel does somewhat to the detriment, or at least at the expense of, its customer—but what do the trunk's owners have to say about being used as a medium for hotel advertisements? Some rebelled, some grumbled, and some went so far as to threaten to withhold tips if their luggage was not spared. They were a very small minority; the majority was indifferent and just let it be. Once the labels became overabundant, they would ask their valets to clean off the trunk. Collectors abounded too, and some were even a bit obsessed, with inevitably varied personal preferences. Some would allow the luggage handler to stick the mini-posters wherever he wanted but would formally forbid the trunk maker to touch them when he was inspecting the trunk. Others, knowing that luggage handlers often tried putting their stickers over those of unrelated hotels, would insist on overseeing the application of the mini-poster on the trunk, making sure that it was well placed between slats that would protect it and that its size or colors did not clash with those of its neighbors. Finally, there were others who asked to be handed the mini-posters and slid them under the binding inside the trunk lid. Every time the owner opened the trunk he could look at them. This type was a dilettante, but his mini-posters remained intact. I've left the fake traveler for last. On his new trunk he would stick labels he had collected here and there or had asked friends to bring back. He wished to travel, but more likely than not he's visited only Deauville or Nice and has never sailed to the Americas."

PARIS RITZ HOTEL Z

BELLEVUE PALACE BERNE

HOTEL GALLIA PARIS
CHAMPS ÉLYSÉES

HOTEL CENTRAL ZÜRICH
PAUL ELWERT PROPR.

HÔTEL EUROPE MILAN
L. BERTOLINI

HÔTEL REGINA: VENISE

CLARIDGE'S HOTEL
PARIS

GRAND HÔTEL Paris

GRAND HOTEL ET DES ILES BORROMÉES STRESA
ROMEO OMARINI
LAC MAJEUR

HOTEL Majestic
19 AVENUE KLÉBER
PARIS

CONTINENTAL PALACE HOTEL SAN SEBASTIAN

The Vuitton home in Asnières. The stained-glass windows, whose floral motif was inspired by Art Nouveau, were made in 1897 by Janin, the master glassmaker from Asnières.

The great Exposition des Arts Décoratifs

Infatuated with Art Nouveau in the early 1900s, Gaston-Louis turned to Art Deco in the 1920s. He collaborated with the great artists of the period, including Legrain, Puiforcat, Conversat, Rulance, and Lalique, to design travel cases in the tradition of French luxury goods.

The travel case, which at Louis Vuitton also goes by names like kit or travel bag, has a long, rich history. It has evolved from a simple, practical object into a veritable work of art. In the Middle Ages it was a plain case in which useful grooming accessories or "mouth objects" for oral hygiene were arranged. With time and the perfecting of manners and custom, it became more refined and distinguished. By the eighteenth century the case had acquired the status of a princely gift. Its manufacture demanded the expertise of several trades—cabinetmaker, ivory carver, goldsmith—using costly materials like precious woods, ebony, ivory, silver, vermeil, mother of pearl, and tortoiseshell.

One of the masterpieces of the genre is Queen Marie-Antoinette's travel case. In the 1770s, when Louis XVI ascended France's throne and his young wife played the role of arbiter of elegance, the silversmith Jean-Pierre Charpenat designed for her a set of silver and porcelain toilet and travel articles made by Sèvres. These pieces and their case were extremely refined. Whatever the uncertainties of travel, anyone traveling with such luggage would be able to create a voluptuous comfort, even in a mediocre inn. The ewer and the silver bowl and the bottles of perfume or eau de Cologne would enable travelers to refresh themselves from the tribulations of the road. Hairbrushes, shaving brushes, scissors, and mirrors made grooming easier, as did many other specialized items for hand care, hairdressing, and trimming beards, moustaches, and sideburns. Glasses, miniature place settings, fine porcelain cups, and all kinds of silver containers were enticements to exquisite light meals, complete with coffee or hot chocolate—which were still exotic and rare beverages then. Sometimes the travel case would include a writing surface, ink, a few candlesticks for the evening, and secret compartments for storing jewelry and important papers.

Design excellence. Travel cases created by Gaston-Louis Vuitton were part of the tradition of luxury goods that triumphed in Europe in the eighteenth century. These fine works drew on a number of trades, including furniture and jewelry making, clothing design, and silversmithing. Vuitton produced several models in the 1920s. The 1923 Torino garment bag for women was made of crocodile and sealskin. Inside were seven bottles of cut crystal and silver plate, nine round or rectangular boxes, three silver-plate brushes—for clothes, hair, and shoes—three leather-covered boxes, a case, a leather comb, and a blotting pad of the same material. The tea case of 1926, which the maharajah of Baroda acquired to take tiger hunting, was made of cowhide. It contained a porcelain and silver-plate service, with everything needed for an impromptu tea in a clearing while awaiting the tiger: cups, saucers, goblets, bottles and boxes, teapots, water and cream pitchers, knives, forks, teaspoons, napkins, and a tablecloth. All that was needed was a clean stream to wash all these lovely implements after use. Sometimes customers offered inspired ideas, as did the elegant Lady Addison, a loyal customer of Louis Vuitton. She had a distinctive, original style, a pronounced taste for Mario Fortuny dresses, and an almost exclusive passion for purple morocco leather. She had all kinds of boxes and cases made from it in what the company soon called "Addison purple." In 1928 she ordered, among other extravagances, a bottle case in purple morocco leather, for transporting eau de Cologne. It was fitted with two five-quart cans, exact replicas in silver plate of the gas cans then in use. In 1929 the famous French singer Marthe Chenal, who played Carmen on stage and off, had a travel case with a flap front: The vertical section contained a row of bottles,

powder, and soap boxes, while the front section that closed horizontally contained an array of brushes and manicure accessories set around a small mirror. One can imagine her gazing into the glass and singing to herself, like Jules Massenet's heroine Thaïs, "Tell me that I am beautiful and that I will be beautiful forever!" The Marthe Chenal set became a Louis Vuitton classic, as did the case the Polish pianist Ignacy Jan Paderewski ordered in 1929. It was made of brown crocodile and red morocco leather. Inside was a set of cut crystal bottles with vermeil stoppers, a vermeil shaving brush, monogrammed ivory hairbrushes, and a fifteen-item manicure set in ivory and steel.

The wonderful kits (called *nécessaires* in French) were great successes in the 1920s. Truly a necessity for the traveler, they also elevated daily life to gracious heights. The writer Vladimir Nabokov immortalized his travel kit in his book *Speak, Memory,* describing it as a tender witness and a heroic actor in an epic that spanned the twentieth century, Europe, the Atlantic Ocean, and the breadth of America.

"On this gray winter morning in the looking glass of my bright hotel room, I see shining the same, the very same, locks of that now seventy-year-old valise, a highish, heavyish, *nécessaire de voyage* of pigskin, with 'H. N.' elaborately interwoven in thick silver under a similar coronet, which had been bought in 1897 for my mother's wedding trip to Florence. In 1917 it transported from St. Petersburg to the Crimea and then to London a handful of jewels. Around 1930 it lost to a pawnbroker its expensive receptacles of crystal and silver, leaving empty the cunningly contrived leather holders on the inside of the lid. But that loss had been amply recouped during the thirty years it then traveled with me—from Prague to Paris, from St. Nazaire to New York and through the mirrors of more than two hundred motel rooms and rented houses in forty-six states. The fact that of our Russian heritage the hardiest survivor proved to be a traveling bag is both logical and emblematic."

Art meets industry. The delicacy, elegance, and sobriety of these cases reinforced Art Deco as the style in vogue in France in the 1920s. A reaction to the excesses of Art Nouveau—remember Paul Morand's ironic remarks about the 1900 Exposition Universelle—Art Deco used simple, unadorned lines and geometric shapes. It assured the primacy of the structure over its ornamentation, favoring lively colors and sharp contrasts. The straight line usurped the arabesques and the intertwining lines (suggesting ivy or morning glories, for example) that had invaded the art world at the beginning of the century. Art Deco was related to contemporary aesthetic revolutions that celebrated bold lines or geometric shapes, including constructivism, fauvism, cubism, and futurism. Although it was not very influential in painting and sculpture, it had a broad impact on architecture. Among the Art Deco masterpieces still standing in Paris are the 1926 La Samaritaine department store by Frantz Jourdain and Henri Sauvage and the Palais de Tokyo. Art Deco also found fertile ground in the applied arts—furniture, notably the work of the cabinetmaker Émile-Jacques Ruhlmann, glassworks, ceramics, posters by Adolphe-Jean-Marie Mouron Cassandre, illustrations by Georges Lepape, and silversmithing.

Gaston-Louis Vuitton's interest in Art Deco drew him into collaborations with great artist-decorators, including the silversmith Jean Puiforcat, bottle set makers like Legrain and Cless Brothier, and Jean Dunand, who created fancy goods and lacquer ware. He displayed the fruits of these joint projects in a beautiful showcase devoted to the new style, the 1925 Exposition des Arts Décoratifs et Industriels Modernes in Paris. Its aim was to establish "the collaboration between artists and industrialists on new foundations." Gaston-Louis was vice president of the exhibition, where the company had a spectacular stand. As Henry-Louis recounted, "It was decorated in green and silver tones to highlight the articles displayed. On each side of the entrance were travel articles, leatherwork, and silverwork. Next were trunks displayed on steps and, in the background, the Excelski automobile trunk, which contained a large garment bag for dresses and clothing, two small

Previous pages: The Paris exposition of 1925, for which Gaston-Louis served as vice president, marked Art Deco's apogee. Sober, straight lines, and geometric forms succeeded the fluid, sinuous curves of Art Nouveau. The public thronged to its opening to discover new industrial and artistic innovations.

Louis Vuitton's stand at the exposition, with its elegant lines and harmonious colors, displayed remarkable items like the Milano case.

Opposite: The Milano was one of the masterpieces Louis Vuitton displayed at the exposition of 1925. The case was lined with red morocco leather and outfitted with cut crystal bottles with vermeil stoppers, as well as ivory brushes and toilet accessories that were finely carved with geometric motifs in Art Deco style. The Milano is part of the collection of the Louis Vuitton Museum in Asnières.

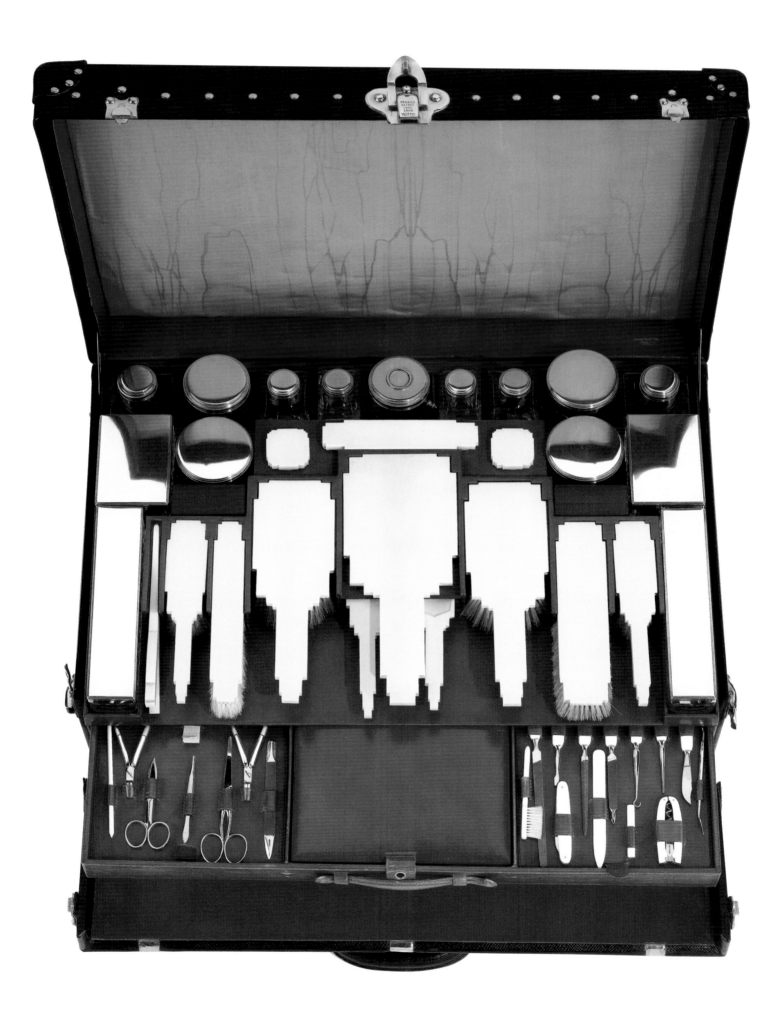

linen cases, and two equipped kits. Visitors could also admire a library trunk with a special case for a typewriter, but the loveliest item presented was surely the Milano set. This was a kit with a front flap covered with pigskin and lined with red morocco leather. It contained more than fifty items. The arrangement of the items was particularly remarkable. The brushes slid into thin slots that held them a few millimeters from the tray, to protect the bristles from being damaged by contact. Underneath were two drawers for fine lingerie." Other remarkable displays at the exhibition included the fabulous jewels Cartier and Van Cleef & Arpels showed at the Grand Palais, and the designs by the great Parisian couturiers—Worth, Jenny, Madeleine Vionnet, Jean Patou, and Jeanne Lanvin—at the Pavillon d'Élégance, which was built by Armand-Albert Rateau. The designer Paul Poiret set up shop on three barges parked on the left bank of the Seine: *Délices* was equipped with a luxurious restaurant and a space for exhibiting perfumes; *Orgues,* decorated with paintings by Raoul Dufy, was used for fashion shows, and *Amours* was used as the couturier's apartment.

Vuitton diversifies. Gaston-Louis felt such an affinity for Art Deco that he began to design items that were very different from the Asnières workshops' traditional output—objects for the adornment of daily life instead of for travel. In the Pavillon de Marsan in July 1924 he exhibited furniture and accessories that had "a completely sedentary vocation," including a dressing table and manicure set made of pear wood and ivory. "Opening the lid reveals a large beveled mirror and triggers the action of a drop-down shelf. The user can now access all the ivory and vermeil accessories, each fitted in a slot on a tray that keeps them in order. On each side are two small dishes in vermeil that can be pushed aside when the user wants to make the piece of furniture look like a precious case. Near this manicure table is a dressing table and seat made of ebony encrusted with rosewood and shell. The ensemble is presented on an extraordinary monkey-skin rug in red, violet blue, and gray, which matches the color of the table and its accessories." In the same spirit of diversification, Gaston-Louis created the first Vuitton perfume, Heures d'absence, in 1926. It was presented in a clever box designed as a small golden milepost, evoking the idea of travel.

Another expression of Gaston-Louis's creativity was the expansion of the Vuitton collection into everyday objects.

Above, from left to right, are bottles designed by Cless-Brothier in 1922: Le Bébé, in frosted crystal with a vermeil stopper; Femme aux tambourins; a view of Pierrot from the back; and a bottle embellished with a bicolor border and silver stopper.

Below: A dressing table by Legrain after an idea of Gaston-Louis Vuitton, with crystal bottles with vermeil stoppers and ivory trim.

Opposite: An illustration from the 1922 catalogue "Du Cadeau ou La Bonne Manière," entitled *La Touche de rouge ou Devant la coiffeuse (A Touch of Red or In Front of the Dressing Table).*

Louis VUITTON, Editeur.

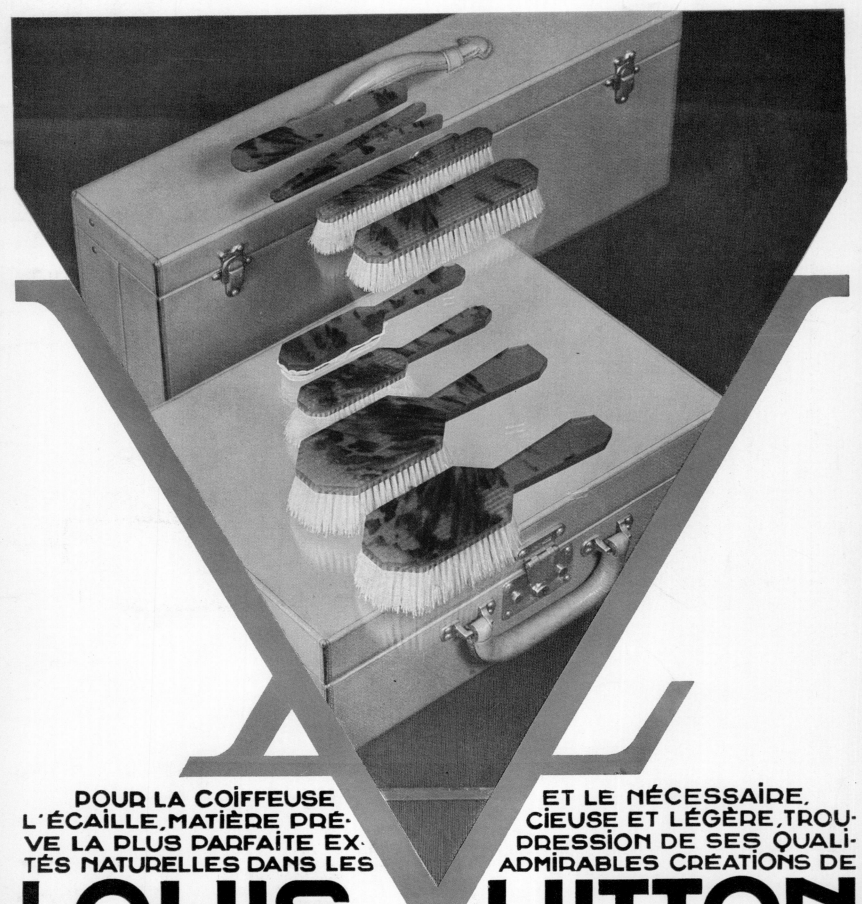

POUR LA COIFFEUSE
L'ÉCAILLE, MATIÈRE PRÉ-
VE LA PLUS PARFAITE EX-
TÉS NATURELLES DANS LES

ET LE NÉCESSAIRE.
CIEUSE ET LÉGÈRE, TROU-
PRESSION DE SES QUALI-
ADMIRABLES CRÉATIONS DE

LOUIS VUITTON
PARIS 70 CHAMPS ELYSEES
NICE 12 AV. DE VERDUN . CANNES 10 R. DES BELGES
VICHY RUE DU PARC . LONDON 149 NEW BOND STREET

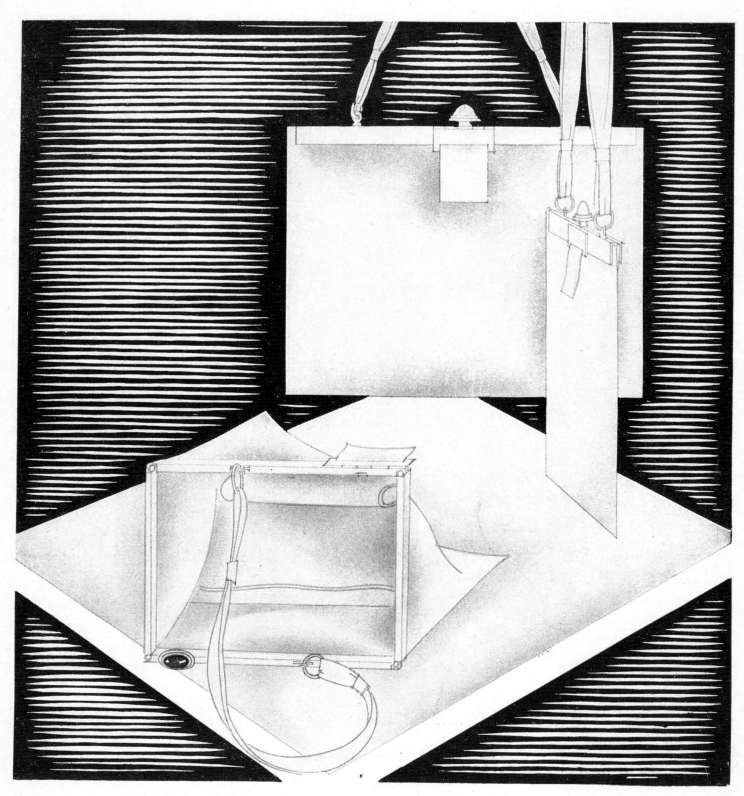

Le sac à main, sac de théâtre, de ville ou de sport, est d'un choix délicat entre tous ; il doit observer, tout à la fois, les tendances de sa mode propre, l'harmonie de la toilette dans son ensemble, les goûts ou habitudes personnelles, et la multiplicité des modèles ne fait qu'accroître l'embarras, la seule solution étant de " prévoir " le sac, comme l'on prévoit la robe, le chapeau, le soulier, tant il est vrai que l'achat du dernier moment ne donne jamais pleine satisfaction. C'est ce que sait bien l'élégante clientèle de Louis VUITTON, certaine de trouver chez ce fin maroquinier le conseil et l'idée qui réaliseront, en quelques jours, le sac désiré.

LOUIS VUITTON
70, Champs-Élysées — PARIS

LONDON	CANNES	NICE
149, New Bond Street	10, Rue des Belges	12, Avenue de Verdun

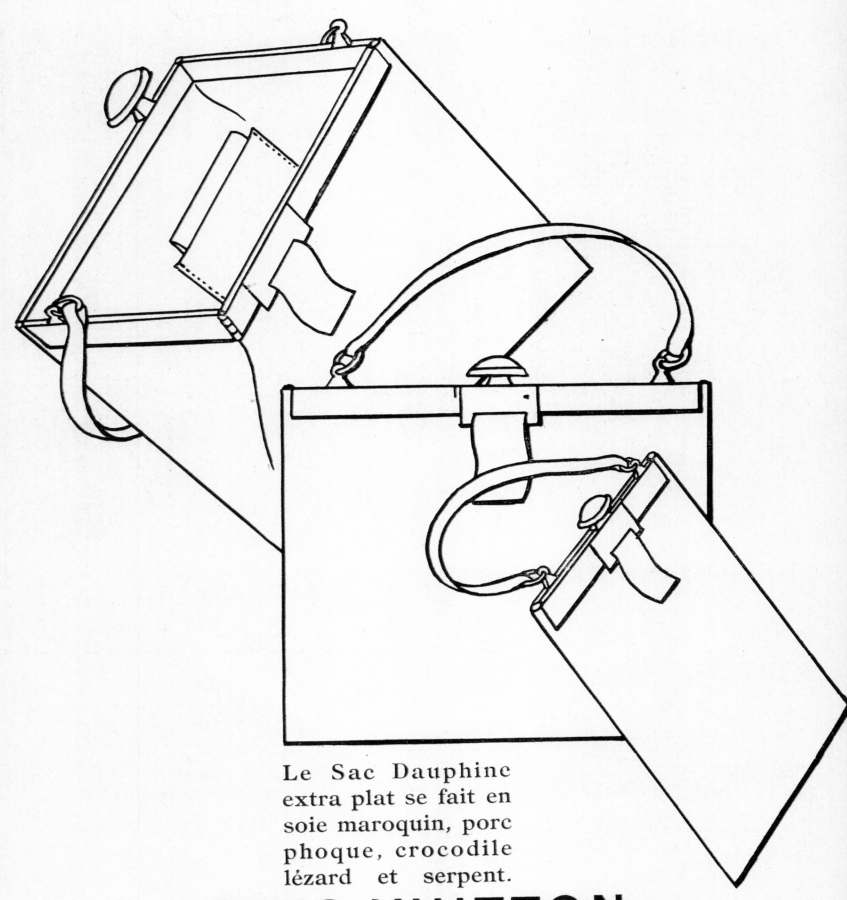

Le Sac Dauphine
extra plat se fait en
soie maroquin, porc
phoque, crocodile
lézard et serpent.

LOUIS VUITTON
70, Champs - Élysées - PARIS
NICE CANNES VICHY LONDON

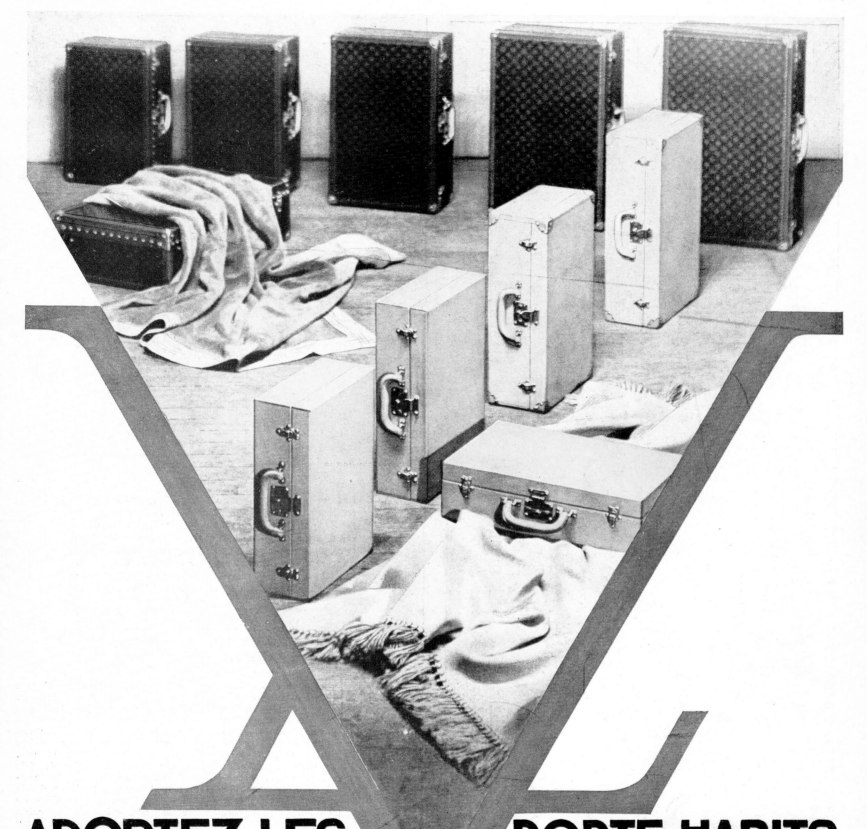

Previous pages: Advertisements for hairbrushes and toiletry kits, 1929; the Dauphine bag, about 1926; the extra-flat Dauphine bag, 1926; and suitcases, 1930.

Above: A yo-yo demonstration in the window of the Champs-Élysées store.

Opposite: The Sinaïa (top left), a large case outfitted for women. The brushes and silverwork are contained in a movable shelf, leaving the bottom for lingerie. Top right: A flat toiletry case for men covered inside and out with toadskin. Bottom left: Secretary desk, with a collapsible table in the door, hanging file drawers, index card files, and a typewriter. Bottom right: Radio trunk, with an antenna installed in the lining of the door, which could be pivoted to improve reception.

The maharajahs' India

In 2003 Louis Vuitton established itself in India with the first luxury goods store to open in Delhi. A second Indian store opened in Bombay in 2004. The company thus renewed its connection with Indian customers—descendants of the maharajahs who were loyal patrons in the 1920s. Today Louis Vuitton is as interested in traditional India as in modern India. People in the news and Bollywood stars frequent the new stores.

Above, clockwise from top left: A trunk made for the maharajah of Kapurthala; the maharajah of Baroda; sacred elephants during an official ceremony; a trunk made for the maharajah of Kashmir's polo gear.

Opposite: A special order made for the maharajah of Baroda in 1926, this tea case contains the following: two cups, saucers, and coasters; two bottles; two round, covered pots; three cake or sandwich boxes; two large and two small goblets; one silver tray; one teapot; one portable stove; one pitcher; one flask; one hidden compartment.

Scents of elsewhere

Gaston-Louis launched Heures d'absence, the first Louis Vuitton perfume, in 1926. It was like an invitation to travel. Other perfumes—Je, tu, il, Réminiscences, and Sur la route—would follow.

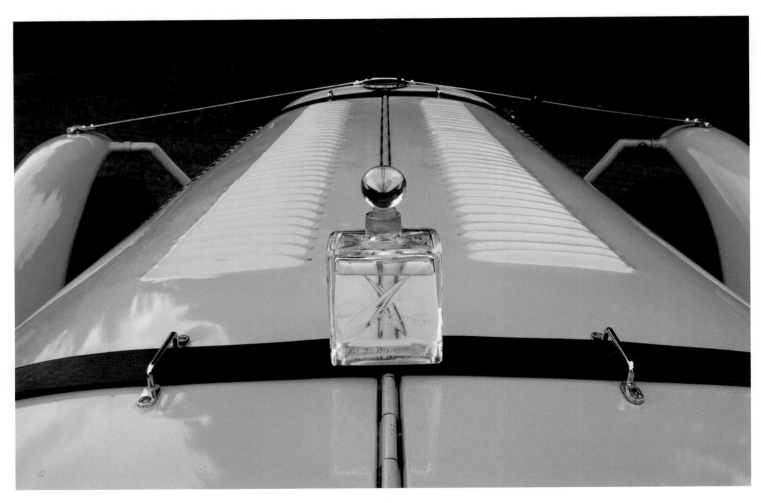

Above: In its bottle of smooth and frosted crystal, Heures d'absence—the perfume Gaston-Louis Vuitton created in 1926—perches elegantly on the hood of a Delage 3-liter car. This unique car, from the collection of Josy and François Jolly, won many prizes in 1939.

Opposite: The triple bottle of the perfume Je, tu, il and its Art Deco box.

Following pages: Heures d'absence perfume and its box, shaped like a milepost, created in 1926 (left); photos by Jean-Loup de Sauverzac. Advertisement (right) in the program for the Monte Carlo opera, January–April 1928, the Ballets Russes season.

Savoir choisir et savoir donner...

A ce problème délicat de l'art de faire plaisir et de bien acheter, Louis Vuitton offre l'aimable solution de ses créations universellement réputées: trousseaux de malles et de porte-habits, nécessaires de voyage, trousses et flaconniers, ainsi qu'un choix impeccable de portefeuilles, portebillets, sacs de dames, cannes, couvertures, et son premier parfum... Choisir chez Vuitton c'est la Bonne Manière

LOUIS VUITTON
NICE – 12 AVENUE DE VERDUN
PARIS – CANNES – VICHY – LONDON

GASTON-LOUIS

The colonial empire on display

The 1931 Exposition Coloniale Internationale, organized by Maréchal Lyautey and held at the gates of Paris, represented the apogee of France's overseas adventure. Following the tradition Louis had established at the 1867 Exposition Universelle, Maison Louis Vuitton took an active part in the event.

The French colonial empire was at its height. Even though there were signs of its demise amid rising demands for national independence, particularly in Indochina, the decolonization movement did not really begin until after the Second World War. The French empire overseas included the departments of Algeria, the colonies in Africa and Asia, the protectorates, and a few territories entrusted to it by the League of Nations. In total, it encompassed four million square miles and a population of about sixty-five million. The exhibition in Vincennes was a showcase for the empire. Following the principles of the world's fairs, where the whole world was represented, concentrated, and staged in microcosm, Vincennes offered some spectacular views and reconstructions. The most incredible was the replica of the Khmer temple of Angkor Wat.

Steps from Queen Ranavalona's palace. Louis Vuitton's exhibit was installed on a lane leading to the simulated palace of the queen of Madagascar, which seemed straight out of a Cecil B. DeMille Hollywood megaproduction. Henry-Louis recounted, "Just beside the reconstruction of Queen Ranavalo's [sic] palace, which housed products from Madagascar, a tree was enclosed in the Vuitton pavilion! Gaston wanted to preserve this ash tree because quite a number of years before, when it was no more than a bush, he had spent an autumn afternoon painting its blazing colors, and his wife had asked him for this little canvas as a gift. The tree would again witness Gaston taking up the brush on the eve of the opening. The decorator in charge of the design office, who had proposed an imposing totem at the pavilion's entrance, didn't dare climb the ladder to touch up the statue's eyes. Gaston had to do it himself, a can

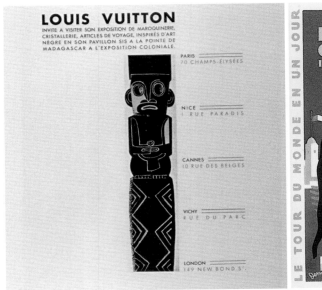

Exoticism and African art came into fashion and were celebrated at the Exposition Coloniale of 1931. Left: Louis Vuitton's invitation and the exhibition poster designed by Robert Lang.

Opposite: The exhibition presented riches from France's colonial empire, including a spectacular reconstruction of the Khmer temple of Angkor Wat, photographed by Jacques-Henri Lartigue, a Buddhist pagoda (still standing today), camel races, folkloric dances, foods from faraway lands, canoe trips, and more.

of paint in one hand and a brush in the other. As night fell, he held a tiny flashlight between his teeth so everything would be ready for the official inauguration the next day."

The exposition's sparkling showcases at the Porte Dorée and in the Bois de Vincennes brought visitors under the spell of a primitive world, which they liked to believe was close to humanity's origins. They strolled the exhibits bewitched by tom-tom drums, by "Negresses with lip plates" and solid gold jewelry that deformed the ears, and by seductive Khmer dances celebrating the combat between the "white monkey" and the "black monkey." All this was found next to very real lions, elephants, and giraffes, which were just acclimating to the brand-new Vincennes zoo. This colonial "other world" displayed an energy that mixed refinement and savagery. It was both fascinating and troubling, at the very moment that the so-called civilized world was entering a period of economic stagnation, moral crisis, and political brutality.

Exoticism comes into fashion. The Exposition Coloniale permeated the atmosphere from the first preparations for the event. Exoticism became fashionable. Gaston-Louis, who we know had a taste for collecting and art objects, was as infatuated as the artists and aesthetes by indigenous cultures, and especially with African art. It had already been several

Ebony, ivory, elephant, crocodile, and lizard skin: Louis Vuitton's products and exhibition pavilion (the exterior is shown above; the interior, opposite) were directly influenced by African art.

years since the avant-garde had passionately welcomed once unknown or unappreciated forms of artistic expression from faraway countries. Music like jazz, ethnic instruments, and African masks brought a refreshing primitivism to the works of European painters, sculptors, and composers. Gaston-Louis was sensitive to these currents of expression. He collected representative items, which he asked friends to bring back from their travels. In March 1931, two months before the exposition debuted in Vincennes, he opened an African salon in the store at 70 Champs-Élysées: "Beside authentic statuettes and traditional jewelry from all of French Africa, visitors saw the premiere of a varied and original collection of cut crystal bottles inspired by African masks and totems. The motifs were also incised or in relief on stoppers of ebony, ivory, and precious metals."

Exoticism inspired some of the company's most memorable creations. The Asnières workshops made luggage and cases from rare skins whose very names were invitations to adventure and faraway travel. Elephant skin was used for two wardrobes, one lined with red morocco leather, the other with green. Encrusted buffalo toad skin was used in the lid of a flat case. An American woman ordered a case of green-tinted ostrich skin with lizard lining and blond tortoiseshell trim. A crocodile skin case with a front flap was fitted with vermeil accessories. Such rare objects inspired dreams of journeying to the marvelous lands of lore.

The Roaring Twenties

A jazzy, fun-loving lifestyle took root in Paris and on the Côte d'Azur in the 1920s, imported by two now legendary Americans, Gerald and Sara Murphy, who inspired F. Scott Fitzgerald's *Tender Is the Night*. Some of the other leading figures of the day—writers like John Dos Passos and Ernest Hemingway, artists like Pablo Picasso and Fernand Léger, the impresario Sergey Diaghilev, and composers as diverse as Igor Stravinsky and Cole Porter—were clients of Maison Vuitton.

"It was a narrow escape!" The end of the long and bloody First World War brought a widespread sense that the world had survived a catastrophe, a euphoria, and an immense desire to enjoy life—to energetically rush forward and try to forget the war's horror. The idea was to escape sorrow through pleasure, to spend without counting, and to improvise, free from the constraints of daily life. It was brilliant, light, and intoxicating—but could also be seen as a headlong rush to nowhere, an escape from reality at any cost. Women adopted a newly fashionable tomboy look, with short haircuts and slim, more athletic figures. And a dance craze broke out like never before.

The brief, sparkling moment known as the Roaring Twenties went by another name in France, with a different nuance: the *années folles,* literally "the crazy years." The novelist F. Scott Fitzgerald was a principal player in and lucid witness of the period. Like many of his compatriots he went to Europe to flee the suffocating atmosphere of an America Gerald Murphy described as in the grip of Prohibition's virtuous demons. "You had the impression that the conservatives were in the saddle, and that a government capable of voting for the Eighteenth Amendment [establishing Prohibition] could do even worse and no doubt would. Life in the United States became more straitlaced than it had ever been." Enriched by the success of his first novel, *This Side of Paradise,* published in 1920, Fitzgerald went to France with his young wife, Zelda. They quickly made their way to Paris and settled at the Ritz. Sumptuous parties, palaces, and sports cars were all part of this "golden" couple's magnificent life. Fitzgerald's second novel, *The Beautiful and Damned,* is steeped in this particular atmosphere, but the exhilaration of living, the frenzy of spending, the lack of constraint, and even the cynicism were so many masks for melancholy and despair.

The Murphys' golden age. In the spring of 1924 the Fitzgeralds met another American couple, Sara and Gerald Murphy—two loyal customers of the Monogram and the store at 70 Champs-Élysées. Sara, the eldest daughter of an ink manufacturer in Cincinnati, was cultured and cosmopolitan. Gerald was the son of a Boston merchant. They made an elegant pair. Following the aesthetic shock he experienced in Paris in 1921, as he stood before the works of Braque, Picasso, and Juan Gris, Gerald devoted himself to painting. He and his wife quickly occupied an eminent position in Paris's artistic world. "Every day was different. There was an almost tangible feeling of tension and stimulation in the air. There was an endless series of new exhibitions, a recital by Les Six, a Dada happening, a masked ball at Montparnasse, the premiere of a new play or ballet, or one of those fantastic Parisian 'soirées' given by Étienne de Beaumont in Montmartre—we didn't miss one, and everyone was there. Interest in all that was happening was so passionate that it made up an activity in its own right." Through their friend the musician Cole Porter, the Murphys discovered the Côte d'Azur and Cap d'Antibes in the summer of 1923. Up until 1917 the English, Germans, and Russians took over the place, but only during

Rev your convertible's engine and make for the Côte d'Azur. In the 1920s every moment was lived as if it were the last, with an indulgence in sudden impulses, rolls of the dice, casinos, the Riviera, passing fancies.

the winter, which was mild, and a few weeks in the spring; they deserted their villas as soon as the hot weather arrived. It was the Americans who launched the Côte d'Azur in the 1920s as a place to spend the summer, enjoying water "the color of jade and amethyst," the beaches dazzled by light and heat, and the mild evenings. The Murphys decided to buy a villa located just under the Antibes lighthouse. It was called the Villa America—also the name of one of Gerald Murphy's paintings. There the couple received European and American friends: the Picassos, the Hemingways, Dos Passos, Archibald MacLeish and his wife, the Fitzgeralds, Rudolph Valentino, Fernand Léger and his wife. In *Living Well Is the Best Revenge* Calvin Tomkins evoked this paradise-scented time: "Those close to the Murphys found it nearly impossible to describe the quality of their life, and how charming she was to friends. The beauty of their fragrant garden, overlooking the sea on the Cannes side, and the mountains in the distance; Gerald's impressive record collection (everything from Bach to the latest jazz); the exquisite food that seemed to suddenly appear at the right moment; the passionate attention that the Murphys gave to their guests' enjoyment, which gave them such obvious pleasure"—all this contributed to an exceptional, enchanting atmosphere.

The Keepall, the modern luggage. The Keepall, which became a Vuitton classic, was a true sign of the changing times. It was a supple, light travel bag that could hold a great deal and be folded flat—the type of bag you can grab and quickly fill with clothes, a scarf or kerchief, a toiletry kit, just the necessities for a trip planned in a flash, an impromptu party, a little getaway to La Baule, to Biarritz, or to Monte-Carlo to gamble at the casino. During the summer of 1924 the Fitzgeralds met up again with their friends the Murphys in Antibes. They would soon be able to go boating together. Vladimir Orloff, the set designer for Diaghilev's Ballets Russes, was passionate about naval architecture and had built the Murphys a superb 115-foot schooner, the *Weather Bird*.

At the opera in Monte-Carlo that season, Diaghilev and his company performed a ballet-operetta, *Le Train bleu,* to a score by Darius Milhaud (forsaking the libretto by Jean Cocteau). The title referred to the famous train that transported pleasure-seeking, happy-go-lucky Parisians from the Gare de Lyon to the Mediterranean. What was the subject? There was not much to it: Some athletes land on a beach, where they spread joyous dis-

According to Calvin Tomkins, Gerald Murphy (above, with Pablo Picasso) and his wife, Sara, were "at the heart of everything that was going on." They were among the first to frequent the Côte d'Azur in summer. In their Villa America at Cap d'Antibes they received a number of artist friends, notably Pablo and Olga Picasso, and invented the bathing suits swimmers everywhere would adopt. The Murphys purchased some thirty Louis Vuitton items between 1922 and 1931, including ten garment bags, four cabin trunks, three hat trunks, a flower trunk, and three cashmere shawls.

Opposite: Prototype of the modern overnight bag, the Keepall was one of the first pieces of multipurpose, light, supple luggage. Very convenient, it symbolized a new way of traveling. It was made at first of cotton fabric, then in supple Monogram canvas, leather, and other materials. It has become one of the most popular Louis Vuitton articles—and one of its icons.

Below: The Murphys' customer record.

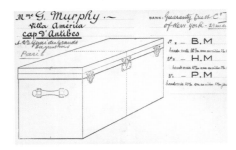

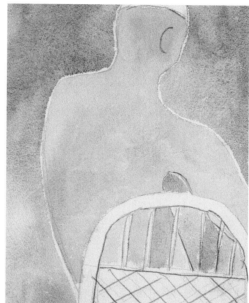

order. It had an unbridled "music hall" ambiance, with a rapid sequence of antic acrobatic movements, an evocation of beach games, and a procession of adventurers and hedonists: Characters in the ballet included high-class prostitutes like Perlouse and gigolos like Beau Gosse. Coco Chanel designed the bathing suits and beach outfits. Bronislawa Nijinska interpreted the role of the tennis player, which was inspired by the legendary French champion Suzanne Lenglen (another Vuitton customer), with her characteristic silhouette, her long skirt pleated for twirling, and her wide white headband. The sculptor Henri Laurens created a geometric set decor using bathing cabins. The stage curtain reproduced in large format the *Deux femmes courant sur la plage,* a small gouache on wood by Picasso. The painting shows two modern, statuesque bacchantes launched heedlessly at full gallop into a savage dance. *Le Train bleu* was a mirror of an era, its energies, frivolities, and beauties. The Monte-Carlo audience fully appreciated it, and the show was a triumph.

The party's over. Black Thursday. The American stock market crash of October 1929 was the first warning, the whistle signaling that playtime was over. A grave and anguished period had begun. Dark clouds were gathering. New catastrophes were in the making, which made the crazy, Roaring Twenties seem like a suspension in time. It had been an era between parentheses, with very special light that was both fragile and intense, the changing, uncertain light of dawn or twilight. Gerald Murphy had to give up his luxuriously bohemian life as an artist. The Murphys returned to the United States in 1934. Gerald succeeded his father as the head of Mark Cross, a luxury goods store in New York, over which he presided for twenty-two years. Fitzgerald, who had returned to America earlier, published *Tender Is the Night* in 1934. The book is full of details borrowed from the life he and Zelda shared with the Murphys between 1924 and 1929, and characters in all his works evoke aspects of Fitzgerald's own life. After a meteoric rise, the title character in *The Great Gatsby* saw his trajectory crash, and the rich society that had celebrated him was entirely indifferent to his murder. Dick Diver, the protagonist of *Tender Is the Night* and a stand-in for Fitzgerald and Murphy, fights to support his psychologically delicate wife, finds himself abandoned once she is cured, loses his footing, and escapes into alcoholism. Like a kind of brother to them, Fitzgerald survived his former glory as best he could, never completing his last work, *The Last Tycoon,* while Zelda after 1930 took refuge in madness.

Opposite: The train headed to the Côte d'Azur practically reverberates with the chords of Darius Milhaud's ballet-operetta *Le Train bleu.*

The Murphys cruised the Mediterranean on the *Weather Bird,* their 115-foot black schooner, and in 1934 had the painter Fernand Léger and his wife, Jeanne, onboard. While sailing to Corsica, Léger painted these portraits of Gerald and Sara (above right). Gerald Murphy, himself a talented painter, is today considered one of the forerunners of American Pop art.

Aesthete and collector

A knowledge of luggage's history and tradition nourishes present and future inspiration and provides a clear perspective on innovation. With that in mind, Gaston-Louis compiled one of the largest and most important collections of historic travel goods.

Georges Vuitton used what he could learn from books to sketch the development of travel items through the ages. Gaston-Louis followed in his footsteps, but as a collector—an aesthete who liked to go on the hunt, take possession of concrete objects, and feel under his fingertips the patina of age on a piece of wood, the wear of leather, the cold touch of metal. He liked to imagine how a chest or travel case had been used, inventing its history, who had once owned it, and what was stored in it. He began collecting chests at the beginning of the twentieth century, and through them a whole world unfolds. One era follows the next, and civilizations cross.

Gaston-Louis (shown here in 1913) was always fascinated by trunks, whether made of leather, wood, or metal, covered with inlay or decorated with lacquer or paint. He carefully maintained albums with details about each item in his collection—with a photo, description, dimensions, origin, date.

Opposite: A display of his collection at the museum in Asnières, which includes travel articles he gathered from around the world. The oldest pieces date from the fourteenth century.

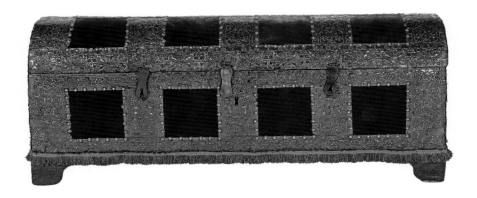

From top to bottom: Swiss trunk from the late sixteenth century, which Gaston-Louis purchased at the Hôtel des Ventes in 1925. Koran chest, Spain, late fourteenth century. Bonnet trunk of wood and metal lined with fabric, Rouen, Normandy, late eighteenth century (a recent acquisition of the Gaston-Louis Vuitton Collection).

From top to bottom: Cabinet trunk made of black leather and iron, with inlay, interior in inlaid wood, and secret drawers, Netherlands, late sixteenth century. Leather trunk for top hat, France, eighteenth century. Seventeenth-century Japanese trunk of shagreen and lacquer, with fans painted on the outside and a golden tree painted inside, purchased by Gaston-Louis at the Hôtel des Ventes in 1923.

The conquest of America

Georges Vuitton had brought Maison Louis Vuitton to the New World at the 1893 World's Columbian Exposition in Chicago, where Vuitton's goods were classified "hors concours" (outside competition) due to their outstanding merit. The event also brought Georges Vuitton in contact with John Wanamaker, who began selling Vuitton products at his beautiful department stores in New York and Philadelphia in 1898. Gaston-Louis followed his father's steps across the Atlantic to secure the company's position there.

Georges returned to the United States in 1904, a trip that strengthened the company's influence on the other side of the Atlantic. He first went to Boston, where Jordan Marsh & Company had been selling Vuitton goods for several months, then to the Saint Louis World's Fair to preside over the jury for travel items. Next he took a pleasure and study trip aboard a showboat on the Mississippi River, then headed by train to San Francisco, Canada, Chicago, and New York. The fruit of his journey was the opening of two Louis Vuitton branches in 1905, one at Marshall Field & Company in Chicago and the other at Roos Brothers in San Francisco. In the years before the First World War, Louis Vuitton opened several more branches across the Americas: in Buenos Aires in 1906, Montreal in 1907, and Washington, D.C, and Buffalo, N.Y., in 1912.

American magnates. The Louis Vuitton outlets across the Atlantic were all the more successful since wealthy Americans were already captivated by the brand; many had traveled to Europe and purchased goods from the Paris store. Among the company's customers were leaders of industry and finance, entrepreneurs who had amassed colossal fortunes within a few decades, people with names like Carnegie, Ford, Vanderbilt, Guggenheim, Pierpont Morgan, Hearst. Phoebe Hearst—whose husband, George, was a mining magnate and son William Randolph was a newspaper tycoon (and inspiration for Orson Welles's film *Citizen Kane*)—shopped at the Vuitton store regularly beginning in 1878. Both Georges and Gaston-Louis described the impression she made at 1 Rue Scribe: "All dressed in black, with a traditional old-ladies' cap tied under the chin, an air more than simple, and always accompanied by young girls, she would enter the store timidly. This woman, who was modesty itself and who beneath this guise hid an extreme kindness, every year invited several young American women from modest backgrounds on a trip to Europe. She offered them everything, and she would not allow them to return to America without a set of Vuitton luggage." Another American customer was James Gordon Bennett, owner of the *New York Herald*, which his father had founded, and co-founder of the Associated Press. An extravagant personality and an avid sportsman, he liked—in addition to traveling and luggage—yachting, including such challenges as racing in the America's Cup. He also founded an automobile race that began in 1906 and an aeronautic balloon competition, both of which were named for him and still take place today.

The earliest "jet set." After the 1914–18 war devastated Europe, the United States rose as the world's great power. Georges traveled there again, accompanied this time by his eldest grandson, Henry-Louis. Ocean liners were at their peak of luxury and comfort. The great waves of emigration to the New World had slowed down, allowing floating cities like

Previous pages: The *Normandie* in New York harbor. At the end of the nineteenth century ocean liners reduced the travel time between Europe and the New World. Louis Vuitton luggage was found on all crossings, and Maison Louis Vuitton was represented in America beginning in 1898.

Opposite, from left to right and top to bottom: Henry Ford and his son Edsel in 1933, photo published in *Illustration*. John D. Rockefeller Sr. with John D. Rockefeller Jr. in 1925. John Pierpont Morgan, American financier. Customer record for Mrs. A. Carnegie. George J. Gould—owner of several casinos—and his family. William Randolph Hearst and his two sons, William Randolph Jr. and John Randolph. Gloria Vanderbilt (left) and her aunt Gertrude Vanderbilt Whitney, sitting on their Vuitton trunks in 1939. Irving I. Bloomingdale—owner of the eponymous stores—and his wife.

Gaston-Louis Vuitton recorded John Pierpont Morgan exclaiming, as he looked at the company's customer register, "It's the most extraordinary directory of American high society ever seen on the continent."

DATE	LOCK	Nº	DETAIL OF GOODS BOUGHT
1894			
10 April	03426	42857	75 bas cuirée cad.
—		43750	8.2 - 90 bas
1898	A C		
17 Mai	07939	108567	90 bas coins cad. S.V.
—	E W	108368	13ᵃ maue / S.V. 4 chᵗ name sage chau

NAME Mᵉ A. Carnegie

BANK

Standard — 852

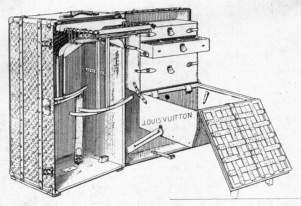
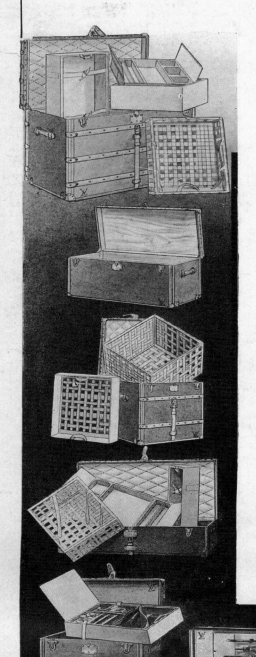
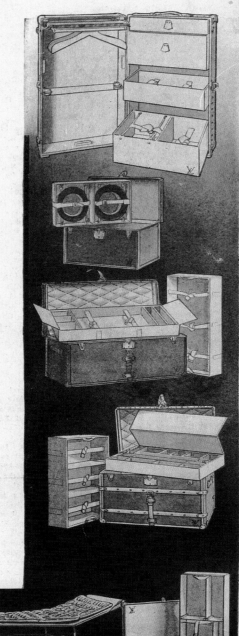

America's most prestigious stores chose to offer Louis Vuitton trunks and travel articles, including John Wanamaker (whose Philadelphia store is shown at right) beginning in 1898.

Opposite: An advertisement published in *Town & Country* magazine in 1922 suggests how Louis Vuitton trunks were considered "must-haves" during travel's golden age.

the Compagnie Générale Transatlantique's legendary *Normandie* to transport the most select people, the crème de la crème—writers, journalists, artists, movie stars, financiers, and politicians. Although the word "jet" did not yet exist and ocean liners still reigned over transatlantic crossings, this truly was the world of the jet set. On one of these liners in 1934 the French actress Lili Damita, a platinum blonde hoping to conquer New York and the California studios, met Errol Flynn, actor and confirmed womanizer, and succumbed to his charms.

Between 1919 and the economic crisis of 1929 the Louis Vuitton empire expanded in North America. Branches opened in Los Angeles in 1919, Toronto in 1925, Detroit in 1928, and Rochester, Pittsburgh, and Baltimore in 1929. Locations in new cities brought new customers, including dynastic families like the Fords and Kennedys, stars of the industry getting under way in Hollywood—Lillian Gish, Mary Pickford, Douglas Fairbanks,

Charlie Chaplin, and Gloria Swanson—adventurers like Charles Lindbergh, and artists like Ernest Hemingway and Gerald Murphy.

Official supplier of the American Embassy in France. After the Second World War the company had to win back ground it had lost, in France and elsewhere. Gaston-Louis Vuitton took up the task of championing the company's past and present fame. Since America's leading names supported the French trunk maker's reputation and recognized its excellence, why not make the endorsement official? On 10 March 1955 Gaston-Louis sent this request to the United States ambassador: "Since the creation of our company, we have had the privilege of supplying an elite American clientele in France, and according to Mr. Pierpont Morgan himself, 'Vuitton's files are the most complete blue book in Europe.' We were curious to look at a list of American ambassadors in France since 1872 (our prior records were destroyed during the war and the Commune of 1871), and we saw that almost all of them were customers entered in our sales books. Mr. Whitelaw Reid (customer since 1880), Mr. James B. Eustis (since 1884), Mr. Horace Porter (since 1889), Mr. Jefferson Coolidge (1893), Mr. Robert McCormick (1903), Mr. Robert Bacon (1903), Mr. Henry White (1909), Mr. Myron T. Herrick (1914), Mr. Walter Edge (1925), Mrs. Jesse Isidor Strauss (1928), Mr. C. Douglas Dillon (1932), Mr. David K. Bruce (1939), Admiral W. D. Leahy (1941), Mr. Jefferson Caffery (1947). Reassured by this uninterrupted confidence, we would be particularly happy to be able to call ourselves 'Suppliers of the American Embassy in France.' I dare to hope that you will not refuse us this honor."

Whole generations of Americans won over. A less formal but very touching episode after the war contributed to the brand's prestige in the United States. It took place on Saturday, 21 July 1956, at the store on Avenue Marceau. A very large American with "a somewhat rugged" appearance entered the store, a multicolored rosette in his buttonhole. In English he explained that he wanted a bag for his wife. Then he began asking more general questions to learn more about the company. The discussion continued in the office of Gaston-Louis Vuitton, who provided information about the family and the company history. The American finally confided in Gaston-Louis: He had been making a three-day inspection tour for the Ford Motor Company and was taking advantage of the opportunity to shed some light on a childhood memory. He had always heard his parents talking about Louis Vuitton. He had come to learn about the company, although he had to admit he was not yet rich enough to make a purchase. Gaston-Louis led him to the cashier's desk where, to his great astonishment, he found records of the purchases made by his mother, when she was still Miss L. Wallace, and by his father, Mr. C. A. Morell Miller. Gaston-Louis remarked enthusiastically, "It is deeply moving to see how, in some American families, the position of Louis Vuitton has remained absolutely exceptional." As a smart businessman he added, "There's a force here that has not been cultivated enough and should be, something on which we should base all the current advertising and all future actions." If that force had not been sufficiently cultivated before, a host of high-quality, famous, and loyal American customers—from the director Stanley Donen to actors like Henry and Jane Fonda, Jerry Lewis, and Lauren Bacall—was on hand to alleviate the problem.

Until the stock market crash of 1929, Louis Vuitton reinforced its success across the Atlantic with branches in New York (Wall Street is shown opposite), Philadelphia, Boston, Chicago, San Francisco, and Buenos Aires.

A fresh start after the war

The Second World War disrupted the family business. Foreign contracts were cancelled. The Asnières workshops were unable to supply the Paris, Nice, and Vichy stores. But within a few years Gaston-Louis Vuitton and his sons would restore the company to its former glory.

The collapse of 1940 and the German invasion unleashed for many French people a time of fear, waiting, and struggling for day-to-day survival. For others in France it was instead a period of revolt and resistance. Sometimes fracture lines appeared within a family, as some members supported Premier Philippe Pétain, who favored collaboration with the occupying Nazis, and others listened to those like General Charles De Gaulle and his entourage in London, who encouraged them to fight for a brighter future. The Vuitton family was not spared those wrenching divisions: Some members subscribed to the archetypal view of Pétain, built by his followers with skill and tenacity, as France's savior and protector, the old oak tree drawing his vigor and his faith from the ancestral land. Others in the family more lucidly saw through Pétain's ideological pretenses and joined those who eventually prevailed in reclaiming France's dignity. Such divisions can have lasting effects and they are no doubt at the root of tensions among Gaston-Louis's three sons. Henry-Louis's younger brothers, the twins Claude-Louis and Jacques-Louis, never tried to hide their Gaullist sympathies. Claude-Louis joined the Second Armored Division in 1944 and fought in its ranks during the German campaign in the spring of 1945. Other members of the family joined the resistance. Denyse Vuitton's husband, Jean Obligator, was confined in a concentration camp for his activities and survived, but René Gimpel, Louis Vuitton's grandnephew and an eminent art dealer, died during deportation on 1 January 1945.

The liberation. The liberation brought a business revival. In January 1945 *Vogue* magazine, which reported on the activities of the grand couturiers and luxury goods designers in Paris, returned to print after a four-year absence with the publication of a special issue, *Vogue Libération*. A moving article by Alexandre Astruc celebrated the return of France and its capital to free thinking and creativity after being entrenched in a "deathly silence" during the long years of war and occupation: "Time seemed to have stopped in this desolate Paris, torn by the sinister sounds of fifes, crossed by the dismal procession over which floated the swastika's shadow. The city was mute, but everyone knew that hidden in its silence its real soul was beating. Now the veil has lifted on a city that is learning to find its face in peace a little at a time. Huge lines press at the doors of the cinemas, which the great American movies are filling again with their moving shadows. Theaters released from enemy propaganda are welcoming once more the efforts and dreams of youth and the spirit."

Beginning in 1946 Gaston-Louis Vuitton energetically promoted the renaissance of the luxury goods industry in France. In the spring he founded an association with a straightforward name: Luxe. As for the Maison Louis Vuitton, its activities were fully revived within a few years, as the supply of raw materials like wood, leather, and canvas returned to normal. Gaston-Louis called on all the family forces, dividing tasks among his three sons. Henry-Louis was in charge of sales, at the head of the Paris store (the Vichy store closed in 1957); Claude-Louis took over manufacturing in Asnières; and Jacques-Louis managed administration and finances. One sign of the company's regained luster was the order from the Élysée Palace for a wardrobe to accompany Vincent Auriol, president of the Republic, on his official visit to the United States in 1951.

New location, new customers. In 1954, the Maison Vuitton's hundredth anniversary, Louis Vuitton left the Champs-Élysées building for a private mansion at 78 bis Avenue

Opposite: Some well-known customers. From left to right and top to bottom: Vincent Auriol, president of the French Republic, preparing for a trip. King Khalid of Saudi Arabia, receiving Queen Elizabeth II in Riyadh. Yvette Labrousse, Miss France 1930, who would become the Begum by marrying the Aga Khan. Customer record of writer Ernest Hemingway. The Aga Khan at Auteuil, in 1935. Prince Ali Khan at the time of his marriage to Rita Hayworth. Guy and Marie-Hélène de Rothschild in 1960.

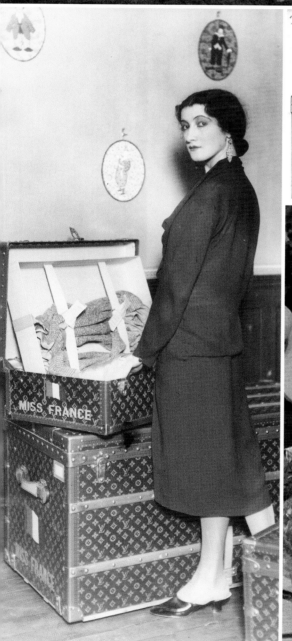

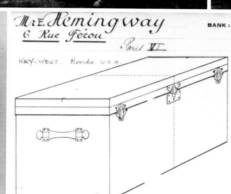

Mr Hemingway
6 Rue Férou
Paris VI
KEY-WEST. Florida U.S.A.
BANK: GUARANTY TRUST C

Right: In 1954, at the time of its hundredth anniversary, Louis Vuitton set up shop at Avenue Marceau in Paris. This new address was a sign of the company's renaissance.

Opposite, from left to right and top to bottom: Tennis champion Suzanne Lenglen in 1922. Jean Borotra, at a Wimbledon championship. Hélène Rochas, photographed by Cecil Beaton in 1970. Record from Balmain, the couture house. Peggy Guggenheim, in the garden of her palace in Venice, photographed by Robert Whittaker. The legendary singer Oum Kalsoum, Cairo, 1967. Christian Dior, photographed in his country house in the south of France by Lord Snowdon. Luggage of the duke and duchess of Windsor; the duke and duchess of Windsor at the Saint-Lazare train station in 1949. Muhammad Ali and his wife.

Below: Diana Vreeland, a major figure in the fashion world, attended all the designers' fashion shows and events. She worked at *Harper's Bazaar* in the 1940s before serving as editor-in-chief of *Vogue* (1962–1971). She was responsible for the creation of the Costume Institute at the Metropolitan Museum of Art, New York.

Marceau, in a quiet and elegant quarter of the eighth arrondissement, near the residential sixteenth arrondissement. The kinds of people now frequenting the "Champs," which had become devoted to entertainment, movies, restaurants, and brasseries, no longer corresponded to the company's traditional clientele. As Gaston's grandson Patrick-Louis Vuitton recalled, "Gaston became aware that the Champs-Élysées store was invaded by non-buyers." Avenue Marceau symbolized a fresh start in the period after the war, the last years of Gaston-Louis's reign. From 1954 until his death in 1970, he divided his days between Asnières in the morning and the store in Paris, where he went by car with his wife, Renée. "At 1:30 p.m. the chauffeur was waiting to drive them," Patrick-Louis remembered.

The new premises meant a new generation of customers, as well as long-term, loyal clients like Sacha Guitry, the actor and dramatist; King Farouk of Egypt and the royal family; Mahmoud Fakhry-Pacha, the Egyptian ambassador to France; the Rothschilds; the duke and duchess of Windsor; Victoria Ocampo, a leading intellectual from South America; and the Belgian novelist Georges Simenon, whose character Inspector Maigret had helped make his fortune. The prize for loyalty may go to the Guerlains, a family of great perfumers, who had bought Louis Vuitton luggage since 1898, when the store was located at Rue Scribe. New names were continuously expanding the list of the trunk maker's demanding, cosmopolitan customers. They included personalities from Paris's luxury goods world, such as Hélène Rochas, Helena Rubinstein, Christian Dior, and Hubert de Givenchy. There were also many representatives of culture and the arts: the writers Françoise Sagan, Roger Nimier, Frédéric Dard; the singers Juliette Gréco, Barbara, and Charles Aznavour; the film makers René Clair, Roger Vadim, and Luchino Visconti; the actresses Michèle Morgan, Anouk Aimée, Annie Girardot, Jeanne Moreau, Catherine Deneuve, and Jane Birkin; the actors Jean Gabin, Jean-Paul Belmondo, Alain Delon, Philippe Noiret, and Marcello Mastroianni; Hollywood stars like Lauren Bacall, Kirk Douglas, Yul Brynner, and Jerry Lewis; and flamboyant personalities like the extravagant genius Salvador Dali. Dali would go so far as to take inspiration from the Monogram to create a logo he called the Daligram.

Elite customers from around the world found in the Parisian trunk maker's products taste, quality, and perfection—once lost to the turbulence of history—that matched their exacting standards. By way of illustration, consider the comment by Diana Vreeland, another legendary figure and loyal client. Vreeland was the longtime editor-in-chief of *Vogue* in America and a high priestess of fashion whose far-sightedness would give birth to the Metropolitan Museum of Art's Costume Institute in New York. She said, "Is there anything beyond fashion? Allure."

Triumph of the supple canvas

By the dawn of the sixties the rigid canvas the company used was no longer in tune with the times. The winds of freedom were rising. The new wave swept up everything in its path. Luggage followed the trend and became softer. A wide range of leather articles accompanied it.

Since the beginning of the twentieth century the famous Monogram presented itself in the form of a cotton canvas coated with pegamoid. This worked very well for the manufacture of hard-sided luggage. But for supple luggage—the Steamer bag that came out in 1901, the Keepall from the 1930s—Maison Louis Vuitton could not use that coated fabric. It was too stiff to fold and easily split. For supple articles Vuitton had to "make do with a solid brown canvas that was eventually rubberized."

The invention of PVC was a real revolution. Coating linen or cotton fabrics with the new product (heated) preserved their suppleness, increased their durability, and kept the fabrics from breaking when folded or manipulated. The Monogram, Vuitton's universal symbol, could now appear on the canvas of all luggage manufactured at Asnières under the direction of Claude-Louis Vuitton, and the canvas's new flexibility inspired a wide array of new designs. "In 1959 the first model of a semi-supple valise combining canvas and russet leather met with an encouraging reception. This Startos model was followed by new Speedy, Keepall, and Steamer bags. This time it was a triumph, and the word is no exaggeration. From then on, from 1959 to 1965, Henry-Louis Vuitton would create an average of twenty-five new models every year. The 'sac de ville' [handbag] collection became richer with the passing seasons; the 'sac tennis' [tennis bag] coupled with the 'sac gibier' [hunter's game bag]; the use of an ultralight coated fabric and new processes for gluing fabric on leather led to a large range of wallets, cardholders, and leatherwork articles."

Opposite: In 1932 a Champagne producer asked Gaston-Louis Vuitton to develop a bag that was elegant, sturdy, and able to carry five bottles of Champagne (four bottles standing up and one, in the middle, turned upside down). He created the Noé bag, a Louis Vuitton classic. The 1959 invention of the supple Monogram canvas made it a fashion article acclaimed worldwide. Today its proportions have been modified and the Noé is available in different sizes and trims.

Left: In this fashion photo from the sixties, the Noé city bag in supple Monogram canvas appeared with the rigid Cotteville, Bessac, and Bisten suitcases on the embarkation platform for the Mistral, a luxury train that connected Paris and the Côte d'Azur.

The new wave

Cinema's new wave—and Louis Vuitton's supple bags—reflected a new way of thinking and of living. The movies brought Saint-Tropez global renown, and the stars and models who coveted Louis Vuitton luggage helped make the Keepall world famous.

The supple canvas, in harmony with the more casual times, adapted well to the new ways of going out and traveling. Rather than undertaking long excursions, people began enjoying short weekend trips; some took houses in the countryside and invited friends for overnight visits. The fashion was to dash off in a sport coupe to Deauville or to enjoy the Saint-Tropez sun for a day or two—not more. There was no need to be burdened with a heavy trunk; a simple bag was enough. The "new wave" generation of the late 1950s and early 1960s lived at a faster pace, with a freer attitude, an insouciant taste for happiness and pleasure, and a greater spontaneity. The term "new wave" first referred to contemporary cinema. The young French film makers who moved to the forefront of the artistic scene fled the formalism of studios and professional routines, dealt with contemporary subjects, and worked in real settings on location. Under those dramatically different shooting conditions, and with much smaller budgets, they shot with lighter cameras to create original, impertinent, energy-charged visions of the world. Among the eloquent titles were François Truffaut's *The Four Hundred Blows* (1959), Jean-Luc Godard's *Breathless* (1960), Jacques Rivette's *Paris Belongs to Us* (1961), Godard's *My Life to Live* (1962), and Agnès Varda's *Happiness* (1964).

Roger Vadim set the tone as early as 1956 with *And God Created Woman*, presenting his generation with both Saint-Tropez, a place of privileged freedoms, and Brigitte Bardot, an icon with whom his contemporaries could identify. In the blink of an eye she became the archetype of the French woman, desirable and independent, curvaceous and infantile, and radiant with vitality. All the women wore their hair like Bardot. All the men desired Bardot. And the one and only Bardot continued to twirl, her bare feet dancing on the sands of Saint-Tropez. The whole world had its eyes on "Saint-Trop," as the paparazzi filled magazine pages with the extravagances there of the stars, models, and their wealthy admirers. This crowd favored the soft-sided Louis Vuitton bags, especially the Keepall, almost as fetishistic objects, catapulting Louis Vuitton's celebrity worldwide.

Left: Françoise Sagan, author of *Bonjour Tristesse.*

Opposite: The Monogram canvas Keepall (below right) met the expectations of a new clientele that was embodied by the stars of the New Wave, including Brigitte Bardot (top right), in an unforgettable scene in *And God Created Woman;* the film's director, Roger Vadim (top left); and Juliette Gréco, the singer and muse of Paris's Saint-Germain-des-Prés (below left).

Below: Patrice de Colmont's Club 55, a celebrated beachfront restaurant in Saint-Tropez, owes its creation to the making of *And God Created Woman* in 1955.

Already in vogue . . .

From the 1920s on *Vogue* paid homage to the elegant woman. The pages of the magazine's American, French, English, and Italian editions celebrated the trends of the 1960s with models posing with Louis Vuitton handbags and suitcases.

Three photographers left an important imprint on the pages of *Vogue* in the sixties, when the magazine revised its editorial line to take into account new fashion trends and resolutely focused on youth.

The photographer William Klein was an American of Hungarian origin. He began his career in Paris in 1948, inspired by the Dada movement. His fashion images are touched by the cool and distant mood he would later use when shooting the international jet set. He loved movement and spontaneity, taking photographs in the street as well as setting up shots "as incomprehensible as life." By contrast, his contemporary Henry Clarke established a formal elegance. The magazine's principal photographer for more than twenty years, Clarke specialized in Parisian haute couture. He photographed his models as society women, reserved and discreet, in well-thought-out and structured poses. The Englishman David Bailey worked in a contrasting vein. In the sixties, when he was given responsibility for *Vogue*'s fourteen-page feature story, he provided a panorama of "Cool Britannia." "Cool" was the adjective that defined him. He knew more than anyone how to capture the insolence of youth. At one time he contemplated a career in film making and wrote a script for *A Clockwork Orange,* which Stanley Kubrick eventually took over.

Photo from *Vogue*'s French edition by William Klein, 1958.

demandez les
SELLES BAURIAT
Plage de
LES JUMELLES BELLIENI
17, Place Carnot-NANCY
Automobiles
E.J. Brierre
CYCLES
STROCK
PARIS
EXIGEZ POUR L'ALLUMAGE
BASSEE & MICHEL
PARIS
CARROSSERIES
BENARD
GARAGE UNIVERSEL
E. MERVILLE & Cie
6, Rue Saint-Ferdinand, 6
PARIS
VALVES, POMPES, RESERVOIRS
pour Vélos, Autos, Motos
E. Sclaverand
6 Rue Caffarelli
PARIS
BACCHUS
LA RÉPÉTITION
OPÉRA
PEER GYNT
239, BOULEVARD
(Porte-Maillot)
PARIS

Photo by Henry Clarke for *Vogue*'s French
edition, 1955.

Opposite: Photo by Henry Clarke for *Vogue*'s French edition, 1957.

Above: The model Penelope Tree on a train platform. Photo by David Bailey for *Vogue*'s English edition, 1968.

Above: The model Twiggy. Photo by Bert Stern for *Vogue*'s English edition, 1967.

Opposite: Photo by David Bailey for *Vogue*'s English edition, 1969.

Following pages: Photo by David Bailey for *Vogue*'s Italian edition, 1976.

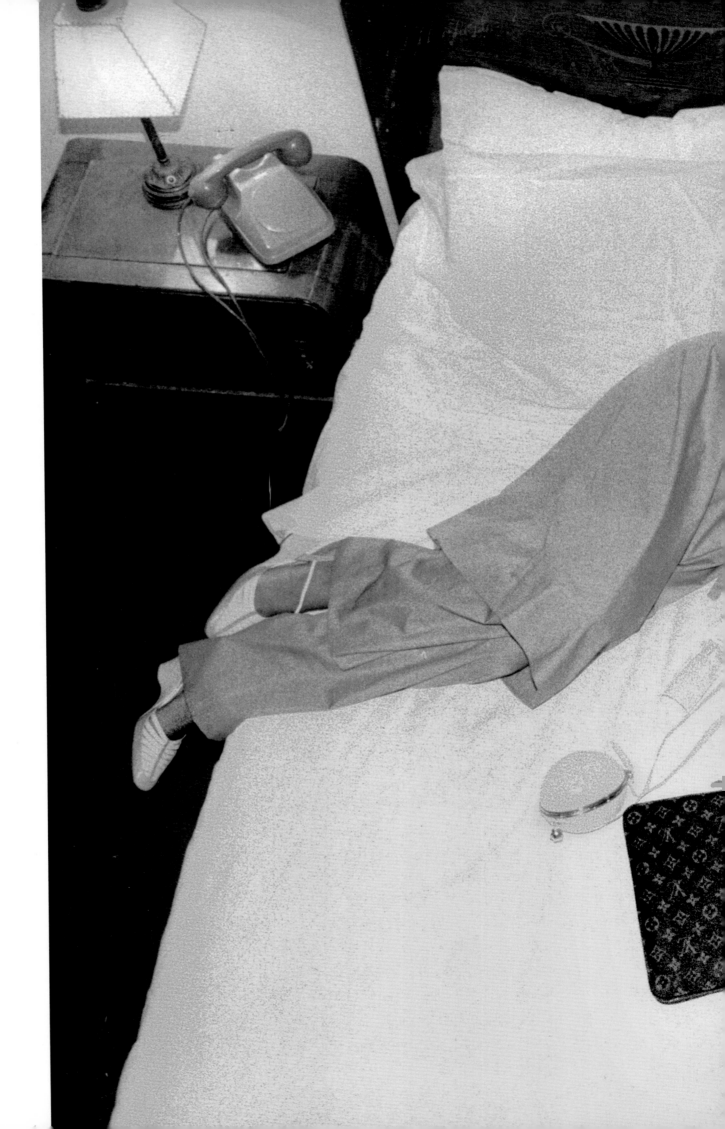

RELAUNCH

Relaunch and international growth

Two exclusive stores and 11 million euros in sales in 1977 grew to 125 stores generating 600 million euros in sales in 1989. With an ambitious business strategy, the company experienced an important period of rapid development.

After Gaston-Louis Vuitton's death in 1970 Maison Louis Vuitton undertook a difficult transition. Always prosperous, the company's growth had stagnated. It operated only two exclusive stores: one on Avenue Marceau in Paris, where customers went in droves, and another in Nice. However, a study showed the company had considerable potential for development. Selling the business was not an option. All Gaston-Louis's children were involved in its day-to-day operations. Henry-Louis, the eldest son, directed sales and the Paris store; Claude, the youngest, was in charge of manufacturing and the Asnières workshops. For the first time the company called upon a manager outside of the family to develop the brand in Japan and Italy, but that did not last long. An enlightened alliance of two of Gaston-Louis's sons-in-law, Henry Racamier and Jean Ogliastro (who were married to the youngest daughters, Odile and Denyse, respectively), with the family's full backing, undertook the company's first efforts to revitalize the business.

The family gets to work. Henry Racamier was sixty-five when he was offered the position of president of Vuitton in 1977. Although all members of the family did not agree on the choice, they deserve credit for having the courage and collective intelligence to choose an uncommon man for the job. Henry Racamier was, like Louis Vuitton, a native of the Jura. He was born in 1912 in Pont-de-Roide. He began his career in the iron and steel industry. When he took over his new functions at Vuitton, he brought his long experience in international business, a rigor borrowed from Germanic models, and an interest in opening the company to the world.

Development of the distribution network. André Sacau, who was appointed general director, was one of the reorganization's engineers. He implemented a new distribution strategy and established the foundations for international growth. Instead of opening franchises Louis Vuitton created its own subsidiaries through local partnerships in other countries. The astute advice of Kyojiro Hata, head of the Japanese subsidiary, led to the successful 1978 opening of the first Louis Vuitton stores in Tokyo and Osaka. The Japanese subsidiary took on the status of a business corporation in 1981. That same year the company opened a third Japanese store, in Tokyo's Ginza district; it has been remodeled and enlarged many times since. The Japanese subsidiary became one of Louis Vuitton's spearheads. For the rest of Asia, the company named Michel Goemans as an associate, opening its first stores in Hong Kong, Singapore, and Guam in 1979. The company pursued expansion in the Middle East with the Chalhoub Group, as well as in Indonesia, Thailand, Taiwan, and elsewhere. The company opened stores in large hotels, which was the best way to reach travelers, particularly the Japanese, who were enjoying new purchasing power. In December 1981 a Louis Vuitton store was unveiled in New York City, on 57th Street. This Atlantic crossing heralded future outlets in North America, while the expansion of the European Union provided new opportunities in countries like Germany, England, and Austria. Louis Vuitton began its conquest of the world.

Stores in the modern era. The creation of the exclusive distribution network enabled the company not only to make considerable profits, but also to control the decor, products, and services in all its stores. In Paris Louis Vuitton opened at a new address, 54 Avenue Montaigne, on one of the city's most prestigious thoroughfares. After crossing a monumental threshold

Previous page: A Monogram collection in a palace vestibule. Photo by Jean Larivière.

Opposite: Facade of the Louis Vuitton store that opened in 1989 at 54 Avenue Montaigne, in Paris's "golden triangle" of fashion.

customers discovered an interior architecture and product display that had been completely rethought since Vuitton's previous incarnations. In London, where the company first established a presence in 1885, the reopening of the shop on Old Bond Street marked a renewal of ties between Louis Vuitton and the British capital. It met with immediate success. Customers included celebrities like Lauren Bacall, Audrey Hepburn, and Joan Collins and dignitaries like the British royal family, Queen Noor of Jordan, and the sultan of Brunei, who bought a shoe trunk one day to hold his wife's jewels. It also attracted a new clientele—the city's golden boys—for whom Louis Vuitton became the favorite brand. As John Davis, assistant manager from 1984 to 1994, recalled, "On Saturday afternoon, the Porsches and Ferraris were double-parked, bumper to bumper, on Old Bond Street. These clients could spend four to six thousand dollars . . . and just as much the next Saturday!"

Obsession for quality. Production increased to meet the demands of the new markets. Workshops and factories opened throughout France, new personnel were trained, and logistics were fine-tuned. Loyal to its principles, the company would not sacrifice the quality of its products on the altar of profits. To the contrary, it imposed increased quality control, even as quantity surged. Guy de Laporte, then the director of communications, explained, "You could manufacture at high costs and sell at high prices on the condition that customers get what they pay for." That insistence on fine quality and full control was why the luggage was produced only in France—according to traditional manufacturing processes, but in ultramodern workshops. Louis Vuitton also developed new leatherwork lines. The Epi line was introduced in 1985, taking its place beside the classic Monogram canvas, which still generated most of the brand's sales.

The advent of communications. Along with the development of its business network and the renewal of its stores, the company decided to forge an image that would conform to its stature. It had to feed the customers' imaginations, simultaneously enriching the Vuitton legend and bringing it up to date. The company clearly defined a corporate personality. Every field of communication was used—advertising, visual merchandising, publications, architecture, store design, sponsorships, patronage—to reflect a consistent identity and convey three ideas: "Louis Vuitton, trunk maker in Paris since 1854," "Timelessness," and "Travel." This identity found its most successful expression in the first advertising campaign entrusted to the photographer Jean Larivière. His unforgettable images—bearing the slogan *"L'Âme du voyage"* ("The Spirit of Travel")—established and upheld the Louis Vuitton legend.

Other ways to connect: sponsorship and patronage. To make its values highly visible, the company decided to cultivate its similarities with another legend, the America's Cup, the celebrated sailing competition. Established in the same year, it was associated with the same world of travel and had the same attachment to tradition, without renouncing any aspect of modernity. The Louis Vuitton Cup was established in 1983 as the mandatory passage to participation in the America's Cup.

Similarly, the company established the Fondation Louis Vuitton pour l'Opéra, la Musique et les Arts in 1986. Rolf Liebermann, former administrator of the Paris Opéra, accepted the presidency of the artistic steering committee, and other eminent personalities contributed their help, including Giorgio Strehler, Sir Peter Ustinov, Hugues R. Gall, Jacques Rigaud, Eva Wagner-Pasquier, Martine Kahane, and Humbert Camerlo. In addition to sponsoring the training of young musicians, the foundation supported the development of contemporary music and contributed to the birth of major works by Pierre Boulez, Pascal Dusapin, Hugues Dufourt, Luigi Nono, and Karlheinz Stockhausen. "There were some fifteen orders for operas, more than fifty orders for musical compositions, and important subsidies for the training of musicians involved in this program," noted Christian de Pange,

Below: Henry-Louis Vuitton and Kyojiro Hata, their wives, and André Sacau at the company's 125th anniversary celebration in 1979.

Opposite: That same year Jacques-Henri Lartigue shot a historic photo—an Eiffel Tower of Louis Vuitton trunks and cases.

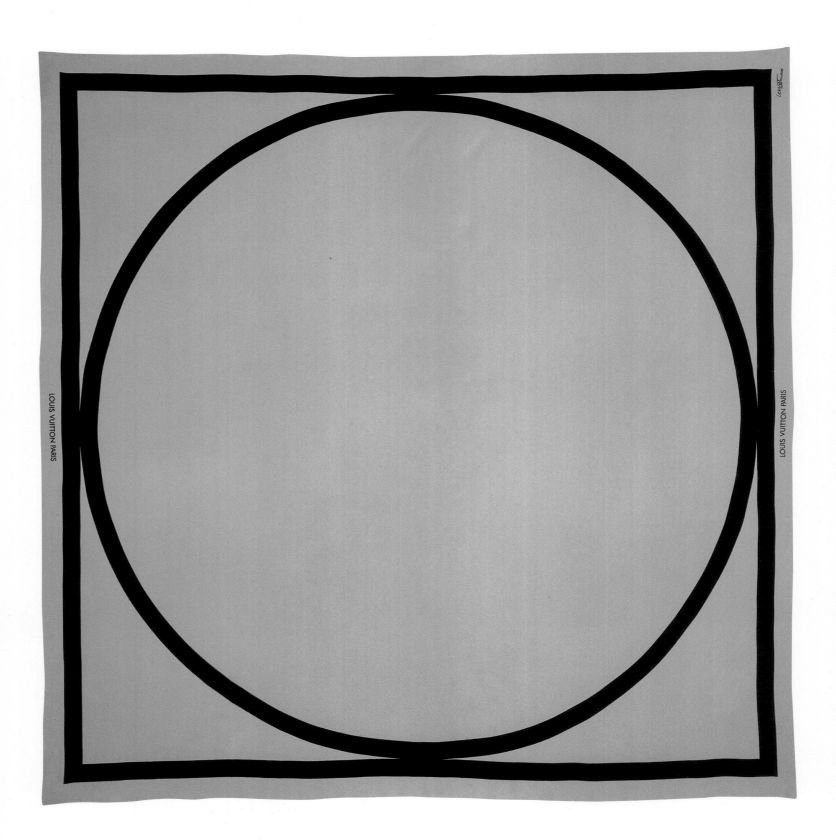

Opposite: "The World Is Round," a silk scarf designed by Sol LeWitt for Louis Vuitton, 1987.

Right: A bottle case in red Epi leather (top) and the Saint-Cloud bag in black Kouril Epi leather (bottom).

Below: Always traveling between New York, London, and the south of France, the English actress Joan Collins, a loyal Louis Vuitton customer.

who was delegate general. It also distinguished itself with high-profile undertakings, such as the gift of a stage curtain, a gigantic canvas painted by Olivier Debré, to Hong Kong's new opera house; worldwide research to form a quartet of Stradivarius violins; and the renovation of the Bibliothèque-Musée de l'Opéra de Paris. All those initiatives have greatly contributed to Maison Louis Vuitton's international reputation.

Birth of the LVMH Group. In 1984, when the company was listed on the Bourse in Paris and the New York Stock Exchange, Louis Vuitton acquired an extraordinary new dimension. It stimulated an incredible fascination around the world. The company had already undertaken a well-thought-out strategy of diversification with the takeover

Left: During Australia's bicentennial celebration in Sydney, Maison Louis Vuitton participated in a hot-air balloon flight.

Below: In 1983 Henry Racamier presented the first Louis Vuitton Cup to the Australians Alan Bond and John Bertrand.

Opposite: The Bibliothèque-Musée de l'Opéra de Paris, renovated by the Fondation Louis Vuitton pour l'Opéra, la Musique et les Arts.

of other prestigious brands, including Veuve Clicquot-Ponsardin (Champagne), Givenchy (apparel, perfume, and cosmetics), and Loewe International (leather goods and ready-to-wear). Luxury goods had become an industry in itself, and Louis Vuitton had quickly become a multinational corporation generating ninety percent of its sales beyond France.

In 1987 a merger of Louis Vuitton and Moët Hennessy (reknowned for fine wines and spirits) gave birth to LVMH, the world's leading luxury brands group. Three years later, at the end of a lively conflict among stockholders, Henry Racamier left the LVMH board. His departure marked a real turning point in Louis Vuitton's history. A new era began, one that would witness the transformation of Louis Vuitton into a global company based on a growth model that would set an example for the entire luxury goods industry.

Jean Larivière, traveler on an epic journey

Rare are the leading brands that have understood the value of associating themselves with the talent of a renowned photographer to build their image. Having given carte blanche to Jean Larivière for some twenty years, Louis Vuitton can boast that it inspired an original body of work that marks an epoch in the history of photography.

Discovery of photography, the first artistic steps. At Jean Larivière's home, toys are everywhere. He has loved them since he was a child in Angers, when, with nose pressed against store windows, he would gaze at all the things he thought he could never possess. His received his first camera later, in the 1950s, when it was an almost classic gift for young people. It provided his first contact with the photograph. Larivière's true discovery of photography took place in the sixties, when he was a twenty-year-old student at the art school in Angers. "I used the photograph like a material," he said, recalling his first steps as a photographer. "I didn't use it for itself, for its capacity for figurative representation, but rather like a palette of colors, pigments, and materials." His first professional endeavors led him to another kind of film—the cinematic type. "As a result of several meetings, notably with an important producer, I started out working in the movie industry. After being Chris Marker's assistant for his movie *Si j'avais quatre dromadaires* [see *Commentaires* by Chris Marker, Du Seuil Publications], I did graphic work for the credits of Alain Resnais's films and in 1966 I collaborated on a collective movie entitled *Loin du Vietnam,* beside Jean-Luc Godard, Agnès Varda, Jacques Demy, William Klein, Claude Lelouch, and Alain Resnais." Three years later, about 1969–70, he by chance crossed paths with a Chilean artist living in France, the painter Roberto Sebastián Antonio Echaurren, better known as Matta, whom André Breton had consecrated as a surrealist painter. Larivière remembered the encounter as if it were yesterday: "Along with that of Chris Marker, it was the most important meeting of my life, because of Matta's exceptional dimension, his culture, his intelligence, his aura. It was Matta who introduced me to Max Ernst." During the same period he met Salvador Dali at the Hôtel Meurice in Paris. "I presented several projects to Dali, including an idea for a movie and the plan for a 'Machine for disintegrating erotic feelings.' Dali really wanted me to build it, but it was beyond my means. I would have had to use expensive materials like silver, ivory, rock crystal, lapis lazuli. I'm definitely going to build this machine now, in homage to Dali."

The meeting with Louis Vuitton. For several years Larivière pursued graphic and photographic research, then suddenly ended that work for personal reasons about 1972–73. He decided to concentrate his artistic activities in only one field, photography. He entered into photography as though it were a religion, choosing to immerse himself totally in the world of the image.

"I stopped reading even my favorite authors like Poe, Kafka, Cocteau, Gide, and Sartre," he said. "I even lost my taste for science fiction. Brown, Lovecraft, and Frank Herbert no longer interested me. Even music had become too vivid. I needed silence. Today I have rediscovered the great jazz men like Charlie Parker, Lester Young, John Coltrane." His asceticism would last twenty years, the time necessary to fully establish himself as a photographer. With the help of Peter Knapp, the Swiss graphic designer and photographer who was an artistic director at *Elle* magazine, Larivière was asked to take over photography for the Charles Jourdan brand from Guy Bourdin, who had been its photographer for fifteen years. His first advertising photos followed.

About 1977–78, at the turning point of his career, he encountered Louis Vuitton through Jean-François Bentz. "I knew Louis Vuitton like everyone else," Larivière recalled. "When I arrived at Rue de La Boétie, Jean Ogliastro, Henry Racamier, and André Sacau were there. I brought some still-life photos of jewelry and a book about India, *The Last Empire*. I explained my vision of Louis Vuitton to them. I remember having told them that, for me, luxury was timeless. I wanted to make photos that were images of the past, present, and future. Both current and timeless, symbols of beauty, luxury, calm, tranquility, and dreams. I didn't want to reflect the excitement of change but rather the opposite, the continuity of things. When I had finished, they consulted among themselves for a moment and finally they gave me carte blanche."

Twenty years capturing "the spirit of travel" on film. Guadeloupe, India, Yemen, Greenland, Cameroon, China, Northern India, Nepal, Myanmar, Chile: Jean Larivière recites his Louis Vuitton campaigns like so many memories, filled with silences and waits for light that could last hours, sometimes entire days. The first campaign was based on three emblematic images: a schooner photographed in Antigua, a small boat on India's Lake Jaisalmer, and an elephant rented for the occasion. The compositions are

Portrait of Jean Larivière by Paolo Roversi, 1984.

sober; the style is bare, stripped of artifice. Each image radiates the same magic, captured in an instant of eternity. The success of the campaign, which was admirably staged by Dominique Grosmangin, was absolute. From there Larivière would traverse the globe, leaving in his wake a thread of inspiration made of powerful images: luggage on an ice floe in Greenland; a Buddhist monk encountered at the far reaches of the world in Ladakh, northern India; toys in the middle of a Burmese landscape. In the world's eyes, Louis Vuitton had appropriated a concept by magnifying it. The "spirit of travel" became a definitive part of its image.

Parallel to the advertising work, Louis Vuitton entrusted Larivière with another, equally passionate mission: to create a kind of mythic memoir expressing Maison Louis Vuitton's legendary side. For Larivière, who loved photography and admired the Flemish painters "because they painted like photographers," it was a grand challenge. He took it up by creating *Oeuvre 1re,* a report on Louis Vuitton's historic factory in Asnières, before its renovation. Next came *Oeuvre 2e,* subtitled *La Comète de Halley* and done on Reunion Island, in the Indian Ocean; *Oeuvre 3e* on the tribulations of a Louis Vuitton store in India; *Oeuvre 4e,* with toys scattered across Patagonia; all the way to *Oeuvre 11,* a current project in China. The photographer's freely creative black-and-white work pays homage to his masters, including Irving Penn, Richard Avedon, Robert Mapplethorpe, and Édouard Boubat, and adds another facet to the company's heritage. He intends to polish that facet like a jewel by "going back to drawing and painting. Because knowing how to use a paintbrush is important for going further into the photographic image."

Left: A moonlit vision of the Asnières workshop, 1984.

Opposite top: A classic toy posed beside the Irrawaddy River, Myanmar, 1991.

Opposite bottom: Camel caravan in Pushkar, India, 1988.

In the Ladakh Mountains, 1987.

Greenland, 1984. Long ago, Louis Vuitton created
a toy wooden bear on wheels; Jean Larivière
discovered it in an attic in Asnières.

On the water's surface, Myanmar, 1993. Two pirogues cross paths and two cultures meet on Lake Inle. The young woman is carrying a Lussac bag made of Epi leather in Tassili yellow.

WORLD LEADER

The benchmark in luxury

By taking control of basics, entering the world of fashion apparel, conquering new markets, diversifying products, modernizing stores, creating a new image, respecting artisanal roots and values—and thanks to the innovative policies initiated in 1990—the company has become a global brand, a leader cited as the benchmark in luxury goods.

A change of eras, people, and points of view. In 1990 the company would experience a profound and rapid renaissance that would give it a new image without altering its fundamental values. What had been a family business quickly evolved into a multinational luxury goods corporation, firmly established in the contemporary world and enriched by 150 years of history. In a changing economy Louis Vuitton increased its capital and became the world's leading luxury goods brand.

The paradox of success. Louis Vuitton can be proud of having thrived through its many decades by entrusting its destiny to visionary managers. Bernard Arnault, the head of the LVMH Group, recognized the need to exploit the company's potential immediately to assure its performance and thereby its longevity. To accomplish this mission, he named Yves Carcelle CEO of Louis Vuitton.

Carcelle, who had studied at the École Polytechnique, was just forty-two years old but had already proven his efficiency and business sense. He was president of Deschamps, the fine linens firm, before taking over as head of strategy and development for LVMH; he is both outstandingly diplomatic and practical. When he arrived at Louis Vuitton he drew up a company inventory: "At the end of the 1980s the company was experiencing extraordinary sales increases. New production facilities were established and new stores were constantly opening. Louis Vuitton's communications were unified globally, due notably to advertising campaigns on the theme of the spirit of travel. On the other hand, there was

Previous page: A luminous globe of Monogram Multicolor canvas at the 2003 launch of the Roppongi Hills store in Tokyo.

Opposite: Bernard Arnault, chairman of the LVMH Group, photographed by Patrick Demarchelier. In the background, two works by Takashi Murakami.

Right: Yves Carcelle, CEO of Louis Vuitton since 1990.

no intensive work on the product and its image. The Monogram benefited from the company's growth and quickly grew without really needing to nourish its own myth. However, its renewal and the perception of its renewal remained weak. It was missing the freshness of innovation."

This analysis was shared by Jean-Marc Loubier, Carcelle's closest accomplice, manager of Louis Vuitton's image, store, and product for ten years, before becoming president of G. "At that time the company's success was based increasingly on appearance. The great majority of people knew the Monogram but not Louis Vuitton. They did not make the connection between the two." The new management devised a new strategy to address that deficit.

The product at the heart of the strategy. Following Bernard Arnault's lead, Louis Vuitton decided to consolidate its market leadership by reinforcing its foundations. All efforts were concentrated on giving the product new dynamism. The existing lines were revitalized and new models were created. Yellow arrived to liven up the Epi leather and reaffirm its colorful identity. The Taiga leather line was created for the classic and elegant man. In 1996 Louis Vuitton revamped its Damier canvas, the company's signature since 1888 and one of the brand's successful mainstays. This design renewal quickly bore fruit and incited the creation of new luggage, including the Satellite suitcases, the Alizé travel bags, and new best sellers like the Alma bag. At the same time the company was taking control of its fundamentals by working on the Monogram, its historic symbol. The Monogram's hundredth anniversary, in 1996, provided a unique opportunity to consolidate Louis Vuitton's leadership in the travel and leather goods sectors.

The Monogram in the limelight. A hundred years after its creation by Georges Vuitton, the Monogram celebrated a grand century. "The usual plan, up until then, for this type of event was to display a series of masterpieces from the past," said Jean-Marc Loubier. "This was exactly what we wanted to avoid, because it would affirm that the past was better than the present. The question was rather to figure out how to make the Monogram become a signature that was once again in tune with the times." The advertising's new slogan affirmed that Louis Vuitton has been surprising the public since 1854. The company brought together an impressive group, including its creative and marketing staffs, several communications

Left: The Taiga advertising campaign, 1997.

Below: Jean-Marc Loubier and Sharon Stone, with whom the company designed a makeup case whose proceeds supported AMFAR's fight against AIDS.

Opposite: The Saint-Jacques bag in Epi leather.

consultants, and fashion world personalities like Jean-Jacques Picart and Hedi Slimane, as a kind of think tank. Together they came up with an outstanding idea: Louis Vuitton would give carte blanche to seven well-known contemporary fashion designers. Each one would create his or her dream travel article using Vuitton's venerable canvas. Yves Carcelle happily remembered this lightning bolt. "Everyone realized that if Azzedine Alaïa, Vivienne Westwood, Manolo Blahnik, Helmut Lang, Romeo Gigli, Sybilla, and Isaac Mizrahi could be inspired to invent extraordinary things with the Monogram, it would definitely prove its incredible modernity." An exhibition of their designs toured all the fashion capitals: Paris, New York, Tokyo, Munich, Rome, Hong Kong, London, and Madrid. In each city an exceptional party was held to inaugurate the Monogram's new era. Collectors fought over the items in stores. The press got involved, rediscovering and promoting the eternal youth of this signature work of modern luxury. This anniversary celebration rang out as an announcement of Louis Vuitton's entry into the fashion world.

Entry into fashion. In 1997 Bernard Arnault decided to move Louis Vuitton into the fashion world. It was a major strategic decision that would give the brand a new dimension. Everyone in the company had to support this evolution, which brought an unquestionable strategic advantage but could have represented a historic rupture for Louis Vuitton, which was then a leather goods specialist and proud of its timeless creations. In 1998 the first ready-to-wear and shoe collections appeared under the inspired hand of Marc Jacobs. The move into apparel actually strengthened the brand's legitimacy and aura of exclusivity. As Jean-Marc Loubier explained, "This overture was indispensable, because if you have an advantage and you don't work on it, you can lose it. The advantage was Louis Vuitton's fantastic commercial success. The Monogram and Epi were not enough as they were. Fashion brought us freshness and lightness." Joining the ready-to-wear world was nevertheless a bet on temporality—the ephemeral seasonality of the collections in every fashion show. "It was a real risk from the standpoint of media and creativity, with the danger of losing the brand's roots and soul and the threat of eroding its economic model," said Yves Carcelle. "Up until then we had followed in the footsteps of the founder, with a great concentration on the travel sector. Our approach was continuity and control of distribution and production. All the ingredients were there, completed by the extremely durable product concept. Those foundations were solid and were still responsible for the brand's

Opposite: The Alma handbag was created in 1992, inspired by a luggage line from the 1930s. Reinterpreted by Stephen Sprouse and Takashi Murakami, available in Epi leather and Monogram Satin, redesigned and enlarged for travel, the Alma quickly became one of the company's icons.

Above right: From the Damier campaign of 1998, the Soho backpack in Damier canvas.

success after 150 years. When Bernard Arnault decided to launch Louis Vuitton into fashion, he kept in mind the founding ideal."

To succeed, the company needed the talents of a strongly committed artistic director whose creative contributions would allow the brand to enter the fashion world by the front door. Bernard Arnault chose the young New Yorker Marc Jacobs, a graduate of the renowned Parsons School of Design. At thirty-four, the award-winning stylist became Louis Vuitton's artistic director. The first ready-to-wear and shoe collections debuted at a 1998 fashion show in Paris before an international press that wouldn't have missed the event for anything. For the occasion Marc Jacobs offered an original version of the Monogram in patent leather embossed with the famous floral motif. Ready-to-wear was already inspiring new materials and new models in leather. Monogram Mini, Monogram Graffiti, and many other new designs met with the same success.

Even in hindsight, the marriage of cultures was never obvious, nor was harmony guaranteed in the coupling of a pragmatic manager, Yves Carcelle, and a creative genius, Marc Jacobs. Nevertheless, the marriage took place—and thrived. As Marc Jacobs immersed himself in the company's codes, his work progressed. Each fashion show and every collection reverberated in increasingly favorable ways. A Louis Vuitton style asserted itself. In 2002, in a dark, gray world, Marc Jacobs created a sensation by providing a naive and joyful interpretation of the spirit of the times. His multicolored bags and accessories, fruits of a collection made with the Japanese artist Takashi Murakami, revealed the season's trend. Yves Carcelle expressed what Marc Jacobs brought to the brand this way: "The Louis Vuitton fashion show became an important highlight of fashion week in Paris. The brand imposed itself as a key player that made fashion on a worldwide scale. It is the real proof that one can think of the fleeting and still keep a very long-term vision."

To mark this new chapter in the history of Maison Louis Vuitton, the company, which had briefly been based at the Grande Arche de la Défense, moved its headquarters in 1998 to the center of the Paris on Rue du Pont-Neuf, in what was formerly the Belle Jardinière department store building. The architect Jean-Jacques Ory restored the Second Empire

Opposite: Isaac Mizrahi, Naomi Campbell, Zhantig, Helmut Lang, Manolo Blahnik, Jérôme Savary, Sybilla, Azzedine Alaïa, Romeo Gigli, and Vivienne Westwood at the Monogram's hundredth anniversary party in 1996.

Above: Beside a giraffe at the Palais de Chaillot Naomi Campbell struts in a bathing suit and shoes coordinated with the bag created by Azzedine Alaïa.

Below: Jean Larivière's 1994 ad campaign, "The Imaginary Voyages of Louis Vuitton."

building and the exterior facade in collaboration with Bâtiments de France. Many observers would have preferred to imagine the headquarters in an elegant mansion in the posh Saint-Honoré district. Once again Louis Vuitton surprised everyone by setting its heart on a location that was unexpected. Bertrand Stalla-Bourdillon, general manager, explained the happy outcome: "We have created our new living space here; we have invested in the area and have had an influence on its development. Everyone has the impression that Louis Vuitton has been here forever—which is not completely wrong since our headquarters is only a few hundred yards from the place where Louis made his start when he first came to Paris."

The image's evolution. Louis Vuitton's image continued to evolve with the times, now newly enriched by contributions from fashion. By increasing the number of products marketed, Louis Vuitton undertook a new path and expressed a more contemporary image. Since the eighties the advertising campaigns photographed by Jean Larivière had forcefully demonstrated a gracious return to the epic and poetic voyage, where the company's spirit has always been anchored. The "toys" campaign for the Monogram's hundredth anniversary and the first ads dedicated to shoes played on unconventional notes, even verging on an impertinent elegance that the company dared to claim as its own. With the arrival of Marc Jacobs the advertising campaigns took on the feel of the fashion collections and found their place in avant-garde design. In 1998 the Monogram Vernis line took shape, along with a campaign thematically centered on the seven deadly sins. Since then Louis Vuitton advertisements have presented scenes of the full product line: leather goods, ready-to-wear, shoes, watches, and jewelry. Extremely sophisticated images by the greatest photographers represent the spirit of the season. Actresses and models including Eva Herzigova, Jennifer Lopez, Naomi Campbell, and Diane Kruger have all incarnated the Louis Vuitton dream woman, changeable and elegant according to the fashions and the seasons. In 2005 the American actress Uma Thurman was Maison Vuitton's model. Marc Jacobs sought a sharp contrast, deciding to "present an ultrafeminine woman in a raw, austere industrial setting.

Uma Thurman is dressed in a sophisticated style, in opposition to an unexpected decor made of cement and concrete."

Vuitton's evolution to fully embraced modernity was also reflected in the field—in the 340 exclusive stores that are the brand's true showcases. "God is in the details" seems to be the credo of Louis Vuitton, which directly controls and manages the architecture, furniture, product display, and services offered to customers in each of its stores around the globe, where five thousand salespeople are on the job. The latest generation of stores is exemplified by the one in Shanghai, renovated in 2004 with a spectacular thirty-three-foot-high glass facade, which made it China's largest luxury goods store. It expresses the brand's complete range, from travel to jewelry, ready-to-wear, leather goods, shoes, and accessories. The new store design serves to present not just product, but Louis Vuitton's underlying image, with tradition and modernity coexisting harmoniously in a carefully designed environment. A wall of old trunks might stand adjacent to the season's ready-to-wear collection; the classic Keepall holds its own with the bags presented at the latest fashion show. The new store concept transforms shopping into a pleasure and enlarges the brand's customer base.

The world's leading luxury goods company further extends its image through numerous sponsorship activities. Perhaps the most visible one is the Louis Vuitton Cup, established in 1983. Success in this elimination heat is required to compete in the America's Cup, the most prestigious international yachting competition. This alliance symbolizes the links between the world's oldest sports trophy and the world's largest luxury brand. Louis Vuitton and the America's Cup reflect similar values involving travel, overcoming obstacles, tradition, and technology, and they share a spirit of conquest. Tycoons and nabobs put all their energy, reputation, fortune, and time on the line to go after the holy grail of the yachting world—and many of these captains of industry are also loyal to Louis Vuitton. Athletes, adventurers, and the powerful all come together to compete, participate, or simply admire the race's incredible spectacle. The single purpose is to win the famous silver cup and organize the next edition on the winner's territory. In 2003 the America's Cup returned to Europe for the first time since its creation in 1851. With the Alinghi team, the landlocked Swiss discovered a new sea view; they chose Valencia, on the Spanish coast,

Above left: In Shanghai, China, the Louis Vuitton store illustrates the new retail concept with its 33-foot-high glass facade, 9,687-square-foot space, and full range of products.

Opposite, above: Louis Vuitton opened a store in 2004 on Moscow's Red Square.

Opposite, center: Maharajah Tikka Shatrujit Singh and his son, Maharajah Kumar Suryajit Singh.

Opposite, below: Queenie Dodhi, Yves Carcelle, Shilpa Shetty, and Rebecca Carcelle at the opening of the New Delhi store in 2003.

as the site of the thirty-second edition of the America's Cup, which will take place in 2007. Louis Vuitton remains the event's privileged partner. A new and ambitious four-year schedule of preliminary regattas began in 2004; it will enable teams to regularly measure themselves against their rivals and will maintain suspenseful interest among European fans. Louis Vuitton directs the competition's communications, including virtual reality and transmission on the Internet. Innovation is manifest in the organization behind the scenes as well as on the boat decks. Through its energy, passion, and commitment Louis Vuitton has given the sailing competition a dimension no one imagined twenty years ago. It has become an event that captivates the public around the world.

Conquering the world. Louis Vuitton is also unflagging in its pursuit of geographic conquests, continuously opening stores in new markets and new countries. A vigorous development strategy has expanded the brand's retail presence to more than 340 stores in some 50 countries. The expansion is rigorously planned, as Louis Vuitton carefully takes the time needed to ensure that employees in new markets master every aspect of Vuitton know-how. Serge Brunschwig, general manager of the international sales network, understands the value of patience. "From India to Brazil, from Russia to South Africa, at each new store, a long upstream preparation includes the recruitment and training of local staff," he said. "For the Russian market, for example, it took at least five years." When the first store in Moscow opened on Stolechnikov Pereoulok, "the brand was the first to open a store on Red Square without having a local distributor," Yves Carcelle remembered. In China, another emerging country where the brand is intensifying its presence, the scenario was similar. Unlike Russia, which had been cut off from the world by two world wars and a communist regime, China never lost contact with global economic development, thanks to the financial support provided by its emigrants. Louis Vuitton sensed what would be a Chinese Eldorado well before others did and opened its first Peking store in 1992 in the Palace Hotel, a few steps from the Forbidden City. Of course, the company's first encounter with China was nearly a hundred years earlier, in 1907, when the Paris-Peking automobile race crossed the Gobi Desert outfitted with its trunks, which withstood temperatures of -31° Fahrenheit. In China, the company worked year after year to win acclaim and sustain its reputation. In 1998, for example, the Classic China Run helped establish its place in the country. It was the first grand international classic car rally to take place in China. Each leg was preceded by a heritage exhibition that recalled Louis Vuitton's French origins and passion for travel. Millions of Chinese followed the rally and visited the historic retrospective. Some mayors of large cities even granted a vacation day so their citizens could watch the cars pass. Result: Louis Vuitton today has ten stores in continental China, and the Chinese are already the brand's third-largest clientele.

Renewed history. At the beginning of the twenty-first century, no region of the world seems likely to escape Vuitton's continuous expansion. But beyond the business figures, each new store represents a reflowering of the company's roots. A new store often provides the opportunity to reunite with former customers. Well before opening its store on Fifth Avenue, Louis Vuitton sold trunks in New York—as early as the late nineteenth century, through the John Wanamaker store. The brand's establishment in India, first in New Delhi and then Bombay, seemed almost predestined, since that country had sent many illustrious clients to Maison Vuitton, including the maharajah of Baroda and Princess Pudukota. Likewise in Russia, where the imperial family and the court of Czar Nicholas II were long among the trunk maker's most loyal customers. The store that opened in Johannesburg, South Africa, in late 2004 recalled Louis Vuitton's connection with the great expeditions across Africa carried out long ago by Savorgnan de Brazza and Georges-Marie Haardt, captain of the Croisière Noire.

Vuitton's trunks have crossed mountains, seas, and oceans, and its pioneer spirit lives on; it was among the first global luxury retailers to open stores in China, Vietnam, the Czech Republic, and India. It evokes the legendary travel of bygone days by opening stores in celebrated hotels like the Peninsula in Hong Kong, the Oriental in Bangkok, the Metropole in Hanoi, Raffles in Singapore, Mamounia in Marrakech. These stores are integrated into the city's architecture and often enhance its historic heritage. That was the case with the revitalization of the Gump Building in Hawaii, which won Louis Vuitton first prize for best restoration. In Tokyo the company took an active part in creating the new urban district of Roppongi Hills, one of Japan's largest real estate projects in recent years. In Moscow Louis Vuitton opened on Red Square in the Gum shopping center, a historic monument. Similarly, it opened a store in Milan's historic Galleria Vittorio Emanuele II, a sumptuous glass-domed shopping arcade.

Toward new frontiers. The first years of the new century have been marked by the integration of new businesses and the introduction of new products. Watches, jewelry, sunglasses, and fashion accessories reinforce Louis Vuitton's commitment to being a global luxury brand. For Pascale Lepoivre, director of the fashion and leather goods division, "the arrival of ready-to-wear and shoes in 1998 was a turning point. Since then Louis Vuitton has had a continuously renewed product line for women and men, local customers and tourists, who travel and buy in the four corners of the world." By turning to fashion, the company set out resolutely in a new direction, increasingly diversifying its offerings and extending itself to new audiences. After establishing its ready-to-wear and shoe lines, in 2002 Louis Vuitton launched its first watch collection. With an original look, a strong design, and fine-quality clockworks, the Tambour line quickly claimed a position in the watch market. The line has been enriched with new models each year and has managed to compete against leading brands in the category. A new line of watches called Speedy, with a recognizable checked design, debuted in 2005 to keep pace with the times.

Louis Vuitton further pursued its quest for new business by launching its first jewelry collection, Emprise, which has a promising future. In this collection, boldness and tradition go hand in hand; the trunk maker's signature joins with the jeweler's skill. Leather,

Opposite: In 1998 Louis Vuitton organized the first China Run, a classic car rally from Dalian to Peking.

Below: Chinese children during the rally's opening ceremonies.

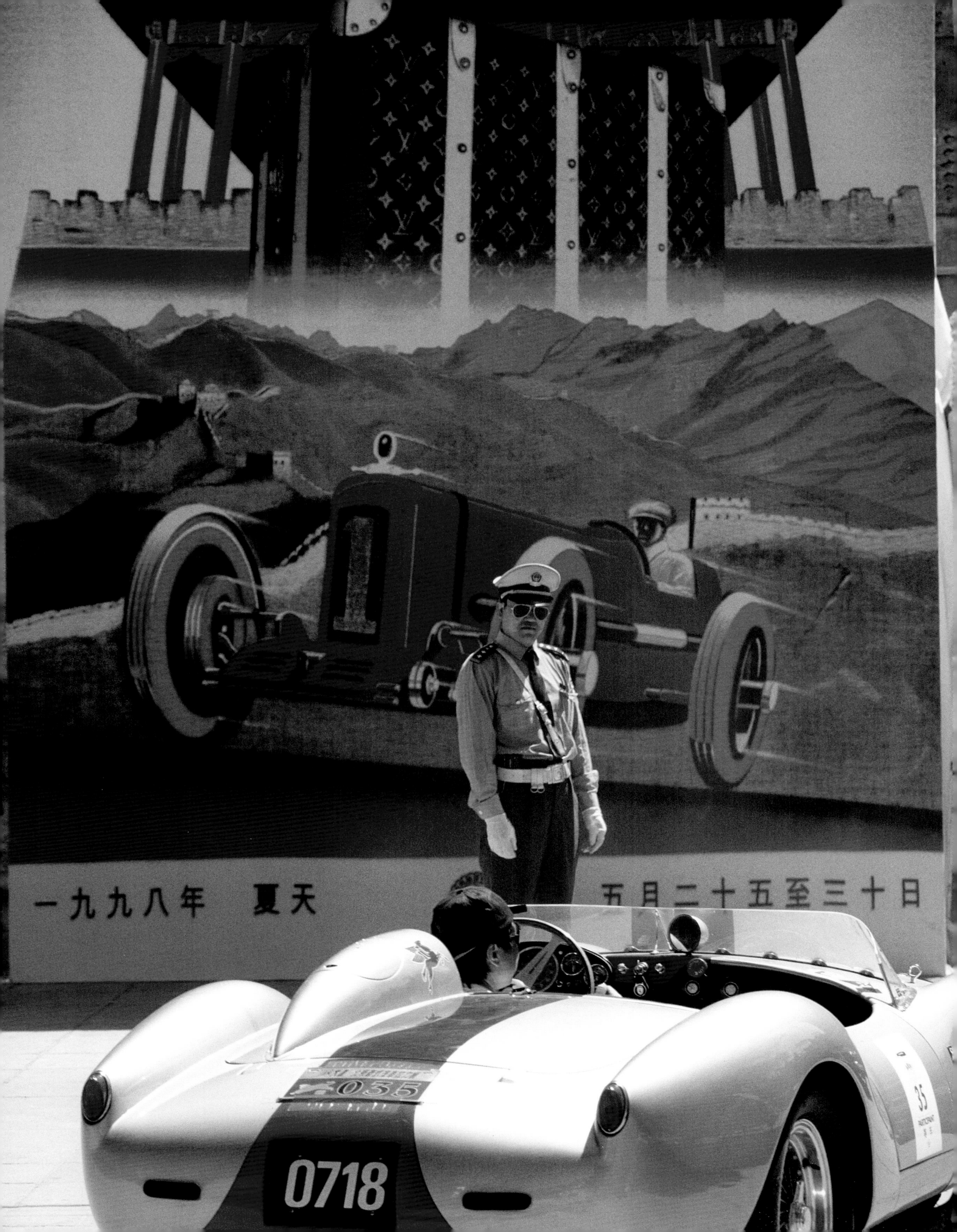
一九九八年　夏天
五月二十五至三十日
035
35
0718

Singapore. Raffles Hotel.

gold, and diamonds—unexpected materials come together. The value of certain exceptional items is as high as $250,000. Nonetheless, demand grows continuously. To meet it, the company must also acquire new skills and production means that are equal to its ambitions. Emmanuel Mathieu, head of the leather workshops, has a demanding challenge before him: to combine artisanal fabrication with the efficiency of industrial production. Since leatherwork skills have been perfected with time, Louis Vuitton has learned to renew itself through original techniques and modern materials. Today the company has fifteen integrated workshops with four thousand employees. The leather workshop opened recently in Ducey, in the bay of Mont-Saint-Michel, joins with the Asnières workshop, which has stood at the gates of Paris since 1859 and was entirely renovated not long ago. At the Paris headquarters on Rue du Pont-Neuf, the design studios benefit from the proximity of the integrated prototype workshops for ready-to-wear and leather goods. Serge Alfandary directs the shoe division, bringing thirty years of experience in the field to Louis Vuitton. Here too rigorous control of production guarantees fine quality. "When we became involved in shoe manufacturing, we bought, transformed, and set up a workshop in the Venice region, which makes all the prototypes and handles some of the production," he said. "We have stakes in several businesses and completely integrated the know-how specific to shoes." Louis Vuitton also has its own watchmaking workshop in Chaux-de-Fonds, Switzerland. Louis Vuitton profits not only from the investment power of the LVMH Group but also from numerous synergies within it. The benefits flow both ways, as some analysts cite Louis Vuitton and its strong profits as the engine of the LVMH Group.

The art of managing success. The fascination that a brand name that first appeared in 1854 continues to exert on the world seems almost inexplicable. That fascination only continues to grow, as measured by sales records beaten every year despite economic crises, terrorist bombings, wars, epidemics, and the decreased tourism that results from them—not to mention the scourge of counterfeiting, against which the company has made considerable strides. Any brakes on the luxury industry's development seem not to affect Louis Vuitton's unabashed health, its global expansion, and its advance on its competitors. By balancing creativity and pragmatism, by taking the risk of opening the company to new businesses, and by preserving an irreproachable product quality, Bernard Arnault's strategy has borne fruit. How to explain this formidable, durable success? Some cite the longevity of Vuitton's know-how; others, the coherence of its development model; and still others, the commitment of its ten thousand employees.

Yves Carcelle, CEO of the company since 1990, set aside business terms like "increase in market share," "percentage of organic growth," and "progression of the operating margin," preferring more humanistic words to evoke "what is really unique about Louis Vuitton: this capacity to combine a respect for lasting values with a completely unbridled creativity. When Marc Jacobs created the Monogram Vernis or invented the Multicolore with Murakami, it was at once totally Louis Vuitton, Monogram, and modern. Our world has always been multifaceted, and today it is even more so. This capacity to enter into a history, to respect the heritage, but at the same time to engage in constant renewal is an extremely subtle balance. This is what makes the Louis Vuitton magic. It is not a sterile vision turned toward a lost paradise, nor a permanent re-creation that ignores the past. It's a rewriting, an ongoing reinvention."

A modern saga of 150 years. More than a century and a half ago a thirty-three-year-old man from the Jura founded his own company and revolutionized the art of travel. Louis Vuitton set himself up as a trunk maker in Paris and adapted his designs to the contemporary world—to the railroad, to ocean liners, to aircraft, and to automobiles in turn. Thanks to his unique know-how, he became the undisputed source for trunks and luggage; his

Opposite, from top to bottom and left to right: Raffles Hotel in Singapore, Hotel Oriental in Bangkok, the Peninsula in Hong Kong, the Metropole in Hanoi, Gump Building in Hawaii, and the Galleria Vittorio Emanuele II in Milan.

Below: Serge Brunschwig and Kyojiro Hata in Hong Kong during the company's celebration of its 150th anniversary.

company met with immediate success that has never wavered in the years since. Few brands can boast that they are still young at such a venerable age. In 2004 Louis Vuitton blew out its 150 candles with panache. To honor the Vuitton saga and celebrate the milestone anniversary, the brand created a spectacular event, placing gigantic monogrammed trunks in the four corners of the world and staging gala parties, where guests learned about the Vuitton story in images projected on a screen thirty yards long. Throughout 2004 the company introduced a number of innovations, proving again how Louis Vuitton turns toward the future while remaining faithful to its roots. The Trianon canvas, which in 1854 was the first canvas the founder created, was reinterpreted and reintroduced by Marc Jacobs 150 years later. A jewelry collection greatly inspired by the traditional trunk's historic signatures was unveiled. Some fifteen stores opened their doors in countries including China, Mexico, Germany, Korea, the United States, Japan, Switzerland, and India—and among them were the world's biggest Louis Vuitton store, in New York, and its smallest sales outlet, in Gstaad, the world's chicest ski resort. The historic Ginza Namiki store reopened in Tokyo, having grown from a simple ground-floor store to occupy a 17,000-square-foot, six-floor building. In the Asia Pacific zone managed by François Delage, the first Shanghai store opened, offering ready-to-wear as well as luggage and handbags. And Maison Louis Vuitton opened its first store in sub-Saharan Africa, in Johannesburg. In Paris, throughout 2004 two monumental trunks were installed on the Champs-Élysées to conceal the titanic renovation that would make the immense store the brand's most prestigious showcase when completed in 2005. History seems to repeat itself: Louis Vuitton opened the

world's largest store for travel articles on this same avenue in 1914, where it remained until its hundredth anniversary move to Avenue Marceau in 1954. It returned to the Champs-Élysées in 1998 with the first store representing its new retail concept, which continues to evolve and become more beautiful. There is no more significant or emblematic place to commemorate the longevity of Louis Vuitton.

Opposite, clockwise from top left: Djemaa el-Fna square in Marrakech; a porter from La Mamounia holding a Damier canvas Ribera bag; the debut of the Louis Vuitton store in Johannesburg in 2004; Winston Churchill in front of his easel.

Right: Speedy DuoJet GMT quartz watch with silver watchband, launched in 2005.

The centennial of the Monogram canvas

In 1996 Louis Vuitton decided to stage an exceptional celebration for the Monogram canvas's one hundredth anniversary. The company invited seven designers to create a superb collection of items using the Monogram canvas, which was displayed in the world's great capitals. The Monogram canvas thus proved once more its incredibly youthful spirit, joyfully expressing itself in the fashion field.

Above left: The Feline handbag—half urban, half jungle—both civilized and savage. Azzedine Alaïa wrapped panther skin voluptuously around the Monogram canvas. Inside, the accessories are stacked like so many exotic charms. Photo Guzman.

Above center: With his music trunk, Helmut Lang gave a surprising twist to what looks like one of Vuitton's traditional vanity cases. The Viennese designer outfitted the inside of this sober and practical cube to hold a globetrotting DJ's music. Photo Guzman.

Above right: Meeting in the rain. Spanish designer Sybilla reinvented the elegant and discreet backpack with an umbrella that opens and magically holds in place, protecting the walker while leaving the hands free. Photo Guzman.

Opposite: Azzedine Alaïa, photographed by Jean-Paul Goude.

 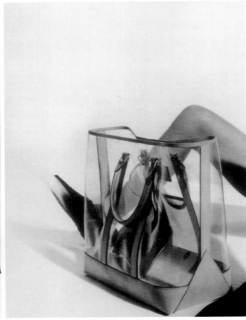 

Above left: Manolo Blahnik's small trunk of simple, almost severe shape opens in two, like a fruit. The compartments, lined with pink leather, hold shoes, a toiletry case, and a small evening dress—suggesting a tempting, brief escapade. Photo Guzman.

Above center: Isaac Mizrahi plays with the idea of transparency with a minimalist plastic shopping bag trimmed in russet leather and containing an elegant Monogram handbag. Photo Guzman.

Above right: Romeo Gigli's backpack, with a solid frame and leather straps across the Monogram canvas, suggests the quiver of an urban Amazon, or perhaps a light amphora. Photo Guzman.

Opposite: Vivienne Westwood's design attaches to the small of the back to enhance a callipygian beauty, or can be held by the hand or hung from the shoulder. The false-bustle bag, with its two symmetrical pockets suggesting two sassy curves, wittily combines sex appeal and practicality. Photo Inez van Lamsweerde and Vinoodh Matadin.

Rebounds

Louis Vuitton has continued to surprise since 1854. To celebrate the 1998 World Cup soccer championship, Louis Vuitton created a Monogram canvas soccer ball, made in a limited and numbered series. The company then gave the balls to writers, artists, show business stars, members of the media, sports figures, business executives, and politicians, who posed with them. Give me a ball, and I'll tell you who I am. . . . And so *Rebounds* was born, a photographic portrait gallery in the form of a book, whose proceeds went to UNICEF.

Above, clockwise from left: French actor Gérard Depardieu during the shooting of the film *Balzac,* with two Monogram canvas balls; photo Xavier Lambours. American actor John Travolta in Hollywood; photo Pascal Dolemieux. Spanish director Pedro Almodóvar at home in Madrid; photo Xavier Lambours.

Opposite: The actress Maggie Cheung in the swimming pool at Hôtel Costes in Paris. Photo Xavier Lambours.

Louis Vuitton celebrates its 150 years

In 2004 Louis Vuitton celebrated its 150th anniversary with a drum roll, placing its trunks in eye-catching spots all over the world. At galas in New York, Hong Kong, and Tokyo, several thousand guests learned about the roots of the ever-alert company, which has endured through time and shaped fashion. Also that year, Louis Vuitton decided to grow by renovating two icons of its history: The Asnières workshop and the Champs-Élysées store were reborn and reopened in 2005.

Dominating the bay in Hong Kong and surrounded by buildings in the business district, a giant Monogram canvas trunk commemorates the trunk maker's 150th anniversary.

Left: In Tokyo on 2 September 2004 an Eiffel Tower of trunks rose on the stage in front of a projected image by Ryuichi Sakamoto.

Above: Monumental signage celebrating Louis Vuitton's 150th anniversary cloaked the Champs-Élysées store during its renovation.

FASHION

How Louis Vuitton entered the Fashion World
By Ruben Toledo and Paul-Gérard Pasols

The house

The House was born with the beginning of the crinoline time. The young Louis Vuitton was "Layetier". He packed the beautiful dresses of the "Elegantes". He became the favorite "Layetier" of the Empress Eugénie as a real specialist. This gave him the idea of creating his own company in 1854.

Near the first Louis Vuitton Store, 4 rue Neuve des Capucines, Charles-Frederic Worth opened 7 rue de la Paix, his first boutique. Worth invented the "Haute Couture". He was the first to put his own signature on his creations. He also invented the "mannequin cabine". Louis Vuitton and Charles-Frederic Worth were close friends.

Like Worth who dared to put his signature on the clothes he created, Georges Vuitton (Louis's son) in 1896 dared to create a canvas bearing Louis Vuitton's initials. It is the Legendary Monogram Canvas, which is the symbol of the HOUSE. Its creation is one of the founding elements of modern luxury.

Vuitton's customers are the most elegant, the most demanding, the most sophisticated in the world. For these travelers, Louis Vuitton creates trunks, luggage, bags and accessories which perfectly protect all these personal and precious effects, and which are made to be adapted to all kinds of transport. Since 1900, the HOUSE has been creating shawls made of the finest cashmeres for the earliest drivers, clutches, traveling rugs, ... and such.

Fashion people have always been Louis Vuitton's customers and friends.

Paul Poiret, Madeleine Vionnet, Jeanne Lanvin, Gabrielle Chanel, Christian Dior, Marcel Rochas, Jean Patou, Hubert de Givenchy, just to drop a few names, ordered creations Louis Vuitton.

From the beginning, the most famous signatures in the fields of Press and Fashion are contributing to the legend of Louis Vuitton such as Diana Vreeland and Anna Piaggi.

In 1996, to celebrate the 100 th anniversary of the Monogram Canvas, LOUIS VUITTON requested 7 celebrated designers of the Fashion Avant-Garde to invent some new creations made with the monogram canvas. the 7 designers are :

Helmut Lang
Azzedine Alaïa
Vivienne Westwood
Romeo Gigli
Manolo Blahnik
Isaac Mizrahi
Sybilla

These creations were shown in Paris and all over the world throughout the entire year of 1996. They were met with high success everywhere. These seven creations are the Symbol of LOUIS VUITTON's engagement with fashion. It is at this time that Bernard Arnault decided to launch LOUIS VUITTON in the fashion field, and to do so, in 1997 he hired MARC JACOBS

Marc Jacobs, the genesis of a style

An eminent representative of a new generation of designers, Marc Jacobs brought Louis Vuitton into the fashion world in its own right. Here is a look at the remarkable itinerary of the young New Yorker who conquered Paris.

You grew up in New York.
I was born in New York City in 1963, on the East Side and, in later years we moved to the West Side. We lived in different neighborhoods, then went to Long Island before returning to New York City. I grew up near Central Park and I have always considered myself a true New Yorker. My parents, my grandparents, and my great-grandparents were all from New York.

What are your fondest childhood memories?
To grow up in a city like New York is a very enriching experience. Today I consider it a kind of blessing. I've been around people from all over the world, with all religions and sexual preferences. My parents never taught me that one thing was better than another. I believe that they were very liberal, like my grandparents. For them, you could become anything you wanted to be. They were nonjudgmental and had no prejudices about how a boy or girl should be. I was immersed in a liberal environment. To grow up in New York really opens your mind. It enabled me to fully discover European culture, which is very anchored there. For me, nothing was insurmountable. I didn't think in terms of authority.

Was your family religious?
No. Not at all.

What did your father do?
My father was impresario of William Morris, the agency, where he was president. My father and mother also met there. Personally, I had no desire to enter that business. In my family there was no set vocation, so I had to decide for myself. I was already attracted to fashion when I was very young, no doubt for the romanticism it implied. I remember when I was nearly thirteen years old, I was very aware of everything happening. I saw beautiful young people, so well dressed, and thought of them not as decadents but rather as hedonists in their lifestyle, dressing very chic to go out to nightclubs, or to Saint-Tropez. It was in this period that a maternal uncle who traveled a lot spoke to me about Parisian life and its nightlife. I was so fascinated that I remember asking my grandmother to buy me European fashion magazines. I waited impatiently for Paris *Vogue*, *Spécial*, and other magazines. When I was fifteen I spent a great deal of time in the Fiorucci boutique. On 59th and 60th Streets were a lot of men's stores. From this period of my life I have an image of young people wearing silk shirts. I can't very well remember whether it was just a mental image or a reality, but I saw fashion as a beauty contest, a kind of spectacle given by people who loved dressing up. I said to myself that it must be wonderful to think about what you are going to wear to the party next day. Without being cliché, that thrilled me.

Among your father's acquaintances, did you ever meet any great artists?
I was probably too young to remember in detail, but there's no doubt that my parents liked to invite people to our house. Many artists visited us, but I can't say whether any were famous or not. Above all I remember the atmosphere at the time, my mother dressing to go to shows. When you're a child, you think it's a kind of party, an invitation to live life to the fullest. For me it's a very beautiful and positive memory.

In 1997, at age thirty-four, Marc Jacobs took over Louis Vuitton's artistic direction. Within a few seasons his fashion shows became one of the hottest tickets of Paris's fashion week. Below: In his New York apartment, 1986.

Later you went to Parsons School of Design.
Yes, I took classes at the art and design school, where some well-known people also went, like the artist Antonio Lopez, Calvin Klein, and Betsey Johnson, I believe. The school reminds me a bit of the movie *Fame*. To be accepted there I had to pass a test that emphasized creativity: I had to create a self-portrait, a landscape, and work on other set subjects. When I found out I was accepted, I was ecstatic, because I could devote myself entirely to fashion. I began to draw and had the profound desire to create clothing someday.

What then was your first experience in this field?
It took place very early. At middle school, in the manual and technical arts department, I took courses in industrial drawing. When no one else was home, a young woman took care of me. She wore work clothes that gave me the idea to create an outfit entirely covered with service station badges. At twelve years old, dressed like that, I was in style, as only older people dared to be. That was my first experience in fashion.

Did anyone close to you encourage this vocation?
My father passed away when I was seven years old. I was raised by my paternal grand-

Marc Jacobs speaking with Paul-Gérard Pasols in London, 2004: "Fashion is an invitation to live life to its fullest . . . something very beautiful, very positive."

"I saw fashion as a kind of spectacle given by people who loved dressing up."

mother, who always encouraged me in everything I did. I wouldn't say that her influence was determining, but she was a woman who had a lot of class and an innate sense of fashion. We sometimes went shopping at Bergdorf Goodman. She used to match her handbags to what she wore and loved life with a very European sensibility. For example, she had to have good hangers for her dresses, which she took great care of. She also said that one good outfit was better than three mediocre ones. One big thing she taught me was that quality was more important than quantity.

Very interesting. Does your first memory of Louis Vuitton go back to this period?
Yes, and still thanks to my grandmother. I should tell you that her opinions were pretty rigid. According to her, an elegant woman should not use a Vuitton handbag as an everyday purse. These handbags were reserved for travel. Moreover, she had a Speedy that she only used for these purposes. In the same way, she couldn't understand why a handbag should carry initials. That is why my first idea of Louis Vuitton was that it was a very chic way to travel but surely not what an urban woman would carry. Since then my opinion has changed somewhat!

On leaving Parsons School you created your own company?
When I was sixteen years old, as a student, I worked for Charivari, a store on the Upper West Side of New York. I went there after class and every weekend to earn a little spending money, to buy drawing supplies and a few articles of clothing. For me, it was a chance to meet people in the fashion world, because it was pretty well connected, for a store. Before leaving Parsons, I completed my final study project: sweaters handmade by my grandmother, according to my drawings and inspired by geometric works by the English artist Bridget Riley. Barbara Weizer, the buyer at Charivari, loved my sweaters. She took me on my first trip to Japan when I was twenty years old. From Tokyo we went to Hong Kong to have the sweaters manufactured, then Barbara sold them at Charivari and several American department stores like Neiman Marcus. These sweaters were noticed, which really launched me into fashion. Bill Cunningham photographed them, the *New York Times* published an article, and Carrie Donovan, also a graduate from Parsons [and the *Times* style editor], showed them. These designs benefited from a lot of publicity in New York.

After that you worked with Robert Duffy.
Robert Duffy was present during my final exam at Parsons. At that time he worked for a company on Seventh Avenue and wanted to launch a line of clothing that was young and contemporary. Robert convinced the directors that I was the perfect designer for the job. I began by creating a collection called Sketchbook, named for the company that hired me.

Next you went to Perry Ellis?
Yes. In 1989 I went to direct the women's collection and Robert became the press agent

for the women's department. Perry Ellis was someone whom I admired and respected enormously. He renewed the trends in the United States with a very young and charming fashion style, a very inspired approach . . . a style far from Calvin Klein, Donna Karan, and Ralph Lauren, which were quite classic and based on what women wore to work. Perry Ellis was a dreamer. He could be inspired by reading a book like the *Canterbury Tales,* by watching a movie like *Chariots of Fire,* or by the twenties, thirties, or forties for his Russian collection. His clothing was American in spirit but he added a whiff of Europe, a touch of fantasy that few American designers have.

And while at Perry Ellis you created the famous "grunge" collection?
Yes. I believe it was my last collection for Perry Ellis. In fact, without my meaning for it to, it turned into a big scandal! It was interesting to see such different opinions—many people loved it, and others really hated it. I believed very strongly in that collection and even today I am very attached to it. Visually, I recognize that it was a little too "noisy." It was my vision and my interpretation of street clothes, with the imperfection that I've always

"My first idea about Louis Vuitton: It was a very chic way to travel."

loved. It was also a reflection of the attitude of young people toward fashion, a look that we see in the work of photographers like Corinne Day, Juergen Teller, and David Sims. I had noted this change in the way models like Kate Moss or Cecilia Chancellor were photographed. This period was also very rich in terms of art, photography, and music. And you know that I have always been inspired by music and those who make music.

On this subject, where does music fit in?
I love music! That's where. Before creating my grunge collection I was a big fan of the group Sonic Youth. I didn't know them personally but soon we became true friends. Most people imagine that musicians aren't interested in fashion but, on the contrary, they're very involved. They too bring their creative contributions to the beauty of life.

After Perry Ellis, you created your own company with Robert Duffy?
Yes, we created our own company without much money. We started up in a small loft at 113 Spring Street in SoHo. It was a nice little place. It was just Robert and me, one person for patterns, a designer, and two dressmakers. Denudo was in charge of production and someone else managed sales and public relations. Now we're in a larger space at 72 Spring Street.

At this time, you were already famous. Anna Wintour loved you, for example.
Anna Wintour was always a great fan of my collections. At my first show for Perry Ellis, you know, she was already there encouraging me. When she worked for *House & Garden*—before becoming editor-in-chief of *Vogue*—she tried to bring fashion to her magazine. She often talked about what I was doing and always encouraged young fashion designers.

And how did you meet up with Louis Vuitton?
We were first contacted by Concetta Lanciaux. Then Mr. Arnault and his wife came to one of my shows. I remember showing them what I was working on. It was an autumn collection. My clothes were obviously very simple but required considerable finishing work. Many ideas were borrowed from European couture but expressed in a less ornamental style. I showed Mr. and Mrs. Arnault how I made my clothes, the precision and accuracy of the finish work, done by hand, the material we used, all imported from Italy, France, Germany, and Switzerland. I don't know whether they were impressed by my work or by my celebrity in the fashion world, but they seemed quite seduced. They proposed to Robert and myself a possible collaboration with LVMH. We had many discussions: Would I be good for Dior? For Givenchy? For Loewe? Finally, I knew it was Mr. Arnault who had the idea to entrust me with the artistic direction of Louis Vuitton, working with Yves Carcelle and Jean-Marc Loubier.

I've seen your drawings from this period.
They were just ideas that expressed my enthusiasm for the project, for the new challenge.

Opposite: Robert Duffy and Marc Jacobs in New York, 1989.

Below: Marc Jacobs wearing a "Happy Face" T-shirt on the runway, 1985

"Everything we create celebrates the history of Louis Vuitton and contributes to its present."

Then you moved to Paris.

I was thrilled. You know, the first time I went to Paris I was seventeen years old and I loved it! I was studying the history of apparel for a school project. By the end of the week I stopped going to classes so I could discover Paris myself. I wanted to visit the Louvre without a guide telling me to look at such-and-such a painting. I even went to several conferences given by designers and I especially remember the one by Sonia Rykiel. That summer we had gone to Yves Saint Laurent's and we talked a lot about his work. It was an enormous pleasure, a true dream. I was so in love with Paris that I extended my trip, and when I finally had to go I was really sad to leave all those extraordinary, colorful, eccentric people. At that time I had long hair and wore bracelets, my dress was a little extreme, with overalls, slightly crazy sandals. People looked at me like I was some kind of weirdo, without really knowing that I was an American. In any case, I knew I was going to miss the Café de Flore.

Is there anything that you do not like about Paris?

Nothing. I love everything in Paris. I love the supermarkets, I love to walk in the streets, I love my life here, I love the parks, the museums—everything!

Well then, you've become a real Parisian.

No, I am not a Parisian. I'm a New Yorker who only sees what's good in Paris. In this city, my life is perfect, full of charm. Perhaps this is not complete reality, because I'm not really part of the French system. I like to work here every day, as part of a wonderful team, for a brand as respected and as magical as Louis Vuitton.

Wonderful! What do you have to say about your first collection for Louis Vuitton? Somewhat surprising, right?

Yes, I know! (Laughter.) It was difficult and I had a certain apprehension. I did not want to do everything people expected me to do or put the logo on everything. When I saw the first trunk in Trianon gray canvas, I said to myself that that's how Louis Vuitton got started. That's how we too are going to start. With grays and whites, with a logo hidden inside the clothing. People were disappointed because they expected a collection that was a little more jazzy, more glamorous. They wanted a flashy Monogram style. But I believed that we should design the collection as it had been, to show that we were loyal to the company's humble beginnings, even if some people would not understand the reference to the brand's origins. Since then my team and I have worked on the Monogram for every fashion show, to get out of the past by expressing the expectations of today's clients. We reinvented the Monogram on patent leather in 1998. The motifs disappeared, becoming nearly invisible, but the handbags were just the opposite, very visible, with a shiny, brilliant surface, in bright colors. A year later, we created the Mini Monogram in denim.

The success was enormous. And the next year you called on Stephen Sprouse.
Yes, it was a kind of homage. This may sound silly, but one of my major artistic references is a work by Marcel Duchamp called *L.H.O.O.Q.* You know, Mona Lisa with a moustache. Asking Stephen Sprouse to draw graffiti on the Monogram was going as far as Duchamp did when he defaced a classic work. As though doing this made the original stronger, cooler, energetic, and punky. That may seem daring, but in fact it was a kind of celebration that showed how much we loved the Monogram. This collaboration was fantastic.

You were a friend of Stephen Sprouse.
I had always admired Stephen as an artist. When I started to design, he was already one of the young New York artists who had a very affirmative vision of fashion. He worked with beautiful materials; he was a truly magical character for whom I had a profound respect. I had always dreamed of doing something with him, and I am someone who never abandons his dreams.

Getting back to New York: Did you ever meet any of the famous people who developed the fashion world? Like Diana Vreeland or Charles James?
No. My generation is more like Anna Wintour.

Louis Vuitton was the first company to establish itself in fashion, leather goods, and shoes at the same time.
Yes, that's true. But you know, our way of working was very positive and constructive, with total respect and healthy irreverence. I respect the world of Louis Vuitton but I want to bring to it a parallel world that honors the past but is always open to the present. The future does not really interest me; I do not know what is in store for us. The past teaches us important things. I have an almost romantic attachment to the past. The present shows us where

we are, which is the most beautiful place to be. With our team, everything we create celebrates the history of Louis Vuitton and contributes to its present.

Certainly. But today what difference is there between Marc Jacobs and Louis Vuitton?

The two companies are completely different. Louis Vuitton has a very strong, graphic image. It's a true icon. It is important that it be recognized immediately. As to the Marc Jacobs collections, only initiates can recognize my signature. Moreover, I like it that way. My clients appreciate my clothing because they have the impression that no one knows exactly what they are wearing. For Louis Vuitton, by contrast, the brand has to be very strong, very affirmative. I want to hear people say: "That's the season Louis Vuitton did this or that, the Cleopatra season, the Scottish, the Russian, etc."

And your inspiration for Louis Vuitton—*Belle de Jour*, for example?

You know, I have some rather special ideas about what is French. For example, when I saw the drawings of Kiraz, this treatment of the comic book seemed so French. I thought it was good to do the same with Louis Vuitton—an approach that was a bit flirty, young, and gay, with color and lack of discipline, in the style of Kiraz. But you're right, there were also other sources of inspiration, like *Belle de Jour*. It's an excellent reference, very typical, almost an icon, in a French style that interests me.

The film *Lost in Translation* and Scarlett Johansson touched you.

In this film Scarlett seems a little like the character of Sofia Coppola. Sofia is one of our clients who has always inspired me. In real life Scarlett Johansson is a very glamorous starlet; she likes to be quite made-up. In *Lost in Translation* she plays a role that seems somewhat like the real Sofia Coppola.

"Drawing graffiti on the Monogram was going as far as Duchamp did when he defaced the Mona Lisa."

Opposite: The American artist Stephen Sprouse (left) drew graffiti on the Monogram canvas for a limited-edition bag collection, 2001. Models carrying Monogram Graffiti luggage opened the summer 2001 women's fashion show (right).

Below: Marc Jacobs's artistic reference: Mona Lisa with a mustache (L.H.O.O.Q.), a work by Marcel Duchamp after Leonardo da Vinci, 1919.

With Peter Copping we talked about your campaigns, how well prepared they are, how perfect.

Yes, I like the idea of perfection. Perfection is not something real; it's like a fetish. I even believe there's something perverse about it. (Laughter.) Peter, Jane, the whole team, and I went to see the Alfred Hitchcock exhibition at the Georges Pompidou Center. That greatly inspired us. This was still a way of playing with the ideas. This woman who seemed perfect but who, underneath her cold exterior, is really sexy and passionate.

You directed your first ad campaign for Louis Vuitton in 2000 in New York with Inez Van Lamsweerde and Vinoodh Matadin, right?

I love this campaign, it's really wonderful. With Inez, we're inspired by people who are typically French. There was Colette with a little Jane Birkin mixed in, some glimpses of berets. I also am inspired by *Jill* magazine and the work of Babeth Djian. This campaign is a reflection of everything I got to know in Paris in the 1980s, of all my Parisian memories. Everything I loved is there.

Jennifer Lopez was a new period for Louis Vuitton advertising.

I don't consider it a turning point. This collaboration was just a fun idea. I had already worked with Stephen Sprouse, Julie Verhoeven, and Takashi Murakami, so why not work with a pop star, who also is an actress and sexy. It was amusing to direct Jennifer. I was sure it was a great idea, but I didn't particularly want to inaugurate a new way of doing things in our advertising.

And with Takashi Murakami?

With Takashi it was an intuition; there was no great plan behind it. I had seen his exhibition at the Cartier Foundation. His contemporary style was nice and intriguing, joyful and full of color, and he had an almost fetishistic interest in mangas. This unexpected encounter was a little like "Hello Kitty," the accessories line for jet-set children. Inviting Takashi to work with us pleased me, all the more so because he had a profound respect for our brand. And Louis Vuitton has such a large market in Japan. Takashi adored the idea of redesigning the Monogram. Together we had lots of back-and-forth, drawings, conversations, colors.

You discovered Japan.

Yes. I can't generalize too much, but I have always been well received by people who were very interested by what's happening elsewhere, especially in Tokyo. They have such a passion for fashion that there's even a fantastic fan club. For these people it's very serious. When people are that passionate about what you do, your favorite films, the last book you read, how can you not give them some of your time? They have such a thirst to know everything.

"*The way we work is very constructive, in total respect and healthy disrespect.*"

And your competitors? You worked with Tom Ford.
(Laughter.) I don't have any competitors! I met Tom when I worked at Perry Ellis. There was this collection I had designed, a business style called Portfolio, and a casual line, Perry Ellis America. Tom at that time was a little different from the Tom we know today. He was really fantastic, creative but with a decidedly classical taste. He never lapsed into the vulgar or mediocre. I said to myself that he would be the perfect person to develop the casual line, by adding a touch of sensitivity and class to the line, instead of shapeless jeans and T-shirts. He worked at Perry Ellis for several years—two years, I believe—then he joined Gucci at Dawn Mello's request.

You also met Yves Saint Laurent.
Yes, I had the opportunity. For me it was a dream. You know, Yves Saint Laurent and his vision of the world, the people surrounding him, how he dressed women. It was that magic that inspired my dream of becoming a fashion designer.

Two more questions, about your personal tastes. Food, for example.
I like prepared dishes because they're fast. I love French, Italian, American, Chinese, and Thai food.

What about wine?
No. I no longer drink wine, because I like it too much. So I don't drink it anymore.

In closing, what would you say about your team?
It's great! The first person I met was Peter, who I really liked right away. The way he talks, the things he showed me. . . . I appreciate the references he keeps in his personal album—drawings, pieces of material, photos. I thought he was ingenious. Then I met Jane and Camille, and after that all the others. But at first it was Peter, Jane, and Camille.

And Alfred?
Yes, Alfred, he's my dog. There is also Daisy, my little dog.

By the way, do you speak French?
No, just a little.

Above: The trunk maker's hundred-year-old canvas meets one of contemporary art's leading figures. Takashi Murakami reinterprets the Monogram canvas in his own way, covering it with cherries for summer 2005.

Opposite: "Fairy Tale" handbag, 2002. The English illustrator Julie Verhoeven brings Louis Vuitton into a magical and poetic world of children's stories, with patchwork covering the Monogram Mini canvas.

Above left: The model Colette, photographed by Inez van Lamsweerde and Vinoodh Matadin, in the first ad campaign directed by Marc Jacobs, 2000.

Above right: In the Paris design studio, a photograph of Jennifer Lopez and Marc Jacobs by Mert Alas and Marcus Piggott. Photo of the photo by Marina Faust.

Opposite: Sketch by Marc Jacobs, photographed by Marina Faust.

Following four pages: Eye Love Monogram canvas case, waiting to be unpacked (photo, Marina Faust); magazines, books, and mail on Marc Jacobs's work table unpacked (photo, Marina Faust); Marc Jacobs's Fantasy Dog, a unique Monogram canvas bag on a Damier Sauvage rug unpacked (photo, Marina Faust); Kate Moss wearing the Charm Bracelet, the first piece of jewelry designed by Marc Jacobs (photo, Inez van Lamsweerde and Vinoodh Matadin).

GAS BOOK 13
JULIE VERHOEVEN

Mark Jacobs
Louis Vuitton
2 Rue Du Pont Neus
Paris France 7500/

cover star. **guinevere** photographed by **craig mcdean october 1999**

.80 US$7.50

uplift

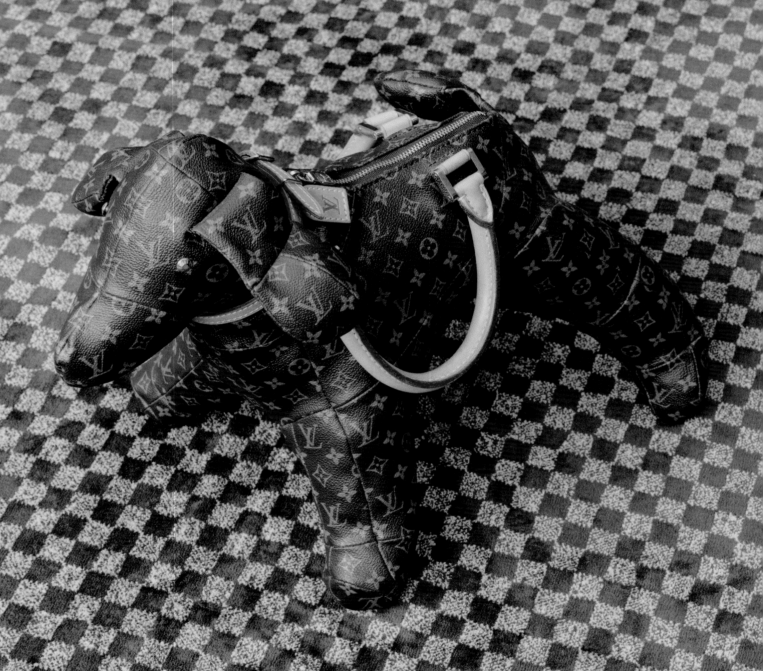

What they say about Marc

What does Marc Jacobs bring to fashion? What has he brought to Louis Vuitton? What about him strikes you the most? Six journalists answer these three questions.

Marc and fashion

ANNA WINTOUR, American *Vogue:* No other American designer has so successfully fused the street style of New York with a reverence for making beautiful fashion. I've long been fascinated by the fact that, for someone who has been portrayed as such an iconoclast, Marc has always loved to use fabrics and techniques that have an almost old-fashioned charm to them. In fact, he almost seems to relish the idea of things being old-fashioned, or frumpy, or clumsy; he manages to find an elegance, even a sexiness, in them. He has a knack of making the conservative seem cool—who would have thought about wearing pleated skirts until he brought them back?—and making the cool seem conservative. Women of all walks of life lust after his chunky-zippered bags. Like the best designers, he has an obsessive eye, an eye that's kept in focus with the help of his close circle of female friends. His relationships with Sofia Coppola, Zoe Cassavetes, Rachel Feinstein, and Elizabeth Peyton are more than just professional associations. His connection with them attunes him to not only their taste and style, but also to the worlds of art, movies, and pop culture.

SUZY MENKES, *International Herald Tribune:* Marc Jacobs is a designer who has caught the vibe of his generation. He is fascinated with his own era, especially the 1970s, and he was one of the first designers to understand the power of "vintage" dressing. For both his Marc Jacobs and Marc collections, he takes pieces from the past but remakes them and mixes them in a modern way.

BABETH DJIAN, *Numéro:* Marc reconciled New York cool and Parisian chic. Season after season he successfully meets the challenge to offer a fashion that goes directly from the runway to the street, without ever sacrificing the part about the dream.

JANIE SAMET, *Le Figaro:* From the first hand-knit stitch in 1984 to the last ultrasophisticated fashion show, Marc Jacobs has in twenty years seriously stirred up the mysteries of international fashion. Craftsman of an opulent, insolent pragmatism and of a fusion—which succeeds because it does not shock—of casual, the street, and glamour, whose radical components he knows how to analyze. He has become a driving force of New York design under European influence.

ALICE MORGAINE, former editor-in-chief, *Jardin des Modes:* Bill Blass, Geoffrey Beene, Donna Karan, Calvin Klein . . . American fashion had barely started to exist beyond sportswear when Marc Jacobs came on the scene in New York. Very young, he had already assimilated the history of fashion. He is teeming with audacity. At Carla Sozzani's, at Corso Como 10 in Milan, he presented, in silence and in person, simple clothes with this something more that defines his fresh, free, new vocabulary.

PIERRE LÉONFORTÉ, *Les Échos:* A certain wildly sophisticated innocence. The insolence of luxury but updated. Woman according to Marc is a Lolita who plays with her own style, makes her own rules, who has the charm of childhood and the refinement of maturity: tuxedos, puff sleeves, English embroidery, luscious cocktails, nursery rhymes, and stolen kisses from a fragile and dangerous little girl.

Marc and Louis Vuitton

ANNA WINTOUR: Marc has brought a truly modern sense of luxury to Louis Vuitton. He understands the way that women (and men) want to live now, which means that he understands that they want their luxury to look a little humorous, or not too flashy, or even, occasionally, to be completely over the top. He divined that Louis Vuitton's future wasn't going to be in steamer trunks, wonderful though they are, but in quirky, intriguing accessories

Opposite: Marc Jacobs, in a polar bear costume, with Sofia Coppola during a Christmas reception at New York's Rainbow Room, 2003.

Below: Marc Jacobs and Catherine Deneuve—an encounter of New York cool and Paris chic.

that can be used every day. What's really striking is the way he has invented a new inventory of classics of the House, especially in the collaborative reworkings of the iconic Monogram print by the late Stephen Sprouse or Takashi Murakami. But, in a way, I think the question should also be, "What has Louis Vuitton given him?" That Marc got the chance to work in Paris, to put together his Vuitton ateliers, to be able to immerse himself in a new country and new culture—all of this has had a profound effect on his work. His experience in Paris has made him push himself harder and harder. When I look at his Vuitton collections for 2004, I see a designer at the peak of his creative powers.

Suzy Menkes: For Louis Vuitton, he has had to invent a clothing image. He has brought a youthful, almost childlike, sense of sweetness to luxury products, especially for his collaborations with Stephen Sprouse on the graffiti bags and with Takashi Murakami for the colorful prints.

BABETH DJIAN: At Vuitton Marc is not content just to give legitimacy to a style born from a travel bag: He has made an empire of it. He reinvented the Monogram on candy pink patent leather, with Stephen Sprouse's graffiti, and Murakami's mangas. The bubbling synergies at Vuitton between the different collections for women and men have made it a unique and exemplary model.

JANIE SAMET: Marc Jacobs has transformed in a few seasons a venerable company purring about its pedigree like a prized, fat, purebred cat into a kind of urban wildcat that can run in the streets just as well as in palaces—design with aplomb. Visibly freed of constraints and knowing how to balance his acceleration effects, he has since 1997 propelled Louis Vuitton to the rank of a creative, trend-setting, and universal brand. Toying with and foiling the usual rules, he has worked mainly at a mischievous and lucrative redeployment of the brand's identifying details and spearheaded communications that are tied to

Above, top: Camille Miceli is responsible for Marc Jacobs's personal communications, Louis Vuitton's fashion shows, and the design of accessories and jewelry.

Above, bottom: Pharell Williams, the American hip-hop artist, collaborated with Marc Jacobs to create a collection of sunglasses for Louis Vuitton's summer 2005 fashion show.

Opposite: Marc Jacobs and Kate Moss—half angel, half devil.

big Hollywood studio campaigns. This effervescent dramatization of stars with offbeat looks, like Christina Ricci or Scarlett Johansson, is part of the determination to make Louis Vuitton a superstar of uncompromising chic.

ALICE MORGAINE: Marc Jacobs had a dream. Vuitton fulfilled it. By hiring him and giving him the freedom to play with the logo and with the long-established image, the trunk maker asserted itself as a fashion brand.

PIERRE LÉONFORTÉ: The brand is historic. It was necessary to emerge from the history and tease the old woman so the name could become the number one desire of a young generation that doesn't have memories, only wants. The facelift succeeded beyond all hopes for a brand that is blowing out its 150 birthday candles today with a burst of laughter and charm. Especially gifted in accessories, Marc Jacobs has made a mythic piece of luggage the starting point for fashion, whether bags, crazy shoes, plaids, muslins or English embroidery, "sweet" suits, golden leathers, tuxedo blouses, or puffy sleeves. And, thanks to him, the Vuitton canvas has become a permanent spectacle and a treasure hunt for its fans.

What is striking about Marc

ANNA WINTOUR: Perhaps the most striking thing about Marc is that he hasn't changed at all. It seems hard to believe, but I've known him as long as he has been designing. Despite all of the setbacks and challenges that he has faced along the way, he's still as enthusiastic and as passionate about fashion as he was when he started. He has also resisted playing the role of the star designer. There are none of today's trappings of fame: no bodyguards, no limousines, no personal trainers. Perhaps the most telling illustration of this was when Marc and I sat together at a recent dinner thrown by Parsons School of Design to honor him. It was touching to see him looking so blown away by the attention of the school's students, who do see him as a star. The reason for his attitude is, I think, that there will always be a part of Marc that's the Manhattan kid who worked after school at Charivari and dreamed of making the best clothes in the world.

SUZY MENKES: Although the image sometimes seems to stray far from Vuitton's travel roots, the fairy tale element in embroidered white leather boots or the recent Scottish castle inspiration give the collections a unique image.

BABETH DJIAN: Marc knows where he's going. He already presented the bohemian coolness of downtown Manhattan with his grunge collection for Perry Ellis. And if today's SoHo no longer resembles the SoHo of fifteen years ago, Marc's style—changeable, elusive from one season to the next—has never stopped accompanying change. Always in step with the times, Marc is very smart.

JANIE SAMET: I love his "inconspicuous" side. He reminds me of a kind of Irving Thalberg, the famous MGM producer who looked like a lawyer and built a cinematic miniempire from prestige, glamour, image, and marketing ploys. Marc Jacobs could have come from the same world.

ALICE MORGAINE: It's less well known that Marc Jacobs excels in the shoe category. With a rounded toe, fine and light, and the sole sometimes including the heel, his shoes are recognizable among a thousand others.

PIERRE LÉONFORTÉ: What strikes me is his modern romanticism, his way of playing with sportswear, glamour, and the sexy clean without falling into the obvious. He is in love with fashion, and it is this that makes him happy. What stays with me is his youth and his capacity to adapt. A multifaceted couturier, he changes styles like changing a shirt. Every season, every collection, is another surprise. So the press and the customers await with great expectations. It never looks the same, and his work is full of fun. This way he has of being both an American from Paris and a Parisian from New York really endears him to us. He is always at home, whether in Tokyo, London, Hong Kong, or Sydney. He's international.

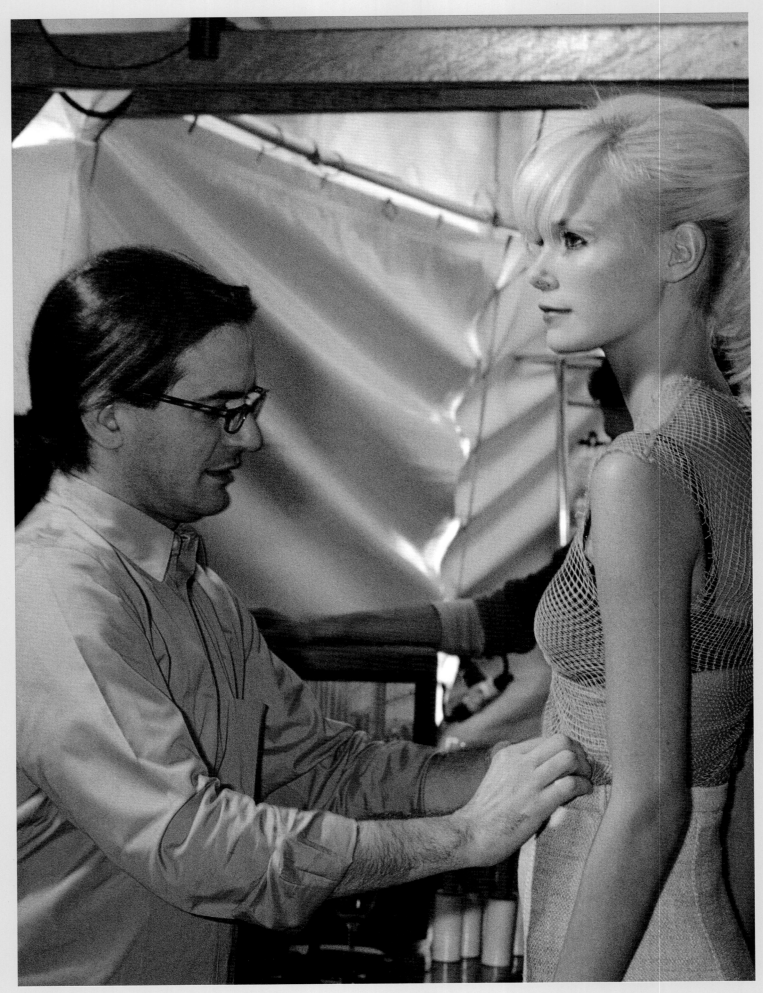

Spring/Summer 2003

On the runways

Spring/Summer 2005

Spring/Summer 2005

Spring/Summer 2000

Spring/Summer 2001

Spring/Summer 2000

Fall/Winter 2000–2001

Fall/Winter 2003–4

Spring/Summer 2004

Spring/Summer 2003

Spring/Summer 2003

Fall/Winter 2004–5

At the ready-to-wear studio

Each season has its fashion show. And each collection has its inspiration.

At the ready-to-wear studio, a small, very involved team works intensely

alongside Marc Jacobs.

Observe, listen, read, feel, capture what's happening now: All design starts by this process of absorption. Marc Jacobs and his designers are constantly on the lookout for new ideas, drawing inspiration from everything. From the Paris flea markets to London libraries, from stores in Tokyo to Hollywood movies, their research leads them on a sensory quest across the globe. Jane Whitfield and Peter Copping have worked with Marc Jacobs on women's collections from the start. "The creative process can change from one season to the next," Copping said. "We retrace our steps and rummage through an idea until it finds its place in a collection. One day it's the paintings of James Tissot or Scottish romanticism that inspire us. The next day it's the gold of ancient Egypt or the vibrant colors of the circus. We mix our strokes of inspiration to obtain the spirit that we want to give to the collection." The company's heritage of course remains a source of inspiration. It is a legacy full of ideas just waiting to be brought up to date.

Simultaneously, the team researches fabrics and materials, which leave a firm imprint on the ready-to-wear lines. Marc Jacobs likes to play with unexpected combinations. Gauzy pleats and gold-plated ostrich skin, silk velvet and shaved mink, sequined embroidery and printed satin—the inexhaustible range of materials brings out the designer's creative impulses. In their ephemeral union, luxury takes on the aspects of the quotidian; silk, organza, taffeta, and cashmere blend their nobility with cotton and linen's natural simplicity.

The actual design process extends over an extremely intense, brief period, a month at most, which to the entire staff feels like a marathon. "Working under emergency conditions serves us well," Copping said. "There is a kind of energy that circulates among us." Marc Jacobs prepares a collection with sketches, annotating his drawings with explanations about the inspiration, materials, or construction details. The silhouettes are designed, adjusted, expanded upon, and then brought to the dressmaking and tailoring workshops. The first fittings on models provide another occasion to modify the contours, the choice of fabric, the details of a button. The days wind down and the excitement mounts until the very last moment, just before the fashion show. On the runway fifty models set the season's tone. Another story begins. But the customer still has to wait four months before she can wear her dream clothes.

Clockwise from left: Peter Copping, studio manager, works with Marc Jacobs on women's ready-to wear; Jane Whitfield, style manager; Louison Martin, tailoring workshop supervisor; Françoise Poirier, dressmaking workshop supervisor; Nicolas Lepoutre, materials research coordinator. Photos by Marina Faust.

Peter Copping discusses the collections

Fall/Winter 1998–99
I don't really know how to describe the first show. Marc has spoken about it a lot because it was heavily criticized. The clothes were rather minimalist and at the same time luxurious, with beautiful fabrics and lovely details. To be completely honest, I don't think I would have done the first show the way it was done. I would have imagined a sexier woman, a little crazier, also a little more French.

Spring/Summer 1999
I joined the team with the second show. I think it was a little wilder. It was inspired by the drawings of the French illustrator Kiraz. The Louis Vuitton woman became international but retained certain typically French characteristics. In this show the outfits were really enhanced by models like Colette or Caroline Martin.

Fall/Winter 1999–2000
This collection created a certain freedom and heralded what the Louis Vuitton woman would become. We worked a lot with skunk. Many of the details attracted attention and the impact was felt all the way to the street. The look I prefer is not necessarily the strongest one, but I adore Laura MacDaniels in this outfit. I think it's supercool. I really like the graphic side, the red leather boots and the black skirt.

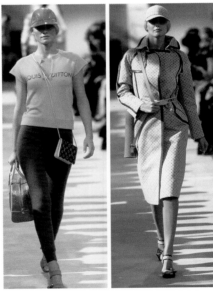

Spring/Summer 2000
This collection launched our first work on the logo. We created the Monogram Mini, used on the bags and the clothes, in lovely color combinations. Other brands have followed us since then. After this fashion show, they were even inspired by some of our ideas to design new clothes. I really like the look Gisèle wears, her small Monogram Perlé bag, her yellow T-shirt playing off the colors of the Monogram canvas.

Fall/Winter 2000–2001
Here we studied the clothes of the eighties, when Marc was often in Paris. At that time there was a magazine called *Jill*. Marc was able to buy a few issues. We were inspired by them, as well as by all the eighties culture. It was the first time we worked on more ample silhouettes. Marc saw it as somewhat of a challenge because he was used to very fitted styles, so he had to work keeping the effects of volume in mind.

Spring/Summer 2001
Stephen Sprouse was there every day for a month and became a team member in his own right. I like the ensemble where Stephen drew graffiti by hand on long white gloves. He also designed a print for a little tank top. When you look closely, there are roses, but they're worked into camouflage colors. We wanted to give a feminine aspect to the combat theme.

Fall/Winter 2001–2
Russia inspired us for this collection. The men with their black fur hats and their boots, a little like Cossacks. We added sunglasses and briefcases for a touch of mystery, like a fashion spy who came out of the cold. We tinted the furs very slightly with blue. I rather like this little blouse with its fur buttons.

Spring/Summer 2002
This is a slightly bohemian collection. For the bags we collaborated with Julie Verhoeven. Her designs evoke children's stories. It was after the events of September 11. Marc was in New York then. In one sense this collection showed its adaptability to the situation, because it was romantic and not aggressive. It was very moving for people. Maybe they needed gentleness at that moment. Personally, I really like this embroidered lambskin.

Fall/Winter 2002–3
This collection was inspired by Hitchcock. We played with the idea of this very chic but cold Hitchcockian woman and we associated it with sports clothes, leather, and motorcycle pants. We also made parkas. The spirit of sports clothes mixed with a certain Hollywood chic.

Spring/Summer 2003
Takashi Murakami gave color and mischief to the Monogram. After having seen his exhibition at the Fondation Cartier, Marc thought it would be interesting to work with him. The historic Monogram is two-tone, and we wanted to carry that idea through in a few dresses and in a variety of colors. It's a very feminine collection, inspired by the fifties. This ensemble is one of my favorites. The silhouette evokes the fifties but the skirt is made of latex. We worked in London with manufacturers of fetishistic clothes.

Fall/Winter 2003–4
It's a bit of a sixties theme we worked with here. With the idea of a very self-possessed woman, somewhat in the image of Joan of Arc. We were also inspired by medieval armor, like for this breastplate embellished with plastic bubbles. We added the cashmere jackets. Everything is interpreted in a very sixties way, with a geometric cut.

Spring/Summer 2004
This is a very glamorous collection inspired by the Hollywood megaproductions of the fifties. I'm thinking in particular of *Cleopatra*. Gold is omnipresent and on different materials—a gold-plated ostrich skin coat or a panne velvet sweater. The fabrics wind around the body in very ancient constructions. We added a yachting touch, with figures in navy blue and white.

Fall/Winter 2004–5
For this Scottish collection we worked a lot with plaids in many different materials and constructions. I rather like this unusual mix of Scottish romanticism sprinkled with a touch of rock. James Tissot's paintings also inspired us; he captured the elegance of the women of his times so well, with their jabots and their wide-brimmed hats.

Spring/Summer 2005
We wanted to create a joyous and festive collection in the image of the circus. The colored prints take on something of the forties spirit, with a very light tone. Ballerina skirts are worn with small tops fitted with puff sleeves. Marc called on Takashi Murakami once again, who drew cheerful cherries on the Monogram canvas. It's like a wish for springtime.

Opposite: The models' final parade.

ADVERTISING

The evolution of the image

Is it because Louis Vuitton has been surprising the world since 1854 that its image remains so unique? Its image, born as the "Spirit of Travel," modernized with the "Toys" campaign, diversified with the launch of ready-to-wear and shoes, has never stopped evolving. Its essential stylistic components—sophistication, vaunted elitism, and impertinence—remain its exclusive domain.

Through the 1980s the "Spirit of Travel" campaigns nourished the company's image by focusing on its legendary identity. Exotic landscapes and traditional rigid luggage recalled the golden age of aristocratic travel and put Louis Vuitton on a pedestal, like a temple on a mountaintop. In the early 1990s it became apparent that the brand needed greater accessibility and warmth. Jean-Marc Loubier, then the director of marketing and communications, gave the Euro RSCG agency its first instructions: "Up until now Louis Vuitton has based its communications on its identity. Now the company's story must be told through its products." From this challenge was born a surprising campaign in which Jean Larivière played with scale and proportion, photographing classic toys together with Vuitton products. The images winked at travel with a wit that was right on target. From that point on, Louis Vuitton wanted the creativity of its advertising to surprise, without sacrificing any of its identity.

The centennial of the Monogram, in 1996, presented another opportunity to reinforce the company's impertinent imprint, with new products and new advertising. A year later the Dutch photographers Inez van Lamsweerde and Vinoodh Matadin spearheaded a remarkable campaign that added a dose of visual shock to Louis Vuitton's communications. Models made up with Monogram eye masks bit into pens designed by Anouska Hempel. An experienced team was behind the scenes, with Vuitton's Jean-Marc Loubier and Isabelle des Garets and the agency's Paul-Gérard Pasols and Maurice Betite, art director. Other successful campaigns followed. The photographer Bruno Dayan colorfully interpreted the seven deadly sins to launch Monogram Vernis leather. For the first shoe campaign Hervé Haddad made a series of images so provocative that some people, like Maurice Betite, called them "porno chic." Some of the ads even had to be pulled from magazines. But the campaign's impact was considerable.

In 2000 Marc Jacobs supervised the art direction of his first campaign for ready-to-wear, a black-and-white photographic puzzle. Since then the designer has been involved in helping Louis Vuitton reinforce its stature as a luxury and fashion brand. The campaigns follow the rhythm of collections and represent the diverse product range, including leather goods, ready-to-wear, shoes, watches, and jewelry. Sophisticated images incorporate the season's spirit and express the different fashion show themes. The "Fairy Tale" campaign revisited the stories of Snow White and Cinderella and inaugurated a fruitful collaboration between Marc Jacobs and the British photographers Mert Alas and Marcus Piggott. In 2003, in the cold heart of winter, Eva Herzigova incarnated a Hitchcockian heroine, directing an anxious look to the sky or hurrying to cross a snow-covered railroad track. Jennifer Lopez, Kate Moss, Scarlett Johansson, Diane Kruger, and Uma Thurman have all embodied the Louis Vuitton woman: desirable, elusive, changeable, and elegant, according to fashion and season.

Previous page: Stephanie Seymour, photographed by Inez van Lamsweerde and Vinoodh Matadin in 1997, for the launch of Doc and Cargo pens. The "Writing" campaign made a strong impression and remains one of the most emblematic Louis Vuitton campaigns.

Right: The "Rapetout" motorcycle, photographed by Jean Larivière for the "Louis Vuitton Imaginary Voyages" 1994 ad campaign. On the passenger's shoulder is an Epi leather bag in Tassili yellow.

The "Centennial Designers" campaign, photographed by Les Guzman, 1996. Travel bag in Monogram canvas designed by Manolo Blahnik.

The Monogram Vernis's "Seven Deadly Sins" campaign, by Bruno Dayan, 1998. Allegories of Gluttony and Jealousy.

Epi leather campaign, by Raymond Meyer, 1999.

Previous pages, above, and opposite: Shoe campaign by Hervé Haddad, 2000.

Above: The "Fairy Tale" campaign, by Mert Alas and Marcus Piggott, Spring/Summer 2002.

Following pages: Charm Bracelet campaign, with Kate Moss photographed by Inez van Lamsweerde and Vinoodh Matadin, 2002.

Above and opposite: Fall/Winter campaign 2002–3. Eva Herzigova, photographed by Mert Alas and Marcus Piggott.

Following pages: Fall/Winter campaign 2003–4. Jennifer Lopez, photographed by Mert Alas and Marcus Piggott.

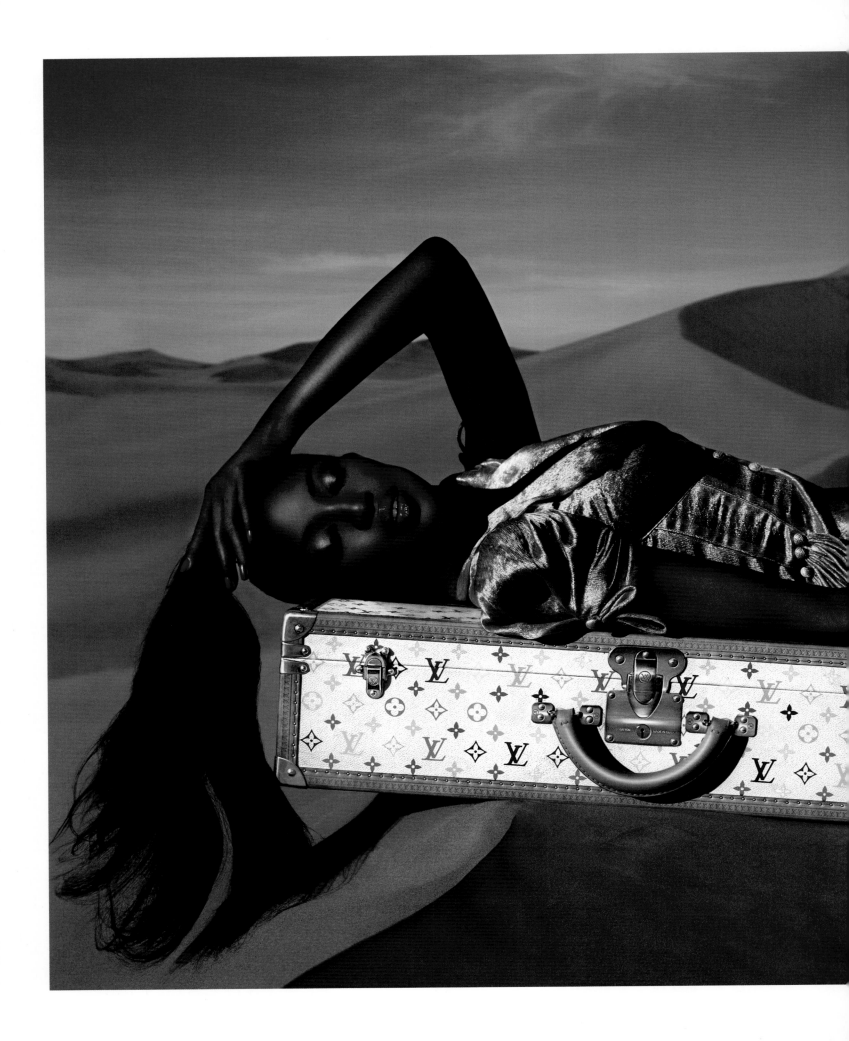

Spring/Summer 2004 campaign. Naomi Campbell, photographed by Mert Alas and Marcus Piggott.

Emprise jewelry campaign. Natasha Poly, photographed by Inez van Lamsweerde and Vinoodh Matadin, 2004.

Above, clockwise from top left: Private discussion between Marc Jacobs and Peter Copping, with Françoise Poirier, workshop supervisor, nearby; actress Christina Ricci relaxes during a break with a friend and her daughter; waiting for shots in a corridor; waiting in the parking lot.

Opposite: Marc Jacobs supervising campaign shots at Royal Park Studio, just outside London.

Fall/Winter 2004–5 campaign. Christina Ricci and Hayden Christensen, photographed by Mert Alas and Marcus Piggott.

Following pages: Spring/Summer 2005 campaign. Uma Thurman, photographed by Mert Alas and Marcus Piggott.

ARCHITECTURE

Stores and architectural creativity

At a time when the biggest fashion houses were calling on great architects, Louis Vuitton distinguished itself by "positive excess." In number, size, and style its new stores constituted a true body of architectural creativity.

Among the various expressions of the Louis Vuitton spirit, architecture occupies a special place—and a historic place, with an architectural tradition cultivated since 1914. That was the year Louis Vuitton unveiled its building on 70 Avenue des Champs-Élysées, an Art Nouveau masterpiece. The company has always held strong attachment to the places and buildings that have grown with it, particularly the most symbolic one: the Asnières workshops, built in 1859. And today the company's architecture collectively constitutes the brand's most prestigious showcase. Up until 1998 the stores were small and exclusively sold travel articles and leather goods. With the introduction and commercial success of ready-to-wear, shoes, watches, and jewelry, the retail inventory dramatically expanded, making it necessary to completely rethink the stores' size and organization. In the first years of the twenty-first century the world witnessed the birth of Louis Vuitton's "global" stores—new temples dedicated to the brand—and the dawn of an architecture specific to the company.

Light and open. The first store of this new era was built in 1999 in Nagoya, Japan. Larger, more airy, lighter, and more vibrant, it prefigured the company's next architectural iterations. As David McNulty, head of Louis Vuitton's architecture department, explained, "The challenge is to optimize every square foot while maintaining the right balance between the full presentation of every product line, the furnishings, and the customer's well-being. Our ultimate goal is to make stores that are not stores—public places open to the world, to the city, where visitors feel a range of sensations but never that they are in a large store."

Previous page: In 2003 Louis Vuitton opened an unprecedented store in the new Roppongi Hills district of Tokyo. Its facade of glass tubes seems like a mirage. The architecture enlivens the whole district with the pleasures of fashion.

Above: The store in Nagoya Sakae, Japan, built in 1999, introduced a completely new approach to architecture for the display and sale of Louis Vuitton products.

Opposite: Five years later the forty-ninth Louis Vuitton "global" store opened on the corner of 57th Street and Fifth Avenue in New York. A symbol of the brand's power, it presents all the company's product lines in more than 12,900 square feet on four floors.

Opposite: With its split levels connected by a huge stairway that runs the full height of a luminous wall, the interior architecture of the Louis Vuitton store on New York's Fifth Avenue emphasizes light and fluidity.

Above: The Louis Vuitton store in Roppongi Hills, Tokyo, encapsulates the idea of transparency. The building's interior is completely covered with a second skin that echoes the lining of Vuitton's legendary trunks.

It's an exciting paradox, especially because the stores' surface area is continuously expanding. When the Louis Vuitton "global" store opened in New York at the corner of Fifth Avenue and 57th Street in 2004, it was the largest in the world, with 12,917 square feet on four floors. The following year it lost the title to the store on the Champs-Élysées.

A Louis Vuitton style. Despite the stores' growing size, the goal was to give customers the illusion of traveling seamlessly through an inviting, multifaceted universe. To that end, the architects of each project were deeply committed to rethinking several essential components of the stores' architecture: the facade, the interior spaces, and the systematic exploitation of the brand.

In Nagoya, for example, they covered the store with a double envelope, giving the exterior a mysterious moiré effect. In fact, it is difficult to discuss the "exterior" when the distinction between outside and inside is so blurred, so elusive to the eye. From one store to the next, the facades are continuously being refined, implementing increasingly sophisticated techniques of metal weaving. As David McNulty explained, "The trend is to conceive the facades as mysterious, moving works of art in their own right. We try to enhance the transparency, the fuzziness, and the play of optics by taking our inspiration from pop art or kinetics." Perhaps there is an analogy between Louis Vuitton's architecture and its fashion, between building materials and clothing fabric.

At the same time, important work has been done on the stores' interiors and spatial organization. The store in Tokyo's Omote-Sando neighborhood resembles a stack of

glass trunks. The architect seems to have crossed time and space to extrapolate from the company's historic trunks their very essence, then rendered it in three dimensions. By segmenting a vast space into smaller interconnected spaces (much as Vuitton's large trunks were organized into distinct sections), he invited the visitor to discover private corners within a great universe and to circulate fluidly among the store's different levels, without encountering boundaries.

The other key element of the stores' architectural style is the omnipresence of the company's graphic codes. The founder's initials and the Monogram and Damier patterns are everywhere—on the facade and the interior walls, and in the windows. But they are more than simple decorative motifs: The architect subtly exploited the letters, diamond shapes, diamonds in squares, and encircled four-petal flowers as structural elements of the interior design and the architecture itself.

An architectural work in progress. Most of the fifty to sixty construction projects Louis Vuitton undertakes every year involve the renovation of existing stores. Only five to ten are entirely new developments. However, David McNulty pointed out, "Generally, a renovation leads us to rethink a store from A to Z. On the Champs-Élysées, for example, everything was gutted to gain more floor space, creating the equivalent of a store with four stories. And the reorganization of the entrance from Avenue Georges V was important work." The architecture department frequently calls on outside architects for these projects, with a determination to merge cultures by forming international teams. "The com-

The Omote-Sando store in Tokyo (opposite) was Vuitton's forty-fourth location in Japan. Designed by the architect Jun Aoki, it presents wide-open interior spaces like the VIP Room (above), where items for special order are displayed in miniature. The store design allows visitors to pass freely from one floor to another, sometimes without even realizing it, and is meant to distract, surprise, and continuously charm.

Louis Vuitton's omnipresent coat of arms comes in infinite variety. Each component can be used as a decorative graphic element, like the Monogram flower behind the curtain of metal beads in the Kobe Kyoryuchi store (above). Or it can be used as a structural architectural element, as in the Roppongi Hills store in Tokyo (opposite top). Without the motif, the style is more staid, as in the women's shoe department (opposite bottom) in the store at 22 Avenue Montaigne in Paris, designed in 2003 by the American architect Peter Marino.

pany builds stores that bear the signature of Louis Vuitton and not that of the architect," McNulty said. "That is why we prefer to work with young architects on their way up, rather than with established stars." They have included Jun Aoki, an associate of the American architect Peter Marino, who worked on the Fifth Avenue building in New York, Kengo Kuma, Philippe Barthélémy and Sylvia Grino, Kumiko Inui, and Aurelio Clementi. From one project to the next the architects constantly push the technology further, together creating a diversified body of architectural work that clearly carries the Louis Vuitton label.

Transformation of city centers. The opening or reopening of a store is always a major event for the company, and also for many of the local residents. While work is under way, the construction is disguised by huge enclosures resembling giant trunks (like those used during the renovation of the Champs-Élysées store), which draw attention and generate traffic. And—as demonstrated by the excitement that prevails day and night at the store

Above: The store exteriors, like the one in Kobe Kyoryuchi, Japan, are vigorously reinterpreting Louis Vuitton's historic patterns.

Opposite: The stores' interior design harmoniously combines the modern with the vaunted past. In the store at Ginza 1 Namikidori in Tokyo, trunks that seem to have traveled through time are suspended, as though weightless, across the wall's full height.

in Roppongi Hills, Tokyo—Louis Vuitton needs only to move into a district to bring it to life. It transforms the area by attracting other luxury brands as well as large crowds, for whom the store becomes a gathering place as practical as it is prized.

The company's headquarters in Paris has had a similar impact on its surroundings. It occupies the former La Belle Jardinière department store on Rue du Pont-Neuf. The building renovation was entrusted to a Parisian architect, Jean-Jacques Ory, who was also responsible for the LVMH Group headquarters on Avenue Montaigne, and the Ory-Gomez Agency designed the interiors. The headquarters have a more austere appearance than the stores, but only from outside. Pass through an immense twenty-six-foot-high wooden door and find offices that are both functional and lively, characterized by both serenity and creativity. By bringing together at this location teams that were formerly dispersed, and by installing several of the group's other brands in neighboring buildings, Louis Vuitton has transformed the historic district. And by giving it a new energy, Vuitton has given it back a soul.

Louis Vuitton stores become landmarks, meeting places, and addresses that can't be ignored. They fascinate even during renovations, as was the case at the Ginza store in Japan (above), artfully camouflaged by Takashi Murakami.

Opposite: The finished product.

A new generation of workshop

In 2004 Louis Vuitton had thirteen leather goods workshops—ten in France, two in Spain, and one in the United States. Though each has its own personality, they all share several attributes.

To provide the staff with optimum working conditions, the workshop's location is of primary importance. For that reason the company has since 1997 located its buildings exclusively in country settings, away from congested areas. The only workshop in an urban setting is Louis Vuitton's historic workshop in Asnières-sur-Seine. To preserve a true artisanal spirit, each workshop is designed for a maximum of twenty-five people. If the work force expands beyond that threshold, the company builds an independent workshop nearby, with its own storage warehouse, employee lounge, administrative offices, and company restaurant. In terms of architecture, each building is designed to meet the needs of a skilled, precise manufacturing process. There are always skylights to capture and diffuse natural northern light. The number of each structure's load-bearing columns is limited, so that machines can easily be moved according to production needs. Aesthetically, all the factories reflect an interest in integrating the structure with the landscape.

The Ducey I workshop (above left) in La Manche, France, occupies a 43,000-square-foot space in the middle of a copse. Two walls of glass and two domed skylights flood the interior with natural light. The company restaurant, on the second floor, offers panoramic views of Mont-Saint-Michel (above right), 7.5 miles to the west.

Opposite: The Asnières workshop, built in 1859, was Louis Vuitton's first factory. The property has been redeveloped and enlarged several times since 1993. Architect Gilles Carnoy modernized the interiors while retaining the traditional architecture and its integration with the surrounding town. The expansions were inspired by late-nineteenth-century shapes and techniques, like riveted steel beams and brick.

Following pages: A lightwell passes through each story of the Asnières workshop, allowing natural light to penetrate the entire building. One of the walls is adorned with a backlit metal mesh whose lines evoke the Damier canvas.

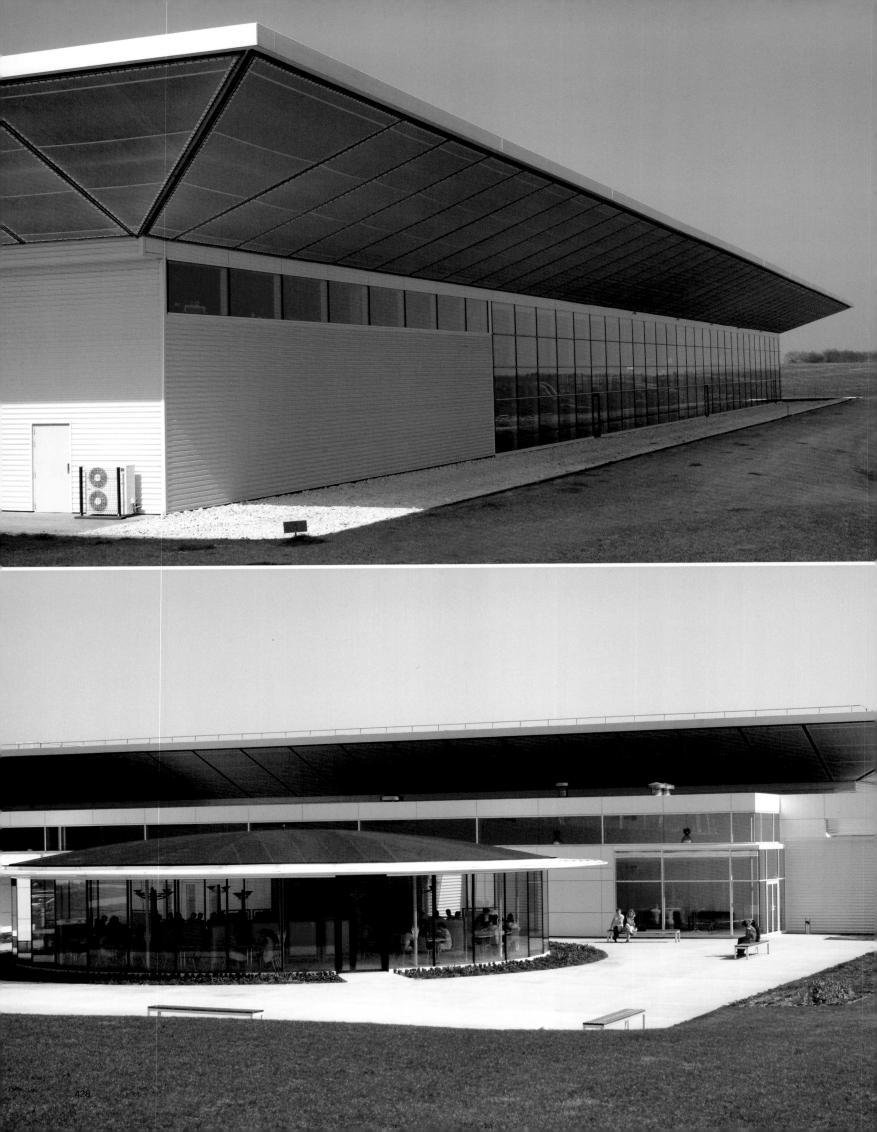

Opposite (top and bottom): In the Indre department of France, the Condé manufacturing workshop was designed along horizontal lines to blend into the surrounding agricultural plains. Transparent walls and a wide overhanging roof give the impression that the building is very light.

Above: In Sainte-Florence, in the Vendée region of France, northern light streams into the workshop. Four skylights shaped like upside-down canoes support the roof (top). This architectural solution made it possible to eliminate supporting columns and free up the workshop's wide interior. The south facade, made entirely of glass and shaded by aluminum screens, is enhanced by two gardens of Japanese inspiration (bottom).

KNOW-HOW

Continuously renewed skills

All expertise develops over time. From the earliest days of Louis Vuitton, trunk makers, saddlers, and leather goods artisans in the company's workshops have polished their precision skills through patient repetition and refinement. Couturiers, shoemakers, watchmakers, jewelers, and other artisans have since joined them to perpetuate the same commitment to fine quality that is the company's heritage.

Asnières, the cradle. The Asnières workshop is the pinnacle of Louis Vuitton's noble trunk-making tradition. Since 1859, when the factory opened just outside Paris, attention to the smallest detail, love of beautiful workmanship, and great pride in the work have reigned supreme. Although the workshops have grown and been modernized over the years, little has really changed. The work is completed at the same pace as ever, and the tools of the trade are not very different from the ones used in the nineteenth century. Asnières, the heart of the Louis Vuitton legend, gave birth to the astonishing trunks of the last century and to custom-made luggage of limitless beauty. Louis Vuitton prides itself in maintaining the tradition of creating luxury goods that serve the art of travel.

For 150 years three traditional crafts have been practiced within the walls of Asnières. Trunk makers, saddlers, and leather goods artisans share a dedication to making the perfect object. They have passed down, from one generation's hands to the next, the patient techniques of woodworking, the gentle handling of leather, the precise hammering of brass. The trunk makers know every step in the process of manufacturing a trunk or a piece of rigid luggage. First of all, they use beech or poplar for the woodwork. Poplar is a soft, solid, and light wood that grows not far from the workshops, in the Oise valley. It is used for the trunk's framework. Beech is used for the exterior slats, to protect the trunk from the shocks of travel. The trunk maker's signature is the hinge in cotton canvas, a cotton rib that distributes the pressure over the entire length of the suitcase better than a metal hinge could. It enables the luggage to open perfectly and offers unparalleled solidity. The craftsman signs each cotton rib, a quality control mark that is quickly covered with canvas or leather. The trunk maker also serves as a case maker, finishing the interior with drawers, frame, and compartments. Ironwork and locksmithing are among the other skills he masters.

The work done at the saddler's workbench has scarcely changed over the long years, either. Leather articles are distinguished by clean-cut hand-sewn edges, the result of a particular technique of saddle stitching. The craftsman slides a beeswax-covered linen thread through the eyes of two needles, one at each end, and has always used a round or triangular boxwood-handled awl to pierce the leather. The saddler uses a trimming knife to thin the edges and keeps the sewing clippers near at hand. These techniques are used to create most of Vuitton's handbags, wallets, change purses, and other supple leather articles. The leather goods artisan cuts and thins the leather to assemble each part of the bag. Each craftsman guarantees the quality of work at each step, which guarantees the product's perfect finish.

The passion for custom orders. Louis Vuitton's great tradition of special orders continues at Asnières to this day, watched over by Patrick-Louis Vuitton, who represents the family's fifth generation in the business. "For my great-grandfather, Georges Vuitton, it was essential that the customer's belongings travel in the greatest comfort," he said. The company has always offered its customers the opportunity to create the travel article of their dreams. From toiletry set to shoe trunk, flute case, jewelry box, travel library, and

Previous page: Cutting a shoe upper from Damier Sauvage in one piece with a scalpel. Photo by Antoine Rozès.

Below and opposite: The historic Asnières workshop outside Paris has manufactured trunks and traditional hard-sided luggage since 1859.

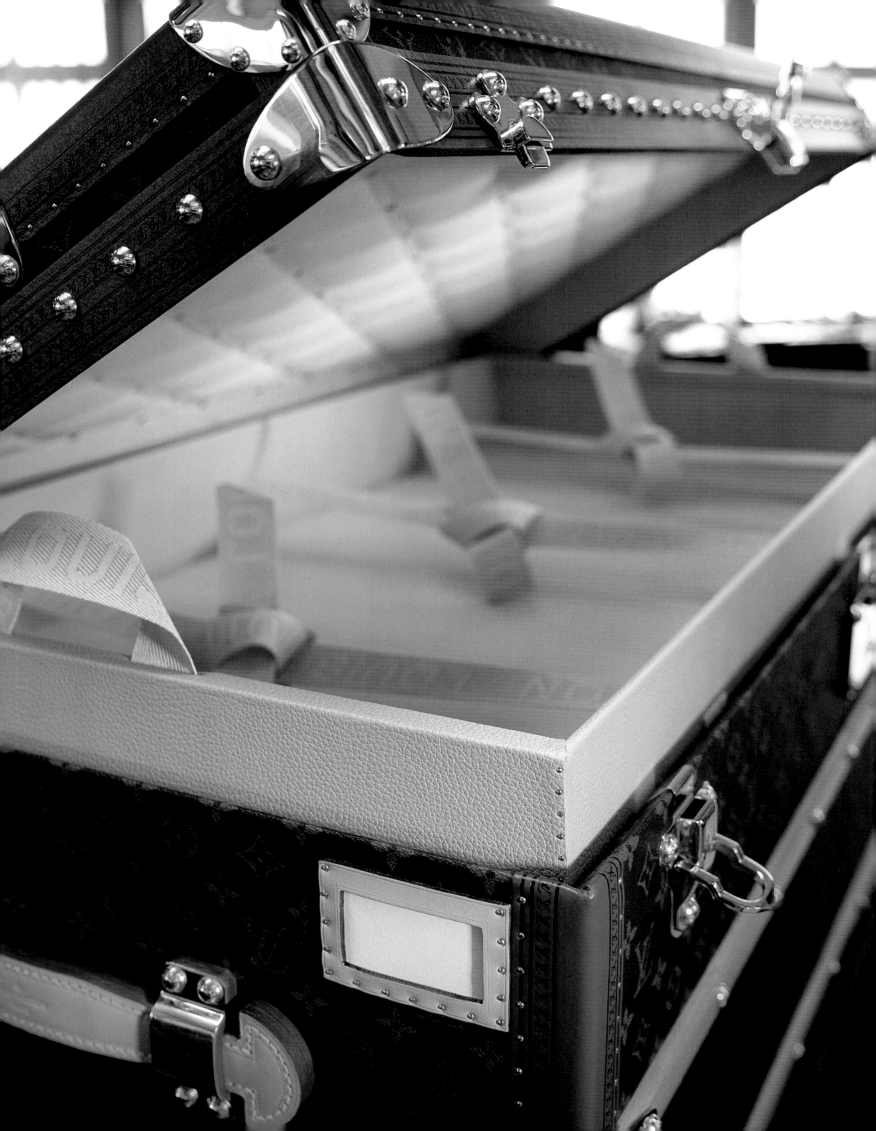

Opposite: A sample of Monogram canvas and the monogrammed plate used to emboss it.

Above right: The Ducey workshop, in the heart of Normandy, is the newest facility devoted to leather.

computer case, more than two hundred curiosities are specially produced each year in this highly precise laboratory, where time seems to have stood still. The manufacture of special orders draws on Vuitton's unrivaled know-how and 150 years of experience. There is only one limitation to customers' wishes: All the items manufactured at the Asnières workshops must be portable. "I refuse to design furniture," says Patrick-Louis Vuitton. "We are into movement. Nothing comes from the hands of one of our craftsmen that can't be easily transported." In Asnières, custom orders are made alongside the latest fashion handbags, which are sometimes more complicated to assemble than traditional trunks—incontestable proof that the ancient methods in no way impede the development of new techniques. The company's savoir-faire has been perfected over time, enriched by experience, and strengthened by difficulties surmounted.

The transmission of skills. Its understanding of excellent manufacturing and strong international development have led Louis Vuitton to open new production workshops outside its historic birthplace. By 1977 the Asnières workshop was too small to meet the demands of a growing clientele by itself. The company expanded its facilities by opening a workshop in Saint-Donat, followed four years later by one in Sarras, in the Rhône valley and not far from Romans, a region famous for its tanners and leatherwork. Since then

Vuitton factories have multiplied throughout France, always built to maintain the human scale necessary for transmitting the ancient crafts to young apprentices. Today thirteen leather workshops employ more than 3,500 artisans who are attentive to the smallest details and trained in uncompromising quality. The company is even bringing its French know-how to workshops near Barcelona, Spain, and San Dimas, California, a few miles from Los Angeles. Every member of Louis Vuitton is aware of the singular heritage that previous generations of trunk makers have bequeathed. Their pride in that heritage informs their daily tasks.

Each of the workshops that opened in the early years of the twenty-first century—in the boscage of Vendée, under the Spanish sun in Barberà, in the Berry countryside near Condé, or by the bay of Mont-Saint-Michel, in Normandy—has a decidedly modern stamp. The Ducey workshop in Normandy is without a doubt the most exemplary. Built amid fields and perfectly integrated with the landscape, the building has an open view of the abbey of Mont-Saint-Michel, a stony pyramid rising above the rushing sea. Each modern, light-filled workshop is designed to provide the ideal working conditions under which the craftsman's skills may blossom. The company fully recognized that the quality of its workshops affects the quality of its products, and its workshops are designed to adhere to comparably high standards.

Improved techniques. Proud though it is of its historic traditions, Louis Vuitton understands that its expertise needs continuous renewal and rethinking. The quality of the company's products has greatly improved with time, said Patrick-Louis Vuitton. "If Louis were to walk through one of our workshops today, I really believe he would be happy to see how the quality of his luggage has improved, enriched by new techniques and new materials."

No truly worthy skill rests on its laurels; it must replenish itself. One way that Louis Vuitton reinvigorated its cozy world of luggage was by introducing fashion in 1998. The company's expanded focus and expanded product line acted like a detonator on its staid heritage. "Everything changed with Marc Jacobs's first fashion show," said Emmanuel Mathieu, the company's manufacturing manager. "It gave the bag a seasonal life cycle."

The creation of new models called for the invention of new skills and cutting-edge leatherwork techniques. The 2005 launch of the Monogram Cerises line is a good indication of the company's resurgent creativity. For this new material Louis Vuitton used the latest silk-screening innovations to obtain a quality of line unprecedented in its canvas motifs. It borrowed a gradation technique from ceramics and developed it for the first time in leatherwork, to achieve a true harmony of color. Each season's fashion shows inspire numerous bags, giving new twists and challenges to the leather goods artisans, who willingly take them on. In this way the technical know-how and fashion creativity intersect, enhancing each other and improving themselves in the process. To realize the designer's dreams, the craftsman daily confronts unforeseen difficulties that only his dexterity and ingenuity can overcome—calling on Louis Vuitton's oldest traditions while also creating new ones.

New skills. Louis Vuitton has recently enlarged its area of competency by creating a structure devoted to each of its new businesses: ready-to-wear, shoes, watches, and jewelry. In 2000 the company opened a shoe workshop in Fiesso d'Artico, near Venice, in a dynamic region of Italy famous for shoemaking. Watchmaking is less subject to fashion seasons' rhythms than to time mechanisms' precision, so Louis Vuitton's La Chaux de Fonds workshops are in the heart of Swiss watchmaking country, near manufacturers of clockworks, dials, casings, and needles. The company also has its own workshop for ready-to-wear prototypes, which works hand in hand with the best French and Italian suppliers. In 2004 Vuitton made a full commitment to producing jewelry, recruiting recognized

Modern and filled with light, the Sainte-Florence workshop in the Vendée manufactures the Alma bag in Monogram canvas, as well as other articles.

experts and entrusting the manufacture of its complex pieces to the greatest workshops in Paris's Place Vendôme. From its very first trunks to its latest shoes, Louis Vuitton's expertise is without a doubt the key to the mythic brand's success. It opens the doors through which its legions of artisans have passed to realize the dreams of customers across the world.

Uncompromising quality. An ever-present aspect of the Louis Vuitton philosophy is a veritable quest for perfection. From each product's conception, every element is tested, evaluated, measured, and compared. A test laboratory at the headquarters on Rue du Pont-Neuf conducts more than two thousand tests every month to maintain or improve the level of quality to the brand's high standard. A bag will be subjected to tropical heat, the heel of a shoe will endure repeated shocks, a piece of fabric will be rubbed a thousand times. Sixty machines reproduce the shocks, pulling, cleaning, and other stresses the product might encounter during its lifetime. The product's reliability also depends on that of the suppliers. Only those who master their manufacturing processes and can prove their performance are brought onboard. The rare problems encountered during production or after a customer's return are systematically studied so improvements can be made. From design to distribution in stores, quality is an imperative that Louis Vuitton cultivates at every level.

Trunk making, the first craft

Today's trunk maker is the repository—and beneficiary—of a long tradition of expertise. Louis Vuitton has cultivated and perpetuated artisanal manufacturing of its trunks and hard-sided luggage since 1854. As in previous centuries, the skilled hands now working at Asnières cut out, form, sew, glue, hammer, and assemble each trunk with profound patience and precision. Their movements have not changed in 150 years.

Above left: Putting a brass buckle on a Monogram canvas cabin trunk with riveted nails.

Opposite: Finishing a secretary trunk made for shirts.

Wood

The strong smell of sawdust infuses the carpentry shop where wooden frames are worked and assembled to give body to the luggage. The carpenter works with three species: the resistant and light poplar, the tropical wood okoume, and the beech that is used for the reinforcing slats. Camphor wood was once used for explorers' trunks because its odor repelled insects. Louis Vuitton continues to combine utility and beauty in the choice of its materials today.

Above left: Poplar plantations along the meandering Seine and Oise rivers. Poplar is used for the hard-sided luggage's framework.

Opposite: Three poplar boards, one raw and two planed (top). Two models of grooves used to make the luggage frame watertight (bottom left). Stack of frame bands waiting to be fitted with bottoms and lids (bottom right).

Lozine

Lozine, an age-old composite of hot-processed and pressure-cured cardboard, cloth, and wood, reinforces and protects the edges of hard-sided luggage. Supple and resistant, Louis Vuitton traditional lozine is the color of aged cognac and bears the famous initials "LV." It now comes in an assorted palette, matching the colors of leather and other luggage materials.

Above: Lozine is available in many colors, to match the leather or canvas used.

Opposite: Printing and marking the logotype on russet leather lozine.

The saddle stitch

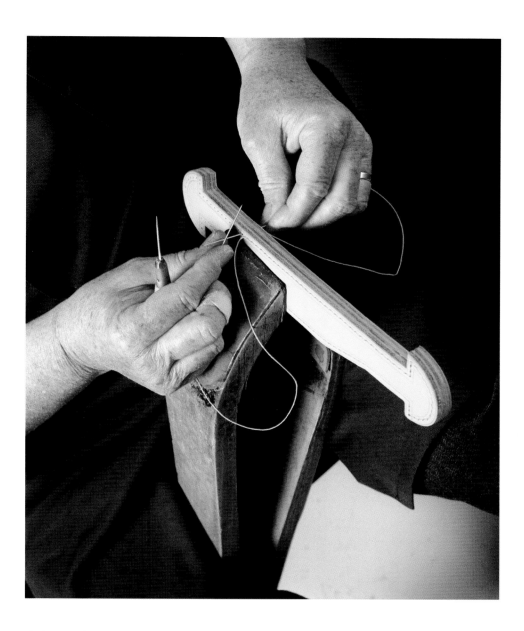

A linen thread covered with beeswax, a needle at either end. Each hand grasps a needle, one also holds an awl, and steadily pierces and crosses again and again. The saddle stitch lives on at Asnières, where it is forever associated with the Steamer bag, a large travel bag completely hand-sewn since 1901.

Opposite: Putting a handle on a Steamer bag. From the preparation of the hemp core to the attachment, a craftsman spends two hours manufacturing a traditional handle.

Right: Saddle stitching the russet leather handle for a trunk.

Leatherwork

Artisanal leatherwork has been enriched by new techniques over time. Thirteen Louis Vuitton leather workshops still practice the ancient handcrafts but have a new rhythm, thanks to recent sewing machines. A new philosophy of product manufacturing has developed without ever compromising quality.

Left: Attaching a handle to a bag at the Issoudun workshop in Indre.

Opposite: Choosing the Damier canvas at the Ducey workshop in La Manche.

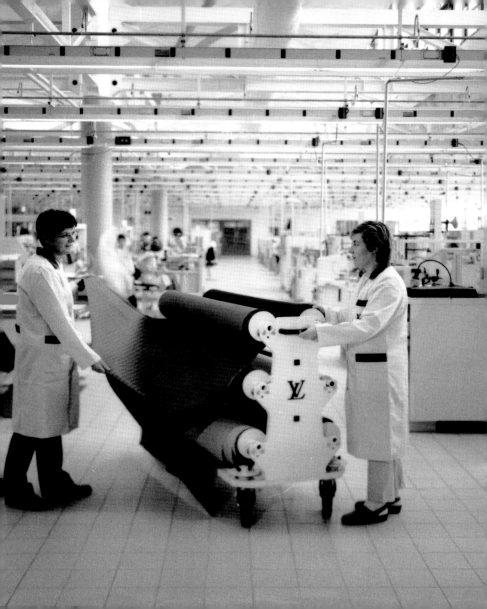

Leather

Louis Vuitton selects only the best, most beautiful skins for its products. Russet leather tanned with natural vegetable extracts, grained leather colored with a thousand pigments, Madras goatskin, or exotic, rare, and precious leathers: The great French leather goods company is very particular when it comes to its materials.

Above left: Round knife used to cut strips of leather from the skins.

Above right: Suhali leathers. During the tanning process, goatskins are soaked in vegetable baths of mimosa, birch, and plum bark. Indian tawers work each skin for seventy days to give it its final grain.

Opposite: Tanning cowhide with vegetable extracts and without surface treatments brings out the leather's fine quality.

Prototype workshop

On the sixth floor of the building on Paris's Rue du Pont-Neuf, a leather goods team brings the designer's sketches to life. This is where all the leather prototypes are made. A few yards away, designers and stylists conceive and draw new models. The proximity of manufacturing and design is unique and it puts traditional expertise at the service of creative fantasy.

Left (top and bottom): All the new models the designers conceive are made in the prototype workshop.

Opposite: Spools of thread in all the colors to match the canvases and leathers.

Ready-to-wear

Nineteen ninety-eight inaugurated a new era for Louis Vuitton's palette of skills. With sophisticated materials, careful construction, elaborate finishing, Marc Jacobs's ready-to-wear designs draw from couture's loftiest traditions. Every collection is designed in-house according to the artisanal rules of the trade before being made in the French and Italian workshops.

Left: Detail from the Winter 2005 collection. Skirt in white silk chiffon, tulle, and Monogram lace.

Opposite: The prototype's first fitting on a model, when final adjustments are made in the studio.

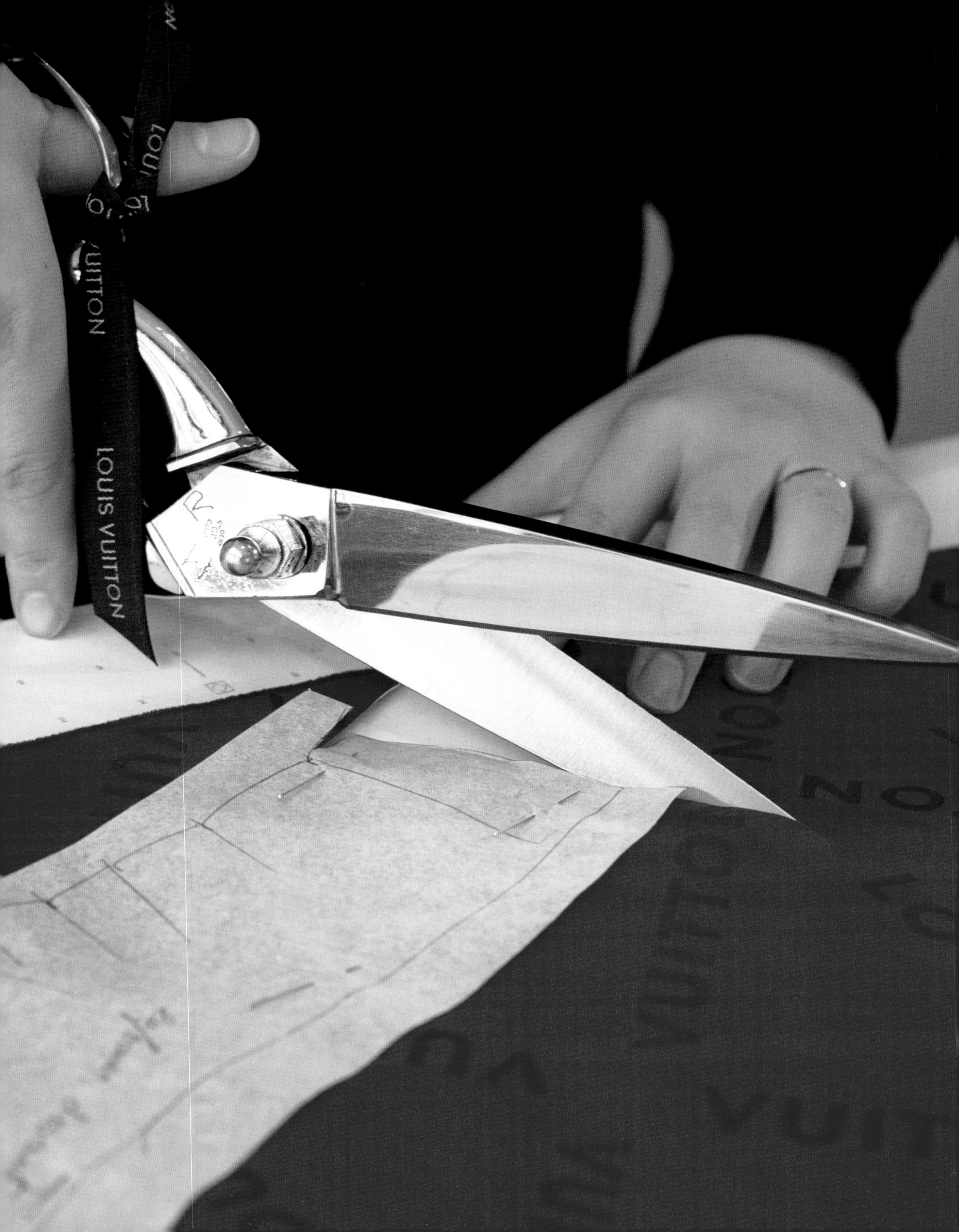
LOUIS VUITTON
LOUIS VUITTON

Opposite: Different pieces of fabric are cut and prepared to assemble various parts of the garment.

Above: The stylist's sketch is studied and translated into three dimensions by a model maker, who creates a muslin model on a mannequin.

Shoes

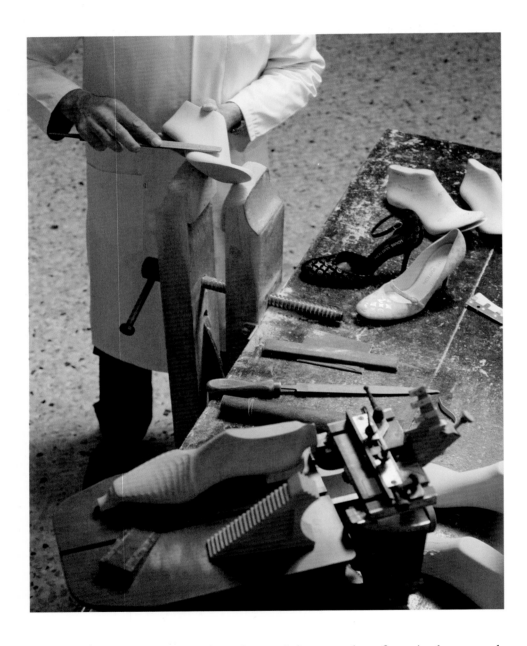

Creating a pair of shoes takes six to eight months of meticulous work from the initial design to the finished product. Applying its leather goods skills to this new business, Louis Vuitton has its own workshop in Fiesso d'Artico, one of Italy's most respected shoemaking regions.

Left: Making the model is the starting point of a shoe. Based on the stylist's design, the model maker chooses the type of last, which he will work with a rasp. The tool attached to the workbench lets him measure the slant of the heel. The tiered tool on the table controls the toe of the shoe and the weight-bearing point.

Opposite: Hornbeam, a heavy, hard wood almost completely free of knots, is traditionally used to make lasts.

Opposite: The "finishing," "make-up," and "dress-up" are all done with care to make the shoe even more beautiful. Making a shoe requires at least 150 separate steps.

Above: A fitting with a foot model allows for adjustments to perfect the shoe's aesthetics and fit. Establishing a consistent fit for the entire collection is an essential step in manufacturing the prototype.

Watchmaking

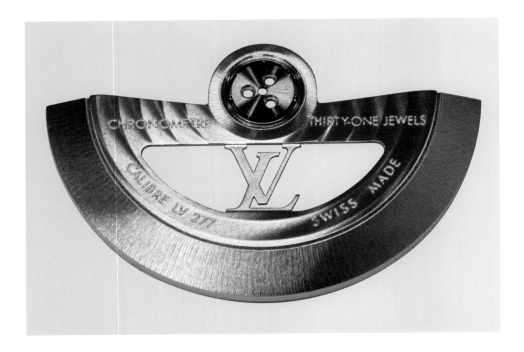

Louis Vuitton's timepieces are the fruit of uncompromising technique. Whether automatics or tourbillions, their movements owe their precision and reliability to the know-how of master watchmakers in La Chaux de Fonds, Switzerland, where the company has its own workshop.

Above left: The oscillating weight of Calibre LV 277.

Opposite: The Tambour automatic chronograph, with sand-colored dial and alligator wristband, photographed by Jean Larivière.

LOUIS VUITTON
STAINLESS STEEL
100M
SWISS MADE
000/277
014810
LOUIS VUITTON
LV 277
CHRONOMETRE
THIRTY-ONE JEWELS
CALIBRE LV 277
SWISS MADE

Opposite: The Calibre LV 277 is an automatic chronograph with an exceptional movement. The rate of its pin lever, 36,000 alternations per hour, puts it among the world's most precise watches.

Above: Adjustments to a timepiece in the Louis Vuitton watchmaking workshop in Switzerland (top). Mounting the clockwork in its case (bottom).

KNOW-HOW

Jewelry

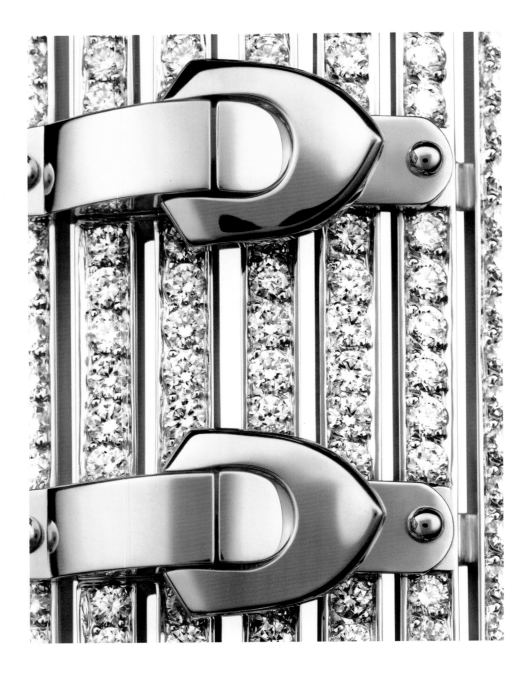

Yellow, white, and pink gold, diamonds, sapphires, emeralds, quartz, cit-rine, and amethyst: Louis Vuitton makes its jewelry of precious metals and the finest stones. In association with Paris's great jewelers and expert gemologists, Louis Vuitton has become part of the noblest jeweler tradition.

Above left: Borrowing from Vuitton's early designs, yellow gold jewelry suggests the trunk's brass locks.

Opposite: From the Emprise collection, the Fleur dog collar, in diamond pavé and gold, with leather ties.

464

Opposite: The jeweler inspects the product's finish with a magnifying glass.

Above: The mini trunk ring of yellow gold and citrine (foreground) requires high-precision technical work because four transparent nails pierce the stone.

Special orders

Louis Vuitton remains true to its origins as a box maker and packer by continuing to create one-of-a-kind goods that meet specific needs. In the age of mass production very few companies have retained mastery of the skills necessary to produce special orders. But, perpetuating its long tradition, Vuitton still makes customized travel articles—unique, beautiful, and practical pieces of luggage that result from a meticulous balance of the customer's wants and the craftsman's know-how.

Above left: Minibar of slate Taiga leather, 2004.

Above right: Patrick-Louis Vuitton, head of the company's special orders.

Opposite, clockwise from top left: Library trunk in Havana Vuittonite, 1926; typewriter case customized with the owner's initials, 1931; dog carrier in Monogram canvas, 1960; Monogram canvas trunk for two bicycles, 1957.

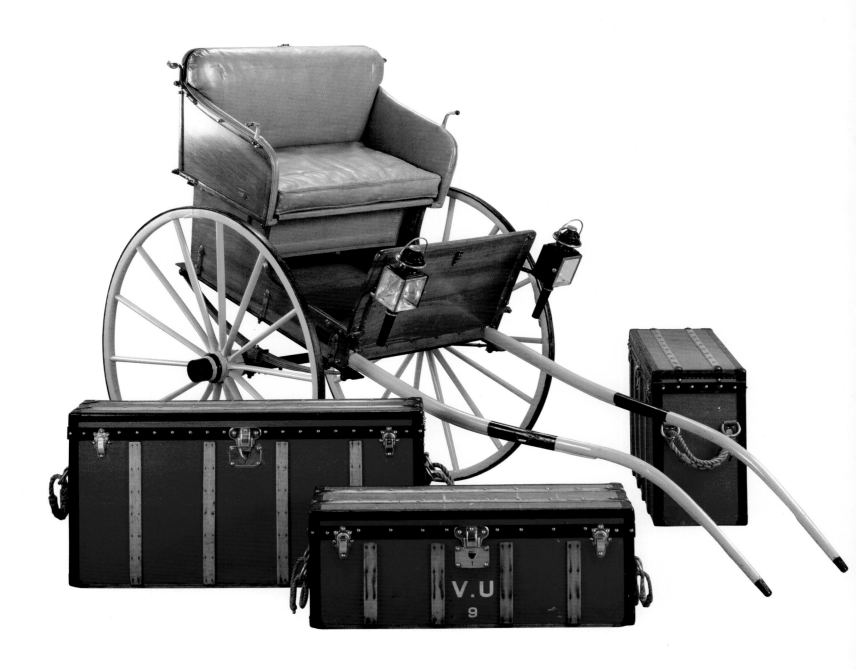

Above: A Frenchwoman planning a 1910 trip to Persia, fearing uncomfortable transportation, ordered a collapsible tilbury from Georges Vuitton. All its pieces fit into three trunks, and the wheels slide into protective covers.

Opposite: To celebrate France's "Year of China" (2004), the Comité Colbert (an association of French luxury goods companies) ordered this Louis Vuitton writing trunk. Covered with red goatskin, it contains a reading stand made of pterocarpus, a rare wood once used for Chinese furniture, a travel guide to Peking, several leather notebooks, and a red lacquer fountain pen.

MALLE SECRETAIRE STOKOWSKI LV / CG NOIR   SPE.

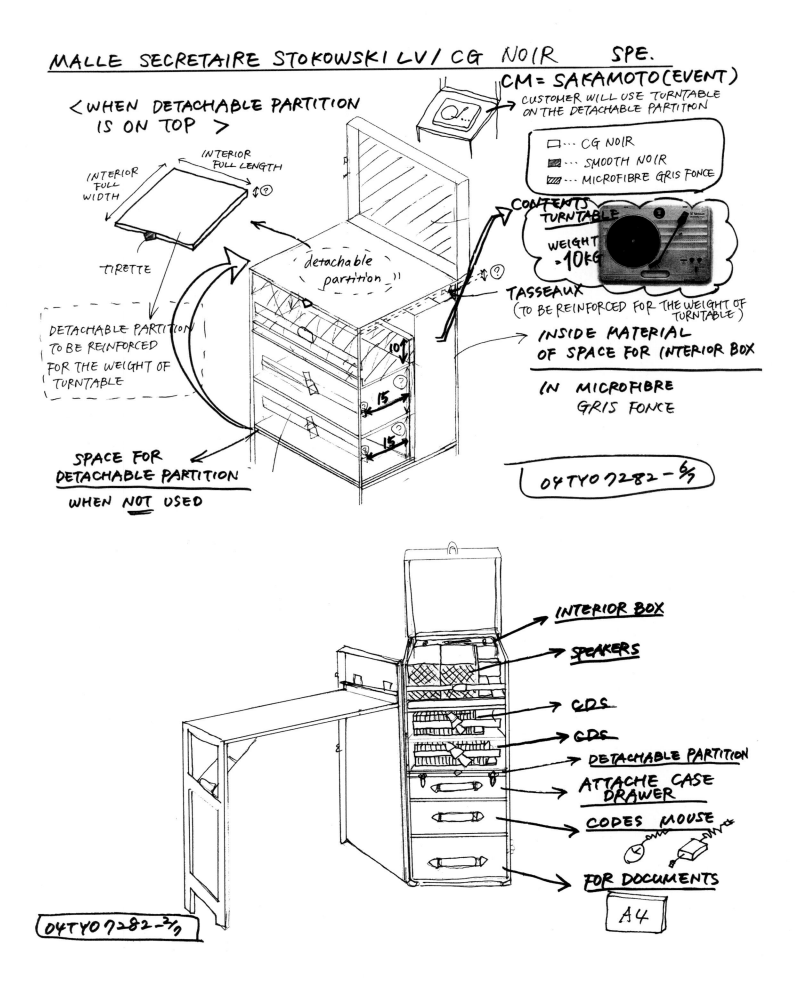

< WHEN DETACHABLE PARTITION IS ON TOP >

INTERIOR FULL LENGTH

INTERIOR FULL WIDTH

↕②

TIRETTE

DETACHABLE PARTITION TO BE REINFORCED FOR THE WEIGHT OF TURNTABLE

detachable partition

SPACE FOR DETACHABLE PARTITION
WHEN NOT USED

CM = SAKAMOTO (EVENT)
CUSTOMER WILL USE TURNTABLE ON THE DETACHABLE PARTITION

☐ ··· CG NOIR
▨ ··· SMOOTH NOIR
▧ ··· MICROFIBRE GRIS FONCE

CONTENTS TURNTABLE
WEIGHT -10KG

TASSEAUX
(TO BE REINFORCED FOR THE WEIGHT OF TURNTABLE)

INSIDE MATERIAL OF SPACE FOR INTERIOR BOX

IN MICROFIBRE GRIS FONCE

10

15 ②

15 ②

↕②

04TY07282 - 6/9

INTERIOR BOX

SPEAKERS

CDS

CDS

DETACHABLE PARTITION

ATTACHE CASE DRAWER

CODES   MOUSE

FOR DOCUMENTS

A4

04TY07282 - 3/9

Opposite: Preliminary sketches for a special order from the Japanese composer and pianist Ryuichi Sakamoto.

Above: The finished product, a Monogram canvas secretary trunk. Designed in collaboration with the artist, it has special compartments, CD storage, and document holders.

For the Summer 2004 men's fashion show (opposite), Marc Jacobs asked Louis Vuitton to make a toiletry set inspired by the 1920s. The classic small trunk (above) is covered with lizard. The interior, embellished with eggplant gray Suhali leather, contains silver bottles and a soap case by the best Parisian silversmiths, a tortoiseshell comb, a clothes brush, a jewelry box, a drawer with movable partitions for razor and extra blades, and, of course, a mirror.

Sober and refined, this chessboard case is made entirely of inlaid lacquered precious woods. The pieces are made of Madagascar ebony and maple, chosen for their strongly contrasting colors. Their classic shapes are adorned with a design element borrowed from one of Louis Vuitton's recurring signatures, the brass nail. When closed, the thirty-two pieces fit into individual compartments. For traveling, the set is protected by a russet leather case.

Louis Vuitton designed this case to protect and carry a collection of sixteen watches. At the top, three moving compartments ensure that automatic watches don't stop. The drawer below holds three watches and conceals a small space for jewelry. On the lower tier, another drawer holds ten wristwatches. The bottom conceals a secret compartment. A russet leather case holds the collector's tools.

Above: This leather and velvet jewelry box has eight drawers under its display tray. Every drawer can be rearranged to adapt precisely to the shape and size of the jewelry it holds. The supple case in multicolor Mini Monogram canvas was made for short trips.

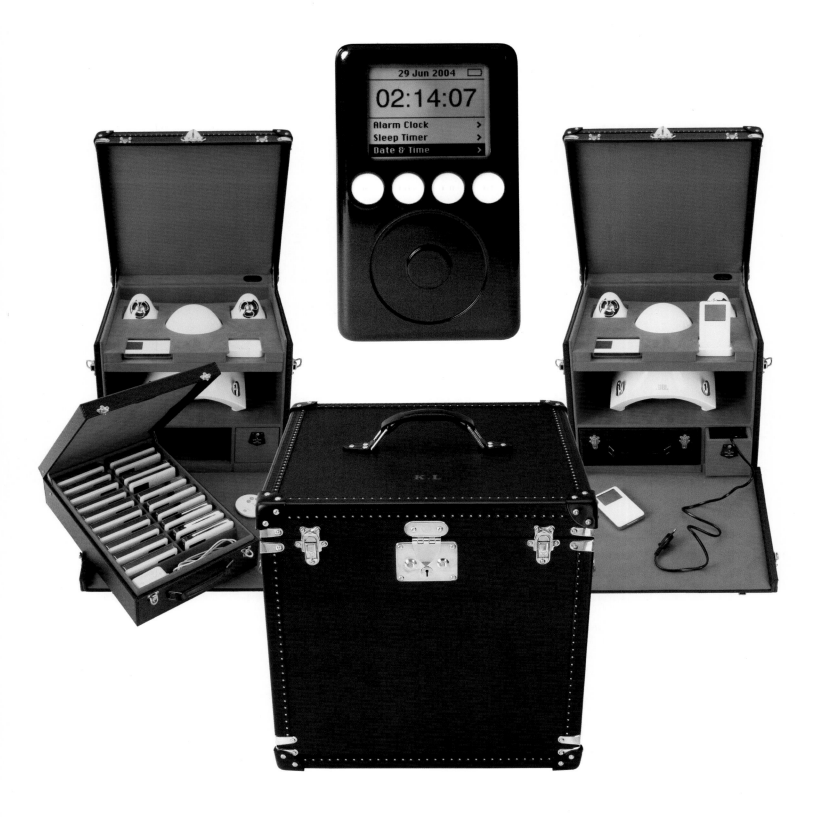

Previous pages: Film director Sofia Coppola travels with her music. Louis Vuitton designed a small trunk of supple leather for her miniature stereo, with side pockets for CDs, screens for the speakers, and multiple pockets for accessories.

Above: This case designed for Karl Lagerfeld carries 40 iPods and their accessories. With a red microfiber interior and a Taiga leather exterior, it bears its owner's initials in red near the handle.

Opposite: With a wink at Louis Vuitton's anniversary, this cake box combines the simple pleasure of presenting a cake with the most extreme luxury. The interior's protective isotherm foam cushions are covered with pink microfiber. A hidden door at the bottom conceals dessert spoons and candles. The lid has a pocket for a birthday card.

LOUIS VUITTON
UGO RONDINONE
VOYAGE D'HIVER

LOUIS VUITTON AND ART

Painters and visual artists

Louis Vuitton's lively interest in contemporary art has been passed down for generations, like an inherited character trait. Today's executives pursue the company's unique relationship with art much as their nineteenth-century predecessors did.

For Louis Vuitton, involvement in the arts is a way of life, a way of doing things, and a way to be at the forefront of cultural currents. Painting and the decorative arts have always infused its designs and been a keen interest. Louis and Georges Vuitton participated in the legendary 1874 exhibition of works by painters who had been banished from the official Salons—"outlaws" like Monet, Renoir, Pissarro, Sisley, Degas, and Cézanne. The show, held at Nadar's photo studio, created a scandal. "A museum of horrors," the press unanimously declared the display of paintings, which included Monet's *Impression, soleil levant*. From that title a journalist came up with the term "Impressionism," which was meant to be a derisive label for the artists' new style.

Continuing to keep pace with the avant-garde, Gaston Vuitton presented the Milano travel kit at the 1925 Exposition des Arts Décoratifs. The kit's bottles and brushes were created in collaboration with the great decorators of the Art Deco period, Legrain and Puiforcat. Some sixty years later, when the company decided to market a line of sixteen silk scarves, it turned once again to contemporary designers—Arata Isozaki, Arman, Sol LeWitt, César, Andrée Putman, Jean-Pierre Raynaud, James Rosenquist, Philippe Starck, Richard Peduzzi, and William Wilson—some already famous, others the company would help make famous.

Whether the company directly solicited them or not, other artists also were inspired by and acted upon the Louis Vuitton image. Its emblematic power has generated unexpected repercussions. Salvador Dali, fascinated by the Monogram, appropriated it in the late 1960s for a series of Daligrams. The same fascination inspired Alberto Sorbelli's performance art. The most spectacular piece, *The Attacked*, took place during the forty-eighth Venice Biennial, in 1999: The artist arranged to be attacked by people armed with Vuitton luggage.

The links between Louis Vuitton and the visual arts continue to intersect in every way. As during the Renaissance, there are now no boundaries among artistic disciplines, only bridges. Robert Wilson, the theater director and visual artist, designed Vuitton's Christmas 2002 store windows, and Ugo Rondinone, the multimedia artist, stepped in in 2004, both recalling the surprising window displays Gaston Vuitton concocted so many years ago.

Previous page: Ugo Rondinone's design for Vuitton's Christmas 2004 store windows. The Swiss artist portrayed the theme of "Winter Voyage" (a reference to Franz Schubert's melancholic song cycle, *Winterreise*), with a mirrored tree and a rainbow-colored light show.

The sculptor Arman (below) created *Luxe, furie et volupté* (opposite) in 1998. Some of his work is based on the reduction of a single object and the exploitation of shock, as in his series of violins and cellos sawed into strips, garbage preserved in a block of resin, and monogrammed soccer balls. It always playfully stirs the senses.

Above: Olivier Debré painting a stage curtain, 1989. (Louis Vuitton, as a sponsor, presented this curtain to Hong Kong for its opera house.) Veering toward abstraction, Debré exposes the real and strips emotion of its anecdotes. He uses a gigantic format to suggest the cosmic dimensions of the real and to contain the movement of time. Debré made his first stage curtain for the Comédie Française.

Opposite, above: Roman Cieslewicz's poster for Louis Vuitton. The Polish poster artist was one of the great graphics masters of the late twentieth century. This work has a touch of Magritte as well as Cieslewicz's hallmarks—the unusual composition, the economy of striking symbols, and the focused expression.

Opposite, below: Salvador Dali and a Daligram, late 1960s. ©ArtsMode Network. Dali reinterpreted Louis Vuitton's Monogram to create his own line of Daligram objects, using his and his wife Gala's initials.

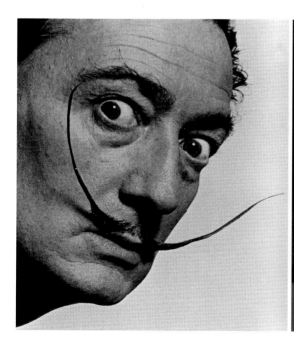

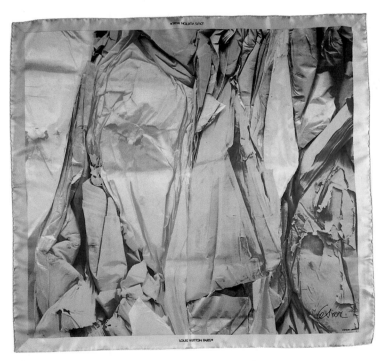

Above: Silk scarves, 1988–95.

James Rosenquist, a champion of Pop art, made large collages in the 1960s denouncing the excesses of consumer culture. In the eighties and nineties the flora surrounding his Florida studio inspired his work. As seen in this silk scarf (top left), he associated tropical flowers with female faces. They are, he said, "ecological and political paintings," that show the fragility of life on Earth.

Sol LeWitt, one of the founders of Conceptual art, has always been attracted to simple geometric shapes. Nothing could seem more alien to his huge murals or cubic sculptures than a Louis Vuitton scarf (top right), but the equivalence is nevertheless remarkable.

The sculptor César is famous for his totems of compressed cars, but his silk scarf (bottom left) is a delicate trompe l'oeil: Crumpled sheet metal becomes crumpled fabric.

William Wilson is a sculptor, painter, video director, poster artist, designer, and illustrator whose work has singular narrative power. His silk scarf (bottom right) presents the conquest of the West as both fairy tale and contemporary poem.

Above: A 2002 work from Wang Guangyi's Great Criticism series. Wang Guangyi, one of the best-known Chinese avant-garde painters of the eighties, launched the Political Pop style. Like Andy Warhol's work, his pictorial series repetitively uses symbols, but with a barbed political point. He presents Maoist workers and peasants with logos of the Western brands that flood contemporary China.

Opposite: Takashi Murakami, *SUPERFLAT MONOGRAM,* 2003. "Louis Vuitton is a fantastic history that heads straight into the future," said Murakami. In 2003 the company produced his first animated film, a magical tale populated by manga characters inspired by Louis Vuitton. Like Alice falling down the rabbit hole to Wonderland, Aya, a Japanese girl crazy for fashion, falls down the checkered throat of a panda bear, beginning a dreamlike voyage through the brand's history. The film was presented at the Venice Biennial.

The artist and director Robert Wilson has collaborated several times with Louis Vuitton. Wilson's 2001 penguin trunk (above left) conveys Wilson's typically original sense of humor as well as his fetish animal, in silkscreen on a black Epi leather trunk. Proceeds from the sale of the trunk went to the Watermill Center, a foundation promoting young artists. Top right: Wilson's Christmas window display and Fluo bags, 2002. Bottom right: Wilson, pictured with Bernard Arnault and his wife, redesigned the LV initials especially for Christmas and created a contemporary collection of bags in fluorescent Monogram Vernis.

Travelers and writers

The travel guide is an indispensable part of the traveler's gear, a practical reference for the best places to go and most exceptional sights to see. It can also be a work of art, enchanting the imagination and leading to a spiritual journey of discovery that parallels the physical one.

Armchair travelers and nomads. Some writers are sedentary, traveling only around their rooms. From this fixed point, this cocoon, they create ever-expanding imaginary circles. Marcel Proust, for example, was a recluse in his Paris apartment. But while hiding himself from outside noises and the bothersome agitation of urban life, Proust pursued a monumental inner vision, rebuilding the world from memories seized from oblivion and restored with all their powers of enchantment. At the end of *Remembrance of Things Past,* the master opus he produced during a voluntary confinement, the Proustian narrator realizes that that which a frivolous social life had relegated to the past could be rediscovered, reconquered, and "won." A work of literary art has the power to capture the wonder and the fleeting sensations summoned by a memory unexpectedly triggered—perhaps by the taste of a madeleine dipped in tea or the sound of a step striking the cobblestones in a courtyard—expressing the true human condition to the world and to individuals. Writing redeems life.

Conversely, some writers are nomads who seem to need physical mobility—who need to move so the spirit can break free. They are captivated by travel plans, departures, momentum, speed! They follow Buddha's precept, "Liberty is in the abandonment of home," meaning that such attachments hold people back and prevent their work from blossoming. Their creative spark and inner fire need to feed on a never-ending voyage. They travel all over the world, seeing travel as a revitalizing panacea. "A change of place is, as if by magic, a new life, with a birth, growth, and death inside the other that is offered to us," wrote Paul Morand, who always had an appetite for travel.

Some of the writers who were travel enthusiasts were regular or occasional Louis Vuitton customers, including the Swiss novelist and poet Blaise Cendrars (1887–1961). A tireless traveler since his childhood—when he was eight he toured Sicily on the back of a donkey—Cendrars patronized Louis Vuitton until he reached old age. In fact, he coined a phrase that is a veritable ad slogan: "To leave is to go to Vuitton." Other writers traveled the world as much on account of their profession as their personal tastes, as was the case with writer-diplomats like Paul Claudel (1868–1955) and Paul Morand (1888–1976). Louis Vuitton's literary customers make a cosmopolitan and varied list: the polished Briton Somerset Maugham; the earthy Frédéric Dard, alias San Antonio; Roger Nimier, the "hussar" of aristocratic ancestry who was hostile to the existential literature that blossomed in Paris in the fifties; and the existentialist Sartre, along with Simone de Beauvoir, a customer before the Second World War.

"Voyager avec." In 1994, to commemorate the hundredth anniversary of the publication of Georges Vuitton's *Le Voyage, depuis les temps les plus reculés jusqu'à nos jours,* Maison Louis Vuitton and the magazine *La Quinzaine Littéraire* launched the "Voyager avec" ("Travel with") book series. It is a collection of works, most of them previously unpublished, by prestigious writers, novelists, and philosophers. They are not all travelers, but their works are all about geographic and poetic discovery. The publisher, Maurice Nadeau, founder of the *La Quinzaine Littéraire,* explained the traits all the writers in the series share, and what distinguishes them from other travelers: "These writers can be very different from the tourist on a packaged vacation, the sales representative who must travel from one place to another, the big businessman in his private jet, the explorer, and, of course, the person

Opposite, clockwise from top left: Ernst Jünger, Vladimir Mayakovsky, Claudio Magris, Jacques Derrida, Virginia Woolf, Valéry Larbaud, and Rainer Maria Rilke, whose works are included in the "Voyager avec" collection through the support of Louis Vuitton.

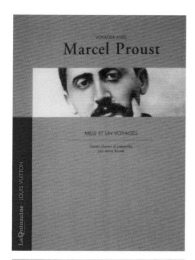

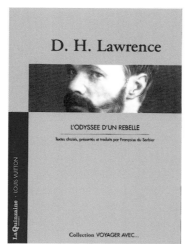

Opposite: Publisher Maurice Nadeau in his office at *La Quinzaine Littéraire*.

Above: Some of the books in the "Voyager avec" series. The collection includes:
Mario de Andrade, *L'Apprenti touriste*
Andrei Biély, *Le Collecteur d'espaces*
Blaise Cendrars, *Le Panama ou les aventures de mes sept oncles (Panama or the Adventures of My Seven Uncles)* and other poems
Jean Chesneaux, *Carnets de Chine*
Joseph Conrad, *Le Port après les flots*
Jacques Derrida, *La Contre-allée*
Philip K. Dick, *Le Zappeur de mondes*
Ernst Jünger, *Récits de voyages*
Valéry Larbaud, *Le Vagabond sédentaire*
D. H. Lawrence, *L'Odyssée d'un rebelle*
Claudio Magris, *Déplacements*
Vladimir Mayakovsky, *Du Monde j'ai fait le tour*
François Maspero, *Transit & CIE*
Paul Morand, *Au Seul souci de voyager*
Marcel Proust, *Mille et un voyages*
Rainer Maria Rilke, *Lettres à une compagne de voyage*
Joseph Roth, *Automne à Berlin*
Natsume Sôseki, *Haltes en Mandchourie et en Corée; Textes londoniens*
Virginia Woolf, *Promenades européennes*

of leisure. Not that the writer has a superior essence, simply a different one. By vocation, by habit, by profession, the writer recalls a feeling, dreams, meditates, rejoices or regrets, approves or denounces—like we all do. But unlike the rest of us, this person puts all this into words. Among all the means of expression, this traveler has chosen the most common one, language, but gives language a very particular turn and uses it so efficiently that we, in the writer's company, also dream, meditate, and become sensitive observers, discovering the world and ourselves."

The varied works in the series feed "on the drunken swirls of the great river of diversity." They express the singular voices of several generations of writers of French, Swiss, British, Italian, Russian, Japanese, German, and Portuguese origin. These books speak to us about the whole world, of encounters, curiosities, and strange civilizations. They speak to us about the plurality of spaces, epochs, and about our common humanity. Each writer conveys a distinct viewpoint with equally distinct language, offering an unparalleled instrument for exploration. The "Voyager avec" series is published in French, with some bilingual editions; for example, Cendrars's text is accompanied John Dos Passos's English translation.

AUTOMOTIVE ELEGANCE

The quintessential car

Louis Vuitton developed an early and lasting passion for automobiles and quickly developed luggage for people traveling the world on four wheels. The company continues to organize adventurous auto expeditions and classic car shows, to the delight of collectors around the world. Both kinds of events are lively celebrations of epic, elegant machines.

A passion for automobiles. Of the various means of transport, automobiles were unquestionably Georges Vuitton's greatest passion. As early as 1894 he attended the Paris-Rouen race, which a steam-powered De Dion Bouton won. Modern engines were still rudimentary then, and everyone was obsessed with breaking speed records. Within a few years those wheezy early monsters were replaced by touring cars and limousines by Voisin, Hotchkiss, Rolls-Royce, and Packard, which strutted along the roadways in chic destinations like Deauville, La Baule, Biarritz, and Nice. Louis Vuitton then designed the first auto trunks, which fit perfectly into the bodywork's curves. The company created other new luggage specifically for automobile travel, such as the ingenious driver's bag, which fit into the center hole of the spare wheel and could be used as a washbasin if required. In 1908, when Ford launched its first mass-produced cars, Georges Vuitton joined forces with the coachbuilder Kellner to design a vehicle that prefigured the modern-day mobile home. The number of auto races and expeditions was multiplying, fueling the technological revolution. In the footsteps of Phileas Fogg, adventurers traveled from Paris to New York, covering 12,427 miles across Russia, Japan, and Alaska. In the great Citroën expeditions organized by the adventurer Georges-Marie Haardt, the cars crossing Africa and Asia were outfitted with trunks specially designed by Georges Vuitton.

Following the route taken by Marco Polo, the Croisière Jaune auto rally left the shores of the Mediterranean in 1931 and headed for the China Sea. Fourteen vehicles and forty men defied the sand, cold, and humidity. Suitcases, Vuittonite bags, trunk-beds, travel

Previous page: A Jaguar C type followed by a Ferrari on the roads of Tuscany, during the 1995 Louis Vuitton Italia Classica.

Left: Three elegant ladies pose in front of a Talbot during a Paris–La Baule race in the Roaring Twenties.

Opposite: A Hispano Suiza, photographed by Jacques-Henri Lartigue, 1922 (top). A Panhard in a classic automobile competition, about 1935 (bottom).

THE LOUIS VUITTON CLASSIC
at Rockefeller Center

Opposite: A poster by Razzia for the first Louis Vuitton Classic at Rockefeller Center, 1996.

Above: At the Château de Bagatelle in 2001, the 1954 Alfa Romeo 1900 BAT 7 won first prize in the Berlinette category.

Below: Peter Giddings's 1935 Alfa Romeo Tipo 8C was the grand-prize winner of the 2000 Louis Vuitton Classic in New York.

kits, leather folding tables—all the luggage bore the Vuitton label. Vuitton's reliable, well-made luggage accompanied the adventurers mile after mile, just as it accompanies travelers today.

Vintage auto shows. Just the mention of certain legendary automobiles, like Bugatti, Delahaye, Packard, or Hispano Suiza, conjures images of classic elegance, pure line, brilliant design, and traveling in style. At the 1988 Pebble Beach Classic Car Show in Florida, three friends with a shared passion for fine automobiles—Antoine Prunet, Arnault de Fouchier, and Christian Philippsen—decided to launch a similar event in France. The Louis Vuitton Classic was born the following year. Every year since, the company has organized exhibitions and competitions of the world's most exceptional cars—both elegant vintage automobiles and cutting-edge car designs—in Paris, London, or New York. English coupes, American limousines, and Italian sports cars share the stage with eccentric prototypes and futuristic concept cars, drawing wealthy collectors and connoisseurs, savvy enthusiasts, and a curious public on a tour of automotive history. At each Louis Vuitton Classic some seventy models are exhibited and numerous prizes are awarded in categories like design, history, restoration, category, and general condition. Some people will sacrifice everything to restore their dream automobile in a dusty garage, with the secret ambition of competing one day. A jury of experts awards the official prizes in each category and the public votes for its favorite among all the handsome machines.

503

Opposite, from left to right and from top to bottom: Clotilde Courau, actress and princess of Savoy, at Bagatelle in 2002; British actor Jeremy Irons with Portuguese actress Barbara Guimaraes; designer Andrée Putman in front of a 1928 Oméga VI; actor Donald Sutherland and his wife in the Jardins de Bagatelle, 1997; actress Kristin Scott Thomas and a 1956 Renault Étoile Filant; Bernard Arnault, chairman of LVMH, with Bertrand Delanoë, mayor of Paris; actress Cyd Charisse at Bagatelle in 1992, in front of Prince Eugene of Sweden's Mercedes-Benz; Patrick-Louis Vuitton and his son Benoît-Louis in front of Marilyn Monroe's 1956 Ford Thunderbird.

Above: The 2002 auto show at the prestigious Hurlingham Club.

Exceptional cars, exceptional places. The Parc de Bagatelle, just outside Paris, and the courtyard of the Château de Bagatelle are favorite settings for the Louis Vuitton Classic. The most extraordinary parade of automobiles has crossed the grounds there: Rolls-Royces belonging to maharajahs, the Bugattis of kings, princes, and stars of the silver screen. In 1991 Louis Vuitton teamed up with Britain's eminent Hurlingham Club to organize that year's event at its Georgian clubhouse in Fulham, west of London. English lords roared in on their motorcycles like James Dean. In 1996 the Louis Vuitton Classic was held in New York for the first time, in the heart of Manhattan, at the plaza of Rockefeller Center. Private galas, parades of cars along Fifth Avenue, and official ceremonies punctuated the three-day exhibition, which was certainly one of the event's most memorable. European jewels like Bugatti and Ferrari were joined by beautiful cars from America's golden days of automaking—Buicks, Fords, and Cadillacs. Almost two million visitors attended the unforgettable show, which was so successful that the Louis Vuitton Classic has returned to Rockefeller Plaza five times.

The myth lives on. Every year the Louis Vuitton Classic is themed to celebrate a different aspect of the mythic automobile, from high-powered, record-breaking race cars to Hollywood stars' convertibles. Who hasn't dreamed of driving off with Clark Gable in his Duesenberg or dashing away on an escapade with Marlene Dietrich in her Cadillac V16, hair blowing in the wind—just like in the movies? In 1998 the theme was aviation, a tribute to all the Icaruses who dreamed of flying off in a car over the sea. The strange Leyat

Hélica, conceived in 1922 by one of the first aircraft manufacturers, was included in the exhibition. It resembles a plane without wings, with the shape of a keelson and a propeller in front.

Although the magnificent designs of the past have a proud and prominent place at the Louis Vuitton Classic, it also highlights the current automotive world's creativity and technical mastery with important displays of cars of the future. Eager to innovate, contemporary manufacturers outdo each other in the inventiveness of their concept cars. The latest models of Aston Martin, Mercedes, BMW, Alfa Romeo, and Peugeot are on display, featuring the work of the world's best engineering and design departments. In 1995, for example, Renault presented Initiale, a concept car that was a harbinger of the lines of today's cars. It also inspired Louis Vuitton to design luxurious and functional luggage to go with it: Two suitcases and a high-tech vanity case were created and exhibited with the Renault Initiale. And in 2005 Pininfarina celebrated its seventy-fifth anniversary by presenting Enjoy, a high-powered two-seater whose production was limited to seventy-five cars. Louis Vuitton's innovation department, directed by Xavier Dixsaut, designed the vehicle's interior, completing it with an array of futuristic accessories.

Above and opposite: The 2004 Louis Vuitton Classic, in the gardens of Waddesdon Manor, Buckinghamshire. Ron Langston (opposite) owner of the 1961 Manx Norton 30M 500C—English style meets the indomitable machine.

Four-wheeled adventures. Louis Vuitton continues to fuel the automotive adventure by organizing extraordinary rallies in faraway countries with beautiful landscapes. On 9 April 1993, after months of preparation, sixty-eight competitors from fifteen nations began their drive from Singapore to Kuala Lumpur. The Vintage Equator Run is a three-day 528-mile expedition across Southeast Asia. The teams left behind the five-star comforts of Raffles Hotel and embarked upon the misty, dusty tracks of the Malaysian jungle, through colonial villages and rubber tree plantations. The vintage cars could not stand up to the rough roads, and stopovers in Malacca and Port Dickson were organized to deal with mechanical problems. It was an unrushed race that offered a good excuse to contemplate the luxuriant vegetation.

Two years later and a few thousand miles away, in sunny Italy, another rally took to the road in Tuscany. The 1995 Louis Vuitton Italia Classica reenacted the history of the automobile. Passionate collectors from across Europe sampled the pleasures of late summer on the roads through Chianti, stopping off at superb patrician villas and enjoying the small villages lining the coast roads between the island of Elba and the Maremma region. The journey ended in Siena, an ancient town whose annual race, the Palio, features galloping horses rather than purring vintage cars.

The following year Louis Vuitton sponsored the Tour du Léman in Switzerland, with more than thirty teams participating. All the cars were built before 1905, which made the rally more challenging than usual. On 13 September 1996, the cars set out from Geneva's Promenade des Bastions on a 112-mile journey around Lake Geneva. Guy Michelin (a descendant of the family that founded the famous tire company), drove the Éclair, a Peugeot with a 4CV Daimler engine that was built in 1895—the first automobile fitted with pneumatic tires.

Above: A 1927 Bugatti Type 40 on the Malaysian jungle trails, 1993.

Opposite: Razzia's poster for the 1993 Louis Vuitton Vintage Equator Run, from Singapore to Kuala Lumpur.

L'ÉLÉGANCE AUTOMOBILE

Opposite: Crowds push forward to see a 1960 Jaguar XL 150S pass through town during the 1998 Louis Vuitton Classic China Run (top). English automotive luxury meets Chinese communism (bottom).

Above right: A Bentley driving past rice fields during the China Run.

Below: A Chinese child at the wheel of a 1956 Mercedes-Benz 300SC that was in the Louis Vuitton Classic China Run.

Chinese adventures. In 1998 Louis Vuitton took a daring chance and staged one of its greatest adventures in the Peoples' Republic of China. Despite the organizational challenges, the 808-mile China Run actually took place, with fifty cars entered in the competition. The expedition went from Dalian to Beijing, with many escapades off the beaten track. The participants saw spectacular shorelines, salt plains, expanses of rice fields, breathtaking mountains, and landscapes that looked completely untouched by civilization. In one remote area where there were no hotels, Louis Vuitton erected a village of Mongolian yurts next to an enormous lake for the night. Along the route the competitors encountered the Qing emperors' Summer Palace and the Great Wall of China, which they had to cross to reach Beijing. Passage through towns could be difficult, as carts, delivery bicycles, donkeys, and countless bicycles thronged the streets. But it was the adventure that counted most, not record-setting times. The Chinese people were even more fascinating than the journey. They turned out in thick crowds to smile and wave as the cars drove past. With each stopover the public's enthusiasm intensified, to such an extent that some mayors offered their constituents a day's legal holiday to watch the fascinating caravan pass. On 30 May the Chinese police escorted the cars through Beijing as far as the Forbidden City. As a beautiful 1955 Chrysler Windsor passed a portrait of Mao hanging from the Gates of Eternal Harmony along Tiananmen Square, the contrast in cultures was evident. But the cultures never clashed, as communist China opened to the rest of the world.

For more than a hundred years cars have occupied a special place in people's lives. They stoked the enthusiasm of pioneers, challenged the daring of drivers, inspired the inventiveness of engineers, and impassioned the movie stars. Thanks to their devoted owners, vintage cars bear magnificent witness to the automobile's history and evolution. And Louis Vuitton continues to prepare new rallies, always moving in new directions.

THE LOUIS VUITTON CUP AND THE AMERICA'S CUP

The Louis Vuitton Cup

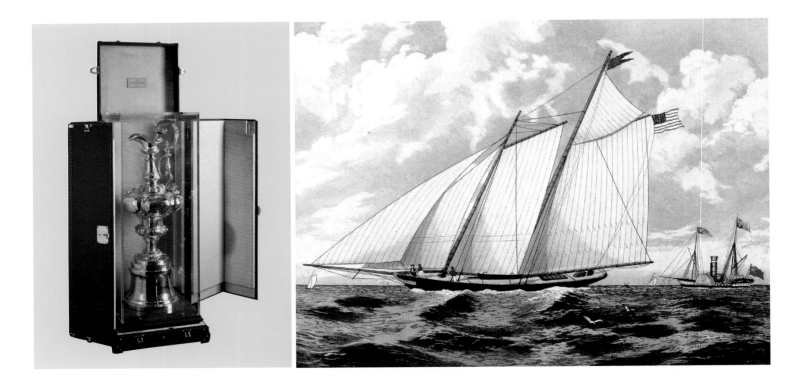

Since 1983 teams wishing to challenge the holder of the America's Cup, the trophy for the world's premier sailing competition, have had to first win the Louis Vuitton Cup. Over the years Louis Vuitton has become increasingly involved, transforming a friendly competition into a major modern event that attracts enormous media coverage and greatly contributes to the international success of the America's Cup.

Founded within just a few years of each other—the America's Cup in 1851 and Maison Louis Vuitton in 1854—the two historic entities ran their separate courses for almost 130 years. Then, in 1983, their destinies crossed.

1851: birth of the America's Cup. The legendary yacht race has a storied history that begins in England. In fact the word "yacht" is thought to derive from a sailing vessel, a *jacht* built in the Netherlands, that was a gift to the seventeenth-century English king Charles II. King Charles participated in the first known regatta when he raced his yacht *Catherine* against his brother the duke of York's yacht *Anne*. The king won. The word "regatta" comes from the Venetian *regata*, which originally referred to a gondola race but came to signify a race of rowboats or sailboats that traditionally followed a course around buoys. Competitors were judged by the boat's performance at different speeds and, above all, the crew's maneuvering abilities. The first official regatta was held in England in 1826, when yachting really took off. The nineteenth century saw a tremendous growth of yacht clubs, which were reserved for the aristocracy. The yacht race was an English inven-

Previous page: The Louis Vuitton Cup.

Above: *America* (right), the schooner from the New York Yacht Club, humiliated the best of British yachting at Cowes in 1851, under the eyes of Queen Victoria. The legendary America's Cup (left), the oldest sports trophy in the world, takes its name from that victory.

Opposite: In 1920 the New York defender *Resolute*, with its white hull, and the English *Shamrock IV* prepare to confront each other.

tion, as well as a symbolic demonstration of Britain's long naval tradition and dominance over the world's seas.

In 1851 the members of the Royal Yacht Squadron (founded in England in 1815) challenged their counterparts from the New York Yacht Club to a race from Cowes, on the Isle of Wight. The American club, founded in 1844, was still very young, but its director, Commodore John Cox Stevens, was proud and audacious. He decided to accept the English sailors' challenge, although many people—including the American ambassador to Paris—tried to convince Stevens that his certain defeat would humiliate not only him but also his country. On 22 August 1851 sixteen competitors lined up at the start of the Cowes Regatta to sail "around the Isle of Wight, passing inside the buoys called No Man's and Sandhead and outside the lightship called the Nab." Among the cutters (one mast) and schooners (two masts) was the distinctive black hull of *America*, the yacht from New York. It was the first international regatta in history. The American victory was unquestionable: The *America* finished more than twenty minutes ahead of the first British boat, the *Aurora*.

1870–95: Anglo-American duels. A legend was thus born, with its own heroes and its own language: words like "syndicate," "challenger," "defender," and "challenge." "The Cup's syndicates are made up of financiers, owners, sponsors, and crews wishing to implement a project. There are syndicates to defend the Cup—the defenders—and syndicates to win the Cup—the challengers. Each challenging syndicate can also be called the challenge."

The object of their desire is a silver cup—the Holy Grail of yachting. On two occasions, in 1870 and 1871, the Englishman James Ashbury vainly attempted to repatriate the Cup. The Canadians also tried their luck but were crushed twice, in 1876 and 1881. From then on, and for many decades—from 1881 to 1962—the duel played out exclusively between the United States and Great Britain and among yachts that were specially designed for the race. During this period the boats' size and performance evolved, ultimately becoming large, luxuriously fitted "sailing machines" designed to win. One of the most distinguished naval architects of the time was the American Nathanael Greene Herreshoff, or "Captain Nat." He dominated the America's Cup scene from 1891 until his death in 1938. In 1893 he designed the *Vigilant*, which beat the British challenger's *Walkyrie II*. Two years later he designed *Defender*, "one of the most handsome monsters ever built—37.49 meters [123 feet] overall, 26.95 meters [88.5 feet] at the water line, and a 5.8-meter [19-foot] draught. With all the care (and aluminum) that Herreshoff put into it, *Defender* had 8 tons more ballast than *Walkyrie III*." That did not keep him from beating the challenger, however, to the great displeasure of its owner, Lord Dunraven.

1899–1937: the clash of the tycoons. The British aristocrat was a sore loser, and his bitter remonstrations led to his exclusion from the New York Yacht Club, which had made him an honorary member. The episode marked the end of an era. Blue-blooded nobles gave way to a new elite—the kings of finance, banking, and industry—in the race to victory. The America's Cup became the privileged pursuit of tycoons. An exceptional figure among them was the Irish tea baron Sir Thomas Lipton. Determined to challenge the Americans, he lined up five yachts between 1899 and 1930, all named *Shamrock*. Five challenges—five defeats. The first two *Shamrocks* came up against the resistance and superiority of *Columbia*, a 131-foot sloop Herreshoff built for John Pierpont Morgan. He was heir to the family of bankers and industrialists who had founded the United States Steel Corporation, the first American steel trust, in 1901. His family members were longtime loyal Louis Vuitton customers.

In 1920 Sir Thomas Lipton almost won. His *Shamrock IV* was faster than the American defender, *Resolute*, and it won the first two regattas. However, a disagreement onboard—a rivalry between two helmsmen—prevented it from turning technical superiority into final victory. In 1930, for his last appearance in the competition (by then held in Newport,

Opposite top: One of the legendary "sailcloth cathedrals," the *American Defender*, winner in 1895.

Opposite bottom: From the beginning, the affluent had a passion for the America's Cup. From left to right, the English aircraft manufacturer T. O. M. Sopwith and his wife, Phyllis; Sir Thomas Lipton, tea magnate and owner of five boats called *Shamrock*; and Harold Vanderbilt, a well-known Louis Vuitton customer who triumphantly defended the cup four times.

Opposite: Crowned heads, business magnates, political figures, Olympic medal winners, and film stars came together during the America's Cup. From left to right and from top to bottom: President John F. Kennedy and his wife, Jackie, in Newport, Rhode Island, in 1958; Diana, princess of Wales, in 1987; Juan Carlos, king of Spain and an accomplished skipper; Princess Tomohito of Mikasa, christening the Japanese challenger in 1992; American actor James Coburn in 1995; Larry Ellison, president of Oracle Corporation, with Yves Carcelle of Louis Vuitton.

Above left: In 1974 the old *Intrepid*, made of wood, conceded defeat to the *Courageous*, made of aluminum.

Above right: In 1977 Ted Turner eliminated Australia and kept the America's Cup.

Below: Baron Marcel Bich organized France's first challenge in 1970. He called upon Eric Tabarly to skipper his boat *France*.

Rhode Island, rather than New York), the Irishman was up against another American tycoon, Harold "Mike" Vanderbilt. (Members of the American Vanderbilt dynasty were also keen Monogram supporters.) Harold, the great-grandson of Cornelius Vanderbilt, who had made a fortune from the railroad in the nineteenth century, was head of New York Central and many other railway companies. An accomplished yachtsman and an excellent helmsman, he won the America's Cup three times running, in 1930, 1934, and 1937, on the *Enterprise*, *Rainbow*, and *Ranger*.

1958–80: new challenges, new players. After the Second World War the boats taking part in the America's Cup scaled back. No more excessive sizes, no more sumptuous J-Class yachts with forty men aboard. Smaller models—such as the Twelves (for twelve meters), with a crew of eleven—took the lead. They raced in the regattas for the ten America's Cups held between 1958 and 1987. In 1992 the Twelves were replaced by a new type of boat: the Class America. It is longer—about 20 meters (65.62 feet) instead of 12 (39.37 feet); uses a lot more canvas (the surface area of the sails is considerable—hundreds of square meters); and is lighter. It has a sixteen-member crew plus a seventeenth person (a guest, observer, boat owner, etc.) who does not take part in onboard maneuvers.

Also after the war the challengers became more international. In 1962 an Australian challenge broke the monotony of the traditional Anglo-American duel when *Gretel* from the Royal Sydney Yacht Club confronted *Weatherly*. In 1970 the New York Yacht Club faced a double challenge—from the Australians (*Gretel II*) and the French (*France*), led by Baron Marcel Bich. The Australian tycoon Alan Bond would defend the colors of the Royal Perth Yacht Club and challenge the Americans in four successive America's Cups. In 1974 his *Southern Cross* lost to *Courageous*, skippered by Ted Hood; in 1977 *Australia* was beaten by Ted Turner's *Courageous*; and in 1980 *Australia* was beaten by Dennis Conner's *Freedom*. But in 1983 he would put an end to America's 132 years of dominance.

1983: the first Louis Vuitton Cup and a thunderbolt for the America's Cup.
Prompted by an idea of Bruno Troublé, *Baron Bich*'s skipper in the 1980 America's Cup, Louis Vuitton's president, Henry Racamier, decided to partner with the America's Cup. In

Opposite and above: A dramatic turn of events in 1983. The challenger *Australia II* wins the first Louis Vuitton Cup, then beats the defender *Liberty*, ending 132 years of American supremacy. The America's Cup leaves for the other side of the world. The winged keel was the Australian yacht's secret weapon.

Below: Louis Vuitton's media center team in San Diego, 1992. The America's Cup is the third most televised event in the world, generating two thousand hours of coverage.

1983 he organized the first Louis Vuitton Cup in Newport. Louis Vuitton was both a sponsor and a joint organizer. Seven boats competed. *Australia II* won the competition ahead of the English boat, *Victory*.

Built by Ben Lexel and skippered by the Australian John Bertrand, *Australia II* had a lethal weapon at its disposal—a winged keel. With those wings of victory *Australia II* sailed on to win the America's Cup against the American defender *Liberty*, a boat designed by the Dutchman Johan Valentijne and skippered by Dennis Conner. Australia's unexpected triumph made the cover of *Time* magazine. The interruption of America's historic winning streak was big news, which had a beneficial effect: creating broad exposure for and generating considerable public interest in the America's Cup. The America's Cup and the Louis Vuitton Cup became sporting events of global interest, inspiring the imagination and enthusiasm of people around the world.

1987: Fremantle, Australia—thirteen challengers, six nations. "Like a hero in a western who, despite an injured leg, pulls himself up to shoot down his opponent." That was how Bruno Troublé described Dennis Conner, the man defending the colors of the San Diego Yacht Club and preparing America's return challenge. Since its first race in 1983 Louis Vuitton had become much more involved in the Louis Vuitton Cup, quadrupling its investment. In 1987 the competition received a great deal of media coverage, especially from television, which focused on the rough seas, wind, sun, and distance covered each day. Thirteen challengers were arrayed for the Louis Vuitton Cup in Perth, Australia. *Stars & Stripes*, skippered by Dennis Conner, won, beating New Zealand's *Kiwi Magic* and its skipper, Chris Dickson. Conner secured his revenge against the Australians at the end of the America's Cup in Fremantle, beating Kevin Parry's boat, *Kookaburra III*, skippered by Iain Murray.

1992: San Diego, California—eight challengers, seven nations. At the instigation of Jean-Marc Loubier, the second in charge at the company, Maison Louis Vuitton arrived in San Diego with innovative broadcast technology. Unfortunately, there was not enough wind, and the regattas failed to capture the public's attention. In the final round of the Louis Vuitton Cup, after many complaints throughout the competition, *Il Moro di Venezia*,

owned by Raul Gardini and skippered by Paul Cayard, beat its New Zealand opponent by winning four races to its opponent's three. The Italians returned to Venice, basking in the glow of their victory, and many thought they would come back to crush the *America 3*. The evening before the America's Cup, the architects were allowed to see the Americans' boat, which was usually covered. Afterward the Argentine architect of the Italian boat, German Frers, declared, "We've lost the Cup. They've come up with something." To the great displeasure of Raul Gardini, the Americans once again won the silver cup.

1995: San Diego, California—seven challengers, six nations. Heightening interest in the events, the Louis Vuitton Cup and the America's Cup inaugurated an Internet site in 1995. It was also the year that three defenders competed in the Citizen Cup, one of which was an all-women team sailing the *America 3*, owned by industrialist Bill Koch. The only challenger in the Louis Vuitton Cup capable of standing up to *Team New Zealand* and its skipper, Peter Blake, was *One Australia*, which sank. On the sidelines of the competition, one of the event's highlights was the "Top Gun" party organized by Louis Vuitton. The final excitement was *Team New Zealand*'s victory in the America's Cup over *Young America*, skippered by Dennis Conner. The fabled silver cup went to New Zealand. Some were sorry to see it travel so far, but those at Louis Vuitton believed the distance would attract new interest to the event.

1999–2000: Auckland, New Zealand—nine challengers. New partners joined the Louis Vuitton Cup. The regattas were breathtaking and the suspense gripping. Among the challengers, the Italians in *Prada*, under the aegis of Patrizio Bertelli, snatched victory from the Americans in *America One*, captained by Paul Cayard. *Prada* was expected to win easily, but *Team New Zealand* skippered by Russell Coutts beat *Prada*, and the America's Cup remained in New Zealand.

2002–3: Auckland, New Zealand—nine challengers. The Louis Vuitton Cup celebrated its twentieth anniversary on a much larger scale. For New Zealand, the economic

Opposite and above: In 1987 the races took place in Fremantle, Australia. The American skipper Dennis Conner, at the helm of *Stars & Stripes*, took his revenge and won back the America's Cup, lost four years earlier.

Below: Launching *Il Moro di Venezia*, in Venice, its home port.

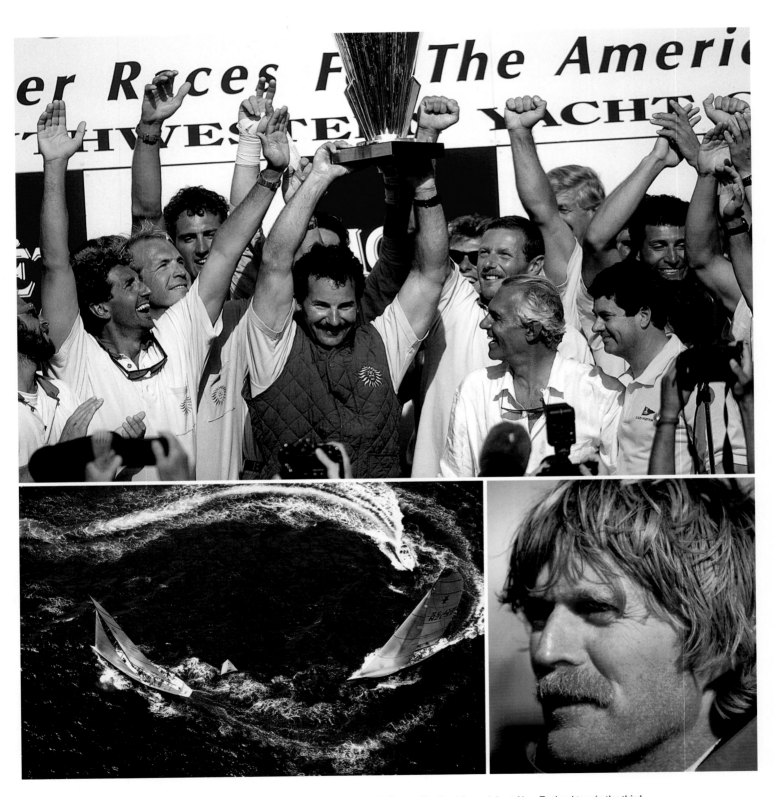

In San Diego in 1992 the Italian boat *Il Moro di Venezia*, owned by Raul Gardini and skippered by Paul Cayard, beat New Zealand to win the third Louis Vuitton Cup (opposite and above, top), but failed to take the America's Cup from the Americans. In 1995 *Team New Zealand*, skippered by Sir Peter Blake, achieved that feat, winning the race and taking the precious trophy to Auckland (two lower images, above).

Opposite and above: In 2003 the Swiss syndicate Alinghi beat the very fast *Oracle BMW Racing,* winning the right to confront the New Zealand defender. *Alinghi* won the next race with panache, and the America's Cup went to Europe for the first time in the event's history.

Following pages: The parade and opening ceremony for the first round of the Louis Vuitton Cup in 2004, with the French challenger, *K Challenge,* entering the ancient port of Marseille. The next America's Cup will be awarded in Valencia, Spain, in 2007.

impact of hosting the Cup twice was considerable, and a Maori official praised the event. In Auckland Bay the Swiss Alinghi team was victorious first in the Louis Vuitton Cup and then in the America's Cup. For the first time in 152 years, the cup went to Europe.

2004–7: Marseille, Valencia—seven challengers. A new program was planned for the thirty-second America's Cup. The Louis Vuitton Cup will include several rounds, from 2004 leading up to 2007, that will select the challenger to race against the Swiss defender, *Alinghi*. Preliminary regattas, fleet racing, and match racing will be held in Marseille and Valencia. In addition to the *Alinghi* "war machine," challengers include the syndicates from the last competition in Auckland—the New Zealanders in *Emirates Team New Zealand*, the Americans in *Oracle BMW Racing*, the Italians in *Luna Rossa*, and the French in *Le Défi*— and three new challengers: the Italian team +39, the French team K-Challenge, with Thierry Peponnet and his men, and the first South African team to compete for the America's Cup— the Shosholoza team, directed by Captain Salvatore Sarno and his skipper Geoff Meek.

This new schedule of events means that, for the first time in the history of the cup, the challengers and the defender will find themselves at the same starting line—three years before the start of the actual event. Louis Vuitton will give its name to the preliminary regattas and 2007 challenger heats, and is the main partner in the finals of the thirty-second America's Cup. Moreover, Louis Vuitton watches will be the competition's official timepieces.

Bibliography

ALLAIN, Maurice. *Encyclopédie pratique illustrée des colonies françaises*. Paris: Quillet, 1931.

ALVAREZ, José. *L'art de vivre à Marrakech*. Paris: Éditions Flammarion, 2003.

APRAXINE, Pierre, and Xavier DEMANGE. *La Divine Comtesse: Photographs of the Countess de Castiglione*. New Haven: Yale University Press in association with the Metropolitan Museum of Art, New York, 2000.

ATGET, Eugène. *L'art décoratif*. Paris: Éditions Flammarion, 2002.

AUDOUIN-DUBREUIL, Ariane. *La Croisière jaune sur la route de la soie*. Paris: Glénat, 2002.

BALDASSARI, Anne (ed.). *Matisse Picasso*. Paris: RMN/Centre Pompidou, 2002.

BAUDY, Francis, Sophie ORIVEL, and Martin PÉNET. *Mémoire de guinguettes*. Paris: Omnibus, 2003.

BEAUNE, Carisse, Gérard BUSQUET, and Jean-Noël MOURET. *Le grand guide du Vietnam*. Paris: Gallimard, 2002.

BENTON, Charlotte, Tim BENTON, and Ghislaine WOOD. *L'Art déco dans le monde, 1910–1939*. Tournai: La Renaissance du Livre, 2003.

BERNARD, Anne-Marie. *Le monde de Proust vu par Paul Nadar*. Paris: Éditions du Patrimoine, 2003.

BLOCH, Jean-Jacques, and Marianne DELORT. *Quand Paris allait "à l'Expo."* Paris: Fayard, 1980.

BLOTTIÈRE, Alain. *Un voyage en Egypte au temps des derniers rois*. Paris: Éditions Flammarion, 2003.

BLUME, Mary, and Martine D'ASTIER. *La Côte d'Azur de Jacques-Henri Lartigue*. Paris: Éditions Flammarion, 1997.

BOISSEL, Pascal. *Café de la paix: 1862 à nos jours, 120 ans de vie parisienne*. Paris: Anwile, 1980.

BOISSIEU, Jean. *Quand Marseille tenait les clés de l'orient*. Paris: Fayard, 1982.

BORHAN, Pierre, and Monica FRESCO. *En bateau*. Paris: La Manufacture, 1991.

BORHAN, Pierre, Jean-Claude GAUTRAND, and Jean-Luc PILLARD. *En train. 150 ans de photographie des chemins de fer français, de vie du rail et de mythologie ferroviaire*. Paris: La Manufacture, 1992.

BORHAN, Pierre, Erick GUDIMARD, and Véronique MARSINI. *En avion*. Paris: La Manufacture, 1992.

BOULAY, Cyrille. *Vacances royales*. Paris: Assouline, 2003.

BUREN, Daniel. *Mot à mot*. Paris: Éditions de La Martinière, 2002.

CHALLAYE, Félicien. *Le Japon illustré*. Paris: Larousse, 1915.

CHERNOW, Ron. *Titan: The Life of John D. Rockefeller, Sr.* New York: Vintage, 1998.

COX, Ian H. (ed.). *The Scallop: Studies of a Shell and Its Influences on Humankind*. London: Shell Transport and Trading Co., 1957.

DARBLAY, Jeanne-Marie, and Caroline DE BEAUREPAIRE. *L'art du pique-nique*. Paris: Éditions du Chêne, 1994.

DE BOTTON, Alain. *L'art du voyage*. Paris: Mercure de France, 2003.

DITTMAR, Gérald (ed.). *Paris sous la Commune par un témoin fidèle: la photographie*. Paris: Dittmar, 2002.

DUAULT, Alain. *L'opéra de Paris. Histoire, mythologie, divas*. Paris: Sand, 1989.

DWIGHT, Eleanor. *Diana Vreeland*. New York: Morrow, 2002.

FERRAND, Franck. *Jacques Garcia ou L'éloge du décor*. Paris: Éditions Flammarion, 1999.

FIERRO, Alfred, and Thomas Shotter BOYS. *Voyage à Paris*. Paris: Bibliothèque de l'Image, 2000.

FISZEL, Roland, Paul-Marie GRINEVALD, and Pierre FAUCHEUX. *Les caractères de l'Imprimerie nationale*. Paris: Imprimerie Nationale, 1990.

FROMENT-GUIEYSSE, George. *Brazza*. Paris: Éditions de l'Empire Colonial et Maritime, 1945.

GAGNAIRE, Pierre. *Sucré, Salé*. Paris: Éditions de La Martinière, 2003.

GAILLARD, Marc. *Paris: Les expositions universelles de 1855 à 1937*. Paris: Les Presses Franciliennes, 2003.

GEOFFROY-SCHNEITER, Bérénice. *Beauté grecque*. Paris: Assouline, 2003.

GEORGEL, Pierre. *Courbet: le poème de la nature*. Paris: Gallimard/Réunion des Musées Nationaux, 1995.

GIMPEL, René. *Journal d'un collectionneur marchand de tableaux*. Paris: Calmann-Lévy, 1963.

GIRARD, Xavier. *Les années Fitzgerald*. Paris: Assouline, 2001.

The Grand Tour. New York: Harmony Books, 1991.

GUERRAND-HERMÈS, Jérôme, Maryline DESBIOLLES, and Michèle GAZIER. *La beauté en voyage*. Paris: Éditions du Cercle d'Art, 2004.

GULSHAN, Helenka. *Vintage Luggage*. New York: Philip Wilson, 1998.

HANKS, David A., Anne HOY, and Martin P. EIDELBERG. *Design for Living. Furniture and Lighting 1950–2000. The Liliane and David M. Stewart Collection*. Montreal: Lake St. Louis Historical Society; Paris: Éditions Flammarion, 2000.

HARRISON, Martin. *David Bailey*. Paris: Éditions de La Martinière, 1999.

Henry Clarke photographe de mode. Paris: Éditions des musées de la ville de Paris,

2002. Catalogue for an exhibition organized by Musée Galliera, Paris.

HOTCHNER, A. E. *Hemingway and His World*. New York: Vendome Press, 1989.

HUGON, Anne. *L'Afrique des explorateurs vers les sources du Nil*. Paris: Gallimard, 1991.

ICHIER, François. *La France des Artisans et des Métiers du Moyen Age à l'époque industrielle*. Paris: Éditions de La Martinière, 2004.

JOBSON, Gary. *An America's Cup Treasury: The Lost Levick Photographs, 1893–1937*. Newport, R.I.: The Mariners' Museum, 1999.

JOHNSON, Ray. *Correspondences*. Paris–New York: Flammarion, 1999.

KAHANE, Martine. *Boris Kochno, Moscou 1904–Paris 1990*. Paris: Éditions de l'Opéra de Paris, 2001.

———. *1909–1929, les Ballets russes à l'Opéra*. Paris: Hazan/Bibliothèque Nationale, 1992.

KELMACHTER, Hélène. *Takashi Murakami*. Paris: Fondation Cartier pour l'Art Contemporain, 2002.

KHIREDDINE, Mourad, and Alain GÉRARD. *Marrakech et la Mamounia*. Paris: ACR, 1994.

KLAPISH-ZUBER, Christiane. *L'arbre des familles*. Paris: Éditions de La Martinière, 2003.

KOLLAR, François. *Le Choix de l'esthétique*. Paris: La Manufacture, 1995.

LABANDA, Jordi. *Hey day*. New York: Editorial RM, 2003.

LAGIER, Rosine. *Il y a un siècle . . . les paquebots transatlantiques: rêves et tragédies*. Rennes: Ouest-France, 2002.

LAMBOURS, Xavier, Luc CHOQUER, Pascal DOLÉMIEUX, Patrick MESSINA, Marcio SCAVONE, Mimi CRAVEN, and Jean LARIVIÉRE. *Rebonds*. Paris: Louis Vuitton, 1999.

LENIAUD, Jean-Michel. *Charles Garnier*. Paris: Éditions du Patrimoine, 2003.

LERI, Jean-Marc. *Musée Carnavalet histoire de Paris*. Paris: Fragments, 2000.

LEVITT, Michael, Carlo BORLENGHI, Bob GRIESER, Sally SAMINS, Kirk SCHLEA, Dean J. SHIER, and Kaoru SOEHATA. *America's Cup 1851 to 1992, The Official Record of America's Cup XXVIII & the Louis Vuitton Cup*. Portland, Ore.: Graphic Arts Center Publishing, 1992.

LÉVY, Sophie (ed.). *Paris capitale de l'Amérique: l'avant-garde américaine à Paris 1918–1939*. Paris: Adam Biro, 2003. Catalogue for an exhibition organized by the Musée d'Art Américain de Giverny.

LINKS, J. G., Deborah Sampson SHINN, Paul FUSSELL, and Ralph CAPLAN. *Bon Voyage: Designs for Travel*. New York: Cooper-Hewitt Museum, 1986.

Le Livre des expositions universelles, 1851–1989. Paris: Éditions des Arts Décoratifs/Herscher, 1983.

LOWE, Jacques. *Le clan Kennedy.* Paris: Éditions de La Martinière, 2003.

MALET, Albert, and Jules ISAAC. *La Naissance du monde moderne, 1848–1914.* Vol. 4 of *Histoire.* Paris: Hachette, 1980.

MARTIN-FUGIER, Anne. *Les salons de la IIIe République. Art, littérature, politique.* Paris: Perrin, 2003.

Masterpieces of the J. Paul Getty Museum. Los Angeles: J. Paul Getty Museum, 1997.

MATTEOLI, Francisca. *Hôtels. Petites histoires de grands hôtels.* Paris: Assouline, 2002.

MENKES, Suzy. *The Windsor Style.* Topsfield, Mass.: Salem House Publishers, 1987.

MIDANT, Jean-Paul. *Viollet-le-Duc. The French Gohic Revival.* Paris: L'Aventurine, 2002.

MORAND, Paul. *La Route des Indes.* Paris: Arléa, 1989.

MUIR, Robin. *David Bailey, Sillage de beauté.* Paris: Éditions de La Martinière, 2001.

OFFENBACH, Jacques. *La Vie parisienne.* Paris: Salabert, 1990.

OTTO VON SPRECKELSEN, Johan, and Paul ANDREU. *La Grande Arche.* Paris: Hermé, 1997.

PANOFSKY, Erwin. *Les Antécédents idéologiques de la calandre Rolls-Royce.* Paris: Le Promeneur–Quai Voltaire, 1988.

PASTOUREAU, Michel. *L'Étoffe du diable: une histoire des rayures et des tissus rayés.* Paris: Le Seuil, 1991.

PENN, Irving. *Passage. A Work Record.* New York: Knopf, 1991.

PERDIGÃO, José de Azeredo. *Calouste Gulbenkian, collectionneur.* Trans. Hélène Bourgeois. Paris: PUF, 1969.

PERRY, George. *Londres dans les années 60.* Paris: Éditions de La Martinière, 2001.

———. *New York dans les années 60.* Paris: Éditions de La Martinière, 2001.

———. *Paris dans les années 60.* Paris: Éditions de La Martinière, 2001.

POZZO DI BORGO, Roland. *Les Champs-Élysées. Trois siècles d'histoire.* Paris: Éditions de La Martinière, 1997.

QUADRI, Franco, Franco BERTONI, and Robert STEARNS. *Robert Wilson.* New York: Rizzoli, 1998.

RAMA, Louis. *Dictionnaire de la technique de la maroquinerie.* Lyon: Centre Technique du Cuir, 1975.

RIHOIT, Catherine. *Brigitte Bardot, un mythe français.* Paris: Olivier Orban, 1986.

RUBIN, James H. *Courbet.* Paris: Phaidon, 2003.

SAGAN, Françoise, and Ghislain DUSSART.

Brigitte Bardot. Paris: Éditions Flammarion, 1975.

SALGADO, Sebastiao. *Exodes.* Paris: Éditions de La Martinière, 2000.

SAVORGNAN DE BRAZZA, Pierre. *Au cœur de l'Afrique vers la source des grands fleuves 1875–1877.* Paris: Phébus, 1992.

SCLARESKY, Monique. *Caprices de la mode romantique, reflets d'un art de vivre.* Rennes: Ouest-France, 2000.

SERVAT, Henry-Jean. *La légende de Saint-Tropez.* Paris: Assouline, 2003.

SIMON, François. *Hôtels de Paris.* Paris: Assouline, 2003.

SMITH, Karen, Yan SHANCHEN, and Charles MEREWETHER. *Wang Guangyi.* Hong Kong: TimeZone 8, 2002.

SPENCER, Charles. *Cecil Beaton: Stage and Film Designs.* London: Academy Editions; New York: Saint Martin's Press, 1975.

STEELING, Charlotte. *La Mode au siècle des créateurs, 1900–1999.* Paris: Könemann, 2000.

STELLA, Alain. *Thé français. Trois siècles de passion.* Paris: Éditions Flammarion, 2003.

STROUSE, Jean. *Morgan: American Financier.* New York: Perennial, 2000.

TERRIER, Agnès. *L'orchestre de l'opéra de Paris de 1669 à nos jours.* Paris: Éditions de La Martinière, 2003.

TEXIER, Edmond. *Tableau de Paris.* Paris: Paulin et le Chevalier, 1853.

TOMKINS, Calvin. *Living Well Is the Best Revenge.* New York: Viking Press, 1971.

TORGOVNIK, Jonathan. *Il était une fois Bollywood.* Paris: Phaidon, 2003.

TULARD, Jean. *Dictionnaire du second empire.* Paris: Fayard, 1995.

URBAIN, Jean-Didier. *L'idiot du voyage. Histoires de touristes.* Paris: Plon, 1991.

VAN DYK, Stephen H. *Rare Books.* London: Scala, 2001.

Voyages en France. Paris: Louis Vuitton Malletier, 1993.

VUITTON, Gaston-Louis. *Voyage iconographique autour de ma malle.* Lille: Imprimerie Lefebvre Ducrocq, 1920.

VUITTON, Henry-Louis. *La Malle aux souvenirs.* Paris: Mengès, 1984.

VUITTON, Louis. *L'Art de traverser le temps.* Paris: Louis Vuitton Malletier, 1996.

VUITTON, Louis (fils). *Le voyage depuis les temps les plus reculés jusqu'à nos jours.* Paris: E. Dentu, 1894.

WALTER, Marc. *Voyages autour du monde.* Paris: Éditions du Chêne, 2001.

WEBER, V. F. *Ko-ji hô-ten, Dictionnaire à l'usage des amateurs et collectionneurs d'objets d'art japonais et chinois* (2 vols.). New York: Hacker Art Books, 1965.

WEISS, Sabine. *Sabine Weiss.* Paris: Éditions de La Martinière, 2003.

"Voyager avec" series

Voyager avec Andrei Biely. Le Collecteur d'espaces. Paris: La Quinzaine Littéraire–Louis Vuitton, 2000.

Voyager avec Blaise Cendrars. Le Panama ou les Aventures de mes sept oncles et autres poèmes. Paris: La Quinzaine Littéraire–Louis Vuitton, 1994.

Voyager avec Claudio Magris. Déplacements. Paris: La Quinzaine Littéraire–Louis Vuitton, 2003.

Voyager avec D. H. Lawrence. L'Odyssée d'un rebelle. Paris: La Quinzaine Littéraire–Louis Vuitton, 2001.

Voyager avec Ernst Jünger. Récits de voyages. Paris: La Quinzaine Littéraire–Louis Vuitton, 1994.

Voyager avec François Maspero. Transit & Cie. Paris: La Quinzaine Littéraire–Louis Vuitton, 2004.

Voyager avec Jacques Derrida. La Contre-allée. Paris: La Quinzaine Littéraire–Louis Vuitton, 1999.

Voyager avec Jean Chesneaux. Carnets de Chine. Paris: La Quinzaine Littéraire–Louis Vuitton, 1999.

Voyager avec Joseph Conrad. Le Port après les flots. Paris: La Quinzaine Littéraire–Louis Vuitton, 2002.

Voyager avec Joseph Roth. Automne à Berlin. Paris: La Quinzaine Littéraire–Louis Vuitton, 2000.

Voyager avec Marcel Proust. Mille et un voyages. Paris: La Quinzaine Littéraire–Louis Vuitton, 1995.

Voyager avec Mario de Andrade. L'Apprenti touriste. Paris: La Quinzaine Littéraire–Louis Vuitton, 1996.

Voyager avec Natsume Sôseki. Haltes en Mandchourie et en Corée précédé de textes londoniens. Paris: La Quinzaine Littéraire–Louis Vuitton, 1997.

Voyager avec Paul Morand. Au seul souci de voyager. Paris: La Quinzaine Littéraire–Louis Vuitton, 2001.

Voyager avec Rainer Maria Rilke. Lettres à une compagne de voyage. Paris: La Quinzaine Littéraire–Louis Vuitton, 1995.

Voyager avec Valéry Larbaud. Le Vagabond sédentaire. Paris: La Quinzaine Littéraire–Louis Vuitton, 2003.

Voyager avec Virginia Woolf. Promenades européennes. Paris: La Quinzaine Littéraire–Louis Vuitton, 1995.

Voyager avec Vladimir Mayakovsky. Du monde j'ai fait le tour. Paris: La Quinzaine Littéraire–Louis Vuitton, 1998.

Chronology

1821 Louis Vuitton is born 4 August at Moulin d'Anchay, commune of Lavans-sur-Valouse in the Jura.

1835 Louis Vuitton leaves his father's mill and sets off for Paris on foot.

1837 Louis arrives in Paris. He is hired as an apprentice by Monsieur Maréchal, box maker/packer. Louis soon becomes head clerk.

1851 Creation of the America's Cup.

1853 Napoléon III marries Eugénie de Montijo.

1854 Louis marries Clémence-Émilie Parriaux.

Opening of the first store, at 4 Rue Neuve-des-Capucines.

1857 Louis Vuitton creates his first trunk model, covering it with Trianon gray canvas.

Charles Frederick Worth, inventor of haute couture and friend of Louis, creates his own company and sets up shop at 7 Rue de la Paix.

Georges Vuitton is born to Louis and Clémence-Émilie.

1859 Louis moves his workshops to Asnières, along the Seine near Paris.

1867 Exposition Universelle in Paris on the Champs-de-Mars. There are 52,000 exhibitors. Louis receives a bronze medal for his designs.

1868 At the Exposition Maritime Internationale of Le Havre a silver medal is awarded to Vuitton's hermetically sealed zinc trunk, made for India and the colonies.

1871 The company leaves Rue Neuve-des-Capucines for 1 Rue Scribe, the former Jockey-Club, which will be its Paris address until 1914.

1872 Introduction of the striped canvas, with vertical bands on a beige background.

1875 Introduction of the Louis Vuitton wardrobe trunk.

1876 The company changes the colors of the striped canvas to alternating light and dark stripes in beige. Beige with beige brown will become the company's graphic signature.

1880 Georges Vuitton and Joséphine Patrelle marry.

Georges takes over direction of the store on Rue Scribe.

1883 Birth of Gaston-Louis Vuitton to Georges and Joséphine Vuitton.

1885 A Louis Vuitton store opens in the heart of London, at 289 Oxford Street.

1888 Creation of the Damier canvas. For the first time, "Marque L. Vuitton déposée" (L. Vuitton registered trademark) appears on the canvas.

1889 Exposition Universelle of Paris, where Maison Louis Vuitton exhibits and receives a grand prize. The event is dominated by the debut of the Eiffel Tower.

Birth of the twins Pierre and Jean to Georges and Joséphine Vuitton.

The London store moves from Oxford Street to 454 Strand.

1890 Creation of the theft-proof tumbler lock, customized and patented by Louis Vuitton.

Maison Louis Vuitton implements an in-house system of social security and pensions for its personnel.

1892 Death of Louis Vuitton at seventy-one.

Georges begins writing *Le Voyage depuis les temps les plus reculés jusqu'à nos jours*.

1893 The company exhibits in the United States for the first time, at the Chicago world's fair.

1894 Publication of Georges Vuitton's book, *Le Voyage depuis les temps les plus reculés jusqu'à nos jours*.

1896 Creation of the Monogram canvas with four motifs: the company's initials; a diamond with a four-petal flower in the center; an enlargement of this flower in positive; and a circle with an openwork flower with four rounded petals.

Georges Vuitton's book earns him the honor of being named officer of the Academy.

1897 Gaston-Louis Vuitton becomes an apprentice at the Asnières workshops.

1898 Introduction of the auto trunk.

Wanamaker department stores begin Louis Vuitton's distribution in the U.S.

1900 Georges relocates the London store from the Strand to occupy a full building at 149 New Bond Street, in a district of suppliers to the royal family.

At the Exposition Universelle of Paris, dedicated to Art Nouveau, Georges is a member of the committees to organize and judge the travel and leather articles section.

1901 Launch of the Steamer bag.

1904 At the Saint Louis World's Fair, Georges Vuitton is president of the jury for travel articles, establishing the company's importance and reputation.

1905 Pierre Savorgnan de Brazza, before leaving for an official investigation in Congo, places an order with Louis Vuitton, including two large trunks-bed with hair mattresses and a portable desk with two secret compartments.

1906 Gaston-Louis marries Renée Versillé.

Launch of the functional and elegant driver's bag.

1907 Gaston-Louis becomes his father's partner. Creation of "Vuitton et fils."

The company outfits a car for the Peking-Paris rally.

Between 1906 and 1908 Louis Vuitton and the Kellner coachbuilding company design a camping car that is exhibited at the Salon de l'Automobile of 1908.

1908 The company opens its third store, in Nice on the Côte d'Azur.

Louis Vuitton outfits a new rally, the New York–Paris, which takes place 12 February–30 July.

1909 Georges Vuitton's twin sons, Pierre and Jean, exhibit their *Vuitton-Huber* helicopter at the aeronautical show in Paris.

Opening of the fourth store, in Lille.

1914 The Vuitton Building: Louis Vuitton opens at 70 Avenue des Champs-Élysées, the largest travel goods store in the world.

The First World War begins.

1920 Gaston, a passionate collector, reader, and writer, presents a speech to the Société Archéologique, Historique et Artistique Le Vieux Papier. It will be published as *Voyage iconographique autour de ma malle (Iconographic Voyage Around My Trunk)*.

Opening of the fifth store, in Cannes.

1923 The Asnières workshops prepare some 150 travel articles for the grand Croisière Noire rally, planned for the following year: garment trunks, outfitted kits, lunchboxes, first-aid kits, camera cases, Thermos cases, driver's bags.

1925 At the Exposition des Arts Décoratifs et Industriels Modernes Louis Vuitton displays the elegant Milano case; the Marthe Chenal toiletry kit; the Paderewski travel kit; and the shoe secretary.

1926　Louis Vuitton creates the item later immortalized as the Maharajah Baroda tea case.

Launch of the first Louis Vuitton perfume, Heures d'absence, followed by Je, Tu, Il; Réminiscences; and Sur la route.

Opening of a store in Vichy, later managed by Gaston-Louis's eldest son, Henry-Louis.

1927　Charles Lindbergh flies from New York to Paris in his plane, the *Spirit of Saint Louis,* in 33.5 hours. After his glorious Atlantic crossing he buys a Louis Vuitton garment bag for his return trip by steamboat.

1930　Louis Vuitton launches the Keepall bag. Developed during the 1920s, the bag meets with great success in the 1930s.

1931　The company outfits the Croisière Jaune (1931–32), which follows Marco Polo's route from the Mediterranean through the Middle East to the China Sea. Hundreds of pounds of materials were kept in Louis Vuitton trunks, cases, travel kits, folding tables, trunk-beds, and many other items made in Asnières.

The company participates in the Exposition Coloniale Internationale in Paris. Louis Vuitton's stand was entirely conceived by Gaston-Louis Vuitton. The roof is supported by a twenty-foot totem pole that impresses visitors.

Introduction of the Noé bag.

1936　Georges Vuitton dies at age seventy-nine.

Creation of a secretary-desk especially for the orchestra conductor Leopold Stokowski.

1954　Hundredth anniversary of Maison Louis Vuitton, which leaves the Champs-Élysées for a new store at 78 bis Avenue Marceau.

1959　Discovery of a new coating process for the Monogram canvas, enabling the development and launch of a line of supple products.

1970　Death of Gaston-Louis Vuitton at the age of eighty-seven.

1977　Creation of the holding company Louis Vuitton S.A. Henry Racamier, Gaston-Louis's son-in-law, assumes the presidency. Establishment of a new international strategy centered on the control and integration of distribution.

The company begins its collaboration with photographer Jean Larivière for the "spirit of travel" campaigns that stamp its image.

Opening of a second leather workshop, in Saint-Donat, France.

1978　Louis Vuitton opens its first Japanese stores in Tokyo and Osaka.

1979　Louis Vuitton opens its first stores in Hong Kong, Singapore, and Guam.

1981　Creation of Louis Vuitton Japan and opening of a store in Tokyo's Ginza.

Opening of the store on New York's 57th Street.

Opening of the Sarras workshop in France.

1983　Creation of the Louis Vuitton Cup, a qualifying race for the America's Cup. The first event is in Newport, Rhode Island.

1984　Louis Vuitton is listed on the stock exchange in Paris and New York.

Opening of the first South Korean store, in Seoul.

1985　Launch of the Epi leather line.

1987　Merger of Louis Vuitton with Moët Hennessy and formation of the LVMH Moët Hennessy–Louis Vuitton Group.

Louis Vuitton Cup in Fremantle, Australia.

1988　Launch of a line of silk scarves designed by contemporary artists.

Opening of the Issoudun workshop in Indre.

1989　Opening of the store at 54 Avenue Montaigne, Paris.

Introduction of the Louis Vuitton Classic, a classic car show and competition. The first event is in the Bagatelle gardens, just outside Paris.

1990　Henry Racamier leaves the board of LVMH Group. Bernard Arnault, chairman of LVMH, names Yves Carcelle president of Louis Vuitton Malletier.

Opening of the Saint-Pourçain workshop in Allier, France.

1991　Louis Vuitton Classic in Hurlingham, England.

Opening of the Barberà del Vallès workshop in Spain and the San Dimas workshop in the U.S.

1992　Launch of the Alma bag, inspired by a luggage line of the thirties.

Opening of Louis Vuitton's first Chinese store, in Peking.

Louis Vuitton Cup in San Diego, California.

1993　Launch of the men's Taïga leather line.

Louis Vuitton organizes the Vintage Rally Equator Run from Singapore to Kuala Lumpur.

1994　To celebrate the hundredth anniversary of the publication of Georges Vuitton's book, the company launches the literary series "Voyager avec" in collaboration with Éditions de La Quinzaine Littéraire.

1995　Louis Vuitton Italia Classica travels the most beautiful roads of Italy.

Launch of the City bag line in precious leathers.

Opening of the third Paris store, at 6 Place Saint-Germain-des-Près.

Louis Vuitton Cup in San Diego, California.

Opening of a second workshop in Saint-Pourçain.

1996　Hundredth anniversary of the Monogram canvas. To celebrate, seven designers (Azzedine Alaïa, Manolo Blahnik, Romeo Gigli, Helmut Lang, Isaac Mizrahi, Sybilla, and Vivienne Westwood) each design a piece of luggage using the Monogram.

The reintroduction of the Damier canvas.

Louis Vuitton Classic at Rockefeller Center, in the heart of New York City.

1997　Bernard Arnault hires young New York designer Marc Jacobs as artistic director, to expand the brand into fashion.

Launch of the Doc and Cargo lines of pens, supported by an emblematic ad campaign by Inez van Lamsweerde and Vinoodh Matadin.

1998　First Louis Vuitton ready-to-wear and shoe collections, designed by Marc Jacobs.

Launch of the Monogram Vernis line.

Opening of the company's first "global" store, its new retail concept, on the Champs-Élysées, Paris.

The Louis Vuitton Classic China Run travels from Dalian to Peking.

For soccer's World Cup Louis Vuitton creates a Monogram canvas ball in a limited, numbered series and publishes a book of portraits of famed persons posing with it; proceeds go to UNICEF.

Introduction of the travel guide series.

Louis Vuitton moves its headquarters to the former Belle Jardinière department store on Rue Pont-Neuf.

1999 Opening of a store in Nagoya Sakae, Japan.

The Louis Vuitton Cup takes place in Auckland, New Zealand.

Launch of the Louis Vuitton city guides.

Opening of the Sainte-Florence workshop, in the Vendée, France.

First men's ready-to-wear fashion show.

2000 Launch of the Monogram Mini line.

Opening of the first store in Africa, in the Hotel La Mamounia, Marrakech.

Marc Jacobs assumes creative direction of the company's ad campaigns.

Opening of a shoe workshop in Fiesso d'Artico, Italy.

Launch of the Graffiti bags designed by Marc Jacobs in collaboration with the artist Stephen Sprouse.

2001 Launch of the Charm bracelet, Louis Vuitton's first piece of jewelry.

The America's Cup celebrates its 150th anniversary on the Isle of Wight.

Opening of a second workshop in Sainte-Florence.

Launch of the Tambour watch collection.

2002 Marc Jacobs collaborates with the British illustrator Julie Verhoeven to design the "Fairy Tale" bag collection.

Opening of the first Louis Vuitton Building in Tokyo's Omote-Sando neighborhood.

Launch of the Monogram Multicolor line, designed with Japanese artist Takashi Murakami.

Opening of three new leather workshops, in Barberà del Vallès, Condé, and Ducey.

The Louis Vuitton Cup is held in Auckland, New Zealand.

2003 Launch of the Suhali line in goatskin.

Opening of the first Louis Vuitton stores in India (in New Delhi) and Russia (in Moscow). Opening of the store in Roppongi Hills, Tokyo.

Twentieth anniversary of the Louis Vuitton Cup, in Auckland.

The company collaborates with artist-director Robert Wilson on the design of the stores' Christmas windows.

2004 The company celebrates its 150th anniversary.

The opening of the Louis Vuitton Building on New York's Fifth Avenue.

The opening of stores in Bombay and on Moscow's Red Square. The opening of the first Chinese "global" store, in Shanghai.

The launch of the Damier Géant line. The launch of the company's first jewelry collection, called Emprise.

The artist Ugo Rondinone designs the company's Christmas windows.

The integration of the watchmaking workshops in La Chaux de Fond, Switzerland.

The Asnières workshops reopen after a year of renovation.

2005 Launch of the Speedy watch line. Launch of the Monogram Cherries line, designed in collaboration with Takashi Murakami. Launch of the Monogram Denim line.

World's fair in Aichi, Japan, is themed "the wisdom of nature." Louis Vuitton's exhibit in the French pavillion outlines the company's environmental efforts.

Launch of the first sunglass collection.

Opening in October of the Louis Vuitton Building on Avenue des Champs-Élysées, the brand's largest store in the world.

Index

Photograph credits

a above, *b* below, *r* right, *l* left, *c* center

8, 10, 12 © Archives Louis Vuitton
14l © Drawing by Isabelle Barthel
14ar © Rapho-Top / Fabrice Soubiros
14br The National Trust, Erddig, Clwyd © AKG-Images
15, 16–17 Moscow, Pushkin Museum © AKG-Images
18l © Archives Louis Vuitton / Antoine Jarrier
18r © Drawing by Isabelle Barthel
19 © Paul-Gérard Pasols
20 © Antoine Jarrier
21 © Collection Roger-Viollet / Paris, Bibliothèque Nationale de France
22–23 Drawing by Isabelle Barthel
25 Paris, Musée Carnavalet © The Bridgeman Art Library / Giraudon / Lauros
26 Versailles, Château de Versailles © AKG-Images / Visioars
29al © Collection ChristopheL
29ar London, The British Museum © The Bridgeman Art Library / Giraudon
29bl © Collection Roger-Viollet
29br Paris, Musée Carnavalet © L'Illustration
30 © Bibliothèque Nationale de France
31 © Collection Roger-Viollet
32 © Marc Walter
33l Compiègne, Musée de la Voiture © RMN / Daniel Arnaudet
33r © RMN / Daniel Arnaudet
34 Paris, Musée Carnavalet © The Bridgeman Art Library / Giraudon / Lauros
35 © Collection Kharbine-Tapabor
36–37 © Archives Louis Vuitton
38 © Les Arts Décoratifs, Musée de la Mode et du Textile / Photograph Laurent Sully-Jaulmes
39 © AKG-Images / Collection Bernard Garrett
40 © Collection Roger-Viollet
42 Compiègne, Château de Compiègne. © RMN / Daniel Arnaudet
43 © AKG-Images / Collection Bernard Garrett
44 © Collection Roger Thérond
45ar Compiègne, Château de Compiègne. © RMN / Franck Raux
45ac © AKG-Images / Collection Bernard Garrett
45ar Compiègne, Château de Compiègne. © RMN / Daniel Arnaudet
45cr © Collection Sirot-Angel
45c © Archives Paul-Gérard Pasols
45br © Bibliothèque Nationale de France
45br Compiègne, Château de

Compiègne. © RMN / Gérard Blot
46al © Diaporama / Photorail
46ac Compiègne, Château de Compiègne. © RMN / Michèle Bellot
46ar © Collection Roger-Viollet
46c © RMN / Jean Gilles Berizzi
46bl © Collection Roger-Viollet
46br © Collection Sirot-Angel
47 © Collection Roger-Viollet
50 © Drawing by Isabelle Barthel
51 © Archives Louis Vuitton
52–53 © Archives Louis Vuitton
54a, 54b, 55 © Collection Louis Vuitton / Antoine Jarrier
56 © Private collection
57 Cliché Nadar / Collection MAP, Archives Photographiques © CMN, Paris
58 © AKG-Images
60–61 Paris, Musée d'Orsay © RMN
62 Cliché Nadar / Collection MAP, Archives Photographiques © CMN, Paris
63 © Roger-Viollet
64–65 Musée Condé, Chantilly © RMN
65b Leemage / Selva
66–67 © AKG-Images / Collection Bernard Garrett
68 © Archives Louis Vuitton
69l Cairo, Compagnie de Suez © AKG-Images
69r Bibliothèque-Musée de l'Opéra. © Bibliothèque Nationale de France
70 Compiègne, Château de Compiègne. © RMN / Daniel Arnaudet
72 © Archives Louis Vuitton
73 © Collection Roger-Viollet
74–75, 76, 77, 78, 79 © Archives Louis Vuitton
80–81 © AKG-Images / Collection Bernard Garrett
82, 83 © Archives Louis Vuitton
84–85 © Collection Pascale Boissel
85b © AKG-Images / Collection Archiv für Kunst und Geschichte, Berlin
86 Bibliothèque Nationale de France. © AKG-Images
87 Paris, Musée Marmottan. © AKG-Images
89 © Collection Louis Vuitton
90 Paris, Musée Marmottan. © AKG-Images
91 © Collection Louis Vuitton
92al © Rue des Archives
92ac © College Art Museum of University of Tokyo
92ar © Rue des Archives
92bl © Archives Louis Vuitton
92blc Paris, Musée d'Orsay. © AKG-Images
92br © Kyoto National Museum
93al © Archives Louis Vuitton
93ac Colmar, Musée Bartholdi. © AKG-Images

93ar, 93lc © L'Illustration
93c © Collection Roger-Viollet
93cr © AKG-Images
93bl Moscow, Pushkin Museum © AKG-Images
93br L'Illustration
94 © Archives Louis Vuitton
96 © The Bridgeman Art Library / Giraudon / Lauros
97 © Archives Louis Vuitton
99 London, National Gallery © The Bridgeman Art Library / Giraudon / Lauros
100, 101, 102 © Archives Louis Vuitton
103 © Collection Roger-Viollet
104, 105 © Archives Louis Vuitton
106 © Collection Louis Vuitton / Patrick Galabert / LB Production
107, 108 © Collection Louis Vuitton / Antoine Jarrier
109–17 © Archives Louis Vuitton
118 © Collection Louis Vuitton / Antoine Jarrier
119, 120 © Collection Louis Vuitton
121 © Archives Louis Vuitton
122–23 © Collection Louis Vuitton
124 Paris, Musée National du Moyen-Âge © RMN / Martine Beck-Coppola
125, 126l © Antoine Rozès
126ar © Elizabeth de Sauverzac
126br Drawing by Viollet-Le-Duc. © D.R.
127a Beaulieu-sur-Dordogne, Abbey Church of Saint-Pierre © AKG-Images / Amelot
127b © Collection Louis Vuitton
128 © Kanagawa Prefectural Museum of Cultural History
128b Drawing after *Ko-ji hô-ten*, Hacker Art Books, New York, 1975
129 © Archives Louis Vuitton
130–31 © Collection Louis Vuitton / Antoine Jarrier
132 © Collection Louis Vuitton / Drawing by Grignon
133 © AKG-Images
134–35 © Collection Roger-Viollet
136 © AKG-Images / IMS
137l © Collection Louis Vuitton / Antoine Jarrier
137r © Collection Roger-Viollet
138 © Roger Schall
139 Archives PLM © Broders / ACCOR (all rights reserved)
140 © Collection Roger-Viollet / Lipnitzki
141 Photograph François Kollar © Ministère de la Culture-France
142 © AKG-Images
143 © Collection Louis Vuitton / Laurent Brémaud / LB Production
144 © Collection Louis Vuitton / Antoine Jarrier
145al © Rue des Archives
145ar © AKG-Images
145cr © Collection Roger-Viollet

145bl © Paul O'Doyle
145br © Keystone
146 © François Lepage
147, 148 © Archives Louis Vuitton
149 Paris, Musée des Arts Décoratifs. © The Bridgeman Art Library / Giraudon / Archives Charmet
150 © Archives Louis Vuitton
151 © AKG-Images
152 © Archives Louis Vuitton / Drawing by Pierre Legrain
153a © Keystone
153cl © AKG-Images
153c © Archives Louis Vuitton
153cr © L'Illustration
153bl © Musée de l'Air et de l'Espace / Le Bourget
153r © AKG-Images / Private collection
154–57 © Archives Louis Vuitton
158 Drawing by Grignon. © Archives Louis Vuitton
159a © Archives Louis Vuitton
159b © Collection Roger-Viollet
160, 161, 162, 163 © Archives Louis Vuitton
164 © L'Illustration
165a Paris, Musée d'Orsay. © RMN / Hervé Lewandowski
165b Collection Louis Vuitton. © Patrick Galabert / LB Production
166 Painting by Paul Huguenin. © Archives Louis Vuitton
167a Drawing by Paguoy. © Archives Louis Vuitton
167b Photograph Otto-Pirou. © AKG-Images
168 © L'Illustration
169 © AKG / Bernard Garrett
170 © Collection Louis Vuitton © Antoine Jarrier
171 © L'Illustration
172, 174 © Archives Louis Vuitton
175 © Collection Roger-Viollet / L. L.
177 © Archives Louis Vuitton
178 © Collection Roger-Viollet / L. L.
179, 180 © Archives Louis Vuitton
181 Collection Roger-Viollet / Boyer
182a Collection Roger-Viollet
182b © Archives Louis Vuitton
183 © Collection Roger-Viollet
184 © L'Illustration
184r, 185 © Citroën Communication
186–87 © Archives Louis Vuitton
188 © Citroën Communication
189–92 © Archives Louis Vuitton
193 © Collection Louis Vuitton / Antoine Jarrier
195al © L'Illustration
195ar © Rue des Archives
195c © Musée Calouste Gulbekian / Studio Mario Novais
195bl © Collection Roger-Viollet
195bc Photograph François

Kollar. © Ministère de la Culture-France
195br © L'Illustration
196 © Archives Louis Vuitton
196al © Keystone
196ar © Les Arts Décoratifs, Musée de la Mode et du Textile, Paris
196cl © AKG-Images / Private collection
196cr © Collection Roger-Viollet / Lipnitzki
196bl © Lanvin estate / DR "Jeanne Lanvin." Photograph Laure Albin-Guillet
196bc © Collection Roger-Viollet / Lipnitzki
197, 198 © Archives Louis Vuitton
200 Archives Louis Vuitton / Drawing by Mich
201–15 © Archives Louis Vuitton
216–17 © Citroën Communication
219 © Collection Roger-Viollet / Harlingue
220–21 © Archives Louis Vuitton
223, 224a, 224b © Collection Louis Vuitton
225–30 © Archives Louis Vuitton
231 © Collection Louis Vuitton
232al © Collection Louis Vuitton / Antoine Jarrier
232ar © Rue des Archives / Agip
232bl © Collection Louis Vuitton
232bc © Collection Roger-Viollet / Harlingue
233 © Collection Louis Vuitton / Antoine Jarrier
234–36 © Jean-Loup de Sauverzac
237, 238l © Archives Louis Vuitton
238r © AKG-Images
239 Jacques-Henri Lartigue © Ministère de la Culture-France / AAJHL
240–41 © Archives Louis Vuitton
243 © Collection Roger-Viollet
244 © Donnelly Collection / VAGA
244b © Archives Louis Vuitton
245 Collection Louis Vuitton. © Laurent Brémaud / LB Production
246 © Rue des Archives
247 © Private collection
248 © Archives Louis Vuitton
249 © Collection Louis Vuitton / Antoine Rozès
250–51 © Collection Louis Vuitton / Patrick Galabert / LB Production
252–53 © Collection Roger-Viollet
254al © L'Illustration
255ar © Rue des Archives
255cl © Rue des Archives / Collection Granger
255c © Archives Louis Vuitton
255cr © Corbis

255bl © Keystone
255bc © SipaPress / AP
255br © Keystone
256, 257, 258 © Archives Louis Vuitton
259 © Agence France Presse
261al © L'Illustration
261ar © Rue des Archives
261c customer record © Archives Louis Vuitton
261cr, bl © Keystone
261bc © Rue des Archives
261br © Keystone
262al © Rue des Archives
262ac © Keystone
262ar © Courtesy Studio Archive of Cecil Beaton
262cl © Archives Louis Vuitton
262c Photograph Robert Whittaker © Gamma / Camera Press / Robert Whittaker
262cr © Gamma / Camera Press
262bl Photograph Lord Snowdon. © Gamma / Camera Press / Lord Snowdon
262bc © Gamma / Camera Press
262bc © Rue des Archives
262br © Gamma / Camera Press
263a © Collection Louis Vuitton
263b © Gamma / Camera Press / Photograph Cecil Beaton
264 © Collection Louis Vuitton
265 © Collection Louis Vuitton / Antoine Jarrier
266a © Paris-Match / Michou Simon
266b © Sacha
267al © Collection Musée Air France / D.R.
267ar, 267bl © Keystone
267br © Collection Louis Vuitton / Alain Beulé
269 William Klein © Vogue France
270, 272 Henry Clarke © Vogue France
273 David Bailey / Vogue © The Condé Nast Publications Ltd.
274 Bert Stern / Vogue © The Condé Nast Publications Ltd.
275 David Bailey / Vogue © The Condé Nast Publications Ltd.
276–77 David Bailey / Vogue © The Condé Nast Publications Ltd.
278 © Jean Larivière
281 © Jean-Philippe Caulliez
282b © Archives Louis Vuitton Japan
283 Jacques-Henri Lartigue © Ministère de la Culture-France / AAJHL
284 © Collection Louis Vuitton / Antoine Jarrier
285l © Sipa / Rex Features / Dennis Stone
285r © Jean Larivière
286 © Arnaud de Wildenberg
286b © Louis Vuitton Media Centre
287 © Pénélope Chauvelot
289 © Paolo Roversi
290, 291, 292–93, 294–95, 296–97 © Jean Larivière
298 © Gamma
300 © Patrick Demarchelier

301 © Philippe Stroppa / Studio Pons
302 © Guzman
302b © Antoine Jarrier
303 © Masahiko Kishino
304 © Collection Louis Vuitton / LB Production
305 © Inez van Lamsweerde / Vinoodh Matadin
306, 307 © Xavier Lambours
307b © Jean Larivière
308 © Antoine Jarrier
309a © Stéphane Muratet / LB Production
309c Martine Houghton
309b, 310, 311 © Antoine Jarrier
312 (from top to bottom and from left to right) © Raffles Hotel (Singapore), © Hotel Oriental (Bangkok), © Peninsula Hotel (Hong Kong), © Metropole Hotel (Hanoi), © David Franzen, © Stéphane Muratet / LB Production
313 © Archives Louis Vuitton
314a © Sacha
314bl Collection Alain Gérard. © ACR Éditions
314br © Stéphane Muratet / LB Production
315 © Mitchell Feinberg
316 © Guzman
317 © Jean-Paul Goude
318 © Guzman
319 © Inez van Lamsweerde / Vinoodh Matadin
320l © Xavier Lambours
320ar © Pascal Dolemieux
320br, 321 © Xavier Lambours
322–23 © Antoine Jarrier
324, 325 © Stéphane Muratet / LB Production
326 © Marina Faust
329, 330–31, 332, 333, 334–35, 336–37, 338, 339, 340–41 © Ruben Toledo for the drawings and calligraphy
342 Collection Marc Jacobs / Photograph George Chinese
343 © Frédérique Dumoulin
344 © Anders Edstrom
346 Collection Marc Jacobs / Photograph Thomas Iannaccone
347 Collection Marc Jacobs / Photograph George Chinese
349a © Collection Louis Vuitton / Laurent Brémaud / LB Production
349b © Archives Louis Vuitton
350l © Antoine Jarrier
350r © Dan Lecca
351 Private collection © AKG-Images / Camera-Photo
352 © Frédérique Dumoulin
353 © Archives Louis Vuitton
354l © Inez van Lamsweerde / Vinoodh Matadin
354r Photograph by Mert Alas & Marcus Piggott photographed by Marina Faust
355 © Marina Faust
356, 357, 358 © Marina Faust
359 Photograph © Inez van Lamsweerde / Vinoodh Matadin, photographed by Marina Faust

360 © Archives Louis Vuitton
361 © Sipa Press / Celeste / Patrick MacMullan
362 © Terry Richardson
363a Greg Kadel
363b, 364 © Archives Louis Vuitton
365 © Chris Moore
366, 367, 368 © Dan Lecca
369 © Frédérique Dumoulin
370 Dan Lecca
371 © Antoine de Parceval
373 © Marina Faust
374al Alvaro Canovas
374ac, 374ar, 374bl, 374b, 375a, 375bl © Dan Lecca
375bc © Frédérique Dumoulin
375bl © Dan Lecca
375bc, 375bl © Frédérique Dumoulin
376l © Antoine de Parceval
376r © Chris Moore
377 © Archives Louis Vuitton
378 © Inez van Lamsweerde / Vinoodh Matadin
381 © Jean Larivière
382–83 © Guzman
384, 385 © Bruno Dayan
386–87 © Raymond Meier
388–89, 390, 391 © Hervé Haddad
392–93 © Mert Alas & Marcus Piggott
394–95 © Inez van Lamsweerde / Vinoodh Matadin
396, 397, 398–99, 400–1 © Mert Alas & Marcus Piggott
402–3 © Inez van Lamsweerde / Vinoodh Matadin
404, 405 © Anders Edstrom
406, 407, 408–9 © Mert Alas & Marcus Piggott
410 © Stéphane Muratet / LB Production
412 © Hiroshi Ueda
413, 414 © Stéphane Muratet / LB Production
415 © Jimmy Cohrssen
416 © Marc Plantec / LB Production
417, 418 © Nacasa & Partners Inc.
419a © Jimmy Cohrssen
419b © Stéphane Muratet / LB Production
420 © Nacasa & Partners Inc.
421 © Jimmy Cohrssen
422 © Archives Louis Vuitton Japan
423 © Jimmy Cohrssen
424l © Jean-Philippe Caulliez
424r, 425 © Antoine Rozès
426–27 © Jean-Philippe Caulliez
428 © Archives Louis Vuitton / Photolouis
429 © Archives Louis Vuitton
430 © Antoine Rozès
432 © Jean-Philippe Caulliez
433 © Eric Leguay
434 © Antoine Rozès
435, 437 © Jean-Philippe Caulliez
438, 439, 440, 441 © Antoine Rozès
442 © Marc Plantec / LB Production

443, 444, 445 © Antoine Rozès
446 © Eric Leguay
447, 448l © Antoine Rozès
448r © Eric Maillet
449, 450, 451, 452, 453, 454, 455, 456, 457, 458, 459 © Antoine Rozès
460 © Stéphane Muratet / LB Production
461 © Jean Larivière
462 © Mitchell Feinberg
463 © Stéphane Muratet / LB Production
464 © Daniel Schweizer
465, 466, 467 © Antoine Rozès
468l © Philippe Jumin / LB Production
468r © Justin Creedy Smith
469, 470 © Archives Louis Vuitton
471 © Roberto Badin
472 © Archives Louis Vuitton Japan
473 © Collection Louis Vuitton / Patrick Galabert / LB Production
474 © Antoine de Parceval
475 © Collection Louis Vuitton / Marc Plantec / LB Production
476, 477, 478, 479, 480–81 © Collection Louis Vuitton / Antoine Rozès
482 Photograph Karl Lagerfeld
483 © Collection Louis Vuitton / Antoine Rozès
484 © Philippe Jumin / LB Production
486 © Corbis / Sygma / Julio Donoso
487 © François Fernandez
488 © Arnaud de Wildenberg
489 © Roman Cieslewicz
489bl © Magnum Photo / Philippe Halsman
489br © La Toile Daligram ArtsMode Network, S.A. 2005
490al © Archives Louis Vuitton
490ar, 490b © Collection Louis Vuitton / Antoine Jarrier
491 © Wang Guangyi
492 SUPERFLAT MONOGRAM created by Takashi Murakami; Producer: Tsuyoshi Takashiro; Co-producer: Takeshi Himi; Director: Mamoru Hosoda; Executive producer: LVMH Louis Vuitton; Illustration: Katsuyoshi Nakatsuru. © 2003 Takashi Murakami / Kaikai Kiki Co., Ltd. All Rights reserved
493l © Collection Louis Vuitton / Élodie Gay
493ra © Archives Louis Vuitton
493rb © Marc Plantec / LB Production
495al © AKG-Images
495ac © Moscow, Pushkin Museum. © AKG-Images
495ar © Gamma / Louis Mounier
495cl © AKG-Images
495cr © Rue des Archives / Horst Tappa
495bl © Leemage / MP
495br © Rue des Archives
496 © Sacha
497 © Collection Louis Vuitton / Élodie Gay (497ac) / Laurent

Brémaud (497bc) / Antoine Jarrier (497r)
498 © Antoine Jarrier
500 Collection Roger Viollet / Branger
501a Jacques-Henri Lartigue © Ministère de la Culture-France / AAJHL
501b Collection Roger Viollet
502 © Razzia
503, 504al © Antoine Jarrier
504ac © Jean-Luce Huré
504ar © Archives Louis Vuitton
504cl © Corbis Sygma / Stéphane Cardinale
504c © Antoine Jarrier
504cr © Jean-Luce Huré
504bl © Antoine Jarrier
504br © Archives Louis Vuitton
505 © Stéphane Muratet / LB Production
506 © Richard Young
507 © David Chancellor
508 © Antoine Jarrier
509 © Razzia
510, 511 © Antoine Jarrier
512, 514l © Collection Louis Vuitton
514r © The Mariner's Museum
515, 517a © The Mariner's Museum / Edwin Lewick
517bl © The Mystic Seaport / Collection Rosenfeld
517bc © Collection Roger-Viollet / Harlingue
517br © The Mystic Seaport / Collection Rosenfeld
518al Corbis / Collection Bettman
518ar, 518cr © D.R.
518cl Corbis / Sygma / Dusko Despotovic
518bl © Gilles Martin-Raget
518br © Bob Grieser
519al, 519ar © The Mystic Seaport / Collection Rosenfeld
519b © The Mystic Seaport
520, 521ar © Gilles Martin-Raget
521al © The Mystic Seaport / Collection Rosenfeld
521b © Bob Grieser
522l © Sally Samins
522r © Gilles Martin-Raget
522b © DPPI / Sea & See / Carlo Borlenghi
523, 524a © Gilles Martin-Raget
524bl © Kaoru Soehata
524br © Gilles Martin-Raget
525 © Franco Pace
526, 527 © Kaoru Soehata
528–29 © Gilles Martin-Raget.

Estate rights

© ADAGP, Paris, 2005 for works by Arman, Roger Broders, Roman Cieslewicz, Henry Clarke, Alexander Alexandrowitsch Deineka, Fernand Léger, René-Xavier Prinet, Pierre Zenobel.
© Succession Marcel Duchamp–ADAGP, Paris, 2005 for the work by Duchamp.

Acknowledgments

This book was conceived and directed by Paul-Gérard Pasols

Assisted by
Anne-Sophie Gouret

Art direction
Dominique Mesnier,
Le Bureau agency

Project coordinator
Antoine Jarrier

Assisted by
Marie-Laure Fourt
Florence Lesché
Mazen Saggar

With collaboration on the text by
Christophe Hardy
Julien Guerrier
France Billand
Eric Mathern
Claude Scasso
Andrew Tucker

Graphic designers
Amélie Boutry
Vinciane Clémens
Fabienne Coron
Nathalie Baetens
Emmanuelle Sion

Iconographers
Claire Ekisler
Marie-Christine Petit
Delphine Babelon
Fany Dupêchez
Elisabeth de Sauverzac
Vonee Reneau

Illustrations
Isabelle Barthel
Ruben Toledo

Archivist
Marianne Hardy

Editorial assistants
Michèle Cohen
Maella Rouellan

Our thanks go to

Yves Carcelle,
Patrick-Louis Vuitton,
Jean-Marc Loubier,

As well as to
René and Geneviève Vuitton,
Patrick-Albert Vuitton,
Denis Millet,
Henri Vuitton,
and Denis Picot;

To the Service Patrimoine
Louis Vuitton in Asnières
and especially to
Dominique Clémenceau
and Marie Wurry;

To Éditions de La Martinière
and especially to
Nathalie Bec,
Dominique Escartin,
Brigitte Govignon, and
Cécile Vandenbroucque;

To Maurice Nadeau,
Anne Sarraute,
Dominique Autrand,
and to La Quinzaine Littéraire;

To Pierre Vidal,
Marie-José Kerhoas,
and La Bibliothèque-
Musée de l'Opéra de Paris;

And to Abdeslam and Wafae Aarab,
Sarah Aarab,
Sophie Adde,
Serge Alfandary,
François d'Andurain,
Nazli Arad,
David Au,
Gabrielle Bellance,
Christine Bélanger,
Albert Bensoussan,
Pascal Boissel,
Aline Boré,
Christophe Brunnquell,
Serge Brunschwig,
Nathalie Canena,
Coline Choay,
Jean-Paul Claverie,
Patrice de Colmont,
Peter Copping,
Isabel Da Silva Ramos,
Hayley Davies,
François Delage,
Caroline Deroche-Pasquier,
Xavier Dixsaut,
Babeth Djian,
Gael de Dorlodot,
Iana Dos Reis Nunes,

Benjamin Dubuis,
François Dulac,
Olivier Dupont,
Christian Duval,
Charles Fabius,
Marina Faust,
Jun Fujiwara,
Claude Furci,
Sophie Gachet,
Isabelle des Garets,
Dominique Grosmangin,
Isabelle Hamelin,
Kyojiro Hata,
Dominique Hisbergue,
Sophie Joubert,
Martine Kahane,
Mari Kawasjee,
Masahiko Kishino,
Georges Kolebka,
Laurent Korcia,
Olivier Labesse,
Rosine Lapresle,
Franck Le Moal,
Pierre Léonforté,
François Lepage,
Pascale Lepoivre,
Martine Levasseur,
Jean-Philippe Martin,
Emmanuel Mathieu,
David McNulty,
Alexandra Mendès-France,
Suzy Menkes,
Camille Miceli,
Akiko Miyamoto,
Alice Morgaine,
Nathalie Moullé-Berteaux,
France Pamouktchinsky,
Maureen Procureur,
Ingrid Pux,
Evelyne Renard,
Ricardo Reyes,
Christian Reyne,
Géraldine Ribeiro,
Xavier de Royère,
Antoine Rozès,
Janie Samet,
Wilma Sarchi,
Franklin Servan-Schreiber,
Bertrand Stalla-Bourdillon,
Régine Sumeire,
Miyuki Tahara,
Madame Roger Théron,
Nathalie Tollu,
Manuel Toro Coll,
Bruno Troublé,
Sacha Van Dorssen,
Heather Vandenberghe,
Inès de Villeneuve,
Robert Wilson,
Anna Wintour,
Margarita Zimmermann;
and to La Mamounia in Marrakech;

And finally to all those who contributed to the realization of this work.

Design coordinators, English-language edition:
Tina Henderson, Shawn Dahl

Library of Congress Cataloging-in-Publication Data

Pasols, Paul-Gérard.
    [Louis Vuitton. English]
    Louis Vuitton : the birth of modern luxury / Paul-Gérard Pasols ;
    translated from the French by Lenora Ammon.
        p. cm.
    Includes bibliographical references and index.
    ISBN 978-0-8109-5950-7 (hardcover : alk. paper)
    1. Vuitton, Louis, 1821–1892. 2. Louis Vuitton (Firm)—History.
    3. Luggage—Design—History. 4. Trunks (Luggage)—History.
    I. Title.

    TS2301.L8P37 2005
    338.7'685'51—dc22

                                                        2005015029

THE ART OF BOOKS SINCE 1949

115 West 18th Street
New York, NY 10011
www.abramsbooks.com